WORLD CINEMAS, TRANSNATIONAL PERSPECTIVES

EDITED BY

NATAŠA ĎUROVIČOVÁ
AND
KATHLEEN NEWMAN

Routledge
Taylor & Francis Group

NEW YORK AND LONDON

First published 2010
by Routledge
270 Madison Avenue,
New York, NY 10016

Simultaneously published in the UK
by Routledge
2 Park Square,
Milton Park, Abingdon,
Oxon OX14 4RN

© 2010 Taylor & Francis
Routledge is an imprint of the Taylor & Francis Group, an informa business

Typeset in Spectrum
by Keystroke, Tettenhall, Wolverhampton
Printed and bound in the United States of America on acid-free paper
by Edwards Brothers, Inc

Library of Congress Cataloging in Publication Data

A catalog record has been requested for this book

ISBN 10: 0-415-97653-7 (hbk)
ISBN 10: 0-415-97654-5 (pbk)
ISBN 10: 0-203-88279-2 (ebk)

ISBN 13: 978-0-415-97653-4 (hbk)
ISBN 13: 978-0-415-97654-1 (pbk)
ISBN 13: 978-0-203-88279-5 (ebk)

For Jean Newman

and

for Garrett Stewart
sine qua non . . .

contents

contents

preface

nataša ďurovičová

The impulse for this volume came from the pairing of a pedagogic dissatisfaction with a historiographic question. Given the rapid and pervasive changes in moving image economies and technologies, the backdrop against which any represented geopolitical entity now appears is the scale of the whole—"the world." Yet the dominant strategy that teaching world cinema most commonly takes is the format of an aggregate of discrete units of national cinemas arranged in a sequence of peak moments, even while presenting them "under erasure" so as to acknowledge the limits of the nation-state paradigm as the basic film-historical unit. How then should the geopolitical imaginary of the discipline of film studies be upgraded to a transnational perspective, broadly conceived as above the level of the national but below the level of the global?

The term "transnational" has since the late 1980s evolved from signaling the generalized permeability of borders to the current usage in which it has taken on, as well, what had been previously meant by the adjective "international." In contradistinction to "global," a concept bound up with the philosophical category of totality, and in contrast to "international," predicated on political systems in a latent relationship of parity, as signaled by the prefix "inter-," the intermediate and open term "transnational" acknowledges the persistent agency of the state, in a varying but fundamentally legitimizing relationship to the scale of "the nation." At the same time, the prefix "trans-" implies relations of unevenness and mobility. It is this relative openness to modalities of geopolitical forms, social relations and especially to the variant *scale* on which relations in film history have occurred that gives this key term its dynamic force, and its utility as a frame for hypotheses about emergent forms.

Gathered in three overlapping parts, the contributions vary in scope, ranging from conceptual inquires in the discipline, through reconsiderations of well-established research questions to shorter, focused analyses departing from the textual level. Chapters in Part One, "The Geopolitical Imaginary of Cinema Studies," take on the current configuration of world cinema, and the geopolitics of the international film history, that is, the institutional patterns of production, distribution, and exhibition on the scale of the national, the regional and the global; Part Two, "Cinema as Transnational Exchange," gathers specific approaches to the representability and/or intelligibility of the global via the cinema; the contributions in Part Three, "Comparative Perspectives," foreground methodological pathways for comparative approaches to the historical study of films in the context of globalization.

Across this threefold thematic clustering, two broad strategies for locating "the transnational" can be discerned. First, there are those approaches in which the formation identified as transnational is a fundamentally spatial construct, reflects a relatively contemporary development within the unfolding process of globalization, and presents itself as directly political. The differential line of this space can range from that comprising a cross-border geography to a fault-line of compression, across which incompatible or incongruent spatial formations are brought into one another's sphere of influence (what in cultural geography would be referred to as "scale jumping"). A second strategy among the chapters foregrounds an agenda that is oriented critically, and diachronically. Methodologically varied, they propose revisions of historiographic narratives that would accommodate the scale of "below-global/above-national."

Sketching first out elements of an intellectual genealogy for the conversion point between "the temporal" and "the spatial" turn in humanities in general, and in film studies in particular, Kathleen Newman outlines several nodal points between theories of power and theories of spatiality, singling out the concept of scale, and tracks the consequences of this disciplinary intersection for film studies. On this account, the inherently circulatory character of world cinema needs to be pursued in studies of the "contact zones" film alone can articulate, and in which—and this is what she sees as the defining and the most promising feature of the scale of the transnational—"not all the relations between center and periphery are uneven."

A distinct working out of the spatial perspective is Mette Hjort's chapter, polemically positioned against what she dubs "the transnational as a term of virtue." As the paradox of its title "the plurality of cinematic transnationalism" indicates, when "transnationalism" appears as a reified a noun, in the singular, it effectively makes room for its very opposite in that it obscures the plurality of its manifestations, the very distinctions it proclaims to be describing, and thereby in fact perpetuates the homogenizing work of globalization. Ultimately Hjort's argument is put in service of a politics of scale—which in some cases can be tantamount to a politics of magnitude. In previous work (especially around Danish cinema) she has extensively argued that, within the framework of media globalization, "small nation cinemas" should be viewed as a distinct political category in which "small" strategically affects the contentious term "national." Implicitly, "national cinema" is here taken not as the site of some recalcitrant essentialism but rather as a forthrightly political project, whose aim is to resist, as best possible, the totalizing logic of a "global film culture." And in order to achieve this goal, films must often be conceived and produced through transnational strategies. Outlined here is a typology of uneven exchanges, of the possible alliances between various kinds of agents reaching across a border to make a larger-than-(small-)national film and in the process creating future conditions for innovative formal and cultural-political projects in which the link between size and importance (itself a gage of scale) could be broken. As has been the case most notably with the Dogme group, "small" can under such circumstances have a global impact. Hjort's diagnostic toolkit could be applied helpfully to, for instance, the chapter by Olivier Barlet, in which he passionately argues against demands for local rootedness and for a "right to hybridity" for African filmmakers. His rejection of the view that to accept economic or institutional support from France is to lapse into postcolonial dependency might via Hjort's typology be read and understood as a situation of modernizing transnationalism.

If "small" is a distinguishing feature in Hjort's analysis of global cinematic formations, "large" can be as well, as Yingjin Zhang's argument shows. Given the array of geopolitical entities claiming a stake in "Chinese identity" (at a minimum the People's Republic of China (PRC), Taiwan, Hong Kong and the various diasporas), in which the scale of statehood, language, cultural and ethnic affiliation or citizenship can not be articulated across any one border, Chinese cinemas scholarship has provided a prime testing ground for the term "transnational." Zhang makes the case for a model in which the national, while not the chief historiographic *telos*, should be retained within "a spatial continuum, stretching from local to global." A (Chinese) film should thus be read out not as a manifestation of any national identity but rather on a spectrum of "regional, national and local specificities, ranging from synergy to contest," an approach he calls "site-oriented transnationalism." Hjort demanded critical attention to the reasons for and the politics of the current proliferation of transnational film historiography; Zhang similarly ends with a reminder that a "site-oriented" approach to Chinese cinemas should also entail awareness of the pervasive geopolitical bias in favor of English-language research about this topic.

Like Zhang, Toby Miller too locates the transnational mutational processes in "site-specific encounters" (undergirded, among other theoretical supports, by the phenomenological concept of "occasionality") as they occur in the Mexican-American border region, and from there in the larger "*gringolandia*." Tracking how distribution, exhibition and the processes of remediation influence a film's reception, Miller details the integrative/ blending/hybridizing forms and formats through which the large Spanish-speaking minority in the United States and the large English-speaking minority in Mexico in turn cause new media compounds, "films plus," to be produced on both sides of the border in a "Latin-centric" manner.

In Miller's model, globalization fundamentally depends on such bottom-up "churning" of media forms that accompanies demographic and market shifts in two linguistically and culturally distinct states, in this case firmly linked by border traffic. Marvin D'Lugo's chapter offers a genealogy of this process in the rise of what he calls "Hispanic transnation," the mediatized imagined community forming during the transition-to-sound era through a musically enabled, broadcast-delivered leveling of Spanish dialects and cultural idioms in the geographically dispersed Latin-American/Caribbean/North-American region.

The "national" on a state-conform scale is largely bracketed out in Bhaskar Sarkar's and Lesley Stern's chapters. Rather, filmic circulation is here tracked on the alternative scale of "the trans-local," a point-to-point contact zone of representational nodes between geographically and culturally vastly distant localities, as well as "the global." In both cases it is also predicated on the much-admired "affective" capacity of the Hong Kong martial arts films to serve as a potent and worldwide transcultural relay, to use Stern's term, their capacity "to move." With an ethnographer's precision and knowledge, she then moves intensely closely to the level of the local, to unpack the politically mobilizing energy of the martial arts aesthetic not through a compatible transfer to another, local, film (as in "influence"), but rather intermedially, as deposited, and maintained, during a particular moment in Zimbabwean history, in the emancipator work and legacy of a provincial *theatre* troupe. For Sarkar, on the other hand, the initial step of moving beyond the level of national (media, film) evolves into a theoretically driven discussion of possible alternative formations "below the level of the global." In sketching a supra-regional "Asian axis" between the "emergent" (rather than fully developed) China and India, with their long

nataša ďurovičová

histories, and assorted non-national cinemas with their specific aesthetic elements, audience formations and economies, Sarkar signals the possibility of "transnational cine-communities and media assemblages that displace an all-encompassing hegemonic mode" with the United States/Hollywood as its center. It is very much this fantasy, or indeed cognitive map, of a world in which the American hegemon has been completely deleted, leaving the protagonists traveling happy together and separate around various points of the Pacific Rim between South East Asia and Latin America without ever once giving any thought to the United States, that in Fredric Jameson's chapter makes up a key representational value of a film like Wong Kar-wai's *Happy Together*.

In several other contributions in the collection, on the other hand, standard accounts of world cinema as aggregate of nation-centric units patterned into coils of norm/deviation are challenged along the axis of diachrony, that is, in the guise of proposing revisions of film-historiographical narratives. If one set of contributions has principally taken on the various political and spatial forms designated by the term "-national," the attention among this second set is on the dynamic prefix "trans-" which as it were heat-seeks, posits effects of non-identity and other structures of uneven development. Here, strategic coinages like *décalage* (Dudley Andrew), "vernacular" (Miriam Hansen) or *translatio* (Nataša Ďurovičová) signal representational dimensions in large-scale cinematic histories that political, inter/nationally centered narratives of globalization have failed to account for.

Andrew's term *décalage*, which he paraphrases as "cinema's constitutive jetlag," is coined to argue that what is commonly termed cinematic networks (laid out between points of films' production and their reception systems) should instead be seen as consisting of a variety of temporal loops, delays, and slippages. In turn, he systematizes these time loops in a narrative of "five phases of world cinema" (of which the national is only one), grouped according to the interdependency and elasticity with which each period could receive and transmit films as circulating phenomena. On Andrew's terms (comparable here with Jameson's formulation of cinematic hybridity as appearing in films " 'shot through' with the future"), cinema is materially defined by the lag time of *décalage*: it is in this foundational time gap that its use as well as its pleasure has been generated. Globalization—marked by instantaneity and full saturation—abolishes this constitutive feature of temporal delay and gives birth to digital cinema, a medium at present aligned but not identical with emulsion-based cinema, and whose "world history" will consist of other temporal forms. It could be argued that Ďurovičová's *translatio* (the term she uses for the amalgam of the linguistic and political apparati involved in all cinematic but also digital translation) does with a semiotic goal what *décalage* does with a phenomenological goal: namely offer terms for revising transnational historiography and "world cinema history" by attending closely to a medium-specific feature (perceptual and affective distance for *décalage*, a sign's localization, point of provenance, for *translatio*) on which cinema's global circulation depends.

Like several other scholars in the volume (Newman, Miller, Stern, Sarkar) Miriam Hansen, too, looks to gage the possible scales of film circulation systems, and to identify nodal points at which horizontal exchanges among films and film cultures may happen. In advancing the concept of "vernacular modernism," her long-standing and resolutely revisionist point of departure is to challenge the relatively more static, normative and top-down operational term "the classical" which has, within film scholarship, mimicked the totalizing aspect of globalization. "Vernacular" is instead a concept conceived as projecting a scale on which local elements are mutually constitutive with a cosmopolitan circulation, where "coeval and uneven modernities connect, intersect and compete." The vernacular is, then, what appears via the substance of expression of the material that makes up fiction film in its reflective, its modernist aspect: contingent elements of mise-en-scene, local sounds, narrative habits and affective structures of "the everyday" that cinema so uniquely well "captures." In turn, these stylistic and also narrative elements may on this account also provide indices of interrelatedness among films—as direct influence, as contemporariness, as reaching for emergent audiences everywhere—that would provide a film historian with more reliable material for a *histoire croisée* of a particular moment.

Because of their attentiveness to this material level, there is a congruence between the comparative stance that both Hansen and Willemen consider to be the master procedure of world cinema historiography. For Willemen, then, the transnational perspective on film history is not derived from empirical observation of cinema's social uses marked by co-presence of different elements or scales (as it is for Miller, or Stern, say); it is, rather, a disciplinary protocol on the level of theory, a combination of all possible (national) research perspectives aiming to systematically describe a semiotic object—cinema.

As a product of later-industrial modernity, all cinema is marked by, and itself reworks elements (labor, capital, body, raw materials, ideology) it shares with other commodity production, as well as elements which vary from period to period and place to place (mise-en-scene, performance, representational forms of image making). The transnational is thus not a "supplement" or a correction to the aggregate of national film histories but rather the historical condition present throughout within a grid of comparison allowing the analyst, and, much more properly, a *team* of analysts specializing in film from an assortment of periods and provenances, to parse and compare. This would involve, for instance, examining the way the materiality of mise-en-scene has been rendered visible in the totality of all cinema—ranging from neutral backdrop to the marked, spectacular destruction scenes known as "special effects." Indeed, João Vieira's chapter on the transnational genre of street kids films in this volume, centered on the changing valances of the figure of the impoverished and violent or abused street child, provides here an instance of parameters for tracing this figure across the historical and geopolitical variations of modern capitalism, from the Dickens/Griffith moment to the present, and across the so-called First and Third Worlds alike.

Closing the volume with Jonathan Rosenbaum's short chapter that interweaves—compares—Jacques Tati's brilliant "failure" *Playtime* (1967) and Jia Zhangke's near-cult *Shijie* (2004), released in 2006 as *The World*, we wanted to end with an exemplary set of questions and of filmic texts, discussed by a critic who has maintained an unfailingly transnational perspective in the face of world cinema's many homogenizing institutions.

acknowledgments

We are very grateful to the authors included in this volume: at conferences and in written exchanges over the years, their work has given shape to this collective inquiry.

We would also like to thank our University of Iowa colleagues in the Department of Cinema and Comparative Literature, Department of Spanish and Portuguese, and International Writing Program for the many conversations about cinema and globalization over the years. The Crossing Borders Program and the Institute for Cinema and Culture, both at the University of Iowa, have been generous with their institutional support. We are especially grateful to Corey Creekmur, Kathy Hall, Dina Iordanova, Franklin Miller, Hamid Naficy, Patrice Petro, Michael Raine, Garrett Stewart, and George Yúdice for their ideas and collaboration at various stages of the project; through it all, Dudley Andrew and Mette Hjort have been good friends and interlocutors. Jane Ferrer, Michael Slowik, and Dennis Hanlon were indispensable in the editing stage, and we owe much to Bill Germano, Matthew Byrnie, and Stan Spring, our kind editors at Routledge, for their support throughout the project.

To our series editors Edward Branigan and Charles Wolfe, thank you for your encouragement and patience.

the geopolitical

imaginary of

cinema studies

notes on

transnational

film theory

decentered subjectivity,

decentered capitalism

k a t h l e e n   n e w m a n

In 2008, about twenty minutes into the television broadcast at the Academy Awards ceremony, actor George Clooney introduced a short film sequence honoring the eightieth anniversary of the Oscars. At the end of the piece, which highlighted moments in past ceremonies when stars were moved by the recognition of their peers and which swept to its minor epic conclusion with an aged Charlie Chaplin thanking the Academy and his fellow filmmakers over Celine Dion's voice singing "My Heart Will Go On" from *Titanic*, the host of the ceremony, comedian Jon Stewart, pretended to be distracted. Holding an iPhone or iPod, he announced he was watching *Lawrence of Arabia*, but that it was better appreciated in widescreen and so he turned the device sideways. It was the perfect joke for the film industry in the digital age, recalling the celluloid grandeur of filmmaking past, referencing, by the film's theme of Middle Eastern wars, the current US military presence in Iraq and Afghanistan, and deflating popular hyperbole regarding new media. Most interesting of all was the gag's recognition, beyond the question of screen size, that questions of geopolitical scale are central to the meaning-making processes of cinema. How a film instantiates the geopolitical imaginary of a particular historical time and place, whom the film addresses and from what geopolitical perspective, and what a film accomplishes as a narrative are understood to be the simultaneous operation of multiple scales. This popular recognition of the centrality of the question of scale has also become a concern for the discipline of film studies.

disciplinary assumptions

Current scholarship on the transnational scale of cinematic circulation now takes for granted a geopolitical decentering of the discipline. Areas once considered peripheral (that is, less developed countries, the so-called Third World) are now seen as integral to the historical development of cinema. The assumption that the export of European and US cinema to the rest of the world, from the silent period onward, inspired only derivative image cultures has been replaced by a dynamic model of cinematic exchange,[1] where filmmakers around the world are known to have been in dialogue with one another's work, and other cultural and political exchanges to form the dynamic context of these dialogues. Audiences outside the United States are understood to have long had access to at least more than one national cinematic tradition, if not several, and their viewing practices are understood to be active engagement, not to be passive reception. Changes in film industries and in film style are now understood not merely to be a response to national conditions and pressures, but also to have, most always, multiple, international determinants. Borders are seen to have been always permeable, societies always hybrid, and international film history to have been key to the processes of globalization. In these early years of the twenty-first century, it is hoped we have better understood the complexities of social structuration than we did in the late twentieth century. Yet, in this recognition of the complexity of the role of the film text in socio-political processes, certain questions raised during the interdisciplinary theoretical debates of the twentieth century remain unanswered. The linguistic turn and the cultural turn, enabled by and enabling the theoretical advance of the decentering of subjectivity, produced interesting questions regarding the relation between the meaning-making processes of art and the determinants of social practices and the trajectories of social change. Yet, until relatively recently, the articulation of the concerns of both the humanities and the social sciences was quite difficult because in neither general area of inquiry had the full implications of the discussions of the nature of globalization been realized: capitalism itself is, and has always been, a decentered practice. Beginning in the 1970s, the sociologists developing world-systems theory were among the first to suggest that the operations of capitalism might be decentered, and, over the subsequent decades, anthropologists, geographers, literary scholars, and political theorists sought to rewrite the conceptualization of power asymmetries: counter-hegemony, subalternity, and discursive formations were key terms of the period.[2] While in film studies there were parallel debates regarding the politics of cinema (particularly regarding ideology and the social divisions of class, race, gender, and sexuality, with the international dimension of these debates concentrated in theories of Third Cinema and their counterpart, theories of Global Hollywood[3]), more pressing in terms of theory were the reconsiderations of temporality.[4] In general, in the humanities, however, by the last decade of the twentieth century, formulations of postmodernity gave way to formulations of cosmopolitanism, inflected by postcolonial theory, and, via the necessary globalism of the latter two projects,[5] matters of temporality were reconnected to matters of space. This spatial turn in the humanities, that is, the inclusion of the theoretical work from the discipline of geography, has made possible, finally, to begin the theoretical articulation of decentered subjectivity and decentered capitalism.

the constitution of texts and societies "prerequisite to any subject [positions] whatsoever"

In discussing the mutual constitution of the textual and the social, or subjectivity and structuration, as a matter of power asymmetries and uneven development, it is useful to consider the links across some thirty years between the writings of Michel Foucault and David Harvey, theorists from areas of academic inquiry that deploy theories of representation quite differently. We remember that, in preparation for his discussion of the "anatomo-politics of the body" and the "bio-politics of the population" as practices of sovereignty in the final chapter "Right of Death and Power over Life" in *The History of Sexuality, Volume I* (1978), Foucault argues regarding "Method" that

> power must be understood in the first instance as the
> multiplicity of force relations immanent in the sphere in
> which they operate and which constitute their own
> organization; [. . .] Power's condition's of possibility [. . .]
> which also makes it possible to use its mechanism as a grid
> of intelligibility of the social order, must not be sought in
> the primary existence of a central point [. . .] it is the moving
> substrate of force relations which, by virtue of their
> inequality, constantly engender states of power, but the
> latter are always local and unstable.[6]

This definition of method permitted literary and film studies to consider print and audiovisual texts as "grids of intelligibility," whose textual operations, particularly narrative operations, served as sites of multiple and overlapping discursive formations. Given subjectivity is constituted in language, narratives are then the evidentiary sites of simultaneous, multiple subject positionings, those of reception of readers or viewers as well as those of enunciation of authors or filmmakers, both active positions of engagement; thus narratives become sites of structuration, effecting multiple subject positioning, including uneven relations of power, and any act of communication produces a concatenation of subject positions in language. The spatial terms are used advisedly because power hierarchies are necessarily spatialized. This was one of the points of greatest concern to geographers when reading Foucault's work: they viewed spatial dispersion or mapping of power as a material practice, not as the secondary order, for them, of metaphor.[7] For theoretical work combining the insights of the humanities and the social sciences, textual operations necessarily reveal the "sphere" in which force relations operate not to be a *place* in which force relations operate, but rather the always ongoing constitutive process by which social relations are assigned, located (spatialized), delimited, and, ultimately, transformed, whether by cooperation or under the sign of violence. Foucault was concerned with state power and the control of the means of violence within and by nation-states, what Nicos Poulantzas described, in the same period, as violence at the heart of the State,[8] but he knew discursive operations to be constitutive, not merely derivative. However, he was more concerned with the intelligibility of specific discursive formations rather than the articulation, one to another, of formations, that is, rather than with the articulations of the "grids of intelligibility" at multiple scales, including those above and below the national scale.

David Harvey, to the contrary, finds himself as a geographer obligated to consider the operation of power at multiple scales of both historical and contemporary capitalism because, not only are geo-economic exchanges multidirectional but capitalism itself operates via the simultaneity of multiple territorial delimitations, among them, local, national, international, world-regional, transnational, and global scales. In *Spaces of Global Capitalism: Towards a Theory of Uneven Geographical Development* (2006), Harvey writes:

> A central contradiction exists with capitalism between *territorial* and *capitalistic* logics of power. This contradiction is internalized within capital accumulation given the tension between regionality and territorial class alliance formation on the one hand and the free geographical circulation of capital on the other.[9]

He describes the shift in wealth, over the latter years of the twentieth century, to scales beyond those of the nation-state, through "accumulation through dispossession," wherein economic operations that in the past served to accrue wealth within a nation-state now facilitate the accumulation of wealth by transnational elites. His work addresses what Giovanni Arrighi, in *The Long Twentieth Century: Money, Power, and the Origins of Our Times*, a work of historical sociology published in 1994,[10] theorized as either the emergent fifth long century of capitalist development (overlapping phases of material and financial expansion, incorporating new territory into the political-economic system, with each long century marked by the competition between two major state powers, with the last competition being that between the nation-states of the United States and the Soviet Union) or the transformation of the capitalist world-economy into something else all together. Thus, Harvey and Arrighi, building on world-systems theory, reveal the decentering of capitalism that was not readily apparent to scholars in film and literary studies in the heyday of Marxist cultural theory in the 1970s and 1980s. In addition, the easy conflation of the terms globalization and capitalism of recent years (where once globalization was thought to include other kinds of flows and exchanges[11]), makes clear that agency within (or of) capitalism is not confined to class agency and, therefore, the nature of resistance and revolution are redefined also to operate at multiple scales, well beyond the "overthrow" an unjust political system seen as a worthy goal in yesteryear.

While both Foucault and Harvey stress the unevenness of power relations at the center of their arguments, neither seek to find a way describe with precision the relationship between multiple determinants of social transformation. Inequality, oppression, counter-hegemony, alternity . . . one and all are seen to operate under the sign of a complexity too great to be parsed. Thus, the similarities in Foucault's and Harvey's projects highlight the extent to which, in both the humanities and the social sciences, the question of collective agency within a complex system of multiple, simultaneous scales remains insufficiently theorized.

international film history, transnational film theory

One of the problems we face, of course and as always, is the language we employ to describe complex systems and histories. For example, John Urry, in *Sociology Beyond Societies: Mobilities for the Twenty-First Century*, takes much the same position as Harvey, arguing in the section "Complex Mobilities" of the final chapter, that

> billions of individual actions occur, each of which is based on exceptionally localized forms of information. [. . .] these local actions do not remain simply local since they are captured, represented, marketed and generalized elsewhere. They are carried along the scapes and flows of the emerging global world, transporting ideas, people, images, monies and technologies to potentially everywhere. Indeed such actions may jump scapes, since they are fluid-like and difficult to keep within any channel. Interestingly since some connections can exist between the local and the global and this

results from an increased reflexivity about those interconnections partially developed through the media. [. . .]

In general though the consequences for the global level
are non-linear, large-scale, unpredictable and partially
ungovernable. [. . .]

The emergent global order is one of constant disorder
and disequilibrium.[12]

Whereas Urry emphasizes the elusiveness of the articulations of the
determinants of social transformations, making almost impossible the
description of the processes of social structuration as they relate one to
another, Saskia Sassen, as a counter-example (also from the perspective of
sociology), did attempt to describe the articulation of multiple determinants
in her chapter in Arjun Appadurai's 2001 edited volume titled *Globalization*:

A specific kind of materiality underlies the world of
new business activities, including those that have been
digitalized. Even the most globalized and dematerialized
business sectors, such as global finance, inhabit both
physical and digital space. Such firms' activities are
simultaneously partly deterritorialized and partly deeply
territorialized; they span the global, yet they are strategically concentrated in specific places.

The strategic geography of this distribution fluidly
traverses borders and spaces while installing itself in key
cities. It is a geography that explodes conventional notions
of context and traditional hierarchies of scale. It does so, in
part, through the unbundling of national territory. We can
therefore understand the global economy as materializing
in a worldwide grid of strategic places, uppermost among
which are the major international business and financial
centers. This global grid can further be understood to
constitute a new economic geography of centrality, one
that cuts across national borders and across the old North-
South divide.[13]

We can see in both these examples how difficult it is to describe with
rigor dynamic social processes, yet phrases such as "hierarchies of scale,"
fortunately for film theory and international film history, imply new, more
complex "grids of intelligibility," though ones slightly different than those
that preoccupy sociological and economic theory, and preferably ones with
a better vocabulary for the social sciences and the humanities combined.
Truly interdisciplinary theoretical and historical analyses, ones erasing the
divide between the humanities and the social sciences, that is, between the
theorists of meaning and the theorists of society, must make explicit their

assumptions regarding representation and other social practices, the mediations between text and social context, the multiple determinants of social changes, and the role of language and other sign systems in the constitution of societies, including the social divisions they instantiate internally and across societal boundaries. This will require a shift in film studies much like the one we remember Mary Louis Pratt advocated for linguistics at the University of Strathclyde "Linguistics of Writing" conference in 1986, when she discussed

> a linguistics of contact, a linguistics that placed at its centre the workings of language across rather than within lines of social differentiation, of class, race, gender, age.

> The distance between langue and parole, competence and performance, is the distance between the homogeneity of the imagined community and the fractured reality of linguistic experience in modern stratified societies.[14]

Pratt introduced the phrase "contact zone" in this essay, remapping social structuration not along the lines of (reified) social divisions, but rather at the points of (linguistic) interaction (much in keeping with the shift away from binary social divisions throughout the periods of post-structuralism and deconstruction). What would happen were we to do the same today for film studies, if we were to consider the geopolitical scales of cinematic exchange to operate as contact zones? What, for film studies as a discipline, would be these points of contact or interaction that occur simultaneously on multiple scales? The disciplinary changes might be far reaching. Interestingly, we can already perceive once the discipline began not to equate all of international film history with Global Hollywood (and its European counterpart), that is, as a variety of (unidirectional) impositions from one region onto other regions, we necessarily also began to redefine such basic concepts and periodizations as modernism and postmodernism for the United States and Europe, taking in account the cinematic and other cultural exchanges between world regions and moving beyond any tendency to reduce the centers and peripheries of present-day capitalism to the past familiar binary of cultural imperialism.

What is now at stake in film studies is the question of how motion pictures register, at formal level of narrative, broad and long-term social transformations, that is, changes in the capitalist world-economy at the regional and global scales and over multiple decades. While this is a question of recognizing ongoing inequalities and how they may articulate one with another, it also must be a question of how film registers, and therefore serves as evidence of, equality among and between peoples over and against the hierarchies of capitalism. We must ask whether the scale of the transnational evidenced in a cinematic text may operate differently from all other scales, whether it may be the one scale, because it operates "above the level of the national but below the level of the global," wherein the connections established between the here and now of relatively distant locales overcome all the uneven relations of power of other scales such as the national, regional, continental, or international scales.

In sum, the transnational film theory that is now emergent in the field asks that, first, questions of representation necessarily involve establishing the relation between decentered subjectivity and decentered capitalism, and second, analyses of the politics of cinema consider the possibility that the simultaneity of geopolitical multiple scales registered in film texts may mean that not all the relations between center and periphery are uneven.

notes

1. Hamid Naficy employed the concept of transnational exchanges productively in his paper, "Interstitial/Transnational Mode of Production and National Cinemas," delivered at the Society for Cinema and Media Studies conference in London, March 31 to April 3, 2005.
2. See Immanuel Wallerstein, *The Modern World System: Capitalist Agriculture and the Origins of the European World-Economy in the Sixteenth Century* (New York: Academic Press, 1974); Wallerstein, *The End of the World as We Know It: Social Science for the Twenty-First Century* (Minneapolis, MN: University of Minnesota Press, 1999); Giovanni Arrighi, *The Long Twentieth Century: Money, Power, and the Origins of our Times* (London: Verso, 1994). See also John Urry, *Sociology Beyond Societies: Mobilities for the Twenty-First Century* (London: Routledge, 2000); Ernesto Laclau and Chantal Mouffe, *Hegemony and Socialist Strategy: Towards a Radical Democratic Politics*, trans. Winston Moore and Paul Cammack (London: Verso, 1985); Arjun Appadurai's edited collection *Globalization* (Durham, NC: Duke University Press, 2001).
3. See Anthony R. Guneratne and Wimal Dissayanake, eds. *Rethinking Third Cinema* (New York: Routledge, 2000), Jim Pine and Paul Willemen, eds. *Questions of Third Cinema* (London: British Film Institute, 1989), and Toby Miller et al., eds. *Global Hollywood 2* (London: British Film Institute, 2005).
4. See Garrett Stewart's assessment of the contributions of Gilles Deleuze in *Framed Time: Toward a Postfilmic Cinema* (Chicago, IL: University of Chicago Press, 2007).
5. See Carol A. Breckenridge, Sheldon Pollock, Homi K. Bhabha, and Dipesh Chakrabarty, eds. *Cosmopolitanism* (Durham, NC: Duke University Press, 2002), and Kwame Anthony Appiah's *Cosmopolitanism: Ethics in a World of Strangers* (New York: W.W. Norton, 2006).
6. Michel Foucault, *The History of Sexuality, Volume I: An Introduction*, trans. Robert Hurley (New York: Pantheon, 1978), 92–93.
7. See, for example, Neil Smith, "Homeless/Global: Scaling Places," in *Mapping the Futures: Local Cultures, Global Change*, ed. Jon Bird et al. (London: Routledge, 1993), 87–119.
8. Nicos Poulanztas, *State, Power, Socialism*, trans. Patrick Cammiler (London, Verso, 1980).
9. David Harvey, *Spaces of Global Capitalism: Towards a Theory of Uneven Geographical Development* (London: Verso, 2006), 107, original emphasis.

10. A second, updated edition is announced for 2009.
11. For an overview, see Jonathan Xavier Inda and Renato Rosaldo, eds. *The Anthropology of Globalization: A Reader* (Oxford: Blackwell, 2002).
12. John Urry, *Sociology Beyond Societies*, 208.
13. Saskia Sassen, "Spatialities and Temporalities of the Global," in *Globalization*, ed. Arjun Appadurai (Durham, NC: Duke University Press, 2001), 271.
14. Mary Louis Pratt, "Linguistic Utopias," in *The Linguistics of Writing: Arguments Between Language and Literature*, ed. Nigel Fabb et al. (New York: Methuen, 1987), 48–66, pp. 61 and 51.

on the plurality

of cinematic

t w o

transnationalism

m e t t e   h j o r t

There is much talk these days in film studies of cinematic transnationalism. And given the ubiquity of transnational arrangements in the world of contemporary filmmaking, and the undeniable transnational dimensions of earlier periods of cinematic production, the use of "transnational" to describe production or distribution practices, sources of funding, casting decisions, thematic concerns, or the complex identities of various film professionals (to name but some of the more obvious candidates) often has an aura of indisputable legitimacy. At the same time, the term "transnational" does little to advance our thinking about important issues if it can mean anything and everything that the occasion would appear to demand. There is anecdotal evidence to suggest that a number of film scholars are tiring of the steady incantation of "transnational" and are beginning to ask themselves whether the very cinematic phenomena currently being described in 2009 as transnational would not, just some ten years previously, have been discussed in terms of a now allegedly outdated national cinemas paradigm.

It is fair to say that to date the discourse of cinematic transnationalism has been characterized less by competing theories and approaches than by a tendency to use the term "transnational" as a largely self-evident qualifier requiring only minimal conceptual clarification.[1] Oftentimes the term functions as shorthand for a series of assumptions about the networked and globalized realities that are those of a contemporary situation, and it is these assumptions, rather than explicit definitions, that lend semantic content to "transnational." While I would wish to contend that a wide range of questions associated with national cinema models remain pertinent today (although they may need to be taken up in ways that reflect changed circumstances), I do believe that the "transnational turn" in film studies has an important contribution to make. In the current discourse, however, the term "transnational" has assumed a referential scope so broad as to encompass phenomena that are surely more interesting for their differences than their similarities. As a result, and quite against the intentions of those who use it, "transnational" ends up playing a strangely homogenizing role that brings to mind Hegel's sarcastic reference to the "night in which all cows are black," as a response to thinking in which conceptual distinctions are effaced rather than properly developed. Therefore, if this turn is to be productively sustained it is imperative that scholars find a *principled* way of distinguishing between what counts as transnational and what does not.

It would be helpful in my view to use the term "transnational" as a scalar concept allowing for the recognition of strong or weak forms of transnationality. On this model a given cinematic case would qualify as strongly transnational, rather than only weakly so, if it could be shown to involve a number of specific transnational elements related to levels of production, distribution, reception, and the cinematic works themselves. For example, a *cinéma beur* film such as Mehdi Charef's *Daughter of Keltoum* (*La Fille de Keltoum*, 2001) appears to be strongly transnational inasmuch as transnationality is operative on several levels at once: the film is a co-production involving France, Belgium, and Tunisia; the film's distribution is supported by the Global Film Initiative; the director's identity is defined by what Yasemin Nuhoglu Soysal identifies as "postnational citizenship,"[2] French and Arabic are spoken in the film; and complex belonging shaped by multiple national cultures is a core component of the film's thematics. Yet, *Daughter of Keltoum* is by no means the norm, and it is not difficult to think of many examples of films that involve only weak forms of transnationality. It is the discussion of these films in transnational terms that is giving rise— among certain film scholars and students, and certainly among colleagues in other disciplines—to the suspicion that the discourse of cinematic transnationalism is driven to a significant extent by fashion, which is not, of course, to say that it will not be with us for a long time.

Equally helpful, I believe, would be a distinction between marked and unmarked transnationality. A film might be said to count as an instance of marked transnationality if the agents who are collectively its author (typically directors, cinematographers, editors, actors, and producers) intentionally direct the attention of viewers towards various transnational properties that encourage thinking about transnationality. This kind of process may involve the foregrounding or making salient of certain elements through camerawork or editing, but it may also involve an intensive use of those narrative techniques and devices that allow certain ideas to be constituted as fully developed themes. It is worth pointing out that there is no necessary connection between strong forms of transnational filmmaking and marked transnationality, for there are many examples of films with transnational themes, made within a purely national framework of production and oriented in the first instance towards an audience defined in national terms. Finally, it is important to remember that some forms of cinematic transnationalism are invisible at the level of work-immanent analyses and can be brought to light only through contextualizing research focused, for example, on issues of production. A distinction between the external or relational properties of a work and its immanent properties is suggestive here inasmuch as it foregrounds a connection between the discernibility of properties and distinct cognitive tasks, with some being oriented towards the cinematic work as such and others towards knowledge of various contextual determinants. Transnationality is not a marked element in the case of a film like Andrea Arnold's *Red Road* (2006), and the film's legitimate description as a strong form of transnational filmmaking becomes apparent only once attention is directed towards the production context, which is characterized, as we shall see, by an unusually robust commitment to transnational collaboration of a very particular kind. Also, in some cases films are unintentionally transnational at the level of work-immanent properties as the result of transnational arrangements in the context of production. "Euro-pudding," I take it, is a derogative term that references a chaotic transnational mix that was never meant to be made salient but intrudes on the viewer's awareness as a result of a failure properly to contain transnationality on the level of production. Intention is thus a helpful tool when trying to sort through what does and does not count as genuinely transnational filmmaking, for presumably a film with marked work-immanent transnational features, that is also the result of a significant degree of transnational collaboration, is a better candidate for description as transnational cinema than a film that is deemed to be unsuccessful because it fails to hide its genuinely transnational provenance.

Let me say a few words about the question of value in the context of today's discourse of cinematic transnationalism. The assumption, much of the time, seems to be that "transnationalism" is the new virtue term of film studies, a term that picks out processes and features that necessarily warrant affirmation as signs, among other things, of a welcome demise of ideologically suspect nation-states and the cinematic arrangements to which they gave rise. However, once we begin the task of uncovering the social models that underwrite different types of transnationalism we soon realize

14

that some transnationalisms are far more appealing than others. There is nothing inherently virtuous about transnationalism and there may even be reason to object to some forms of transnationalism.

What is needed, in my view, is not some stipulative definition that strictly rules out certain possible meanings of the term "transnational," but a detailed typology that links the concept of transnationalism to different models of cinematic production, each motivated by specific concerns and designed to achieve particular effects. If, for example, a given instance of transnationalism is believed to qualify as experimental rather than opportunistic (to introduce two terms that will be explored further below), then the task of identifying contributions that have aesthetic, artistic, and possibly political or social value follows quite naturally. The point is not to suggest that progress lies in the elimination of the variety of cinematic transnationalism in favor of one particular type, but to call for a far more polemical and less unitary discourse about cinematic transnationalism. Questions of value cannot be assumed to be settled in advance in connection with cinematic transnationalism, and distinctions as to worth must thus themselves be made central to the ongoing discussion. My own view is that the more valuable forms of cinematic transnationalism feature at least two qualities: a resistance to globalization as cultural homogenization; and a commitment to ensuring that certain economic realities associated with filmmaking do not eclipse the pursuit of aesthetic, artistic, social, and political values. As we shall see, there are a number of different types of cinematic transnationalism that combine genuine hybridity, traceable to distinct national elements, with norms such as solidarity, friendship, innovation, or social and political progress. It is my aim, then, to try to draw attention to these particular types of transnationalism and to suggest why they warrant description, analysis, and ultimately affirmation. It is no doubt possible to think of many more types than those proposed here, just as it would undoubtedly be fruitful to think through the question of cinematic types in connection not only with production, but also reception and distribution, among other things. These legitimate avenues of research will, however, need to be explored in the context of a much larger and possibly collaborative project. In the present context, the goals are far more modest: to make the case for conceptual clarification in the discourse of transnationalism; and to propose some production-based types that have a genuine purchase on actual cinematic phenomena while also providing a basis for principled discriminations as to value or worth.

a typology of cinematic transnationalisms

It is important to note that the categories included in the proposed typology highlight tendencies that are not necessarily mutually exclusive. There are, for example, actual cases in which elements of what I call affinitive transnationalism figure together with aspects of experimental transnationalism,[3] just as there are cases in which affinitive and milieu-building transnationalisms are jointly present. It is also worth mentioning that whereas many typologies are generated through the manipulation of various general categories, the approach in what follows is to describe telling instances of actual cinematic transnationalism in such a way as to suggest certain conceptual and categorical distinctions. Unlike Max Weber, who focused on ideal types having no perfectly matching empirical concretizations, the emphasis here is on the conceptual implications of actual cases.[4] The proposed typology includes epiphanic transnationalism, affinitive transnationalism, milieu-building transnationalism, opportunistic transnationalism, cosmopolitan transnationalism, globalizing transnationalism, auteurist transnationalism, modernizing transnationalism, and experimental transnationalism. These are all terms of art, coined with the intent of signaling the underlying orientations of various cinematic transnationalisms.

epiphanic transnationalism

In epiphanic transnationalism the emphasis is on the cinematic articulation of those elements of deep national belonging that overlap with aspects of other national identities to produce something resembling deep transnational belonging.[5] The term "epiphanic" signals the extent to which this form of transnationalism depends on a process of disclosure that is also somewhat constitutive of the depicted commonalities. The idea is to bring shared culture that may not actually be fully or focally recognized as such into public awareness, to make it salient and thus a more significant dimension of citizens' self-understandings. The example I have in mind is that of the early Nordic Film and TV Fund (NFTF), a body that was created by the Nordic Council in 1990 in an attempt to promote narratives that would make manifest, and so strengthen, various Nordic commonalities.

The NFTF's initial mandate was to foster a culture of co-productions that would be attuned to the promise of a particular epiphanic film, Bille August's award-winning *Pelle the Conqueror* (*Pelle Erobreren*, 1987). An adaptation of the first part of Danish writer Martin Andersen Nexø's four-volume work by the same title, August's *Pelle* explores emigration from Sweden to Denmark in the nineteenth century through two central characters, Lasse (played by Max von Sydow) and Pelle (played by Pelle Hvenegaard). Nordic policymakers noted that the long canonized *Nordic* literary classic referenced interconnected Swedish and Danish identities and cultures in ways that made Swedish and Danish cinematic cooperation natural and rational and the joint interest of Swedish and Danish audiences in the resulting adaptation highly probable.

The epiphanic transnationalism of Nordic co-production policies in the early 1990s was prompted by the globalizing strategies of Hollywood, especially the ultra-high-budget film.[6] This particular example of epiphanic transnationalism emerges, then, as a form of nationally motivated reactive globalization, one articulated and codified at the supra-national level, where the search for effective strategies of counter-globalization was deemed most likely to succeed. The guiding intuition on the part of the NFTF in the early 1990s was that there is strength in numbers understood both in economic and cultural terms. The result was a strategy designed to pool monetary resources and to stimulate a mutual awareness of shared interests, histories, and identities through the exploration of intersecting national heritage cultures that were to figure in the relevant films in the form of what we might call hyper-marked transnationality: the whole point of early NFTF-supported transnational collaboration was precisely to make Nordic viewers focally aware of the issue of transnational, Nordic belonging.

affinitive transnationalism

Affinitive transnationalism centers on "the tendency to communicate with those similar to us,"[7] with similarity typically being understood in terms of ethnicity, partially overlapping or mutually intelligible languages, and a history of interaction giving rise to shared core values, common practices, and comparable institutions. Here too the Nordic Film and TV Fund is relevant, for from the mid-1990s onwards this body relinquished its commitment to marked transnationality through the thematization of shared (heritage) cultures in favor of a model focused quite simply on stimulating Nordic networks through the circulation of film practitioners, films, and monies. Underwriting this new model of transnationalism was a concept of ethnic, linguistic, and cultural affinity that was believed to make cross-border collaboration particularly smooth and therefore cost-efficient, pleasurable, and effective.

Affinitive transnationalism need not, however, be based uniquely on cultural similarities that have long been recognized as such and are viewed as quite substantial, but can also arise in connection with shared problems or commitments in a punctual now, or with the discovery of features of other national contexts that are deemed to be potentially relevant to key problems experienced within a home context. In such cases there is often a retroactive invention—usually sincere and not necessarily deluded, but at times rhetorically maudlin—of shared culture to justify or explain the problem-based collaboration that provides the focus for agents' energies.[8] Relevant in this connection are some of the Scottish and Danish films that were produced in the early years of the twenty-first century: David MacKenzie's *The Last Great Wilderness* (2002) and Lone Scherfig's *Wilbur Wants to Kill Himself* (2002), for example. These films are the result of transnational collaboration between Glasgow-based Sigma Films, founded by David MacKenzie, Alastair MacKenzie and Gillian Berrie in 1996, and Copenhagen-based Zentropa, created by Lars von Trier and Peter Aalbæk Jensen in 1992. The transnational collaborative venture involving Sigma and Zentropa warrants description as affinitive inasmuch as it arises from a sense of mutual awareness regarding the problems that are endemic to many *small-nation contexts* and minor cinemas. The Sigma Films website revealingly refers to the Scottish and Danish companies, not only as partners, but also as allies,[9] suggesting a somewhat embattled position within the landscape of contemporary cinematic production. Interviews with key figures associated with the two companies and their collaboration draw attention to the challenges faced by small nations—with or without statehood—but they also produce a discourse centered on some of the cultural commonalities that allegedly derive from these challenges. There seems to be a strong need to identify such forms of shared culture as a way of explaining the rewarding and even inspiring dimensions of the problem-driven collaborative arrangement.

milieu-building transnationalism

Of particular interest in the present context is *Advance Party*, a rule-governed, collaborative, low budget project involving the shooting of three films in Scotland. *Advance Party* is very much part of the effective history of Lars von Trier's successful Dogma 95 initiative, itself an attempt to develop an artistically innovative and economically viable small-nation response to Hollywood-style globalization. Interviews with Sigma Films in 2006 confirmed that the Scottish company approached von Trier in 2003 about a collaborative, transnational, Dogma-style project that would be specifically designed to develop the film milieu in Scotland.[10] The Danish filmmaker has been adept at devising artistic undertakings that have a milieu-developing function, and that effectively serve as a complement, or even alternative, to cultural policy as a result.[11] In the case of *Advance Party* the aim was to transfer some of the positive features of the thriving Danish film milieu to Scotland, where sufficiently comprehensive cultural policies and support in the area of film are deemed to be lacking by Sigma Films, who thus believe that the task of developing a viable film milieu to a significant extent falls on the shoulders of the practitioners, be they producers or filmmakers.[12]

Advance Party is a three-film project, with films envisaged by first-time feature length directors Andrea Arnold (who released the award-winning film *Red Road* in 2006), Morag McKinnon and Mikkel Nørgaard. Von Trier's rules for the project specify that all three films will share the same actors and characters, although the weight assigned to a given character may vary from film to film, just as the directors are free to develop these characters within the context of quite different genres of filmmaking. Further constraints include location shooting in Scotland, limited budgets, and six-week shooting schedules. Lone Scherfig and prolific scriptwriter-turned-director Anders

Thomas Jensen were responsible for providing the brief character sketches with which all three directors were required to work, and, at least in theory, for offering some guidance and assistance as these directors sought to transform the outlines into fully developed scripts.

Interviews with Gillian Berrie and Anna Duffield at Sigma Films, and with Lone Scherfig and producer Marie Gade at Zentropa, brought to light the systematic links between the nature of the constraints and the overall goal of milieu development. The requirement that participating directors should be first time feature filmmakers was identified as a response to Berrie's view of the transition from short to feature length production as particularly difficult in the Scottish context. The Scottish location requirement was viewed as an attempt to provide valuable feature filmmaking opportunities for Scottish actors and thus as a form of capacity building. The collaborative dimensions of the project, it was claimed, were an attempt to foster the kind of networks that are the result of well-established film schools. Berrie especially viewed the absence in Scotland of an institution such as the National Film School of Denmark as problematic, the existence of the National Film and Television School outside London being no adequate substitute for a Scottish institution for reasons that were not spelled out, but are not difficult to surmise. Finally, the creativity under constraint concept that is a feature of both Dogma 95 and the Advance Party initiative was construed by all interviewees as a crucial philosophical principle with particular relevance for all small-nation film practitioners. What emerges through close study of the Advance Party project is a model of transnational collaboration aimed at jointly developing solutions to particular problems that hamper the development of thriving film milieus. The commitment in the Sigma/Zentropa case to institution building is evident in the two film towns that these companies have created: the Govan Film Town in Glasgow and Filmbyen in Avedøre, the former being directly inspired by the latter.

opportunistic transnationalism

A fourth type of transnationalism, opportunistic transnationalism, contrasts strikingly with the first three types. While all four forms of transnationality to an important extent arise as a result of financial imperatives, the epiphanic, affinitive, and milieu-building types of transnationalism reveal a resistance to purely economic thinking that opportunistic transnationalism does not. In the case, for example, of epiphanic and affinitive transnationalism, economic constraints and related challenges become the starting point for a project of cultural collaboration with intrinsic worth. Opportunistic transnationalism involves giving priority to economic issues to the point where monetary factors actually dictate the selection of partners beyond national borders. Opportunistic transnationalism is all about responding to available economic opportunities at a given moment in time and in no wise about the creation of lasting networks or about the fostering of social bonds that are deemed to be inherently valuable. Peter Garde, director of finance at Zentropa, puts the point as follows: "We traipse about Europe like gypsies and set up camp wherever we happen to find financing opportunities and the best locations."[13] Cited in the present context, this remark makes clear that a given production company need not be wedded to a single model of cinematic transnationalism, but may be committed to a range of transnational practices. Indeed, Zentropa provides evidence of a commitment to at least four types of transnationalism: affinitive, milieu-building, opportunistic, and experimental transnationalism.

cosmopolitan transnationalism

If we look to the scene of independent Chinese filmmaking, we note a fifth type of transnationalism, one defined by the cosmopolitanism of the particular individuals who exercise executive control over the filmmaking process. A good example of cosmopolitan transnationalism is the work of Evans Chan. As Gina Marchetti remarks, "Chan is a New-York based filmmaker, born in mainland China, bred in Macao, educated in Hong Kong and America, who makes independent narrative films primarily for a Hong Kong, overseas Chinese, 'greater China' audience."[14] Multiple belonging linked to ethnicity and various trajectories of migration here becomes the basis for a form of transnationalism that is oriented toward the ideal of film as a medium capable of strengthening certain social imaginaries. The emphasis is on the exploration of issues relevant to particular communities situated in a number of different national or subnational locations to which the cosmopolitan auteur has a certain privileged access. A brief description of just some of the key works helps to make this point.

In *To Liv(e)* (*Fau sai luen kuk*, 1992), a family drama focusing on a young magazine editor becomes a means of reflecting on the implications of the Tiananmen Square massacre in 1989 and on Swedish actress Liv Ullmann's actual condemnation of the Hong Kong government's decision to deport a number of Vietnamese boat refugees in 1990. Speaking as a "third world intellectual/filmmaker," Evans identifies the point of his remarkable film as follows:

> Liv Ullmann presented herself as the angel of European High Culture when she visited Hong Kong at an inopportune time and spoke on an issue in the most abstract humanitarian terms, seemingly oblivious to the history of the refugee situation and the political context in which it became Hong Kong's cross to bear.[15]

Journey to Beijing (*Buk jing*, 1998) documents a four-month philanthropic walk from Hong Kong to Beijing organized by the Hong Kong Charity Sowers

Action in an effort to raise monies for education in some of the poorer areas of rural China. Cutting between Hong Kong and New York, the thriller *Crossings* (*Chor oi*, 1999) explores some of the real-life issues confronting many immigrants and exiles in their new life worlds. In *The Map of Sex and Love* (*Qingse ditu*, 2001), Wei-ming, a gay Chinese-American filmmaker, returns to Hong Kong from New York in order to shoot a documentary about Disney's new presence in the Special Administrative Region in the form of a theme park. Wei-ming becomes involved with Larry, a dancer and choreographer, and the two befriend the emotionally fragile young woman, Mimi. When Wei-ming's American lover makes reference, in a phone message, to reports of Nazi gold in Macao, where Wei-ming's father worked as a gold welder, the three friends travel to the former Portuguese colony to speak to the old man who does indeed recall an atmosphere of illegality associated with the precious metal. *Bauhinia* (2002), which is set at the edge of 9/11's Ground Zero in New York, uses the conflict-ridden but ultimately hopeful interactions between two young Chinese lovers to explore China's one child policy, the stereotyping of mainland Chinese women by affluent Hong Kongers, and Chinese attitudes towards US immigration policies.

While by no means locked into a set of purely personal experiences, these films do at some level reflect the movements of their director and the particular mix of national, transnational, and postcolonial commitments and opportunities to which these trajectories give rise. "Cosmopolitan," rather than "exilic," strikes me as the appropriate term for what Hamid Naficy might call Chan's "accented" transnational cinema inasmuch as this director has the freedom to move back and forth between different sites, where a certain highly enabling insider status is available to him.

globalizing transnationalism

Globalizing transnationalism often finds a starting point in the putative inadequacy of national sources of film finance and makes transnational appeal oriented asymptotically towards global appeal the mechanism for recuperating the high costs of supposedly unavoidable international co-productions. The premise underwriting globalizing transnationalism, namely that filmmaking must be astronomically expensive to succeed at the task of securing viewers, is, of course, open to dispute, as the programmatic back-to-basics initiative of the Dogma 95 collective has shown. Whereas members of the sixth generation Chinese filmmakers regularly reference the Dogma initiative in interviews and casual conversations and typically eschew a conception of film as both expensive and spectacular, some of the filmmakers belonging to the older fifth generation currently appear to endorse the assumptions driving transnationalism in its globalizing form. The result is a number of fifth generation films in which spectacular production values secured through transnational capital flows combine with many of the genre- and star-based vehicles of transnational appeal in what is clearly an effort to gain access to major distribution networks beyond China.[16] Zhang Yimou's martial arts epic, *Hero* (*Ying Xiong*, 2002) is an example of these globalizing transnational films. *Hero* was produced by Beijing New Picture Film, Elite Group Enterprises, Zhang Yimou and Hong Kong film distributor turned film producer Bill Kong (who also helped finance *Crouching Tiger, Hidden Dragon*). The film was shot by Wong Kar-wai's long-time Australian cinematographer, Christopher Doyle, and features internationally bankable Hong Kong stars (Tony Leung Chiu Wai, Maggie Cheung, Jet Li, and Donnie Yen) alongside mainland actors in a visually spectacular story that is characterized by the director as "commercial" in its thrust.[17] "Commercial," the exchange with the interviewer makes clear, identifies the aspiration to recuperate costs through an audience appeal that extends well beyond the territories where the *wuxia* genre is held somehow to be an indigenous cultural element.

It is generally agreed that the model informing a production such as *Hero* is that of *Crouching Tiger, Hidden Dragon* (*Wo hu cang long*, 2000), a Columbia Pictures, Good Machine International and China Film Co-Production Corporation martial arts film directed by Chinese-Taiwanese-American filmmaker Ang Lee. *Crouching Tiger* was the "top grossing Chinese language film in all of Asia as an aggregate territory" in 2000 with box office receipts of over $17 million in Asia alone,[18] the film's success being attributable, as Sheldon Lu convincingly argues, to the following factors: a preference for Hollywood-style techniques over those, for example, of Third Cinema; the absence of various types of pathos associated with displacement and alienation; a romantic and sentimental take on the *wuxia* genre; a remarkable cast with numerous pan-Asian stars; and the filmmakers' canny ability to draw on various funding and distribution channels. The integral link between high budgets and the need for maximal reach and appeal makes globalizing transnationalism (or what Sheldon Lu calls "commercial transnational cinema") a close relative of the kind of cinematic processes that produce global cinema. Indeed, globalizing transnationalism is in many ways oriented towards the kind of global cinemagoer whom Charles Acland associates with widespread assumptions in the mainstream commercial film industry about "points of commonality across national boundaries."[19]

22

auteurist transnationalism

The next two examples of transnational filmmaking are both instances, although quite different, of omnibus filmmaking. Popular in the 1960s, this often awkward genre of filmmaking has been revived in recent times, resulting in various forms of transnational filmmaking that are interesting for contrastive reasons. Much as in the case of cosmopolitan transnationalism, the driving force in auteurist transnationalism is an individual director who is very much attuned to film's potential for personal rather than formulaic expression. Whereas cosmopolitan transnationalism emerges as the virtually unshakeable effect of a lived experience of the limits of national belonging and citizenship, auteurist transnationalism arises in a more punctual, ad-hoc manner when an established auteur and icon of a particular national cinema—in my example Michelangelo Antonioni—decides to embrace a particular kind of collaboration beyond national borders. The collaborative gesture addresses itself in the first instance to accomplished individuals, all carefully selected as film auteurs in their own right, rather than to various companies and institutions with an interest in developing transnational markets. Auteurist concepts are operative at many levels in auteurist transnationalism: an auteur figures centrally in the initiating phase; auteurs play a decisive role throughout the executive phase; and the collaborative endeavor is designed to revive or boost the auteur-based status of one or more of the participating filmmakers.

Eros (2004), a 104-minute-long omnibus film involving thematically interconnected contributions by Wong Kar-wai, Steven Soderbergh, and Michelangelo Antonioni, provides a clear example of how a somewhat thin or abstract concept of the transnational can be made to serve essentially auteurist goals. The idea for *Eros* was originally proposed by Paris-based producer Stéphane Tchal Gadjieff who had worked with Antonioni on *Beyond the Clouds* (1995). Influence, it appears, was a guiding concept as Gadjieff and Antonioni sought to identify suitable directors for their project, for the goal was to secure the participation of two much younger directors who were on record as having expressed a sincere debt to the Italian filmmaker. The result of the three directors' anthologizing efforts, quite clearly, was to be homage to the aging auteur, Antonioni. The Italian filmmaker initially expressed an interest in working with Wong Kar-wai and Pedro Almodóvar, but the latter was subsequently replaced by Steven Soderbergh when the Spaniard chose to focus on the controversial issue of sexual abuse involving children.[20] *The Hand* (Wong Kar-wai), *Equilibrium* (Steven Soderbergh), and *The Dangerous Thread of Things* (Antonioni) are loosely linked by interstitial drawings by Lorenzo Mattotti and by a theme song entitled "Michelangelo Antonioni," sung in Italian by the Brazilian singer Caetano Veloso. Wong's sensuous narrative about a courtesan (Gong Li) and her tailor (Chang Chen) has received high praise from critics whereas Soderbergh's tale of an advertising man's sessions with his psychiatrist tends to be viewed as superficial and only mildly engaging. Antonioni's contribution about a rich, bored, and constantly squabbling couple in Tuscany has drawn only critical comments, none of which, unfortunately, are unfair.

Auteurist transnationalism of the *Eros* kind betrays only a passing and in many ways tenuous interest in the transnational. The attempt, it appears, is to engage a now ubiquitous transnational tendency, but to do so in a way that keeps the messiness (or more positively, hybridity) of many genuinely transnational connections at arm's length. Discrete, autonomous works from Hong Kong, the United States, and Italy coexist in a single trans-national frame, but at no point does the dynamism of genuine transnational interaction infuse the works through surprising connections, striking combinations, innovative shifts in style, and so on. Entirely absent throughout, for example, are the kinds of auteurist effects generated by newly appropriated devices, which can be traced, through inherently intriguing patterns of flow, to sources at some once significant remove from the relevant director's national nexus. The idea that the influence of a genuine auteur might be worth tracking through interconnected, contrasting works that would highlight the results of transporting certain styles of cinematic work to new, partly national contexts is by no means uninteresting. To succeed as a form of engaging, substantive trans-nationalism, however, an auteurist endeavor such as *Eros* must relinquish the relatively noncommittal strategy of mere juxtaposition in order, among other things, to pursue the much more demanding task of genuine rather than nominal artistic collaboration. What seems strikingly absent in this instance is the marked transnationality that the project seems to require.

modernizing transnationalism

Whereas theories of modernity once took for granted the idea that modernity is reached by means of a single path resulting in a particular set of features, the emphasis following the ground-breaking work of Charles Taylor and other members of the Center for Transcultural Studies is now on multiple modernities and the various processes through which they arise.[21] Societies, it is now recognized, modernize at different times, in distinctive ways, and in response to various local impulses and developments. Following the multiple modernities line of argument, "modernity" is a term that can be legitimately used with reference *both* to the collapse of ontological hierarchies and the emergence of civil society and market-driven economies in eighteenth-century Europe, *and* in connection with the current workings of democracy in a strictly caste-based society such as India.[22] What is interesting for present purposes is the way in which the paths of modernity at times intersect with developments that are transnational in their thrust.

In the context of film, modernizing transnationalism arises when a significantly transnationalized film culture becomes a means of fueling, but also signifying, the mechanisms of modernization within a given society. The pursuit of modernity can be articulated in many ways and need by no means find expression only through such standard markers of modernity as health, income, and literacy. Decisions designed to nurture film, and especially a film culture that looks beyond the framework of the purely national in order both to reflect and forge transnational connections, can serve to crystallize some of the regulative ideals that animate a rapidly changing society. Asia, not surprisingly, is a likely site of modernizing transnationalism, for it is here that we find booming economies coupled with an understanding of what George Yúdice refers to as culture as a resource.[23] The continued prospect of remarkable economic growth on a regional level makes tangible the possibility of Asian leadership in a global arena, especially considering the significant problems currently faced by the various societies of Western modernity. Modernization in many Asian contexts is not simply a matter of securing prosperity, for progress is also measured in terms of international recognition for noteworthy contributions in the area of culture, broadly construed. The Hong Kong government's attempts, since the beginning of the new millennium, to create an image of Hong Kong as a world-class city through a turn to the arts rests, for example, on the symbolic capital associated with culture. The crisis-ridden proposal to develop West Kowloon as a cultural mechanism for transforming Hong Kong into Asia's world city is part of a post-Handover process of reinvention on the part of the former colony *and* an element in an ongoing narrative of progress. That Hong Kong's brand, as a global city, might somehow include the idea of culture, is an idea that commands considerable support. What is controversial, however, is how culture, and especially artistic culture, is to be understood. Equally difficult is the problem of deciding what is to count as truly progressive or innovative institution building in the art world today.[24] In the present context "modernizing transnationalism" designates the confluence of a conception of cutting edge cinematic practice as essentially transnational with a concept of culture as a resource for modernization and recognition.

A concrete example of what I have in mind when I speak of modernizing cinematic transnationalism may be helpful at this point. The South Korean film industry witnessed what the film scholar Bérénice Reynaud describes as "unprecedented modernization" in the 1990s.[25] This dramatic development of the South Korean film industry was largely the result of a wide range of government-based initiatives. The official desire, more specifically, was to see South Korea emerge at "the cutting edge of international film culture" (1), and the creation of the Chonju/Jeonju Film Festival is to be understood in this light. As Reynaud points out, the festival has featured "homages to Asian (Hou Hsiao-hsien) or European ... *auteurs*" while hosting events devoted to the very quintessence of cinematic newness, digital filmmaking. Of particular interest, however, is the omnibus film initiative that Jeonju launched in 2000. Produced by Jeonju, the first omnibus film had a strong trans-Asian dimension, encompassing works by Chinese director Zhang Yuan and the Korean directors Park Kwang-Su and Kim Yun-Tae. In the second omnibus film commissioned by the Festival we witness a clear intention to promote a form of film culture that registers as cutting edge precisely because it is internally distanced from the concepts of the national that underwrite both national cinema and many a conception of international film. To solicit contributions by Jia Zhangke, Tsai Ming-liang, and John Akomfrah, as

Reynaud insightfully remarks, is to provide a shared transnational platform for filmmakers who cannot be neatly contained within their own national cinemas:

> Jia continues to operate illegally in China—his work produced via a small company in Hong Kong ... and through foreign financing. As a Black British, Akomfrah still occupies a marginal position in England. And finally Tsai Ming-liang is marked by a double exile—as a diasporic Chinese born in Malaysia, he came to Taiwan as a young man to study and make films (2).

In both cases, the omnibus films are designed to highlight and forge transnational connections, the very commitment to transnationalism being itself understood as an indicator of a forward looking and progressive approach to cultural policy and institution building.[26]

experimental transnationalism[27]

A guiding assumption throughout has been that some forms of cinematic transnationalism are more worthwhile than others because they promote certain social, political, artistic, or aesthetic phenomena that we value highly. Experimental transnationalism, it would seem, is a prime candidate for consideration in connection with deeper issues of value, the *logic of experimentation* being necessarily linked to artistic, social, or political values, depending on the nature of the experiment in question. In the case of *The Five Obstructions* (*De fem benspænd*, 2003), which serves to illustrate the idea of meaningful experimental transnationalism, the commitment, as we shall see, is to artistic value. The project is not without social and political value, but this is realized primarily at the national and international level, whereas artistic value is pursued transnationally.

The Five Obstructions is an 88-minute film and transnational experiment involving Lars von Trier and his former mentor, Jørgen Leth. The film is produced by Zentropa Real, Wijnbrosse Production, Yeslam bin Laden's Almaz Film Production, and Panic Productions, with support from the Danish Film Institute, DR Drama, the Nordic Film and TV Fund, the Swedish Film Institute, Channel 4 and Canal+. Essentially, *The Five Obstructions* documents a process in which Leth remakes his celebrated, modernist, 12-minute short film, *The Perfect Human* (*Det perfekte menneske*, 1967), four or five times (depending on how *Obstruction #5* is interpreted) in accordance with obstructive rules imposed by von Trier. Recalling aspects of the Dogma 95 initiative, the guiding principle of this similarly manifesto-based project is to pull the rug out from underneath the director's feet—in this case Leth's—by imposing the opposite of what he requests, or by prescribing practices that are antithetical to his cinematic style or habitual modes of filmmaking. *Obstruction # 1* reads as follows: "12 frames, answers, Cuba, no set." Leth normally relies heavily on a lingering gaze; to proscribe any shot of more than twelve frames is thus quite literally to impose an alien framework on the filmmaker. The original short film poses a series of questions about the perfect human to which Leth is now to provide answers. Leth admits that he has never been to Cuba, which makes the playfully adversarial von Trier momentarily entertain and then impose location shooting on the island. Finally, Leth indicates that he would like a certain kind of set, and the result is that von Trier "obstructs" him by ruling out a set in this case. We are shown shots of Leth on April 2, 2001 in which he insists that von Trier is "ruining" the film "from the start" by imposing the twelve-frame rule. The result, the usually unflappable Leth quietly fumes, can be only a "spastic film." Documentary footage shot in Havana in November 2001 gives the viewer some sense of how Leth resolves the challenge posed by the obstructions, and subsequent images show him returning to Zentropa on March 21, 2002 to share his remake with von Trier. The latter notes that Leth "looks great," which, he continues, is a "bad sign," for, had the obstructions functioned as they should have, Leth would be looking rather "battered." Having watched *The Perfect Human: Cuba*, von Trier indicates that Leth has passed his first test and offers him vodka and caviar.

Von Trier's second obstruction is designed to "test" Leth's ethics. More specifically, the point is to challenge the distanced look or disengaged observer stance that characterizes much of the filmmaker's work. The rules governing remake number two are: "The most miserable place; Don't show it; Jørgen Leth is the man. The meal." Leth is himself allowed to choose what he considers to be a truly miserable place and opts for the red light district on Falkland Road in Mumbai. In response to the requirement that the misery not be directly shown, Leth uses a translucent screen partially to block off the impoverished scene in which he, as the perfect man originally played by Claus Nissen in the 1967 film, eats a gourmet meal surrounded by poverty, exploitation, and illness. When Leth returns to Copenhagen to show the results to Lars von Trier on September 12, 2002 he is told that he has failed to follow orders, the use of the translucent screen being a clear violation of one of the elements in the overall obstruction. Von Trier underscores the extent of his disapproval and disappointment and indicates that he has no choice but to punish the disobedient Leth. The latter is initially told to return to Mumbai and start over, which Leth insists that he simply cannot do. The result is the "worst punishment of all": a free-style film. *Obstruction # 3* is finally articulated disjunctively ("Complete freedom or Back to Bombay"), but in fact provides no choice, since one of the putative options was ruled out in no uncertain terms by Leth. The free-style task results in a thriller-like film, shot in Bruxelles and featuring the Belgian star, Patrick Bauchau. The guiding thought in von Trier's articulation of *Obstruction # 4* is that Leth is a filmmaker who has undertaken only projects to which he was genuinely drawn and in which he could fully believe. *Obstruction # 4*, which involves Leth remaking *The Perfect Human* as a cartoon, is thus designed to impose a task that would be absolutely unappealing, even loathsome, to Leth. Images from Port-au-Prince in December 2002 provide insight into Leth's strategy in connection with the task at hand, as do subsequent sequences from Austin, Texas in January 2003, where Leth elicits the assistance of Bob Sabiston who transforms "live footage into liquidly shifting planes of colour."[28] Leth and von Trier watch *Obstruction # 4* on two sides of the world (in Port-au-Prince, where Leth lives much of the year, and in Copenhagen), communicating by telephone in order to ensure a perfectly synchronized viewing. Von Trier acknowledges that Leth has managed, yet again, to turn the obstruction to positive effect, and proposes as a result to take control of the final remake. *Obstruction # 5* thus reads as follows: "Lars von Trier will make the last obstruction. Jørgen Leth will be credited as director. Jørgen Leth will read a text written by Lars von Trier."

What are some of the noteworthy features of *The Five Obstructions* and how do they contribute to what I am calling experimental transnationalism? The *funding*, we note, is pieced together from various sources within and beyond the nation-state of Denmark. The *production* of the remakes involves locations in Cuba, Mumbai, and Brussels, as well as a trip to Austin, Texas. While Leth's core production team remains constant throughout, various locals, professional and other, become part of the experiment as it unfolds. The collaboration is not meant to contribute to lasting networks, an aspiration that often accompanies affinitive transnationalism, nor is it meant to articulate shared culture or to pursue some global cinemagoer, as is the case with epiphanic and globalizing transnationalism respectively. Instead, the collaboration emerges quite simply as the *artistically* cogent or necessary thing to do at a given moment in time. It is the experiment and its obstructions, as interpreted by Leth, that provide the rationale for the choice of collaborators and locations. *The Five Obstructions* makes use of *multiple languages* (Danish, Spanish, English, French), as working languages of cinematic production and as languages of expression in the actual remakes. *The Five Obstructions* takes seriously the need for *transnational or even global audience appeal*, but eschews the solutions associated with epiphanic transnationalism (deep culture) or with globalizing transnationalism (quasi-universal psychologies and/or dominant norms of film style). Much as in the case of Dogma 95, the appeal of *The Five Obstructions* is linked to meta-cultural strategies involving manifestos and rules, to the inherent interest of a precisely defined experiment.[29]

It is not difficult to see that *The Five Obstructions* promotes certain artistic values, such as innovation and creativity. Far more puzzling may be the suggestion that this project also involves valuable social and political dimensions. This may be especially true in light of the scandal that Leth's memoirs, entitled *The Imperfect Human* (*Det uperfekte menneske*) generated when they were published in the fall of 2005.[30] Most troubling is Leth's description of a standing arrangement with his Haitian housekeeper that allowed him to have sex with her 17-year-old daughter. Leth's actions and confessions had dire consequences for the filmmaker: TV2 fired him as Tour de France commentator, a role that made him a household name in Denmark for decades; Leth is no longer honorary Danish consul in Haiti; and the Danish Film Institute saw itself obliged to withdraw its financial support for his current film project, although the money has since been granted again, with strict conditions attached. Leth's actions, there can be no doubt, reveal a serious lack of moral and political probity, and certainly cast new light on von Trier's decision in *Obstruction # 2* to test Leth's ethics. While Leth's confessed failings may have implications for how we assess the social, moral, or political value of any project in which he is involved, they do not automatically allow us to conclude that the particular example of experimental transnationalism that *The Five Obstructions* provides has only artistic or aesthetic value. The social and political contribution is, however, primarily to be sought at the national rather than transnational level in this instance.

The social and political significance of the *Five Obstructions* example has to do with the decision of an already successful individual (Lars von Trier) to refuse the more than likely possibility of ultimate success in what Robert H. Frank and Philip J. Cook (1995) call the "winner-take-all society" in order instead to make a gift of his talent and reputation to a colleague (Leth), and by extension, to a small national community.[31] In small-nation contexts, international success of the kind that von Trier has enjoyed, arguably since *Element of Crime* and certainly since *Breaking the Waves*, tends to produce what Albert Hirshman refers to as "exit."[32] Bille August, a figure who is now strikingly absent from the Danish landscape, is a clear case in point: previously unavailable opportunities for especially big-budget filmmaking elsewhere became irresistible, it would seem, following the success of *Pelle* at the Academy Awards ceremony in 1988. In von Trier's case, however, the highly individualistic strategy of exit is one that has been very consciously refused in favor of initiatives that are designed to make the relevant small-nation context a noteworthy site for innovative cinematic work. More specifically, von Trier's many different, and oftentimes manifesto-based, collaborative projects make a virtue of the various ways in which gift and exchange cultures can be combined.[33] The collaborative experiments that von Trier stages are clever marketing strategies and effective tools of self-promotion with clear pay-offs within an economy of exchange. Yet, they are also ingenious devices designed both to profile the insufficiently recognized talents of somewhat less successful small-nation filmmakers and to enhance the flow of reputation associated with Denmark as a nation committed to film culture and capable of producing talented directors and remarkable works. Von Trier's "help a colleague project," as he characterizes *The Five Obstructions* in a conversation that is recorded at the Zentropa Film Town and included in the experimental work, involves a number of different gifts: von

Trier's obstructions create the conditions under which Leth can break with personal style as stultifying habit and can rediscover and realize the promise of his earlier creativity; the collaborative framework transfers prestige from von Trier to the highly competent but much less visible Leth; and, finally, the gifts of reputation, talent, and creative stimulus combine with Leth's contributions to produce an intriguing work that brings recognition to Danish film more generally.[34] The gifts, that is, benefit not only the particular individual whose reputation (and thus range of creative options) is considerably enhanced, but also an entire network of small-nation filmmakers.

Cinematic transnationalism comes in many different forms and promotes a wide range of values, some of which are economic, artistic, cultural, social, or political. Any given instance of cinematic transnationalism may involve the pursuit of more than one kind of value, the various kinds of value being themselves differentially weighted depending on the type of transnationalism in question. In some types of transnationalism, for example, the turn towards the transnational is prompted by economic necessities (and thus values) but the overarching goal is to promote values other than the purely economic: the social value of community, belonging, and heritage in the case of epiphanic transnationalism; and the social value of solidarity in the case of affinitive and milieu-building transnationalism. That cinematic transnationalism is a ubiquitous phenomenon at the beginning of the new millennium is by now an accepted fact. The time is ripe as a result for work on cinematic transnationalism that goes beyond affirmative description in order to distinguish carefully among tendencies that are more or less positive within a larger scheme of things. It may be a matter, for example, of trying to ensure that cinematic transnationalism continues to find diverse typological expression, rather than being reduced to a single, in all likelihood, globalizing, type; or of supporting, with whatever cultural capital and analytic acumen scholars happen to command, those types of transnationalism where pragmatism is constrained by the pursuit of inherently worthwhile goals. Cinematic transnationalism is no doubt the future, but as such it is also an "open" phenomenon with the potential to develop in many different directions. Debates about questions of value and evaluation will be crucial in this connection, as will the articulation of the models, both descriptive and regulative, that underlie the empirical cases that the discourse of transnationality celebrates.

notes

1. There are exceptions to this way of using the term "transnational" and these include John Hess and Patricia R. Zimmerman, "Transnational Documentaries: A Manifesto," in *Transnational Cinema: The Film Reader*, ed. Elizabeth Ezra and Terry Rowden (London: Routledge, 2006), 97–108

(and the editors' helpful introduction); Meaghan Morris, Siu Leung Li, and Stephen Chan Ching-Kui, eds. *Hong Kong Connections: Transnational Imagination in Action Cinema* (Hong Kong: University of Hong Kong Press, 2005); Ella Shohat and Robert Stam, eds. *Multiculturalism, Postcoloniality and Transnational Media* (New Brunswick, NJ: Rutgers University Press, 2003); Sheldon H. Lu, "Crouching Tiger, Hidden Dragon, Bouncing Angels: Hollywood, Taiwan, Hong Kong, and Transnational Cinema," in *Chinese-Language Film: Historiography, Poetics, Politics*, ed. Sheldon H. Lu and Emilie Yueh-yu Yeh (Honolulu, HI: University of Hawaii Press, 2004), and Hamid Naficy's monumental *An Accented Cinema: Exilic and Diasporic Filmmaking* (Princeton, NJ: Princeton University Press, 2001).

2. Yasemin Nuhoglu Soysal, "Citizenship and Identity: Living in Diasporas in Postwar Europe?" in *The Postnational Self: Belonging and Identity*, ed. Ulf Hedetoft and Mette Hjort (Minneapolis, MN: University of Minnesota Press, 2002), 137–51.

3. Mette Hjort, *Small Nation, Global Cinema: The New Danish Cinema* (Minneapolis, MN: University of Minnesota Press, 2005) includes a lengthy discussion of affinitive transnationalism. This earlier discussion makes use of Carly H. Dodd's concept of "homophily," but the term "homophilic" is best avoided as it carries associations that are not part of my understanding of the relevant type of transnationalism.

4. See Richard Swedberg, *The Max Weber Dictionary: Key Words and Central Concepts* (Palo Alto, CA: Stanford University Press, 2005) for a discussion of Weber's concept of ideal types.

5. For a fuller discussion of epiphanic transnationalism, see Hjort *Small Nation, Global Cinema*.

6. On the blockbuster as a globalization strategy, see Tino Balio, " 'A Major Presence in All of the World's Important Markets': The Globalization of Hollywood in the 1990s," in *Contemporary Hollywood Cinema*, ed. Steve Neale and Murray Smith (London: Routledge, 1998), 58–73.

7. Carley H. Dodd, *Dynamics of Intercultural Communication* (Boston, MA: McGraw-Hill, 1998), 178.

8. I am grateful to Philip Schlesinger, who commented helpfully on the concept of affinitive transnationalism in response to a paper focused on *Red Road* and the Advance Party concept.

9. See www.sigmafilms.com.

10. See also "The Advance Party—A Timeline" (www.glasgowfilm.com/redroad/DOWNLOADS/AMENDED%20Advance%20Party%20Timeline.pdf).

11. Mette Hjort, "Denmark," in *The Cinema of Small Nations*, ed. Mette Hjort and Duncan Petrie (Edinburgh: University of Edinburgh Press, 2007), 23–42.

12. For a fuller discussion of *Advance Party* focusing on the milieu-developing features of this transnational initiative, see Mette Hjort, "Affinitive and Milieu-Building Transnationalism: The Advance Party Initiative," in *Cinema at the Periphery: Industries, Narratives, Iconographies*, ed. Dina Iordanova, David Martin-Jones, and Belén Vidal (Detroit, MI: Wayne State University Press, forthcoming).

13. Cited in Jesper Andersen, "Dear Europe", *EKKO* (February 2005).

14. Gina Marchetti, "Thinking Beyond Culture," Part 2 of "Transnational Cinema, Hybrid Identities and the Films of Evans Chan" (http//members.tripod.com/~ginacao/).

15. Evans Chan, "Preface," in *Evans Chan's To Liv(e): Screenplay and Essays*, ed. Tak-wai Wong (Hong Kong: Department of Comparative Literature, University of Hong Kong, 1996), 4.

16. Sheldon H. Lu, *Transnational Chinese Cinemas: Identity, Nationhood, Gender* (Honolulu, HI: University of Hawaii Press, 1997), 9.

17. See the interview with Zhang Yimou entitled "Hero News" in *Southern Daily* (November 24, 2001): 58.

18. Stephen Teo, " 'We Kicked Jackie Chan's Ass': An Interview with James Schamus," *Senses of Cinema* (March–April 2001), www.sensesofcinema.com/contents/01/13/schamus.html

19. Charles Acland, *Screen Traffic: Movies, Multiplexes, and Global Culture* (Durham, NC: Duke University Press, 2003), 11.

20. Almodóvar subsequently went on to direct *La mala educación* (*Bad Education*, 2004) instead.

21. Charles Taylor, *Modern Social Imaginaries* (Durham, NC: Duke University Press, 2004).

22. Sudipta Kaviraj, "Modernity and Politics in India," *Daedalus* 129, no. 1 (2000): 137–62.

23. George Yúdice, *The Expediency of Culture: Uses of Culture in the Global Era* (Durham, NC: Duke University Press, 2003).

24. An official account of the West Kowloon Cultural District can be found at www.hplb.gov.hk/wkcd/eng/public_consultation/intro.htm. Critics of the Hong Kong government's approach to the project include Stephen Chan, Ada Wong, Lung Ying-tai, and Mirana Szeto. Scholars and activists with a special interest in cultural policy, these figures are all working hard to redefine the vision for West Kowloon in ways that will make the project more responsive to the needs and aspirations of the local Hong Kong arts community.

25. Bérénice Reynaud, "Cutting Edge and Missed Encounters: Digital Short Films by Three Filmmakers," *Senses of Cinema* (May 2002).

26. I am very grateful to Chris Berry for putting me in touch with Kim Soyoung, and to Soyoung for graciously sharing her insights about the omnibus initiative.

27. The description of the *Five Obstructions* film was previously published in *Northern Constellations: New Readings in Nordic Cinema*, ed. Claire Thomson (Norwich, UK: Norvik Press, 2005), 111–29. I am grateful to Norvik Press for permission to reprint the passages in question here.

28. Jonathan Romney, "Lars von Trier, Nil, Jørgen Leth, Five," *The Independent*, November 9, 2003.

29. See Mette Hjort, "The Globalisation of Dogma: The Dynamics of Metaculture and Counter-Publicity," in *Purity and Provocation*, ed. Mette Hjort and Scott MacKenzie (London: British Film Institute, 2003), 133–57.

30. Jørgen Leth, *Det uperfekte menneske: Scener fra mit liv* (Copenhagen: Gyldendal, 2005).

31. Robert H. Frank and Philip J. Cook, *The Winner-Take-All Society: How More and More Americans Compete for Ever Fewer and Bigger Prizes, Encouraging Economic Waste, Income Inequality, and an Impoverished Cultural Life* (New York: Free Press, 1995).

32. See Albert Hirshman, *Exit, Voice, and Loyalty* (Cambridge, MA: Harvard University Press, 1970).

33. On the concept of gift culture, see Natalie Davis, *The Gift in Sixteenth-Century France* (Madison, WI: University of Wisconsin Press, 2000); Jacques Derrida, *Given Time*, trans. Peggy Kamuf (Chicago, IL: University of Chicago Press, 1992); Marcel Mauss, *The Gift: Forms and Functions of Exchange in Archaic Societies*, trans. Ian Cunnison, intro. E.E. Evans-Pritchard (London: Cohen & West, 1970).

34. The first issue of *Dekalog*, a series launched by Wallflower Press in 2008, is devoted entirely to *The Five Obstructions* and includes articles by Susan Dwyer, Mette Hjort, Paisley Livingston, Trevor Ponech, Hector Rodriguez, Peter Schepelern, and Murray Smith. Hjort's contribution focuses on the experiment as a problem-solving device designed to remedy a loss of cinematic style on the part of Leth.

tracking "global
media" in the
outposts of
globalization

three

b h a s k a r   s a r k a r

rerouting media circuits

Sometime in the mid-1990s, while pondering on the reception of Hong Kong genre films in my neighborhood in Los Angeles, I was miffed at the way in which the local cine-cognoscenti turned martial arts and ghost films into zany and inscrutable objects from a distant and wacky culture—objects that they loved, *and* loved to lampoon. Knowledge of these "cult" films was cultural capital in these cine-subcultures, raising the hipster quotient of their unofficial members. In a mild fit of Asianist outrage, I noted that martial arts films were typically described as "cool"—a glib designation that was ultimately dismissive "of the reality of Hong Kong, of the lived experiences and sensibilities of its people."[1] An urban, and largely urbane, North American audience fondly ascribed cult value to these "foreign" films through, ironically, a process of cultural devaluation. Similar poles of fascination and disdain would come into play over the next decade with respect to "Bollywood musicals," as these self-styled cosmopolitan audiences discovered and learned to love and laugh at yet another alien culture industry.

During recent trips to Kolkata, my birthplace and a city I still, habitually, call "home," I realized that its educated, urbane spectators (including my former classmates, friends, cousins) harbor the same kind of irreverent, if fond, attitude toward bloated Hollywood productions like *Titanic* (1997) or *Armageddon* (1998)—although they are much less patient with overblown Bombay concoctions like *Taal* (1999) or *Asoka* (2001). Even when they watch "classic" films like John Ford westerns on television or DVD (digital video disc), it is a leisure activity—in local lingo, "timepass"—with little or no concern for the cultural politics of American frontier mythology. Lo Kwai-cheung points to a similar emptying out of racial and ethnic dynamics in the reception of the two *Rush Hour* films (1998, 2001) in Hong Kong. While this duo of transnational blockbusters starring Jackie Chan did well in the Hong Kong market, much of the humor—springing from the misuse of the epithet "nigger" or the more flavorful invective "sweet-and-sour chicken ass"—was lost on local audiences as "they do not have a strong enough idea of racial stereotypes in American culture to understand the gags."[2]

Something is always lost in translation in the transnational circulation of film genres and, arguably, something unintended or unanticipated is gained.[3] As "Bollywood" emerges from its virtual obscurity in the West and becomes a global cultural phenomenon, Terry Zwigoff's indie-film sensation *Ghost World* (2001) uses a rambunctious song number from the Hindi film *Gumnaam* (1965) to introduce its young protagonist during the credit sequence: the camera pans across various windows of a tenement building, finally closing in on Edna dancing to a video clip of the song. A rather mainstream, generic artifact from another culture is deployed, out of context, to not only signal a sensitive young woman's disaffectation with her own cultural milieu, but also imagine an alternative, subcultural realm of belonging. Through its transnational appropriation, conventional and hegemonic Bollywood now becomes a sign of resistance, adding yet another twist to Hindi cinema's own voracious cannibalization of Latin jazz and funk of the mid-twentieth century to produce a populist and baroque version of cosmopolitan modernity.

Transnational cultural circuits abound in such echoes, kinks, gaps, and refractions—complexities frequently subsumed under the imputed global influence of the US culture industry we refer to as Hollywood. Indeed, "Hollywood hegemony" has become something of a cliché, a stumbling block to our understanding of contemporary global cultural networks. It is easy to point out that *Titanic* and *Armageddon* are transnational blockbusters, that the *Rush Hour* films are popular in Hong Kong in spite of their partial illegibility, that *Red River* (1948) or *The Searchers* (1956) are considered "classics" all over the world. But such reiterations stave off more attentive and supple theoretical approaches that are necessary to apprehend the concrete, ground-level intricacies of the transnational circulation and reception of cinematic representations.

In this chapter, I want to pursue the possibility of delineating a transnational media theory that is not held hostage by Hollywood. I do not mean to suggest that Hollywood does not matter; if such a claim would have seemed positively senseless half a century ago (not that anyone considered it then), even now—after the emergence of multiple transnational infotainment industries—it would come across as misguided. The myriad connections and interpenetrations of contemporary global media assemblages preclude claims to cultural exclusivity and Hollywood-shorn authenticity. To appreciate the linkages, one has to simply consider the recent spate of Hindi remakes of US film and television hits—*Kaante* (2002), based on *Reservoir Dogs* (1992), and *Kaun Banga Crorepati?* (2000), the Hindi component of the *Who Wants to be a Millionaire?* (1998) franchise, come to mind—and the Hindi mega-hit sci-fi *Krrish* (2006), with contributions from Hollywood special effects wizards Marc Kolbe and Craig Mumma (not to mention stunts choreographed by the legendary Hong Kong action director Ching Siu-tung, and financing from Singapore) and blatant visual "quotations" from recent Hollywood films like *Underworld* (2003) and *Spiderman 2* (2004). But what if Hollywood's hegemony is strategically bracketed—or, following historian Dipesh Chakrabarty's celebrated intellectual maneuver, "provincialized"[4]—within media theory, so that non-Hollywood cultural circuits come into analytical focus?

We have to be mindful of two sets of analytical questions here. First, what kinds of space-clearing epistemic shifts are in order if we are to undertake such an operation of provincialization? For instance, how must we revise some of our starting assumptions, frameworks, units of analysis: modernity, nation, history, globalization, and even theory, to name the most obvious? To begin with, we must distinguish between two senses of "global media theory"—one having to do with the globalizing of media theory (producing *global* media theory, i.e. knowledge about media that is global and not beholden to one particular locale), and the other relating to the theorization of global media (creating *global media* theory, i.e. knowledge about global media forms and assemblages). The emergence of translocal media forms (satellites, the Internet) and constellations (transnational media conglomerates like Viacom and News Corporation) have, no doubt, made it imperative that we develop global knowledge about media, eschewing or bracketing partially obsolete units and levels of analysis and addressing emergent realities. But this technological and economic imperative is not the only reason why media theory has to "go global." Recent experiences have underscored the necessity of overcoming entrenched assumptions that prompt entire viewing publics to think of CNN as the objective, unbiased voice of reason, and TeleSur or Al-Jazeera as a virulent propaganda machine (or exactly the opposite)—assumptions and value judgments whose roots can be traced back to nineteenth century colonial worldviews and mid-twentieth century Cold War mentalities. A genuinely *global media theory* must engage, and overcome, both techno-economic and political myopias. At a point when the balance of media theory is tilting toward cognitive apprehensions of the techno-rational, the new and the exciting, the intervention of this chapter is to underscore the persistence of the (neo)colonial in both contemporary media assemblages and within academic knowledge production.

Second, what are the potential pitfalls associated with such an approach? For instance, if we focus on cultural conduits that largely bypass Hollywood, if we engage in such a politics of cultural difference, do we not pigeonhole these transnational networks simply as Hollywood's marginal others, thereby limiting their significance? Meaghan Morris stresses the crucial need for "ways to account from multiple perspectives for the *connections* between otherwise disparate and often mutually indifferent film communities that transnational popularity entails;" she also warns us of the danger of reproducing the normative division between Hollywood and its others.[5] Consider the following conclusion to a *New York Times* review of the Hindi sci-fi *Krrish*:

> "Krrish" is overlong, schmaltzy, wholly derivative and sprinkled with underwhelming song-and-dance numbers. Coming from anywhere else, these elements might be considered glaring flaws. In Bollywood, they are not only expected, but often, as in this film, they also appear as virtues.[6]

Dismissing the film summarily, the critic then goes on to claim that its apparent "flaws" are "virtues" in Bollywood; this confounding doublespeak reiterates the established supposition that Bollywood is the "exception" to Hollywood's universalized ("anywhere else") norms.

In what follows, I pursue the problematic nature of extra-Hollywood transnational connections by examining an influential approach within transnational film theory (second section) and suggesting cross-disciplinary perspectives that I believe should inform contemporary takes on transnational media (third section). In the final section, I focus on two moments of cultural exchange that are cogent and compelling indices of a transnational media circuit involving China and India, the two outposts of globalization. I use the term "outpost" in a conscious mobilization of its two senses of "settlement" and "frontier": China and India have been colonized by the forces of global capital (in the tellingly invasive rhetoric of neoliberal imperialism, they have "opened up"); their incorporation within a global order remains incomplete and tenuous (China continues to be politically repressive, while Indian liberalization keeps getting bogged down in the quagmire of its democratic politics); they are characterized by a certain lawlessness (for example, the problem of "piracy" in flagrant contravention of international patent and copyright laws); and they are now widely seen as the engines of global economic growth. This uneasy status of the two

Asian powers in a US-led world system mirrors the ambivalent position of the Hong Kong (HK)-Chinese and "Bollywood" culture industries within the presumed Hollywood-dominated global media formation.

beyond exceptionalism and multiculturalism

Film theory originating in Europe or the United States, and focusing on Hollywood, European art cinema, Soviet revolutionary cinema and a handful of Japanese masters, has managed to masquerade as universal film theory, thanks largely to the twentieth century political economy of global knowledge production. The theoretical benchmarks derived from these specific cinematic traditions cannot account for Asian or Latin American popular cinemas which, in spite of the past decade's attempts to globalize knowledge structures, continue to be dismissed as heavy-handed and unsophisticated, and remain marginalized within English-language film history.[7] In his discussion of the legendary Hindi film *Devdas* (1955), Ravi Vasudevan demonstrates that the mise-en-scene and editing in the sequence of the hero's reunion with his childhood love, Paro, are crucially motivated by local cultural norms and visual and aural idiolects.[8] For instance, Paro's first glimpse of Devdas after a long separation consists of his feet in a doorway: as Vasudevan points out, this framing of the feet in a low-angle shot from Paro's point of view, in tandem with the flute music associated with the mythic romance between Radha and Krishna, harnesses the cultural notion of the male lover as an object of reverential devotion. My American undergraduate students append to this useful discussion a translational confusion: they think, on the basis of a western film idiom established by countless thrillers and horror films, that Devdas is a murderous villain about to attack Paro. One possible response to such "misreadings" is to argue that Hindi cinema is a unique and exotic case marked by its fundamental alterity from either Hollywood or European modernist cinemas—a response that no serious scholar of cinema will espouse at this point. Another approach is to claim that Hindi (or Bengali or Telegu) cinema has developed its own language and semiotic, and must be judged "on its own terms." Some scholars, like Corey Creekmur, maintain that the second approach leads necessarily to a claim about Indian cinema's exceptionalism, so that the Euro-American standards remain normative.[9] While I do not wish to insist on Indian cinema's radical alterity in relation to a presumed set of purely Western norms, I would like to hold onto the concept of cultural specificity as a key measure of any particular cinema: thus, an account or discussion or investigation of Indian cinema must historicize its codes and conventions not only in relation to international influences but also in terms of local cultural traditions. Attentiveness to specificity need not lead to an argument for exceptionalism. All the same, I am in emphatic agreement with Creekmur's provocative assertion that any theory of film must account for

Bombay cinema (or Mexican or Egyptian cinema), without treating it as an anomaly, if it wants to convincingly speak for "cinema" as "an international form of popular entertainment."[10] As I see it, the primary challenge confronting a translocal media theory is one of achieving a general applicability while being able to capture the continual negotiations and articulations through which local media forms come into being.

The naturalized and unquestioned preeminence of Hollywood is a logical corollary to a set of interlocking political, economic and social paradigms in terms of which we map modernity. A common definition of globalization as the latest stage of imperialism, that is of the unrelenting march of capitalism across the globe, produces understandings of the global that must always refer back, in affirmation or negation, to a worldwide hegemony now widely (mis)represented by the term "America." In the cultural arena, all endeavors and exchanges are seen either to consolidate Hollywood's hegemony, leading to the centralization of global media and the homogenization of cultures, or to offer resistance, marking the partial triumph, real or imagined, of the local over the global. In either case, culture is being crucially defined in relation to a hegemonic order. Without ignoring the connections and interpenetrations of the contemporary world, one can still ask: must all transnational flows and experiences remain beholden to this deterministic relationality to the capitalist, industrialized West?

If to speak of the "American" is to invoke not only one particular national horizon but also the universal, then the "transnational" is, for all practical purposes, reduced to a transcending of every other national imagination in the service of an emergent uniformity. Contemporary globalism is then tantamount to the triumph of one localism (the American) over all other localisms. Interestingly, this very insight presents a way out of the unilateral, totalizing, and inevitable trajectory of capitalist or US-led globalization: it is possible to imagine the currently subordinate localisms vying for a more hegemonic position, even transforming themselves into alternative globalisms. While China and India are two important and obvious cases in point, other post-national constellations of challenge and resistance (non-governmental organizations (NGOs), legal aid counsels, environmental movements) are becoming increasingly significant: these new formations are being heralded as insurgent cosmopolitanisms and counter-hegemonic globalizations.[11] What can we learn from these novel assemblages of the transnational and the global, and what new approaches to media do they call for?

A detour through contemporary media theory might help by throwing into sharper relief for us the kinds of analytical shifts that are in order. I begin with an interrogation of a prominent body of critical scholarship associated with Ella Shohat and Robert Stam, media theorists whose work has had a seminal impact on my own intellectual formation. Their 1994 book, *Unthinking Eurocentrism*, had a profound effect on media studies, revealing the operations of—and delineating the challenges to—colonialist and racist epistemes in audiovisual representations. Yet, for all its incisive criticism and its engagement with Third Worldist media, this crucial and timely intervention was limited by its location within US academia: while attempting to forge an intellectual and political alliance with media practitioners and movements all over the globe, the book couched global cultural questions in multiculturalist terms integral to the US public sphere. At that point, I ascribed this epistemic compulsion to the demands of writing an effective and field-transforming textbook aimed at a particular audience (the "field" in question being US media theory posing, no doubt, as global media theory). But even after the academic world has become sensitized to the global politics of knowledge production, Shohat and Stam have persisted with this multiculturalist paradigm in their work on transnational media; their valiant attempts to justify this approach lead only to further analytic problems.[12] Thus, in the introduction to their co-edited volume, *Multiculturalism, Postcoloniality and Transnational Media*, they state that it is the term "multiculturalism" (as opposed to "postcoloniality") that best captures the challenges constituting a contemporary "seismological shift: the decolonization of European power structures and epistemologies."[13] At first glance, this formulation appears to be a regression from Shohat and Stam's earlier project of "unthinking"—i.e. dismantling—Eurocentrism. Now "European power structures and epistemologies" are basically rethought and recast ("decolonized") through a multiculturalist lens, continuing the post-Enlightenment narrative of European self-realization, of progress. When they state that "a radical version" of this multiculturalist project "calls for revisioning world history and contemporary social life from a decolonizing and anti-racist perspective" (7), they appear to be echoing Latin American scholars of postcoloniality—especially Walter Mignolo's emphasis on the necessity of a "decolonial imagination" for thinking with, against, and beyond Western epistemologies.[14] The decolonial gesture makes sense for the Americas, where local worldviews and life processes could not inform colonial modernity to the extent they did in the Arab world and Asia; in Egypt or Indonesia, for instance, decolonization involves a critical engagement with postcolonial syncretism.[15] My point here is that significantly divergent histories of various regions do not allow for the unproblematic, universal mobilization of either the "decolonial" or the "multicultural."

Shohat and Stam are aware of the limitations of "multiculturalism": they concede that the term is an "empty signifier onto which diverse groups project their hopes and fears" (6). In their estimation, critics from the Right attack multiculturalism as a continuation of 1960s revolutionism that seeks to destroy the norms and canons of the Euro-American world, and threatens to balkanize American (or French, or Dutch) society. Detractors from the Left see multiculturalism as a distraction from the real conflicts of class and political economy, and blame it for splintering radical movements.

In settler colonies like Canada and Australia, multiculturalism is associated with official programs "designed to placate ... and empower minorities" (6). (Shohat and Stam seem to distinguish US multiculturalism from its Canadian and Australian counterparts, thereby reserving a more radical-popular role for it. One could, of course, point to the politics of US Affirmative Action and various measures of socio-economic restitution aimed at Native American groups.) In each evaluation, multiculturalism refers back to, and is in dialogue with, a "national culture." Where does the *transnational* come into play in these negotiations? At various points (as on pages 4 and 12), Shohat and Stam suggest that multiculturalism is a force in various countries, and a comparative and coalitionary framework allows for a transnational multiculturalist project. It is one thing for multiculturalist tendencies and pressures to exist in Brazil, India and Nigeria, it is another to expect the American model of multiculturalism to work, or even to apply, in these disparate locations—the authors admit as much (12). What they do not specify is how we can move analytically from local multiculturalisms to a transnational multiculturalist project. A possible clue is provided by Shohat and Stam's definition of multiculturalism as "convenient shorthand for a body of scholarly work ... that critically engages issues of power relations rooted in the practices and discourses of colonialism, imperialism and racism" (6–7). Here, they appear to locate the multiculturalist project in critiques of systemic forces of power and subjugation that are translocal, and that produce world-historical phenomena. But structural similarities (e.g. class struggles) cannot always transcend the difference between historical instances: what precise mechanisms allow local multiculturalisms to congeal as global forces and movements?

In the light of these proposals by Stam and Shohat, one would presume an attentiveness to structural conditions and new global assemblages that might serve as the basis of post-national coalitions; yet, in this introduction to a volume on transnational media, Shohat and Stam barely address the translocal issues and historical complexities that are now central to the disciplines of comparative sociology, world history, and anthropology of globalization (see the following section). As such, multiculturalism remains a vague and slippery term; rhetorical gestures toward experiential complexity and explanatory capaciousness (note the frequent use of words like heterogeneous, polysemic, protean, plural, conjunctural, reciprocal, polycentric, differential, contingent, relational, contradictory, competing, dissonant) further compound its opacity. The heterogeneity and multiplicity held implicit in the concept place all agents, if not on a level playing field, then at least within reach of a horizon of potential equality: the irreducible *agon* of modern history is virtually erased by a liberal projection of *equivalence*. If the question of hegemony (and its transmutations) is deflected, it cannot be contained—let alone "solved"—by this rhetoric of multiculturalism. For instance, the current demand for the revision of history textbooks by Hindu groups in California, on the plea that extant books shortchange Hindu culture and history, can be framed, within the US context, as part of an ongoing debate about multiculturalism.[16] But such a local perspective cannot advance any understanding of this demand as part of a new global hegemonic formation, a resurgent Hindu chauvinist strain of Indian nationalism that seeks to produce its own, totalizing versions of all things Indian.

Ultimately, Shohat and Stam's polemical and agenda-setting call for the "transnationalization and the multiculturalization of the media studies curriculum" (2) betrays a narrower concern. A long exegesis of the cultural politics of race and ethnicity (2–4), the twin obsessions of Western European and American academic and political life, and a manifest concern about the American audience's limited awareness of the world at large (5) frame this polemic. The catalytic impetus behind their reinscription of media studies is clear in the conclusion to the first section: "At this point in history, *as a consequence*, transnationalizing media studies has become a political and pedagogical responsibility" (5, my emphasis). One is left with a strong sense that their location of culture—and critique—is steadfastly American, that the operation of "transnationalizing" is to be pressed in the service of one particular national domain. One locale remains central to, and animates, this translocal imperative. I am reminded of a cover story in the independent-liberal Los Angeles news magazine, *L.A. Weekly*, from the early 1990s. The feature, in attempting to establish Los Angeles as part of the global South, declared that the metropolis was "the capital of the Third World." The center of any world, even the Third World, had to be located back in the United States: well-minded coalitional politics unwittingly devolved into a more ambivalent, perhaps even ironic, form of US-centrism.

Just as multiculturalism within one nation-state recognizes differences, parades minorities and promotes a politics of identity, all the while maintaining the naturalized dominance of one ethnic position,[17] similarly a transnational multiculturalism would seem to institute a hierarchical global order in which a few ethnically and culturally similar nations retain a locus of primacy and privilege. Global multiculturalism would appear to provide the cultural basis of neocolonialism, arranging various local cultures in a global hierarchy, exhibiting them to a cosmopolitan audience as a global menagerie, and fostering exceptionalist nativism and civilizationalism.

Before moving on, I want to hold on to one sentence in Shohat and Stam's introductory chapter: "In a globalized world, it is perhaps time to think in terms of comparative and transnational multiculturalism, of relational studies that do not always pass through the putative center" (4). While their governing framework remains beholden to that very "putative center," and they pay scant attention here to the forces, agents and circuits of globalization, this injunction steers us in a useful direction. Also, there are several chapters in their coedited volume that offer valuable insights into the radical transnationality of contemporary media, and advance new analytical approaches and research paradigms.[18] And to be fair to Shohat and Stam, one must note that in a more recent essay, "Traveling Multiculturalism," they attend to transnational circuits wrought by inter-linked colonial histories (in this case, the constitutive presence of the Black Atlantic in contemporary Brazil, France, and the United States), in order to underscore the necessity of overcoming the narcissistic investment in "nation-state thinking" in debates about race relations and multicultur-alism.[19] Nevertheless, concerns about the imputed equivalence of various locales and the blind spot regarding mutating transnational hegemonies remain.

globalization, imagination and the politics of circulation

A commonplace of contemporary intellectual thought is that we cannot assume an object of study to be simply "out there," that any serious scholarship must pay attention to the ways in which it construes its subject. And yet, in actual practice, this reflexivity is often sorely missing. What contemporary critical provocations should inform the incipient field of global media studies in its dual senses—theories of local or national media in a global, comparative frame, and theories of translocal, global media forms and flows? At stake is the articulation of a politics of global media studies. With this intent in mind, I want to gesture toward certain cross-disciplinary interventions that might prove productive for film studies as a discipline.

The professed "globalization" of contemporary media rests on the claim to something new, both qualitative (scope, nature, form) and quantitative (audience size, intensity of penetration). While there is ample evidence to back up this discourse of novelty, we need to be circumspect about the relentless presentism that marks theories of globalization in general. It is easy to slide into an ahistorical focus on the current conjuncture and give in to hyperboles of novelty, fostering a "new age" approach to social and cultural theory: economics sans history, politics sans memory, and media studies sans media genealogies. Global media theory would then appear to be driven primarily by the notorious capitalist appetite for novelty, raising doubts about its ability to challenge or move beyond a deterministic script of capital. This is why it is important that we supplement theories of technological and industrial developments in media with ideological and political economic analyses, locate globalization in relation to the long *durée* of capitalist modernity, and complicate the very notion of modernity in terms of multiple spatial and temporal horizons. Let me elaborate.

The rhetoric of "being modern" matters in ways that do not always conform to the hallowed modernist virtues of rationality and objectivity: one need only think of the psychic and material effects on entire populations of

43

loaded designations such as traditional, backward, regressive. If the definition of modernity is limited to the post-enlightenment era, then Europe (and, by extension, North America) remains the engine of humanity's march toward progress and emancipation: the rest of the world can, at best, tag on, hoping to catch up someday. As scholars of global history such as Janet Abu-Lughod, Kirit Chaudhuri, and John Hobson have demonstrated, China, India, and the Arab world were already modern in the contemporary sense of the word (comprising the familiar criteria of the flowering of technoscience and the arts, global commerce and exchange of ideas, entrepreneurship and accumulation, and rational-bureaucratic systems of governance) when Europe was mired in medieval darkness.[20] Indeed, it may be argued that an Asian globality, captured in such romanticized invocations as the "Silk Road,"[21] was largely instrumental in motivating European explorations and entrepreneurship: Asia, in other words, was constitutive of European modernity. These studies are significant not because they establish an "Orient first" worldview but because they serve to destabilize an endemic Eurocentrism, revealing the non-linear course of global history. One has to be careful of such world historical reorientations, lest one ends up producing an inverted binary—yet another hierarchical worldview. Moreover, scholarly attempts to reinstate China or India's primacy—that, for one commentator, represent "a kind of retroactive Sinocentrism and Indocentrism"[22]—must be placed in relation to the contemporary capitalist resurgence of Asia: in a sense, these contributions too are underwritten by the movements of global capital.[23] Nevertheless, revelations of earlier moments of oriental globalization complicate the temporal arc of global modernity.

If we limit ourselves to the temporal horizon of the past three centuries, a different set of critical interventions that are primarily spatial in nature come into focus, displacing the centrality of a Euro-American modernity. Scholars such as Charles Taylor and Arjun Appadurai argue that diverse practices of the imagination in different regions of the world, drawing on local cultural resources in tandem with more universalized sensibilities, produce variegated conceptions of modernity and globality.[24] Such considerations of differential imaginative practices split up the idea of a universal modernity into multiple visions and parallel experiences of modernity. From such an analytical vantage point, when South Asian rocket scientists consult astrologers before they undertake personal ventures, it is not a simple matter of regression into superstition: rather, apparently incommensurate practices are taken to constitute a specifically South Asian modernity. Indigenous cultural practices of postcolonial societies, long dismissed as traditional and retrograde when different from European standards, are not necessarily viewed as problems that must be overcome, just as these collectivities are not summarily relegated to the "waiting room of history"—forever falling behind, forever waiting to become modern. In place of a monolithic globality, we now speak of a range of globalities.

Yet another kind of challenge to notions of being modern comes from contemporary science studies, questioning the professed modern penchant for rigorous definitions and rigid demarcations of various categories (nature and culture, human and object, fact and fiction). In actual practice, such modernist distinctions serve heuristic functions and are rarely, if ever, strictly maintained: in Bruno Latour's provocative words, "we have never been modern."[25] Instead, we work with hybrid categories that transcend purist boundaries between disciplines, approaches and attitudes, and bring together presumed opposites—politics and science, nature and technology. In the light of this contention, rational (Euro-American) modernity begins to take on the attributes of a remote ideal, one with limited relevance in quotidian life.

What these interventions tell us is that modernity and globalization are far more complex and variegated phenomena than they are usually made out to be; that the East-West, traditional-modern, regressive-progressive polarities are largely modernist myths which mask significant contiguities across the globe and continuities over time; that these myths have, nevertheless, profoundly influenced—and continue to shape—our worldviews, a core element of which is a lingering impression of Euro-American ascendancy; that we can challenge this hegemony in terms of an understanding of the grand sweep of human history as a series of uneven turns in the fortunes of various regions; and that we can move beyond a persistent colonial mentality by recognizing and holding onto the myriad imaginative negotiations through which various societies mold their own distinctive modernities, their own globalities.

If a utopian note tinges these vital critical insights, both its urgency and its tenuousness become patent in the light of contemporary institutional, material and ideological realities. After the fall of the Communist bloc, a unipolar global configuration of power has come into existence; at the core of this constellation is the so-called Washington Consensus, composed of deregulation, limited government, privatization, and structural adjustment programs. These primarily economic measures come packaged with a set of political frameworks and values—democracy, freedom, rights, choice— that provide a veneer of legitimacy, but which remain largely vacuous slogans.[26] This neoliberal agenda is propagated, even enforced, by international organizations like the United Nations (UN), International Monetary Fund (IMF), World Trade Organization (WTO), World Bank and the G8—whose purported global nature is put to question by the incommensurate influence wielded by the sole superpower. Commentators have argued that neoliberalism is tantamount to neocolonialism: a turning around of the global process of decolonialization—producing a "reverse postcoloniality," as it were.[27]

While anxieties about identity and sovereignty, unleashed by globaliza-tion's radical redrawing of territorialities and communities, have produced a resurgence of fervent nationalisms all over the globe, the very idea of the national has come under critique for a host of ethico-political concerns. This is not the place to rehearse critiques of the nation form and of the state.[28] For my purposes here, it is more important to ask: if the nation-state is a "bad object," in what other ways can the local counter an increasingly Orwellian global order? Partha Chatterjee's point that there is a continuing necessity of speaking from within the nation, even when official nationalisms have proved antithetical to participatory democracy, remains a pertinent intervention.[29] Still, what are the possibilities of fostering decentered translocal solidarities for which inclusion does not imply obligatory subordination? Post-statist alliances and institutions (World Social Forum, NGOs) which operate at a translocal level, provide a space for counter-hegemonic imagination and praxis: various locals come together around their common interests to resist and reverse the processes through which they are marginalized, devalued, taken apart, reconstituted according to "global" norms, and incorporated into the new order. Ideals and institutions that are legacies of post-enlightenment thought and, therefore, inherently Eurocentric, are getting reworked via local ground-level practices. Civil society and the public sphere are now terrains more contested than ever before, facing challenges from parallel systems of social being and alternative paradigms of political culture.[30] Instead of a universal cosmopolitanism, we now speak of actually existing, rooted or insurgent cosmopolitanisms—indicating a range of global *imaginaires* and sensibilities.[31] In place of a hegemonic localism masquerading as an all-encompassing transnationalism, we invoke "vernacular modernisms,"[32] and will into existence multiple "minor transnationalisms" that allow for the transversal production and performance of cultures "without necessary mediation by the center."[33]

The rhetoric of transnationalism does not guarantee the end of inequity and injustice: in fact, it frequently engenders new orders of oppression and exploitation. Thus it is important to ask: as we move beyond the space of the nation, on what basis do we forge new affiliations? Kuan-hsing Chen poses precisely this question, and provides his pithy answer:

> [W]ith what sort of specific subjects could one identify? The male chauvinist Oriental? Upper-class privileged whites? African governing elites who kill their own human rights activists? Or the transnational corporate hybrid subject who rips off all the poor labor on earth? Certainly not.[34]

Instead, he calls for a strategy of "critical syncretism" which involves "becoming others" by "actively interioriz[ing] elements of others into the subjectivity of the self."[35] That is to say, critical syncretism would entail working toward dismantling imperial and hierarchical power relations and ending unequal exchanges. At stake is the creation of a transnational, global order comprising level interactions, horizontal constellations, and a more ethical politics.

Boaventura de Sousa Santos sums it up for us when he claims that globalization continues to be a fundamentally *political* question: its intense and far-reaching transformations cannot be reduced to technical concerns alone.[36] The implications of this assertion are germane to this chapter, and are worth enumerating before we move on. Globalization is an immensely agonistic and stratified phenomenon, whose only certitudes are transience and flux, unforeseen risks and opportunities; therefore, its outcomes cannot be predicted with any measure of confidence. Nevertheless, it is unlikely to lead to the radical homogenization of identities and cultures. Resurgent locales will contest existing hegemonies and new power alignments will come into being, producing new transnational elites and subaltern populations and creating fresh potentials for negotiations and struggles. How can media studies reconfigure itself to intervene effectively in this global field? In the final section, I gesture toward one tentative answer by focusing on media assemblages linking China/HK and India.

between china and india

After three decades of the so-called Asian Miracle, in which Japan, South Korea, and the ASEAN (Association of Southeast Asian Nations) economies held center-stage, China and India—relative latecomers to the global capitalist fold—have emerged as the engines of a long-term Asian resurgence. With their billion-plus populations and well-trained technical and managerial labor forces, they appear ready to set the terms of global economic growth in this century. But there is much ambivalence in global public discourse about these frontier settlements of globalization: while China has posted growth rates of around 10 percent for the better part of the period since the late 1980s, it remains politically repressive and projects an air of secrecy about its socio-cultural policies. If India has seen the flowering of democratic institutions and rights and enjoyed high growth rates since the early 2000s, it has also been plagued by sectarian violence, separatist movements, and strong political pressures that threaten to derail the process of economic liberalization.[37] Detractors of their capitulation to global capital point out that both countries are ignoring the deleterious effects of the rapid transformations on large sections of their populations: they cite untold miseries of peasants and workers negotiating the new regimes of finance, management and governance obsessed with returns, efficiency and formalization, and falling through the cracks into destitution, crime, even suicide. The element of uncertainty about China and India's "performance" is compounded by widespread speculations about their conflicted attitudes toward the so-called Washington Consensus, their positions that are sometimes adversarial to the economic and political interests of the United States and the European Union (EU), and their ability to calibrate—even shape—the terms of global capital. The two emerging powers are endlessly pitted against each other,[38] producing a hyped sense of intense bilateral competition when, in fact, it is the prospect of their cooperation in the fields of energy, communication and commerce that produce anxieties in the rest of the world.

Consider, for instance, the loaded question of global intellectual property rights—a question that congeals around media copyright and patent law infringements. In a twist to their "frontier" status, both China and India have garnered notoriety with regard to film, music, and software piracy. But the issues and arguments are complex and polyvocal: indeed, many would view media piracy as local subversion of global hegemonies in the "para-sites of capitalism."[39] As the well-publicized cases over turmeric and basmati rice patents have demonstrated, attempts to usurp and institutionalize local knowledge in terms of global laws constitute a form of neocolonization: once more, the "settlement" status of India makes it vulnerable to global pressures that turn it into a mere source of "raw materials"—this time, bio-knowledge.[40] Yet, we are seeing initiatives at protecting intellectual property rights against local and translocal contraventions: Bollywood's Yash Raj Films rails against videopiracy at home and abroad; Chinese Anti-Piracy Office announces a hundred-day crackdown on audio-video piracy between July and October, 2006; NGOs and some national governments press the UN and the WTO to protect the biodiversity of the global South from the greedy incursions of transnational corporations.[41] Meanwhile, a new law passed by the Indian Parliament in March 2005, conforming more closely to the WTO Agreement on Trade-Related Aspects of Intellectual Property Rights (TRIPS) threatens to raise the price of HIV drugs in Africa, causing demonstrations outside Indian embassies in various African capital cities.[42]

The patent and piracy wars graphically intimate the vicissitudes of globalization for nation-states like China and India: while they are not quite the underdog "minor" countries, they do have to negotiate translocal institutional arrangements that continue to undermine their sovereignties and to privilege the interests of the more developed North. As they insert themselves into the new world order, as they stake out their increasingly influential positions at governing global fora, can they hold onto earlier transnational imaginations and networks, be it socialist ideals of equity and justice, non-aligned pacifism, or South-South cooperation? Or do these emergent powers have to reinvent and realign themselves completely, severing past transnational affiliations in favor of membership in a more exclusive club of the privileged?

The sheer demographic mass of India and China, the very factor that is vaunted as a mark of their global importance, introduces a further set of contradictions at the heart of their capitalist makeovers: the rapid techno-economic strides cannot mask the rising inequities, the naked disparities between the hegemonic and the subaltern classes, the expanding gulf between metropolitan centers and the hinterlands. While the ruling classes enthusiastically champion the turn towards globalization, the emergence of new coalitions among disaffected economic and social groups is generating internal political pressures.[43] Global media theory, in the dual senses of "globalized media theory" and "theories of translocal media forms and networks," must be informed by these contingencies and complexities.

In the balance of this chapter, I want to provide some sense of the kinds of scholarly projects I am alluding to, by focusing on two moments of cinematic exchange between China and India. Two points, central to my argument, are worth emphasizing here. First, the global, in the true sense of the word, should designate a situation in which each local is shot through with other locals; thus a translocal approach must work to transcend every local, challenging any extant inter-local hierarchy. Second, the instances of transnational cultural exchange I bring up are neither fully outside the purview of, nor completely inscribed by, the nation-state or global capital: rather, they operate at the level of the translocal-popular—the level which, while largely complicit with hegemonic apparatuses, continues to hold as-yet-unrealized promises of democratic imaginations and interventions. By examining this translocal-popular exchange, we can avoid slipping into the problems of exceptionalism, exoticism and containment associated with the multiculturalist paradigm.

Our first locus of cinematic interaction is the post-1980s popularity of the Chinese martial arts genre in the southern Indian state of Andhra Pradesh. Scholars of Asian cinemas have begun to study martial arts as a transnational genre, tracing one locus of interactions between Hong Kong, Hollywood and Indian cinemas.[44] S.V. Srinivas, in particular, has produced remarkably textured accounts of the Hong Kong connections of the cinema of Andhra Pradesh. He addresses not only HK cinema's impact on local Telugu-language films, but also the vibrant fan culture that has developed around the exhibition of HK martial arts films in the region's B-circuit theaters.[45] To begin with, Srinivas points to the banality of cinematic "influence" and of attempts to trace it. Originality has never been an absolute, or even crucial, requirement for Indian (or other) popular cinemas: as a modern cultural medium, cinema has thrived on cross-cultural interaction and pollination. He calls for a shift of focus to "the processes at work in the act of borrowing," which get "obfuscated" by "the tracking of influence" in its misleading "attention to what is trivial."[46] In his work, Srinivas fleshes out the local dynamics of "borrowing" by charting the ways in which aspects of HK martial arts films become constitutive elements of the Telegu mass-film. He explicates the iconic function of the star-hero in Telegu cine-culture, especially his role, as a "bearer of history,"[47] in a regional linguistic identity and politics. Of particular interest is the two-prong crisis that has come to beset Telegu cinema from the 1990s, related to the place of a regional Telegu

49

nationalism vis-à-vis an increasingly confrontational and totalizing Indian nationalism, and to the representation of the star-protagonist. In the film *Bhadrachalam* (2001), it is through the invocation of martial arts that these dual levels of crisis are mediated and symbolically resolved. The star-hero now has to efface his subnational identity and uphold the national in the global arena: he emerges triumphant against a racially white Korean contestant in the finals of a taekwondo championship in Bangkok. Confronting a global opponent, even the hero's arch-rival from his home town becomes his ardent supporter, forgetting past enmity in a fit of nationalist fervor: the global proves to be crucial in producing "a nation free of antagonisms."[48]

Srinivas extends his own work on Telegu cinema's fan culture[49] to produce a compelling account of the spectatorial communities that have congealed around HK martial arts films in the B circuit of film exhibition in Andhra Pradesh.[50] The films are shown when they have already been in distribution for a while, and the extra revenue that is generated is a minuscule portion of the total box office receipts. The "status of the 'film as product' is jeopardized" in the B circuit: the films are "tampered with," with pornographic footage having no relation to the narrative spliced in; the theaters have uncomfortable seating, poor quality sound and projection, and unreliable screening schedules.[51] Nevertheless, the industrial marginality of this scene is incommensurate with its patent cultural significance. Noting that "audiences here are more or less left to their own devices, . . . free to indulge in all modes of excesses,"[52] Srinivas demonstrates that it is through audience activities that HK films take on their local import. There are practically no fan associations dedicated to HK stars, as these clubs have been linked with the local politics of linguistic identity through the historically constructed iconicity of Telegu (and other southern languages—Tamil, Kannada, Malayalam) film stars. Instead, HK martial arts and its stars become the fulcrums of cultural activities ranging from "the mushrooming of schools and 'institutes' offering training in East Asian martial arts,"[53] with explicit allegiances to specific HK stars, to "popular print literature in Telegu" encompassing "self-help books" and "detective novels."[54] Srinivas underscores the democratic nature of these fan activities, transcending caste and class divisions; I would also like to emphasize the dynamics of bracketing a "national" cine-culture centered on Hindi-language ("Bollywood") films and fostering a subnational cine-community through the localized invocations of a transnational cultural realm.

The immense popularity of "Bollywood" titan Raj Kapoor and his film *Awara* (*The Vagabond*, and *Liulanzhe* in China, 1951) in mainland China provides us with a second locus of Sino-Indian cinematic interaction. In his travelogue *From Heaven Lake* (1983), novelist Vikram Seth recounts hearing the hit theme song "Awara Hoon" ("I am wayward") hummed on the streets of Nanjing. Then, traveling through a small town in a more remote part of China, Seth has to perform the song on request at a local gathering:

No sooner have I begun than I find that the musicians have
struck up the accompaniment behind me: they know the
tune better than I do. The tubby man with the twirling
moustaches is singing along with me, in Hindi at that . . . I
am entranced, and, carried forward by their momentum,
pour out the lyrics with abandon . . . When the song ends
the orchestra and audience cheer me back to my seat. I am
giddy with euphoria.[55]

Next morning, this experience has a serendipitous aftermath: a local
bureaucrat issues Seth a travel permit, a rare privilege for foreigners,
allowing his passage through Tibet. Seth's experience is corroborated by
accounts of other visitors to China.[56] My own encounters with Chinese
expatriates in the United States have led to similar moments of immediate
affinity, with many of them breaking into energetic humming, if not actual
singing, of the theme song from *Awara*, or remembering another Hindi film,
Caravan (1971), famous in China as *De Peng Che*.

It is not clear precisely when *Awara* was released in China: it may have
been during the heydays of Sino-Indian friendship in the 1950s when, in the
wake of the decolonization of Asia, Mao's China and Nehru's India were
emerging as important representatives of the geopolitical South. It is worth
noting that *Awara* was a huge hit in the USSR, where it was dubbed into
several regional languages and widely distributed: such unmitigated
adulation must have furnished the film with a certain socialist pedigree.[57]
Therefore, it is not surprising that when China started to "open up" at the
end of the Cultural Revolution (1966–76)—a period in which all forms
of external influence became anathema and the domestic production of
films came to a standstill—Deng Xiao Ping's government looked close
to home for films with a strong social reformist message. It was in the late
1970s that *Awara*, Raj Kapoor and his character Raj (known locally as Laj or
Laji) became household names in China. In the opening minutes of
Jia Zhang-ke's *Zhantai* (*Platform*, 2000), an epic film that vividly captures the
social transformations over two decades, the young protagonists go to see a
foreign film. While we never see the screen, nor any posters outside the
auditorium, the soundtrack makes it clear that they are watching *Awara*. An
irritable father scolds his teenage daughter about her youthful penchant for
all things foreign: evidently, the shift to a cultural receptiveness after the
long collective insularity is going to be hard earned.

The tacit seal of approval from the Soviet bloc clearly facilitated
the Chinese distribution of *Awara*; the social reformist undertones of the
narrative (a debate about nature versus nurture, a proto-feminist critique
of patriarchal oppressions, a pitch for the remarriage of widows
and women's education, an impassioned plea for the social protection and
custody of orphans), and screenwriter K.A. Abbas' socialist leanings

and involvement with the Indian People's Theatre Association (the semi-autonomous cultural wing of the Communist Party of India), added to the film's appeal for the Communist Party of China and the cultural establishment. But beyond this official interest, the enduring popularity of the film still merits scrutiny. To understand how translocal affective communities coalesce around a film, we need to address how it engages a complex web of experiences and affects, commitments and fantasies, structures and belief systems. This requires, ideally, ethnographic research on Chinese audiences and their investment in Hindi films like *Awara* and *Do Bigha Zameen* (*Two Acres of Land*, 1953): it is the kind of project that I have been arguing for in this chapter, but that is beyond its scope. For now, I will offer some observations that are partly conjectural, and partly based on conversations with my friends from the PRC.

Much has been made of the somewhat "Chaplinesque" protagonist Raj, played by the director himself. While Kapoor did develop a clownish, tramp-like persona more explicitly in *Shri 420* (1955) and *Mera Naam Joker* (1970), Raj remains more of a charming scoundrel, a happy-go-lucky conman with a big heart. The similarity to Chaplin's loveable tramp is superficial, as in the awkwardly short trouser length; the rage simmering in Raj is missing from Chaplin. It is primarily his plebeian character, his street-smart ways, and his sardonic criticism of the rich and the powerful that endear him to audiences, and turn him into a cross-cultural icon of populist aspirations. Raj's subjectivity—his humanity—is endangered by Law, both familial-patriarchal and statist-juridical. Judge Raghunath, his biological father, wrongs him time and again: first, he casts out his pregnant mother from their home, suspecting that she is carrying the criminal Jagga's child; then he is disdainful of the boy's friendship with Rita, his friend's daughter, on grounds of his lack of family name and status; finally, he gets embroiled with Raj in an implicitly incestuous romantic triangle, with Rita at its apex. Jagga willingly takes on the role of surrogate father and apprentices Raj to a criminal life, in a bid to disprove the judge's claim that blood is crucial to a person's character—that a felon's son always sinks into a life of crime, while a decent person's offspring grows up to be righteous. Things come to a head in this oedipal family melodrama when Raj ends up murdering Jagga and attacks Raghunath. In the ensuing courtroom battle, Rita—Raj's childhood love and now Raghunath's ward—reveals Raj's true identity and forces Raghunath to acknowledge his own mistakes. Raj goes to jail for a short stint, only after having the chance to make an impassioned speech about every society's responsibility to look after its underprivileged and its orphans.[58]

The melodramatic plot uses song numbers that draw on transnational cinematic elements (musical and fantasy sequences, as in the nine-minute-long dream sequence), and vernacular oral and theatrical traditions (most memorably, a group of folk singers reciting the mythological story of Rama and Sita, and suave women dancing at Rita's birthday party—in both cases, commenting on story events). It uses repetitive and coincidental structures (people keep referring to the debate concerning blood proclivities and social upbringing; Rita and Raj riff endlessly on his "savage" nature; when Raghunath gets suspicious about his wife, he has to preside over a case involving illegitimate pregnancy; Raj keeps serendipitously bumping into Rita; Raghunath's estranged wife gets run over by his car), and brazenly milks the pathos from poignant situations (the young Raj cannot afford a birthday gift for his friend Rita; later, Raj steals the necklace that Raghunath buys for Rita—as one presents her the unwrapped jewelry, and the other hands her an empty box, the necklace becoming the narrative's *point de capiton*, forcing Rita to recognize that her beloved Raj is a thief). The baroque setting (gigantic chandeliers and clocks, ornate bed-stand, gauzy and billowing window drapes) of Raghunath's home, from which his wife and yet-to-be-born son are evicted, underscores not only the twisted intensity of the judge's—and his family members'—suspicions, but also the enormity of the transgression that bars Raj from what is rightfully his. Later, the spiraling staircase, the grand piano, the armchairs and marble statues in Raghunath and Rita's home—all standard cinematic markers of grandeur and power—starkly frame Raj's social marginality.

Perhaps it is these melodramatic elements, thematic and formal, that elicit such fond and passionate responses from Chinese audiences to *Awara*, a film they find at once exotically foreign *and* familiar. One ought to substantiate this argument with reference to settings, characters and myths of Chinese literature and cinema, visual components and styles from architecture and the fine arts, and the musical and performative dimensions of Chinese opera. One ought also to investigate what is it that Chinese spectators take away, and hold onto, from *Awara* and other Raj Kapoor films. It is through such interrogations that we will be able to recognize—and bring into critical consciousness—the already operational transnational cine-communities and media assemblages that displace an all-encompassing hegemonic model. Only through the tracking of such cultural conduits can we hope to foster a global media theory that does not take Hollywood as its presumed epicenter, and reduce all other culture industries to its satellites.

53

notes

1. Bhaskar Sarkar, "Hong Kong Hysteria: Martial Arts Tales from a Mutating World," in *At Full Speed: Hong Kong Cinema in a Borderless World*, ed. Esther Yau (Minneapolis, MN: University of Minnesota Press, 2001), 159.
2. Lo Kwai-cheung, "Double Negations: Hong Kong Cultural Identity in Hollywood's Transnational Representations," in *Between Home and World: A Reader in Hong Kong Cinema*, ed. Esther M.K. Cheung and Chu Yiu-wai (Hong Kong: Oxford University Press, 2004), 76.

3. An interesting case study of cross-cultural misinterpretation is provided by Jinsoo An, "*The Killer*: Cult Film and Transcultural (Mis)Reading," in Yau, *At Full Speed*, 2001, 95–113.

4. Dipesh Chakrabarty, *Provincializing Europe: Postcolonial Thought and Historical Difference* (Princeton, NJ: Princeton University Press, 2000).

5. Meaghan Morris, "Introduction: Hong Kong Connections," in *Hong Kong Connections: Transnational Imagination in Action Cinema*, ed. Meaghan Morris, Siu Leung Li, and Stephen Chan Ching-kiu (Durham, NC: Duke University Press, 2005), 5–6.

6. Laura Kern, "Krrish," *The New York Times*, June 30, 2006.

7. In the first edition of Tim Corrigan and Patricia White's well-received introductory textbook, *The Film Experience*, nine (374–82) out of five hundred-odd pages are dedicated to post-World War II cinemas outside Europe and the United States; there is no mention of Indian cinema of the 1930s and early 1940s; Latin American cinema is wholly subsumed under Third Cinema, in complete disregard of popular cinematic traditions; as for pre-Communist Chinese cinema, the only reference to Shanghai is in relation to the Marlene Dietrich vehicle, *Shanghai Express* (1932). Corrigan and White, *The Film Experience: An Introduction* (New York: Bedford/St. Martin's, 2004).

8. Ravi Vasudevan, "The Politics of Cultural Address in a Transitional Cinema: A Case Study of Indian Popular Cinema," in *Reinventing Film Studies*, ed. Christine Gledhill and Linda Williams (London: Hodder Arnold, 2000), 130–64.

9. Corey Creekmur, "Picturizing American Cinema: Hindi Film Songs and the Last Days of Genre," in *Soundtrack Available: Essays on Film and Popular Culture*, ed. Pamela Robertson Wojcik and Arthur Knight (Durham, NC: Duke University Press, 2001), 376.

10. Influential theories of cinema spectatorship, for instance, need not be "adjusted" to account for the specific "case" of India; to the contrary, Bombay cinema, precisely because it is a mainstream cinema and thus unexceptional, even what one might call emphatically conventional, demands that theories of spectatorship must adequately account for it, if those theories are to remain broadly convincing and generally applicable to "cinema" as an international form of popular entertainment.

(Creekmur 2001: 376)

11. Boaventura de Sousa Santos, "Globalizations," *Theory, Culture and Society* 26, nos. 2–3 (2006): 393–99; Walden Bello, *Deglobalization: Ideas for a New Economy* (London: Zed, 2002).

12. Here I focus on two of Ella Shohat and Robert Stam's more polemical interventions from 1994 and 2003. However, the tendency to privilege multiculturalism runs through their work. See, for instance, Shohat and Stam, "Film Theory and Spectatorship in the Age of the 'Posts'," in *Reinventing Film Studies*, ed. Christine Gledhill and Linda Williams (New York: Hodder Arnold, 2000), 381–401; Stam and Shohat, "Traveling Multiculturalism: A Trinational Debate in Translation," in *Postcolonial Studies and Beyond*, ed. Ania Loomba et al. (Durham, NC: Duke University Press, 2005), 293–316.

13. Ella Shohat and Robert Stam, "Introduction," *Multiculturalism, Postcoloniality and Transnational Media* (New Brunswick, NJ: Rutgers University Press, 2003), 9.

14. Walter Mignolo, "Coloniality of Power and De-Colonial Thinking," introduction to the special issue of *Cultural Studies* 21, nos. 2–3 (2007): 155–67.

15. For an enlightening take on decolonization as "critical syncretism," see Kuan-Hsing Chen, "Introduction: The Decolonization Question," in *Trajectories: Inter-Asia Cultural Studies*, ed. Chen et al. (New York: Routledge, 1998), 1–53.

16. Scott Baldauf, "India History Spat Hits U.S," *Christian Science Monitor*, January 25, 2006; Daniel Golden, "New Battleground in Textbook Wars: Religion in History," *Wall Street Journal*, January 25, 2006.

17. A trenchant critique of multiculturalism's classificatory and exhibitionary complex, tracing it back to the racist ideologies of colonialism, is provided by Ghassan Hage, *White Nation: Fantasies of White Supremacy in a Multicultural Society* (London: Routledge, 2000).

18. See, for example, Brian Larkin, "Itineraries of Indian Cinema: African Videos, Bollywood and Global Media" (pp. 170–92) and Talitha Espiritu, "Multiculturalism, Dictatorship and Cinema Vanguards: Philippine and Brazilian Analogies" (pp. 279–98). Ana López, "*Train of Shadows*: Early Cinema and Modernity in Latin America" (pp. 99–128) provides a corrective to the presentism inherent in the very concept of "global media."

19. Stam and Shohat, "Traveling Multiculturalism."

20. Janet Abu-Lughod, *Before European Hegemony: The World System A.D. 1250–1350* (New York: Oxford University Press, 1989); K.N. Chaudhuri, *Asia Before Europe: Economy and Civilization of the Indian Ocean from the Rise of Islam to 1750* (Cambridge: Cambridge University Press, 1991); John M. Hobson, *The Eastern Origins of Western Civilization* (Cambridge: Cambridge University Press, 2004).

21. Frances Wood, *The Silk Road: Two Thousand Years in the Heart of Asia* (Berkeley, CA: University of California, 2002).

22. Jan Nederveen Pieterse, "Oriental Globalization," *Theory, Culture and Society* 23, nos. 2–3 (2006): 412.

23. The link between Asian capitalist success and the reframing of global economic history becomes obvious in André Gunder Frank, *ReOrient: Global Economy in the Asian Age* (Berkeley, CA: University of California Press, 1998).

24. Charles Taylor, *Modern Social Imaginaries* (Durham, NC: Duke University Press, 2004); Arjun Appadurai, *Modernity at Large: Cultural Dimensions of Globalization* (Minneapolis, MN: University of Minnesota Press, 1996); Dominic Sachsenmaier, Jens Riedel and S.N. Eisenstadt, eds. *Reflections on Multiple Modernities* (Leiden: Brill Academic, 2002).

25. Bruno Latour, *We Have Never Been Modern* (Cambridge, MA: Harvard University Press, 1993).

26. See the various contributions in Richard Applebaum and William Robinson, eds. *Critical Globalization Studies* (New York: Routledge, 2005).

27. Mark Driscoll, "Reverse Postcoloniality," *Social Text* 22, no. 78 (2004), 59–84; David Harvey, *Spaces of Global Capitalism: Towards a Theory of Uneven Geographical Development* (London: Verso, 2006).

28. I have addressed some of these concerns in the introductory chapter of my book, Sarkar, *Mourning the Nation: Indian Cinema in the Wake of Partition* (Durham, NC: Duke University Press, 2009). See also the essays in Geoff Eley and Ronald Grigor Suny, eds. *Becoming National* (Oxford: Oxford University Press, 1996); Mette Hjort and Scott Mackenzie, eds. *Cinema and Nation* (London: Routledge, 2000); Valentina Vitali and Paul Willemen, eds. *Theorising National Cinemas* (London: British Film Institute, 2006).

29. Partha Chatterjee, "Beyond the Nation? Or Within?" *Social Text* 16, no. 56 (1998): 57–69.

30. Writing about the global controversy surrounding the Danish cartoons of the Prophet Mohammed, Saskia Sassen suggests:

> In their dissecting of what is easily represented as clear and completed, such as the right to free speech, they illuminate a world of debates, disagreements, innovations, new struggles that lie ahead in carving out a terrain for free speech that, to use my words, can function in the frontier-zone, one where liberal democracies are but one collective actor.

She argues that we are witnessing the formation of a new frontier-zone, a new globality with new rights and new political subjects/actors:

> Frontier-zones are spaces of imbrication. They are *not* lines where civilisations clash. They are areas of hybridity. What liberal democracies are experiencing is the limits of their closure and of the presumption that the world should like the way they look.
>
> (Sassen, "Free speech in the frontier-zone,"
> *Open Democracy*, February 20, 2006,
> www.opendemocracy.net/
> faith-europe_islam/freespeech_3282.jsp)

31. Timothy Brennan, *At Home in the World: Cosmopolitanism Now* (Cambridge, MA: Harvard University Press, 1997); Bruce Robbins, "Actually Existing Cosmopolitanism," in *Cosmopolitics: Thinking and Feeling Beyond the Nation*, ed. Pheng Cheah and Bruce Robbins (Minneapolis, MN: University of Minnesota Press, 1998), 1–19; Santos, "Globalizations," 397. See also the essays in Leila Fawaz, C.A. Bayly and Robert Ilbert, eds. *Modernity and Culture from the Mediterranean to the Indian Ocean, 1890–1920* (New York: Columbia University Press, 2001).

32. Miriam Bratu Hansen, "The Mass Production of the Senses: Classical Cinema as Vernacular Modernism," in *Reinventing Film Studies*, ed. Christine Gledhill and Linda Williams (London: Arnold, 2000), 332–50; Hansen, "Vernacular Modernism: Tracking Cinema on a Global Scale," Chapter 13 in this volume.

33. Françoise Lionnet and Shu-mei Shih, "Introduction: Thinking through the Minor, Transnationally," in *Minor Transnationalism*, ed. Lionnet and Shih (Durham, NC: Duke University Press, 2005), 5.

34. Kuan-hsing Chen, "Introduction: The Decolonization Question," in *Trajectories: Inter-Asia Cultural Studies*, ed. Chen et al. (New York: Routledge, 1998), 25.

35. Ibid. For a philosophical take on the ethics of globalization, see Peter Singer, *One World: The Ethics of Globalization* (New Haven, CT: Yale University Press, 2004).

36. Santos, "Globalizations," 395.

37. The following are all from covers of influential English-language magazines since 2004: "China's Growing Pains," *The Economist*, August 21, 2004; "Inside Bollywood," *National Geographic*, February 2005; "China's New Revolution: Remaking our World, One Deal at a Time," *Time*, June 27, 2005; "The New India," *Newsweek*, March 6, 2006; "How to Make China Even Richer," *The Economist*, March 25, 2006; "Can India Fly?" *The Economist*, June 3, 2006; "India Inc.," *Time*, June 26, 2006.

38. The media hype has prompted one commentator to quip:

> This argument has become particularly popular as both countries suck up greater amounts of US software and other technical outsourcing work. It's

also fun for people who know very little else about either country to look at the map and say, "Wow, China and India. They're both big countries. They both have huge populations. They're both in Asia." This is like Homer Simpson's school of geopolitics.

(Steven Schwankert, "Stop Comparing China and India," IDG News Service, July 6, 2006, www.infoworld.com/article/06/07/06/ HNcomparechinaindia_1.html)

39. This wonderful phrase is from Timothy Mitchell, *Rule of Experts: Egypt, Techno-Politics, Modernity* (Berkeley, CA: University of California Press, 2002).

40. Vandana Shiva, *Biopiracy: The Plunder of Nature and Knowledge* (London: South End Press, 1997); Ramachandra Guha, *Environmentalism: A Global History* (New York: Longman, 1999).

41. "Members step up demand on GI extensions, disclosure as stalemate continues," *Bridges: Weekly Trade News Digest* 10, no. 22, June 21, 2006, www.ictsd.org/weekly/06-06-21/story5.htm.

42. "Indian Parliament TRIPS Up," *Intellectual Property and Social Justice*, March 5, 2005, http://ip-sj.org/wp/2005/03/30/27/; "HIV Kenya Protest at Patent Law," *BBC News*, March 18, 2005, www.aegis.org/news/bbc/2005/BB050313.html.

43. In 2004, after the ruling Bharatiya Janata Party adopted as its campaign slogan the celebratory phrase "India Shining"—straight from a featured story in the February 21 issue of *The Economist*, the pro-liberalization international weekly from the UK—it lost in the elections, against all predictions, to a coalition of the Congress Party and various leftist outfits.

44. Lo Kwai-cheung, "Double Negations"; S.V. Srinivas, "Hong Kong Action Film and the Career of the Telegu Mass Hero," in *Hong Kong Connections: Transnational Imagination in Action Cinema*, ed. Meaghan Morris, Siu Leung Li, and Stephen Chan Ching-Kui (Hong Kong: Hong Kong University Press, 2006), 111–23; S.V. Srinivas, "Hong Kong Action Film in the Indian B Circuit," *Inter-Asia Cultural Studies* 4, no. 1 (2003): 40–62; Valentina Vitali, "Hong Kong-Hollywood-Bombay: On the Function of 'Martial Art' in the Hindi Action Cinema," in *Hong Kong Connections*, 125–50.

45. See the informative website, "Hong Kong Action Film at the Frontiers of Cinema," http://apache.cscsarchive.org/Hongkong_Action/index.htm.

46. Srinivas, "Hong Kong Action Film and the Career of the Telegu Mass Hero," 113.

47. Ibid., 114.

48. Ibid., 118.

49. S.V. Srinivas, "Devotion and Defiance in Fan Activity," in *Making Meaning in Indian Cinema*, ed. Ravi Vasudevan (New Delhi: Oxford University Press, 1999), 297–317.

50. S.V. Srinivas, "Film Culture, Politics and Society," *Seminar* no. 525 (May 2003): 47–51, www.india-seminar.com/2003/525.htm.

51. Srinivas, "Hong Kong Action Film in the Indian B Circuit," 56.

52. Ibid.

53. Ibid., 43.

54. Ibid., 42.

55. Vikram Seth, *From Heaven Lake: Travels through Sinkiang and Tibet* (London: Chatto & Windus, 1983), 11.

56. See, for instance, Atish Ghosh, "*Awara* in China," *TWFIndia.com*, April 25, 2004, www.twfindia.com/offTrackDetail1_25.04.04.asp, a story about Hou

Wei, a popular performer of Bollywood songs in Beijing, who sang for the Pakistani President Pervez Musharraf and impressed him with her "perfect Urdu." Pallavi Aiyar, "Bollywood's China Link," *The Hindu,* March 19, 2006, www.hindu.com/mag/2006/03/19/stories/2006031900270500.htm.

57. Sudha Rajagopalan, "Emblematic of the Thaw: Early Indian Films in Soviet Cinemas," *South Asian Popular Culture* 4, no. 2 (2006): 83–100.
58. For an extended critical discussion of the film, see Gayatri Chatterjee, *Awara* (New Delhi: Penguin, 2003).

time zones

and jetlag

four

the flows and phases

of world cinema

d u d l e y   a n d r e w

preamble: cinema out of step with itself

Cinema distinguished itself as the twentieth century's genuinely international medium. Far more than literature, so dependent on translation, films from the outset were watched by peoples in the most far-flung areas. Hardly had they invented the *cinématographe* than the Lumière brothers sent it around the world. This apparatus—capturing, processing, and projecting images—was carried like Stendhal's mirror on the backs of operators from region to region where people gazed at pictures of themselves and their surroundings taken just a few days or weeks before. This same footage was then shipped back to Paris which in 1900 functioned not only as a production source but also as a depot and distribution center. Imagine footage shot, say, in the Caucasus packaged for exhibition in Rio de Janeiro and vice versa. Many parts of the globe were touched by the *cinématographe*, each responding to this international phenomenon at its own speed, each stamping it with its own image and its own temporality.

This vast geographical flow of images, as well as the time-lag that inevitably accompanies it, remain still with us today even as the international circulation of cinema has become infinitely more complex. To achieve even the slightest historical understanding of "world cinema," in the following pages I wish to consider two ways to categorize the full phenomenon. First, we should be able to identify the patterns whereby, out of all films produced in the world, a certain set emerged that distributors, critics, scholars, and cinephiles consider to belong to the class of "world cinema." Second, we can note distinct historical phases of "world cinema" that reveal the aesthetic criteria employed, often unwittingly, to define this quite varied set of films which seem to speak to audiences everywhere, that seem to define a global matter. Although I propose five phases that periodize world cinema history (cosmopolitan, national, federated, world, and global), it must be stressed that the notions of cinema running through these phases often overlap and coexist; moreover, I am most interested in the ways in which certain films travel out of phase, for cinema in my view is constitutionally out-of-phase with itself. The critic, the scholar, and the cinephile, not to mention industry personnel, can find themselves repositioned by certain films that rework our very understanding of what the cinema holds out, what it represents, and to whom.

Surely all industries of cultural production can be tracked through geographical flow and historical phases, but not to the extent of cinema. When at mid-century television came along, it scarcely challenged cinema's internationalism, being at once congenitally national and potentially global. Television was immediately licensed by the state and, particularly during the broadcast era, was often fully state controlled. Even today it addresses its audience as national citizens, as in its ubiquitous news programs. At the same time, television can claim true globality because, in principle, everyone alive can simultaneously witness an event like the coronation of Queen Elizabeth II in 1953, or the World Cup every four years, or the annual Academy Awards. The audience for a film, however, even a blockbuster, can only be projected to be worldwide. "Box office projection," though not quite a mirage, is an image of the sum of innumerable actual projections taking place here and there, skipping borders and oceans over the course of what is called a film's "run." The synchronized release of *Star Wars: Revenge of the Sith* aimed to establish a Guinness Book of Records benchmark, a marketing stunt that is an exception proving the rule.

And that rule is that cinema's voltage depends on delay and slippage, what I dub the *décalage* at the heart of the medium and of each film between "here and there" as well as "now and then." This French term connotes discrepancy in space and deferral or jump in time. At the most primary level, the film image leaps from present to past, since what is edited and shown was filmed at least days, weeks, or months earlier. This slight stutter in its articulation then repeats itself in the time and distance that separates filmmaker from spectator, and spectators from each other when they see the same film on separate occasions. The gap in each of these relations constitutes cinema's difference from television. Films display traces of what is past and inaccessible, whereas television feels (and often is) present. We live with television continually as part of our lives and our homes; sets are sold as furniture. Keeping up a 24-hour chatter on scores of channels, television is banal by definition. In contrast we *go out* to the movies, leaving home to cross into a different realm. Every genuine cinematic experience involves *décalage*, jetlag. After all, we are taken on a flight during and after which we are not quite ourselves.

To track changing conceptions about a phenomenon that is forever out-of-phase with itself, we do best to hold fast to a particular domain. I will keep the East Asian region in view and monitor the potential energy accumulating, as it were, on that side of the International Date Line. From time to time (and increasingly) films and entire film movements jump the Date Line on their way to light up screens elsewhere, subtitled or dubbed of course. Spinning the globe until the Pacific Rim faces front represents an academic displacement of its own, since nearly all large-scale assessments of cinema have been made by and for the West, with the "Prime Meridian" running through either Hollywood or Paris. Miriam Hansen follows out in East Asia what she aptly terms "a theoretically inspired *histoire croisée*, a history of entanglement that traces actual interconnections."[1] She reminds us that Western accounts of cinema's development assume all too quickly a continuous narrative with Hollywood's norms as the trunk and mainly European alternatives branching and forking—but always growing—year after year. East Asia's nations, on the other hand, have clearly developed with less synchrony, and sometimes without any visible interaction among them at all. Neither the Chinese nor the Koreans could see a Japanese film for decades after World War II; nor were PRC features viewable in Taiwan, and vice versa.

The staggered development of forms of cinema within East Asia have resulted from far more complex patterns of circulation and influence than anything obtaining in the West. Despite political, economic, and linguistic blockages, films, personnel, money, and ideas have intermittently and increasingly circulated along the Pacific Rim. Moreover, depending on import restrictions and censorship, Hollywood influenced to varying degrees the shape of genres in each East Asian country, as did prominent European imports. This is not to mention the national or ethnic entertainment traditions that distinguish the way films are viewed, say, in distant PRC villages as opposed to Tokyo or to Bangkok. Perhaps the energy and the variety evident in current Asian cinema has been powered by the interface and negotiation of so many cosmopolitan and local forms. Emerging Asian cinemas have been more able than their European or Latin American counterparts to pick and choose among options held out by national traditions at one extreme and Hollywood or European modernism at the other, with intermediate options borrowed from neighbor cultures.

Quite distinct strains of national and regional styles and genres surely tell several histories of East Asian film, each harboring its particular idea of cinema. Just how have such ideas come into being and affected the way films are made and viewed? And where are those ideas to be found? In its first decades, before the existence of institutions like history, criticism, cine-clubs, and festivals, ideas of world cinema were best articulated by distributors and by those intellectuals and journalists drawn to this new art and to the way it visibly was reconfiguring the constellation of social life.

To return to the beginning, but now from an Asian point of view, the Lumière *cinématographe* was thought to complete, less than a half-century later, Commodore Perry's mission of opening up Japan. By 1910 concerned intellectuals and nationalists decried what they felt was unauthorized foreign exploitation: images of Mount Fuji, the Emperor's Palace, and Japanese beauties in ornate kimonos were being seized by the camera and shipped to the West, to be hawked at fairgrounds, interpolated into tawdry dramas, and in every case misinterpreted. At the same time, this spectacular foreign technology was a pipeline through which flowed images of Western customs, values, and commodities that challenged local mores and tempted some Japanese to cast their allegiance with a cosmopolitan community.[2] Soon a second anxiety would grip even those Asians who had joined this community: within a scant twenty years cinema's vaunted internationalism had been stamped with a particular national form, an American one. Hollywood began to set the tempo and express the temporality that spectators everywhere believed to be modern whether they embraced modernity or not. A great many did embrace it. "Vernacular modernism" is what Miriam Hansen terms this emergent and irreverent manner of participating in the twentieth-century life, a manner that took hold in cosmopolitan cities around the world.[3]

the cosmopolitan phase

Tokyo was one such city. In 1918, early in his dazzling literary career, Junichiro Tanizaki exploited to eerie effect the primacy of Hollywood and the internationality of cinema in a fantastic tale called *Jinmenso*. A detective story about a ghost that survives indefinitely on celluloid in old cans, only to be released into the audience during screenings, *Jinmenso* evokes a new cosmopolitan culture in which films from afar, transported like Nosferatu by ship, appear late at night on Japanese screens with disconcerting, sometimes deadly effects. Here is its tantalizing opening paragraph:

> Two or three times of late, Utagawa Yurie had heard rumors
> that a weird and ghastly film, a sort of mysterious drama in

which she played the heroine, was making the rounds in the outskirts of Tokyo, showing in rather infamous theaters in Shinjuku and Shibuya. Apparently, it was a motion picture from the time when she was in America playing all kinds of roles as an actress under an exclusive contract with the Globe Company in Los Angeles. According to someone who had seen it, at the end of the film, the company emblem, a globe, appeared, and in credits, the names of a number of Westerners were mixed in with those of Japanese actors. The Japanese title *Vengeance* was rendered in English as *The Tumor with a Human Face*, and it had a reputation as a superb work of mystery, a work full of aura and artistry.

Of course this was not a first for her; films that she made in America had shown in Japanese movie theaters. In five of six of the films imported from the Globe Company since her return to Japan, she made an occasional appearance, and from early on, caught the attention of her compatriots: her smooth, ample figure ranked her favorably with American and European actresses, and her lovely face tempered Occidental coquetterie with Oriental modesty. In her appearances on the silver screen, she showed a degree of vigor rare in Eastern women, and because she was possessed of pluck and liveliness that enabled her to laugh her way through adventurous scenes, she seemed to excel at roles that required both charm and agility, such as women bandits, dragon ladies, or female detectives. In one film in particular, *The Samurai's Daughter* that played some time ago in the Asakusa Shikishima Theater, Yurie's brilliant performance as the heroine roused the crowd of spectators. The story was about a Japanese maiden named Kikuko who becomes a spy because she must learn the military secrets of a certain country, and who travels all across Europe and Asia in various disguises, as a geisha, as a noble woman, and as a circus stunt rider. As a result of the tremendous popularity of the picture in Japan, last year she received a contract with the Nitto Film Company in Tokyo that stipulated an unprecedented high salary, and thus returned home after her four or five years in America.

Yurie, however, had no recollection of having acted in a production anything like *The Tumor with a Human Face*.[4]

Tanizaki's paranoia about Hollywood was shared by many of his countrymen. Americans, after all, had for some time been capturing pictures of Japan's sacred landscape and circulating them for profit. In the story, the

63

very "face of Japan," Utagawa Yurie, is kidnapped to Hollywood where she serves crass producers. Tanizaki's is a cautionary tale: this actress returns to Japan in *Vengeance* to suck the soul from anyone who dares to watch this film alone at night. It is the prototype for *Ringu* (1998) and *Pulse* (2001).[5] Even more prophetically, Tanizaki pointed to the clandestine itinerary along which movies exert their indefinable and variable effects as they pass from one locale to the next. For as the story continues, the actress, worried about a film she cannot recall having made, tracks down its Tokyo distributor, who gradually reveals that

> it wasn't bought directly from Globe; a certain Frenchman in Yokohama came and sold it. The Frenchman said that he had acquired it along with many other films in Shanghai and had long used it for pleasure at home. Apparently, before he bought it, it was used throughout the colonies in China and the South Seas, where it probably sustained much harm and damage.[6]

Later, the narrator will compare *Vengeance* to Paul Wegener's *Student of Prague* and *The Golem*, early landmarks of German feature film production. How had Tanizaki seen these? More important, how could he be sure that his readers would respond to these references? Clearly Tanizaki wrote for a cosmopolitan class. Symptomatically, he mentioned around this time that he preferred the society of film viewers to that of literati, the former being necessarily more cosmopolitan, even if less sophisticated.[7] Although his own stories could take years to be translated into German or English, he loved the fact that he could view *Student of Prague* in Tokyo shortly after its Berlin premiere, and could see it at virtually the same time that connoisseurs like him might watch it in London or New York. In its opening passage *Jinmenso* imagines an immediate international comradeship of enthusiasts, adventurous men in Tokyo, Shanghai and colonial outposts in the South Seas, all on the lookout for risqué and even dangerous amusements issuing from Los Angeles, and purveyed by a company with a likely name, "Globe Films."[8]

This interplay of the national and the international forces evident in the business practices of both the fictional "Globe Films" and the genuine Lumière Brothers encourages the adoption of another cognate, the *transnational*. Propitiously, the prefix "trans" connotes temporal as well as geographical extension, proposing not just a field to survey but also a process to understand, one that itself fluctuates in history. Successive historical phases (categorized here as cosmopolitan, national, federated, world, global) alter the process and the prominence of cinema's transnationality. In any given phase, producers similar to Globe Films and intellectuals like Tanizaki, as well as theater owners, critics, historians, and governmental officials, share a general sense of cinema's landscape. I aim to monitor the changing norms of world cinema, moving first from its early expansive cosmopolitanism to the national phase that a decade after the Tanizaki tale had tightened borders, erected customs houses, and would demand monolingual dialogue tracks as soon as sound arrived. Of course a certain cosmopolitanism survived during the 1930s, just as nationalism remains very much alive during more recent phases. Multiple notions of cinema always coexist but new notions can be seen emerging to color each phase; I always look for the emerging colors.

the national phase

Far beyond its due, "the national" has dominated conceptions of cinema right up to our own day. One can see it take hold in Japan at the end of the Taisho era in 1926 when "The Pure Film Movement" involving many of Japan's fashionable cosmopolitans at the front edge of modernity dissolved in the face of a nationalist backlash. Tanizaki himself ceased writing scripts, made a decisive sojourn (nearly a pilgrimage) to China, and moved from the secular port city of Yokohama to the sacred temple city of Kyoto. His ingenious and notorious essay of 1933, "In Praise of Shadows," specifically targets motion pictures as a Western invention unsuited to the temperament and even the skin tone of Asians.

Tanizaki's ideological retreat was hardly unique, for the interwar years drew the attention and most often the allegiance of many public intellectuals back to their separate lands and traditions. In 1935, the comprehensive film historians, Maurice Bardèche and Robert Brasillach, did not think twice about mapping cinema along national borders, with chapters on Italy, France, Germany, the USSR, and of course the United States. The communist Georges Sadoul relied on the same national paradigm as these two fascist critics when he countered their assessment of "international competition" with one of his own. These crucial tomes established an institution of film historiography that scarcely changed for fifty years, as textbooks, university courses, and museum screenings continue to parse cinematic output mainly by nation. Every country—the mature ones at least—was thought to have its distinct industry, style, and thematic concerns.[9] When notable personnel immigrate, it is presumed that they at best inflect the national predispositions of the host country that welcomes them. For instance England with its rigid class structure was allegedly a suitable place for someone like René Clair to exercise his charm within the comedy of manners, a genre that already flourished there. And German émigrés darkened what was already the pessimistic style of French poetic realism.

Sound bolstered the cinema's nationalist turn by immediately anchoring every film to a linguistic community and its literature (through the massive adaptation of plays in those first years). Everywhere foreign actors found themselves being replaced by performers from the national theater, since these reproduced the speech patterns and physical gestures of the national community.[10] Actors become familiar, fostering a feeling of familiarity and

65

by extension the self-recognition and affiliation that comprise nationalism. This is how many cinemas managed to flourish under the shadow of Hollywood, despite the latter's incomparable resources in technology, financing, and marketing. Even small national cinemas could modify Hollywood's universally popular genres to deal with local themes and topics. Most important, they could display on screen, as on a mirror, the physical and verbal gestures that comprise the hum of life within the national community. Comedies, for instance, often draw on a repertoire of references, locations, props, linguistic idioms, and actors, sufficient to suffuse an audience in pleasures of self-recognition, turning the movie theater into a large comfortable living room where citizens feel at home, no matter what the quality of the movie.

As would be the case with weekly serials during the age of broadcast television, the routine of genres and the routines of actors kept audiences of the interwar years mainly tuned in to their respective homelands. What Jean-Michel Frodon has dubbed *la projection nationale* merges native spectators into a uniform temporality, one with no lag at all.[11] A single heart beats to the timing of local comedy, throbs to the rise and fall of melodrama, and responds to the rhythm of patriotic works. The heroes of *Triumph of the Will*, *Alexander Nevsky*, *Scipio Africanus*, *Raja*, and *Young Mr. Lincoln* declaim not just to their rapt on-screen listeners but also to a vast audience that comprises what might be called the theater of the nation. Cinema thus extends Benedict Anderson's assertion that national feeling was made possible with the advent of daily newspapers linking readers across the land simultaneously.

Cinema's built-in time-delay, or *décalage*, registered less intensely in most interwar films, but functioned all the same at the collective level, as an issue of national tardiness or prescience. The Italians bemoaned their cinema as being "behind the times," while Hollywood promoted its products as "the next thing" in an inexorable advance in the medium. *Olympia* could be hailed by the Germans as raising the bar in what were effectively an Olympic games of cinema. Those games started in 1934 at the very first competitive festival (Venice) which screened films flying nineteen different flags. How different it had been just after World War I when Tanizaki wrote his short story and when cinema was touted as the international art par excellence. Under the ideology of the League of Nations, cinema promised to be a kind of Esperanto; the entire world identified Charlot, not as British or American, but as the tramp, a universal and modern figure. All too soon, however, the Marx Brothers became known as quintessential Americans, applauded as such, just as, after the success of Pagnol's trilogy, Raimu was hailed around the world as the consummate Gallic character. He represented France.

Of course international concerns drove the cinema even during the 1930s. A "specter of comparison" haunted government commissions and industry personnel as they positioned national industries in relation to one another.[12] In matters of hardware, a few powerhouse states really did exact tribute over

66

entire territories where patents wars were waged for exclusive control. As for films, most were designed to stay at home, with only higher budget features subtitled or dubbed so as to reach an audience abroad. These are the films that competed against each other in the world market (as many as 200 a year from Hollywood, about 30 a year from France, about 24 from Britain, and so on). Hollywood's tremendous lead in sound must have seemed overwhelming to a country like Japan even though it made over 500 movies annually; for only a handful of these thousands ever reached the West. *Page of Madness* director, Teinosuke Kinugase, managed to get his *Jojiru (Crossroads, 1928)* a brief Western engagement, encouraging Kawakita Nagamasa, an importer of European works, to try to reverse the flow by exporting *Nippon*, a three-film compilation (including a Mizoguchi). *Nippon*, however, managed only one-off screenings in Germany and France as a kind of curiosity. Aside from untranslated films playing for émigrés in Hawaii and California, this would be the fate of Japanese exports, including Naruse's sublime *Wife Be Like a Rose*. Having been chosen best film in Japan in 1936, it failed to attract an audience in New York the following year, surely because silent films could no longer play in the West. Later in 1937 Kawakita produced the first Japanese sound film made specifically for export, *The New Earth*, bringing German Arnold Fanck to Japan as director, with Mansaka Itami making a second English/Japanese version.[13] Starring Sessue Hayakawa and 16-year-old Setsuko Hara, this propaganda piece got scathing reviews in Japan but showed widely in Germany and Scandinavia (though not in France, Britain or the United States). As the decade moved to its dire conclusion, this experiment was not repeated, politics having increasingly skewed distribution and production.

National politics would also quickly turn the supposedly "free zone" of the Venice festival into a battleground. While the lineup of films "in compe tition" from 1934 to 1937 was dominated by American and French titles, with a few from Britain and an occasional selection from Czechoslovakia, the USSR, and Germany, after 1937 more German films showed up, plus one each year from Japan. Leni Reifenstahl's *Olympia*, a perfect emblem for the politics of international competition, took the Golden Lion in 1938.

In daily commerce there was more regional than world distribution. Some Czech films, for example, played in Germany, Austria, and elsewhere in Eastern Europe, while Swedish films played in Denmark and so on. East Asia, however, fostered little image exchange. The giant studios in Tokyo, which one might expect to have dominated the region, exploited at most the Japanese colonies of Taiwan and Korea, though showing films unsubtitled there. Few efforts were made to win over a South East Asian or Chinese market, partly for political reasons, at least until the war with the United States had eliminated Hollywood products. After the war, Japanese titles were routinely distributed through the region, and co-productions became feasible.

During this national phase, transnational circulation—whatever its scale—was primarily governed by center-periphery protocols emanating from a few production capitals: Berlin, Moscow, London, Paris, and preeminently Hollywood. Perhaps more than at any other time, films were identified by national origin. The Franco-German co-production *La Kermesse héroïque*, directed by Belgian Jacques Feyder in two language versions, was never thought to be other than a French film. This is how it was identified when the National Board of Review in New York chose it the top film of 1937. Furthermore, like the Academy Awards, they honored this as a "foreign film" within the American context. Japan's *Kinema Jumpo* poll also ranked *La Kermesse héroïque* number one, the third straight French film to carry Japan's highest recognition, though France was never in competition with anything but other "foreign films." Japan's exhibition system effectively put all "foreign films" on a separate circuit, in the urban areas at least, leaving Japanese productions to compete against each other (Naruse and Mizoguchi came out on top in two of those years).[14]

Whether in Japan, the United States, or France, critics and historians before World War II seem generally more insular than industry personnel. Content to take the temperature of world cinema wherever they worked, their presumed cosmopolitanism, while surely greater than that of most of their readers, was pulled back by the magnetic force of the nation with its concentration of indigenous films. The foreign films they did see had already been pre-selected by the business sense of distributors. Still, the presence in major urban centers of at least some films from abroad invited critics to measure the state of world cinema (and of their nation's products) by the speed at which modernity operated in one country as opposed to another. Yet critics invariably write from a national perspective and certainly for a national, or more often a metropolitan audience; after all, as "reviewers" they aim to lead their readers to the most worthy films around, that is, the films currently playing on available screens. Even had they traveled to view the astounding melodramas being made in Shanghai and Tokyo, no American critic in the 1930s would have written about them, since their readers, and most viewers, indeed most filmmakers, kept to local time.

Thus it was only on the basis of what was imported to London that, in his remarkable *Spectator* columns, Graham Greene declared French films to be far and away the most mature in the world. Similarly the numerous French film journals, such as *Pour Vous*, mainly featured directors, stars, and films opening each week in Paris, though they did report the glamor and gossip from Hollywood. As for American critics, when Frank Nugent or Otis Fergusson compared national output, they did so without leaving New York. Only *Variety*, plus a couple of industry publications such as *The Film Daily Yearbook*, maintained reporters on assignment in numerous places around the globe to provide annual statistics and observations about world cinema, one country at a time. These stringers kept tabs on changes in theater ownership, tariffs and regulations, box office activity (prices, number of films, attendance), and the notable successes of local genres, stars, and particular films. France's version of *Variety*, *La Cinématographie Française*, published occasional international assessments to monitor the competition, as did a unique Japanese yearbook from 1935 to 1938.

Although genuine "international criticism" was rare,[15] an exception can be found in Roger Leenhardt who in a brief but brilliant 1938 essay, titled "Le cinéma, art national," agreed with Graham Greene about the strength of the current run of French output, but considered it a minor fluctuation in what had become, since sound, a rather homogenized world cinema. National differences were far more apparent in the silent age, he believed, because the first years of sound were dominated by Hollywood since they were initially best prepared to deal with it. Nearly everyone needed to mimic Hollywood's techniques just to get a sufficient number of sound films on screen; hence the overall similarity of style and genres compared to a decade earlier. In Paris, Leenhardt was in a position to see more types of films than critics elsewhere and on that basis noted "the general upgrading of the average French film and the renewal of this national cinema via a return to the *film d'essai*" which he said was crowned by the flower of "several works that have reached a status that belongs to films of that mysterious international class."[16] He dates the beginning of this resurgence at 1935, attributing it in part to complicated market conditions that flow around the globe in waves. At the current juncture, the tides may favor France but he cautions: "Superiority in cinema moves, like the Davis Cup, from continent to continent, depending on cinematographic ambience, including technical equipment, the education of the public, the overturning of one generation by another."[17] Paradoxically, distinct national traditions, rather than modest fluctuations of a universal norm, would begin to return after World War II in a period that downplayed nationalist fever. Had he written a sequel to his 1938 piece, Leenhardt might well have titled it "Le Cinéma, art international," for after 1946 he was able to reassess historical movements at the Cinémathèque Français and track current trends at Cannes or Venice. But by then he was making feature films, having ceded to André Bazin both his post as critic at *Esprit* and his world perspective on the artform.

the federated phase

The victory of the Allies over the fascist states did not bring an end to the reality of nations; indeed new entities and new rivalries were placed on the world chessboard (East Germany, North Korea, Israel). But the lethal consequences of unrestrained nationalism had been exposed, and alternative ways of conceiving social life were given some chance to prove themselves, most prominently the United Nations. True, the UN was hard put just to maintain a delicate balance among the muscle-bound victors as this chess game escalated into an outright "cold war." But some of its agencies, particularly UNESCO, demonstrating the values of a federation of member states, really did foster initiatives and an ethos that was described as "international humanism" to stand up to uncritical national feeling.

True, the realities of cinema like those of politics were hardly overturned all at once. The USSR, for instance, persisted in its jingoistic socialist realism, produced by an unchanged cultural bureaucracy. And postwar French cinema looks quite like that of Vichy, both in its institutional setup and in its "cinéma de qualité" aesthetic. Most trenchant of all, Hollywood's hegemonic studio system was never stronger than in 1946, its box-office apex. Furthermore, Hollywood films rolled behind American troops to reinforce its unchallenged claim to overseas distribution. Through staggered distribution schedules, a film carved out a reputation at home and was gradually exported to friendly neighbors before venturing into the murkier marketplaces of smaller, more distant, or culturally more hostile countries where it likely had to compete with films from other production centers. At Hollywood's height, even films without much reputation in themselves could be exported on the basis of their genre, stars, and marketing, not to mention the strong-arm tactics of block-booking, more prevalent in 1946 than a decade earlier.

The military vocabulary often associated with big business (tactics, strategies, marketing offensives, trade wars, and treaties), plus the maintenance of personnel in outposts abroad, remind us that as an "idea of cinema," nationalism was hardly broken by World War II. Nevertheless, another idea rose to challenge it, signaled by the word "federation." With Renoir's *La Grande illusion* to prompt me, I have traced this word to its pre-war origins in the French journal *Esprit* and particularly in the thought of the Swiss intellectual Denis de Rougemont.[18] In 1946 De Rougemont sailed back to Europe famous for his Voice of America programs that issued from New York during the war. He quickly took his place at the head of international congresses and he established numerous cultural institutions that are still in place, prefiguring a European Union. A devastated continent looked to peaceful Switzerland for a political idea distinct from those of the superpowers to its east and its west. Eliminating hierarchy, Switzerland has for centuries successfully balanced the partial independence of its many cantons and several linguistic groups. In a symbolic gesture, and as if completing the project instigated in Renoir's beloved film, the very first grand prize awarded at Cannes went to *Die letzte Chance*, a social realist allegory of refugees (speaking four different languages in one virtuoso tracking shot) who struggle to cross into the safety zone of Switzerland, a clear emblem of the United Nations just then being born.

The award also said something about Cannes and about film festivals in general, making good on their declaration of independence from business concerns and promising that films from anywhere could speak as they might choose and be given a chance to make a difference culturally and politically. Hollywood would surely remain the power center of finance and production—the center, that is, of *quantity*—but as for *quality*, this would be monitored at film festivals which would eventually become federated (FIAPF: in English, International Federation of Film Producers Associations). Another federation, this one of film critics (FIPRESCI: Fédération Internationale de la Presse Cinématographique), has always followed the ever-enlarging circuit of festivals.

Federation came as a retort to nationalism, but it should not be conflated with the geopolitical phase at work today, that of "the network." For unlike the network, federalism is anchored in territory, just like nationalism. The problem with the nation, De Rougemont believed, is that it had become an abstraction that cost individuals their freedom and communities their distinctive characters. Moreover national administrative machinery is inevitably centripetal (tax collecting, military conscription) and its energy centrifugal, producing conflicts with other self-centered nations and resulting in colonialism and war. The federal model, on the other hand, encourages cooperation, since its primary unit is the local community where people are more likely to trust each other. For needs that transcend the local, De Rougemont suggests a regional linkage of "united communities" of increasing size; ultimately the United Nations ought to be replaced by a fully federated world of communities.

Played out in the sphere of cinema, the federation model fosters both equality and difference in artistic expression. Hence a "minor" Swiss film could be taken just as seriously as a star-laden Hollywood product. Smaller scale films, including documentaries and amateur works, thrive under the federation idea which is automatically attentive to the cultural distinctiveness of dialects, folklore, topography, and the history of communities. Resisting large theater chains, federalism promotes local control over exhibition, and it encourages alliances among neighboring locales. At the same time, federalism jumps far beyond the level of the state in its attention to the global film community evident at the surprising number of postwar festivals, cine-clubs, and specialized theaters.[19] Such institutions are themselves ordinarily federated, with each festival and cine-club sporting a distinct orientation and tenor, while benefiting from and contributing to the maintenance of neighboring agencies and of the system as a whole.

Each year in a protected arena at Cannes, Venice, Locarno, and Berlin, the Hollywood empire dissolved in the face of more universal aspirations for the art. Often explicitly commanding high moral ground, festivals claimed to be utopias where the appreciation of difference and similarity would contribute to tolerance, coexistence and, of course, a richer cinema.[20] In effect festivals promoted UNESCO's humanitarian goals; they also helped popularize such non-national philosophical movements as existentialism and Zen Buddhism as these traveled in the most trendy movies of the time.[21]

I yoke the federal idea in film culture to the cinematic modernism that André Bazin and Alexandre Astruc recognized as emerging at the same moment. Modernism was—tautologically—the latest stage in "the evolution of the language of cinema," and Bazin found it sprouting internationally, though unevenly on the postwar landscape. Whether this amounted to a genuine revolution transforming cinema as a whole, or was a mirage that fascinated certain critics who looked at things from a particular perspective, the fact is that particularly in Paris a newly ambitious culture of cinema (a film school, journals, books, cine-clubs, the Cinémathèque, festivals, specialized movie theaters) greeted the unmistakable ambition evident in a number of postwar films.[22]

This "federal idea" incubated most successfully in war-ravaged Europe where it served as a defensive strategy to ward off imperial threats from the United States and the USSR. The moral force of film festivals, for instance, lay precisely in their egalitarian pan-nationalism. Hollywood may have been present at Venice and Cannes, but it was put in its place alongside films from any-place-wherever. And its classic studio style was countered by other, newer (i.e. "modernist") styles. Certain accounts from the inaugural Cannes, imbued with this "new idea," explicitly threw European realism in the face of Hollywood's artifice.[23] At the first Cannes festival Bazin recognized a conception of space emerging in tandem with the reconstruction of Europe, and a conception of time that was out-of-step with Hollywood norms, either too fast (*Bataille du rail*) or too slow (*Farrebique*). The discomfort of such films, the *décalage* they engender, measures the friction of modernity rubbing up against and reshaping subjectivity, as characters and spectators find themselves in a physical and moral *terrain vague*.

Over the next decade, as if to seal this ethic, Cannes and Venice consistently rewarded works from Italy and Japan, nations that had been politically and morally obliterated. In short, if not directly opposed to national cinemas (most festivals in fact showcased what each nation submitted) alternative exhibition sites definitely aimed to thwart Hollywood's de facto colonizing of world screens. They took pride in presenting films made *elsewhere* (Mexico, for instance), and *else-wise* (neorealist). Luis Buñuel did not represent Mexico (or Spain); nor did Ingmar Bergman stand in for Sweden. They represented instead the newest trends in cinema as world film artists. Jacques Rivette said it best when, overwhelmed by the sublimity of Mizoguchi, he wrote:

> His films—which tell us in an alien tongue stories that are completely foreign to our customs and way of life—do talk to us in a familiar language. What language? The only one to which a filmmaker should lay claim when all is said and done, the language of mise-en-scène.[24]

Mizoguchi and Kurosawa were the most foreign of masters to take the stage at Venice. Has there ever been a more unexpected festival triumph than that of *Rashomon* at Venice in 1951? This was the first film from beyond Europe and North America to compete since the festival's founding. Compared to Olivier's *Hamlet* or Clouzot's *Manon* (the previous years' winners), *Rashomon* looked muscular, a film that knew what cinema was capable of. Venice became the launching pad for a series of Japanese masterworks, with Mizoguchi's *Saikaku ichidai onna* scoring there in 1952, *Ugetsu* taking the Silver Lion in 1953 and *Sansho Dayu* splitting that Lion with Kurosawa's *Seven Samurai* in 1954. Cannes gave its top prize in 1953 to Kinugasa's *Gate of Hell*. The Japanese moved cinema forward by recuperating what Paul Willemen calls archaic chronotopes and merging them with forms of enunciation,[25] which were as challenging to critics as anything being attempted in contemporary literature.

All these Japanese exports were *jidei-geki* (period dramas) made with special fervor following the injunction on the genre imposed by the American Occupying forces—hence the flavor of archaism. But Kurosawa and Mizoguchi did not simply pour exotic material into Western moulds; indeed it was *Rashomon's* narration, distributed among several points of view (including one belonging to a murder victim), that caused the shock at Venice and that still startles today. As for *Ugetsu*, a critic wrote from Venice of the eerie feeling it conveyed, with its "temporal schema utterly distinct from Western dramatics."[26] Drawing on venerable Eastern traditions, Japan helped renew the modern art of cinema that was just then stepping forward to take the lead in the "universal humanism" that intellectuals everywhere held up in the face of the Korean and Cold Wars. This modern cinema, emerging at festivals and cine-clubs, could be shaped by developments anywhere on the globe, and could in turn enlarge the sensibility of humans everywhere, letting Westerners comprehend the world, for example, from within the feeling-structure of the Japanese, who only a decade before had been deemed essentially non-human.[27]

Meanwhile, in Japan Mizoguchi was thought to lag behind, even if *Sansho Dayu* was ranked by *Cahiers du Cinéma* the best film released in Paris in 1960. In fact, for some time he had stood for the old guard against which Japan's future New Wave directors rebelled. How different film history appears when one spins the globe. Let us look at his assistant, Yasuzo Masamura, who, while relishing his years as the first Asian student accepted into Italy's prestigious Centro Sperimentale, met Mizoguchi at the Venice festivals of 1952–53.[28] Intoxicated by the ambience of the incipient European youth culture, he wrote overviews of cinema that, though praising *Sansho Dayu*, characterized Mizoguchi as a traditional esthete. In Tokyo, even while serving as second-unit director on Mizoguchi's last films, he flaunted his European cachet and talked Daiei Studio into letting him try out subjects that sported a modern rhythm and taboo subject matter. His audacity inspired newcomers Oshima, Imamura, and Yoshida who declared themselves done with the past. Living at a different speed—one they assumed to be Western—they gave voice to the resentful Asian youth of their own generation. Characters in the films of all four directors spout or mumble shocking colloquialisms in films that in 1960 were immediately labeled the Japanese New Wave.

Cinematic modernity thus moved forward as a series of waves in a wide ocean of activity, but progress or development was measured in and by the West. This contradiction can be felt already in 1948 when Jean-Paul Sartre in his essay "Black Orpheus" posited the relation of colonialism (a spatial concept, the *elsewhere* of political economy) and modernism (a temporal concept, the *else-wise* of aesthetics).[29] After Dien Bien Phu in 1954, and caught in a losing situation in Algeria, French cultural hegemony relinquished its authority and its say over the claims of the modern. A tired Europe would soon depend on the energy of ideas coming from or involving its former colonies. But how could European intellectuals credit the "peripheral" without rehearsing the centrism that produces colonial thinking in the first place? This conundrum between history and geography flummoxes every account of postwar developments in world film, even the most politically astute.[30]

European festivals, for instance, fell into the trap Sartre had recognized by inviting nations from beyond the West's periphery to submit films that might have something essential to contribute, something unavailable to those in the center. After all, in the federated model value might in principle appear from anywhere. And yet value could properly be assessed only at Western festivals, and only by Western, specifically Parisian critics. European festivals thus served as a stock market where producers and critics bought and sold ideas of cinema, sometimes investing in futures and trading on the margin, with the quotations registered in *Cahiers du Cinéma*. Despite its core premise, federalism, it seems, needed a headquarters, a European head-quarters, since, despite its egalitarian and international ideology, federalism arose in the context of a European debate. While modern cinema was glad to be enriched by developments around the globe, nearly everyone who followed such things did so in the pages of Paris's *Cahiers du Cinéma* (or London's *Sight and Sound*, or the annual catalogues from Cannes, Venice, Locarno, and Berlin); that is, from the heart of Europe.[31]

A doomed attempt to encompass both space and time in one gesture garbled the key metaphor of the 1960s, "New Wave." For film historians and festival directors each wave, and especially each *new* one, must be considered the next development in history, while, at the same time, as a wave it rolls across oceans and effects change wherever it hits shore. Operating ambiva-lently in these two modes, the various "international new waves" of the 1960s mark the climax of the postwar idea of cinematic modernism through what is in effect a double deterritorialization. First, each new wave had to wrest control from the privileged producers of the national cinema, in an Oedipal struggle of succession. Thus the young French critics, in their revolt against *le cinéma du papa*, took their cameras to the streets; while in Tokyo the revolution occurred within the palace of the studios themselves. Oshima and Imamura, among others, made films for Shochiku. In Prague, a state system had to be bucked. Second, to achieve recognition and identity, every new cinematic movement had to float from its home base and reach international visibility at festivals, then in theaters abroad. New waves certainly abetted each other in an inchoate international film culture, but each took shape as a national struggle. Mizoguchi was the whipping boy of the young Japanese directors who used the French new wave as their whip; yet that French Wave had been inspired by none other than Mizoguchi. To them Mizoguchi had floated his dreamy films from the periphery of civilization, just as in *Sansho Dayu* Kinuyo Tanaka calls to her children from the offshore isle of Sado. But considered locally in Japan, Mizoguchi was central, not peripheral. He held court and needed to be dethroned so that a new wave could flood Japanese cinema with the vitality of youth.

the world cinema phase

European intellectual arrogance fell hard in 1968, helping precipitate the decline of cinematic modernism and of art theaters. And it fell, country by country. In Czechoslovakia the filmmakers slipped away when the tanks rolled in. In France, utopian community action and modernist thought ran up against the combined power of traditional values, backed by government and the interests of capital. Japan's youth fervor conceded two years later, when rallies against the American treaty which had been so much a part of the New Wave in 1960 this time proved disappointing, indeed pathetic. After a spate of brilliant films in 1969 (by Shinoda, Oshima, and Yoshida) all products of the Art Theater Guild—an upstart foreign film distributor supporting radical work—the Japanese new wave was spent, receding into the pervasive doldrums of the 1970s.[32]

From the perspective of the West, the 1970s, this decade when film studies took root in the United States and elsewhere, was utterly unremarkable, except for the New German directors and the new American cinema of Scorsese, Coppola, and Malick. And except for what was then termed the "Third Cinema" of Brazilian *cinema novo*, *nuevo cine argentino*, and Cuban Cinema. All three of these movements were taken to be new waves with directly political, rather than cultural ambitions. Their fates depended to a large extent on the vicissitudes of state politics. They were held up almost to scold the inconsequential spate of genre pictures and (increasingly) soft-porn coming out of Europe. Summing up the French situation in 1981, Serge Daney put it this way:

> The seventies will be known as the post-decade par
> excellence: post-New Wave, post-68, post-modern. No big
> wave, no movement, or school, virtually an aesthetic desert.

You can't tell how this decade looked ahead to the 80s, and we won't know till later what it prefigured. While we wait, I have to hazard a description: neither cold nor hot, just tepid.[33]

Daney did not have long to wait, for the 1980s would see a set of towering waves that in my view surpasses those of the 1960s. In fact, he did not sit back and wait. Leaving *Cahiers* (and French cinema) behind, he set off as a journalist writing for the daily newspaper that Sartre had launched, *Libération*, to locate life and a lively cinema elsewhere. His poignant autobiographical reflections would be called *Itinéraire d'un ciné-fils* and the 1980s indeed found him heading out for North Africa, the USSR, and China.[34] He was not alone. Another *Cahiers* critic, later turned filmmaker, Olivier Assayas, likewise set out to see what cinema looked like elsewhere and up close. He traveled to Hong Kong in 1983 and stood in awe of the films and the spirit he experienced in the region there. The French New Wave, he implied, had been resurrected in Taiwan.

Festivals played a crucial role in this transition, becoming "world" rather than "international" events. The difference is key. Scanning the first twenty-five years of festival submissions, one is struck that no major festival screened East Asian titles except Japanese. Indeed few titles come from anywhere outside Europe (which includes the Soviet bloc). Satjyajit Ray, Glauber Rocha, Torre Nilsson, and a few others were notable—and noted—exceptions. During this period festivals mainly showcased films that had been chosen by each participating nation, and those nations were more limited in number than one might think. After 1968, however, as Marijke de Valck has thoroughly demonstrated, the major festivals under strong leaders actively shaped their own lineup, opening up to far more films.[35]

Gradually in the 1970s an expansive idea of "world cinema" took hold among the traffickers in images. Those in charge of quality control at Cannes decided to enlarge their offerings beyond the official selection, inaugurating the "Quinzaine de réalisiteurs" and later "Un certain regard" so as to expose a greater variety of films coming from no-matter where. In 1972 the Berlin festival initiated the "Forum des Jungen Film" to diffuse attention that had been concentrated on its precious Bears, widening its audience and exposing new directors and directions. Across the Atlantic, Toronto and Montreal (explicitly dubbed "Festival du cinéma du monde") sprang to life in 1975, soon showing more than 300 films annually, very few coming from the United States. Hong Kong's great festival also opened in 1975, and the Panafrican festival FESPACO in Burkina Faso kept the new African cinema in view every other year. It was in 1975 that the Palme d'Or at Cannes went to the Algerian *Chronicle of the Year of Embers*, besting, among other official entries, King Hu's *Touch of Zen* and an avant-garde drama by Tereyama Shinji.

So as the blood drained from the European art cinema (the Italian public service broadcaster RAI stopped sponsoring films in the late 1970s sending the Italian industry into a tailspin, East European states clamped down on the audacity that had bubbled up a decade earlier, and so on), and as the number of art theaters fell off and criticism squandered its authority in what became quite literally academic debates about Hollywood and Europe, it was left to film festivals to present alternative possibilities, possibilities that increasingly were being taken up in the "elsewhere." Sucked into the vacuum caused by the retreat of the modernist art cinema, films from places never before thought of as cinematically interesting or viable surprised Western cinephiles: Taiwan, the PRC, Senegal, Mali, Iran. As for Europe, the most vibrant works could be expected now from its edges, from Yugoslavia on one side and from Ireland on the other.

Quite distinct from the 1960s in their provenance, this second set of waves also functioned in a greatly changed world system. For Hollywood was back, asphyxiating other production sources with its saturation strategy for world distribution in the wake of *Jaws*, then *Star Wars*. Many national cinemas (Italy most regrettably) were already enfeebled by the glut of movies available on television, not even counting the predicted impact of Betamax and VHS tapes. These were only some of the overriding pressures that circulated around the growing number of festivals that were revivified by this onslaught of waves and currents. After *Yellow Earth* astonished the juries at Hong Kong and Hawaii, Western festival directors canvassed the PRC, and by 1986 the so-called fifth generation offerings would be invited annually to Locarno, Berlin, and even Cork, Ireland. Ordinary cinephiles, attending a festival close to home, wherever home might be, could look forward to the *décalage* produced by a journey into the different temporalities of films from distant narrative and visual traditions.

Looking back on this period in 1995, Rey Chow would castigate critics, not to mention filmmakers, for exploiting a graphic version of orientalism, because they dwelt on what she called the "primitive passions" suffered by and through women and marginal groups.[36] For the most memorable successes of 1980s coming from beyond the West, like *Yellow Earth*, went in search of characters and spaces that seemed peripheral to their own nations but which gave those nations their strength and distinctiveness. "Authenticity," a seductive and dangerous term, could still be uttered in the 1980s, indeed could scarcely be avoided by critics looking beyond Hollywood for genuine difference, for discoveries like *Red Sorghum* (Zhang Yimou, 1987), *A Time to Live and a Time to Die* (Hou Hsiou-Hsien, 1985), and *The Cyclist* (Mohsen Makhmalbaf, 1987).

In justifying its extensive 1986 program on Yugoslavia, Paris's Pompidou Center proclaimed this far-flung cinema to be meatier than anything else in Europe, affording "a taste for authentic 'terroir' [that] hasn't caved in completely to the seduction of odorless internationalism."[37] Riding high on this wave was Emir Kusturica whose *When Father was Away on Business* had just taken the Palme d'Or at Cannes. He was already preparing *Time of the Gypsies*, which would jolt the West with narrative tricks drawing on magic realism, Yugoslavian oral epics, Onza Onza rhythms, a grab-bag of cinematic references, and an unruly gypsy aesthetic. Kusturica would have us believe that this film took its inspiration from the Romani grandmother, discovered on location, who fed him many of the fantastical anecdotes that cascade irrepressibly onto the screen. Although the director had grown up in the area, it was through her that he expressed the *décalage* between Sarajevo and the gypsy encampment just outside the city that operates on a different time scheme altogether, a time scheme the film does its best to adopt. Festival audiences entered into this time of the gypsies and were entranced.[38] They counted it as both an archaic and modernist expression, as they had two years earlier when Souleymane Cissé's *Yeelen* likewise put before them epic images emanating from an aged woman who had never before seen let alone acted in a film. And let us not forget the surprising arrival of Abbas Kiarostami at Locarno in 1989 with his limpid *Where is the Friend's House?* Had these directors truly abandoned their modern sophistication in unearthing stories and people from the depths of the countries they come from? Festivals tracked down such "authentic visions" opening up far-off lands, each a "treasure island" to be discovered.[39]

In the 1980s the Pacific Rim became an entire archipelago of treasured islands, each detached enough to spawn its own distinctive and, therefore, irreplaceable cinematic flora and fauna. Take the two richest discoveries of the time, Zhang Yimou and Hou Hsiao-Hsien. Separated by the narrow Straits of Taiwan, these men came from utterly different backgrounds. Even putting aside politics and social formation, imagine the nearly opposite ways each trained for his profession. Imagine, that is, the separate conceptions of world cinema they relied on as they planned their projects, wrote their scripts, designed their mise-en-scene. One might expect those in the PRC, especially following a decade of Cultural Revolution, to be ignorant of films and ideas from abroad; and yet the reverse is true. In the first graduating class of the Beijing Film Academy, Zhang Yimou and his colleagues assiduously soaked up the classic Chinese, Soviet, and Hollywood films that were part of their aesthetic education. Then they devoured the modernist works of Resnais, Tarkovsky, and Scorsese that the China Film Archive screened for them under controlled circumstances.[40] Arguing about cinematic style and mission, often via the Western film theory that was massively translated at the time, they also immersed themselves in Chinese painting and literature, so as to conceive a cinematic form alternative to the newly resuscitated national industry and to international trends as well. Growing up in a walled-off country and then operating outside a market system, the fifth generation could claim to walk an aesthetic high road of their own devising, a high road laid out in large part by teachers and critics, at least till June 1989 and Tiananmen Square.

By contrast, although for decades Taipei has been a buzzing node in the capitalist exchange network, very little of the larger world's film culture filtered down to Hou Hsiou-Hsien in his formative years. He rose within the local industry through an apprenticeship system, not through viewings, reading, and discussion. While he kept the ever present Hong Kong and American pictures in his peripheral vision, he purportedly did not go looking for Japanese or European models and claims not to have been aware of Ozu, Antonioni, or any of the other sources critics imputed to his 1980s' style. Nor had he any idea what "mise-en-scene" connoted, when critics first proclaimed him a master of that style. His inspiration was primarily Taiwan's own (neo)realist literary tradition, giving substance to Angelo Restivo's provocative hypothesis that every new wave begins with the capturing of landscapes, faces, and language that had heretofore been invisible and inaudible.[41] Even if he worked intuitively and without the benefit (or onus) of noisy critical reflection, Hou joined other realists and modernists (Edward Yang most notably) in pressing for an ambitious Taiwanese cinema, supported by the state. In 1986 he was among those who signed a petition to the government explicitly modeled on the 1964 Oberhausen Manifesto that launched the New German Cinema. Peggy Chiao, just back from graduate film studies in the United States, helped draft that document, as did Chen Kuo-fu, editor of a new journal of film studies.[42] These two are the most prominent of several critics who soon involved themselves in production, helping guide Hou's sober, beautiful and increasingly complex portraits of rural Taiwan to European festivals. His masterpiece, *City of Sadness*, unsanctioned by the state censorship board, took the Golden Lion at Venice in 1989, and then returned triumphantly home to become the island's highest grossing film to that date.[43]

I have dwelt on Zhang Yimou and Hou Hsiao-Hsien because they are by far the most famous of a phalanx (or wave) of directors from their respective "Chinas." In later interviews they both recall the 1980s as a time when, working essentially in a collective of like-minded friends, they felt themselves capable of giving expression to muted cultures. However, after these nearly simultaneous and equally thrilling surges had spent themselves, once the waters of not only Taiwan and the mainland but also Hong Kong had mixed at festivals and in the press, their shape and identity wavered.

By 1990 the striking films from Taiwan and the PRC had already drawn so much attention from both the West and from their respective governments that it would be disingenuous to speak of the "natural development" of these movements as if films were being mined or harvested from the land. For hybrids inevitably were concocted, often as recipes to suit the taste of festivals. Thus Zhang's hit *Raise the Red Lantern* (1991) was produced by Hou Hsiao-Hsien himself, who had become interested in mainland productions. The two men could have met at the Hong Kong festival of 1984, and certainly did meet in Locarno in 1985 where *Yellow Earth* (Zhang was its cinematographer) and Hou's *A Summer at Grampa*'s shared the FIPRESCI prize. The jury there, amazed at such accomplished films made in relative isolation and under such different circumstances, understood the full force of that cinema's world context. Well into the 1990s, no major film festival could do without a selection from Taiwan; its difference had become an essential part of the varied landscape of world cinema. But that landscape was rapidly eroding.

from world cinema to global cinema

As a matter of mnemonic convenience, but also alert to the most massive determinations likely to affect cinema in its full complexity, I have divided the eras of cinema with reference to major political dates in the twentieth century: 1918, 1945, 1968, and . . . 1989. The massacre at Tiananmen Square and the fall of the Berlin Wall mark, if not effect, a shift from the world phase to the global. World systems imply transnational operations and negotiations that encourage the spread and interchange of images, ideas, and capital across and throughout a vast but differentiated cultural geography. Global notions, however, like blockbuster films, have nothing to negotiate; they expect to saturate every place in an undifferentiated manner. "Google" is an example of such a concept and global enterprise; whereas "animé" today constitutes a world phenomenon, as does, by definition, "world music." The distinction may play out less visibly in film style than in altered mechanisms of production and distribution, but it operates throughout the full cinema complex.

Returning to Zhang Yimou, he crossed the dividing line of 1989 a rebel in his own country, but gradually reconciled with the Beijing government, to become the architect of state-sanctioned blockbusters, films that use actors from all along the Pacific Rim and play to international acclaim. Hou Hsiao-hsien for his part has become an Asian celebrity. Japan serves as a key location in each of his last three films, and his fans in Tokyo book tours to Taiwan to visit Hou's settings. In Korea he was chosen the first official dean of the workshop of the Pusan Promotion Plan that encourages pan-Asian productions. And so this quintessential artisan of local Taiwanese culture now finds himself at the hub of Pacific Rim cinema. Whereas he had shaped the Taiwanese New Wave of the 1980s through anti-generic, utterly local material, in 2003 he advised young Taiwanese filmmakers to attract a large regional audience by embracing Asian genres like the ghost story, inflecting these with their personal or native styles. But such styles have lost their local footing, since in East Asia casts and crews, like genres, are increasingly mixed. Clearly the New Waves of the 1980s have emptied themselves into the larger basin of regional and then global cinema.

Two words characterize the current situation: entropy and network. No new islands of cinema can be expected to appear out of the mist, given the omnipresence of the World Wide Web and of cell phone communication, accompanying the global flow of videos, many pirated. Anticipation of new work (scanning the horizon for waves) is inversely proportional to the increased speed with which films and information about them has become available. The coastal patrols and customs agents of vigilant governments are unable to outwit today's image traffickers; one can presume that all films are simultaneously and everywhere available to those who care. Hence entropy. Whereas in the 1980s international festivals sought out and showcased work produced in pockets from around the world, in the 1990s those pockets have been networked and the festivals themselves are interconnected.

As late as the 1960s, exported movies traveled by ship—just as did "Vengeance" in the Tanizaki story with which we began—leaving an interlude of weeks between production and reception, when a film's reputation or rumor could precede it and when value could be added through staggered marketing. Those first new wave filmmakers had to read criticism to keep up with the projects of peers, and then go out of their way, often to festivals, to experience what was being made elsewhere. With no video library to consult, only the memory of screenings sufficed, intense viewings followed by equally intense discussions. Even the fifth generation in China was formed this way. But after 1990 video has come to supplement memory, and films spread massively and swiftly. Eventually electronic distribution may obviate all delay, all travel, and the attendant experience of *décalage*.

Under these entropic conditions festivals have come up with a new mission. Not just out to discover new work in a shrunken world, they now have a hand in commissioning it. This is what Geoffrey Gilmore, Sundance's longtime programmer, sheepishly confessed,[44] referring to the Hugo Bals Fund that was put in place at Rotterdam in 1988 to provide seed money to cineastes the festival has a stake in. Ironically, films often eventually screen at Cannes or Venice bearing the Hugo Bals logo that advertises Rotterdam's foresight and investment. Such a shift in function introduces an ethical conundrum: "Many film festivals nowadays look beyond the programming and evaluation of finished products and demand a say in which films are artistically interesting, before they are made."[45] Even without direct festival support, producers and directors today are tempted to shape their work to appeal to the taste of those deciding which films get selected (therefore, in many cases which ones obtain completion money). Moreover, festivals find themselves in league with advertising and distribution, since films that play well (or play at all) on the festival circuit command better DVD deals. This sort of ethical dilemma exacerbates what has always been a problem for critics who, like festivals, are tempted to link their reputations to that of promising filmmakers. Such a feedback system can foster collaboration, in the worst sense of the term.[46]

This interlinked and accelerating economy of a world saturated with films that are available instantly from every place and every time—this world without waiting—describes the state of things in the global sublime. How can we expect the unexpected, when the warming of the cultural atmosphere since 1990 has reduced differences within and among nations, such that new waves will no longer form, at least not with the power and frequency they once did. The vaunted Korean new wave, I would argue, has been an artifact of national promotion. The very first Pusan festival in 1996 was devoted to "The Korean New Wave," a movement that many historians would date to 1997 or even later. Korean cinema was effectively jump-started by a festival that itself was born of an alliance between government and industry (Samsung, and so on). Pusan plays a strategic role in "Hallyu," a sanctioned cultural wave abetted by a coordinated advertising campaign involving fashion, food, music, and television series as well as film. While the French *nouvelle vague* may have taken part in the overall youth movement of its era, it did so on its own terms, whether ironic (Chabrol), corrosive (Godard), or philosophic (Rohmer). That *nouvelle vague* was a critical cinema born of and resulting in written criticism. By contrast, today's waves are more often measured by number of films produced or box office percentage, that is by industry standards. When in the early 1990s newspapers in the United States began replacing their film critics with a standings of movies ranked by (national) attendance figures, democratic taste swamped considered judgment. No reflection, no *décalage* . . . except on the internet where films and directors may now build up the considerable potential energy stored each time someone contributes to an online journal or a blog. This seems a fitting critical complement to a cinema that, we are told, will soon be distributed across the internet.

epilogue: saving cinema

A century ago Tanizaki was 20 years old when he began experiencing the dislocations of modernity that he felt so intensely at the cinema. The urban self-estrangement in the ghost tale *Jinmenso* came by way of "Globe Films," through its pan-Asian distribution. That particular film's ambiguous status as object ("Does it even exist?" asks its star, who cannot recall having made it) along with its eerie, sometimes lethal reception, make it and the cinema as a whole the ideal expression of a young man who discovered that existence does not coincide with presence. Each new film he saw brought Tanizaki an experience of both totality (globe films) and disjunction. The simultaneity he felt with the characters on the screen and with spectators watching it around the world was crossed by the realization that those characters were phantoms of the past and those spectators existed in different time zones.

Waves of cinema later, and despite the inexorable entropy of globalization, we can still be haunted by the *décalage* that Tanizaki prophetically relished as an early cinephile. One of today's most beloved auteurs, Wong Kar-wai, has exploited this feeling, this "mood for cinema," from genre to genre and film to film but never more than in *Chungking Express*, which drips with *décalage*, set as it is four years before the clock runs out on Hong Kong's status as a British Protectorate. Repeatedly rendering such songs as "What a Difference a Day Makes" and "California Dreamin'," Wong Kar-wai contrives to keep his characters from ever quite getting together. Their longing comes across intermittently as a voice daydreaming atop the tangible historical moment recorded on the image track. The climactic scene layers not only voice-over and music atop the image, but also two distinct temporalities within that image. At a nightspot called "California" Tony Leung waits vainly for Faye Wong. A letter is delivered letting him understand that she has in fact left for California, the literal place. While his voice-over calculates that "we were both in California, only fifteen hours apart,"[47] Tony Leung leans against a juke box and looks down languorously, the smoke rising visibly from his cigarette. In slow motion he inserts a coin into the machine while behind him, in his ken and peripheral vision, anonymous figures rush by, speeded up into a blur of motion, producing Wong Kar-wai's signature effect. Like all cities, but far beyond any other, Hong Kong is shown to be in perpetual, unthinking movement; but it also exists as a network of 6 million nodes of consciousness, in each of which it decelerates into reflection and mood. Drama occurs when two or more of these nodes meet and intertwine in the grid of the city's incessant mobility. *Chunking Express* dares to conjoin two plots, one after the other, that scarcely intersect, and in each of which potential lovers miss their intersections as they pass at the wrong times in and out of the fast food joint that gives the film its title in English. Ultimately *Chunking Express*, though shot entirely in a single picturesque *quartier*, expresses the experience of air travel, the experience of flight hostesses who arrive, jetlagged, from overseas and depart soon after for some other California. The film concludes when some time later Faye Wong delivers a love letter personally to Tony Leung, an invitation in the form of a hand-drawn boarding pass, predated by precisely a year. These lonely people, not yet a couple, consider what kind of rendezvous might take place at that scheduled time. This was the question for millions in Hong Kong in the mid-1990s who could not help but experience time in a peculiar way. Wong Kar-wai distilled that peculiar temporality into a quintessential experience of cinema for everyone in the world.

And what of *The World*? Its title brings Jia Zhangke's film forward to close this chapter. At first glance, the director seems to have lavished on his sets and costumes the full budget that had been his reward after a string of underground successes. Japanese and French money supplemented a deal with the Shanghai Film Group and a Hong Kong company that ensured a well-advertised Chinese release, a first for this difficult director. The poster prepared for its Venice festival appearance could serve to advertise world

83

cinema altogether: a beautiful woman in traditional costume stares anxiously at her cell phone while standing amidst key attractions at the World Park that employs her: the Leaning Tower of Pisa, the Great Pyramid, the Taj Majal, the Giant Sphinx of Luxor, the Eiffel Tower. Broken into sections identified as Belleville, Tokyo Story, and Ulan Bator, *The World* makes you anticipate a global spectacle like Wim Wenders' *Till the End of the World* or even the James Bond films that Wenders ironized. But the germ of consciousness, of subjectivity and a discordant temporality, has been introduced.

Does the world now amount to a circumscribed theme park? The film's characters can scarcely leave it though they struggle with family, money, and romantic problems, mainly in its dressing rooms behind the scenes or after hours on the deserted grounds of the park. Imprisoned in "The World," they escape by funneling their hopes into the cell phones they continually consult. In a daring gambit, Jia Zhang-ke inflates the brief text-messages that characters send one another into brilliantly colored full-size animation sequences, where emotions encrypted or decoded burst their tiny screens into liberating CinemaScope. The virtual world accessed via text-messaging has become the only one that counts for those who work inside "The World." Jia Zhang-ke has inverted the norms of scale, giving us miniatures of great monuments on the one hand, and outsized reproductions of cell phone images on the other.[48]

These extraordinary animated sequences might seem to celebrate the intoxicating freedom of the digital universe of which cell phones are a synecdoche, yet, like the theme park, they are circumscribed by the larger human dramas that they interrupt. Jia Zhang-ke stares down postmodern ubiquity so as to register the *décalage* between coexisting temporalities that makes life in China at once painful and compelling in this new century. Look at the film's title shot: an old man, surely from the provinces, carrying a sack on his back, pauses at dawn on his way to Beijing, with the Eiffel Tower looming in the background. Later, a group of the hero's (Taisheng's) acquaintances arrives from Shangxi province to find work in the booming construction industry. They gather and greet each other in front of the large replica of Manhattan, still topped by the towers of the World Trade Center. Taisheng tries to explain urban reality to these villagers, though he himself appears a bumpkin in such a setting. When he and his secret girlfriend Qun take a bus to her hometown, they traverse a changing moral landscape. And when Taisheng's uncle and grandparents come to Beijing to claim his cousin's body (and an indemnity) after a construction accident, their illegible peasant faces bear tangible moral strength. Taisheng needs to translate their provincial dialect as well as their code of behavior to the Beijing bureaucrat.

The mismatch of provincial and urban experience strains Taisheng's relation with Tao, the film's heroine and moral center. But a greater strain comes from his attraction to Qun, which takes him and the film into central Beijing. In her cramped and airless building, rows of workers bend over sewing machines on the ground floor. Two flights of stairs above them, Qun designs clothes for Beijing's new middle class, adapting patterns from European magazines. Her connection to Europe goes beyond this form of simulation, for her husband stowed away on a ship for France years ago and now lives in Belleville expecting her to join him. He is from the sea-coast city of Wenzhou, noted for its intrepid sailors and traders. Jia Zhang-ke thus lays out a demographic sweep of contemporary China, from the northern and western villages still steeped in Confucian tradition and still speaking dialect, to the Mandarin capital which seems to contain the entire world within it, then further east to the coast where Chinese in ever greater numbers are physically going out to the world and sometimes bringing it back. The film's extraordinary shifts in scale replicate what so many, perhaps all, Chinese must deal with today. When an airplane soars overhead, en route from Beijing airport, recently expanded in preparation for the Olympics, Tao exclaims that she has never known anyone who has been aboard anything except the mock plane in the park; yet daily she dresses in the garb of women from India, Japan, or Africa, performing on a huge stage and in front of monuments for crowds of tourists.

Jia Zhang-ke's elegiac camera style teams up with Lim Giong's sad but unsentimental musical score in casting the film's future with the troubled couple.[49] In a universe of pure simulation—Karaoke bars, false romance, and opportunistic sex—Tao is an old-fashioned heroine seeking genuine friendship (with a Russian woman whose language she cannot understand) and abiding love. "You must never be unfaithful. Otherwise," she tells Taisheng prophetically, "I'll kill myself." In following through with such a love-death, Jia Zhang-ke upholds human values that are at risk in the fast-moving capital. He also upholds, by analogy, a way of making films that is faithful to the contract of director to actor and actor to role. The budget he commanded allowed him to indulge in animation, simulation, and special effects. But *The World* is larger than the theme park from which it takes its name; put in Heidegger's old-fashioned way, Being is larger than "The World as Picture."

Much anticipated the following year, Chen Kaige's *The Promise* puts *The World* in perspective, by reversing nearly each of its aesthetic choices. Chen Kaige, who launched the PRC into world cinema with *Yellow Earth*, has joined global cinema twenty years later thanks to the largest budget to date for a Chinese film. Although shot on Super-35mm, *The Promise* depends entirely on CGI (computer-generated imagery) effects which outperform the actors who serve as mere models manipulated by digital sculptors. Jia Zhang-ke employs a digital camera throughout his exploration of the world-become-theme park; yet unlike *The Promise*, his film turns on the subtle performances of actors left to themselves in real time. Toward the end of *The Promise* four characters die, but in an era when nothing need be lost, time is reversed and all come back to life again. Jia Zhang-ke's dead lovers, out of phase with what the world has become, lie inert in the final shot, like Romeo and Juliet, at least until the image fades and their spectral voices whisper in the dark: "This is just the beginning."

Let *The World* be the beginning of a general return to genuine cinema, which Serge Daney claimed has nothing to do with spectacle and everything to do with time, time that passes.[50] Daney would have saluted Tsai Ming-liang's *What Time is It There?*, whose very title implies the incompleteness of being in the world, an incompleteness covered over today by CGI fantasies in which everything is visible and reversible. While so many "global films," like *The Promise* or Zhang Yimou's *Curse of the Golden Flower*, have become avatars of animation, where every effect is precisely controlled, Jia Zhiangke understands that what he and his characters seek to discover can be neither fully present, nor fully controlled; his camera registers the pain of transitions, of absence, and of incompletion in long takes and indistinct lighting. He has made a film about "Life on Earth," the title of another transnational film, an extraordinary one set between Paris and Mali, which expresses in a number of registers so much of what this long chapter has attempted to lay out. As the main character (played by its director Abderrahmane Sissako) asserts in *Life on Earth*, quoting Aimé Césaire, "La vie n'est pas un spectacle, et l'homme qui crie n'est pas un ours qui danse." (Life is not a spectacle, and a screaming man is not a dancing bear.)

In this society of the spectacle, there happily remain films that, while situated in one place and one time, reach viewers elsewhere, all situated differently, all out of phase with themselves and with each other. For nearly a century now, at least since Tanizaki, those who care about cinema have relished the choreographed temporality with which strong films keep us emotionally and politically agile, and within which we slip into moments of coincidence or alignment that intermittently grace the screen and quicken the heart.

notes

1. Miriam Hansen, in Chapter 13 in this volume.
2. See Aaron Gerow, *Modeling Spectators: Cinema, Japan, Modernity 1895–1925* (Berkeley, CA: University of California Press, forthcoming).
3. Miriam Bratu Hansen, "The Mass Production of the Senses: Classical Cinema as Vernacular Modernism," in *Reinventing Film Studies*, ed. Christine Gledhill and Linda Williams (London: Arnold, 2000), 332–50.
4. Junichiro Tanizaki, "Jinmenso," trans. Thomas LaMarre in his *Shadows on the Silver Screen: Junichiro Tanizaki and Silent Film Aesthetics* (Ann Arbor, MI: University of Michigan Press, 2005), 86–97.
5. Ryan Cook has pursued this relation in depth in an unpublished paper, "Private Screenings: Cinematic Metaphors of Infection at the City's Edge: Jun'ichro Tanizaki's 'The Tumor with a Human Face' and *Ringu*," Yale, May 2006.
6. Tanizaki, "Jinmenso," 96.

7. JoAnn Bernardi, *Writing in Light: The Silent Scenario and the Japanese Pure Film Movement* (Detroit, MI: Wayne State University Press, 2001).

8. When Romanized, the Japanese term Tanizaki uses is "Gurôbu Gaisha."

9. See Maurice Bardèche and Robert Brasillach, *Histoire du cinéma* (Paris: Denoël & Steele, 1935). Even Gilles Deleuze adopts this commonplace in *L'Image-Mouvement* (Paris: Minuit, 1983), Chapter 3.

10. Fredric Jameson has argued that every significant national cinema has been built around a stable of theater actors—not stars. Keynote lecture at the conference, Cinema and Nation, Dublin, November 1996.

11. Jean-Michel Frodon, *La Projection nationale: Cinéma et nation* (Paris: Odile Jacob, 1998).

12. Benedict Anderson's highly pertinent book is called *Specter of Comparison* (New York: Verso, 1998).

13. Janine Hansen, "The New Earth, a German-Japanese Misalliance in Film," in *In Praise of Film Studies*, ed. M. Makino, A. Gerow, and M. Nornes (Vancouver: Trafford, 2001).

14. In addition to the many books on Japanese cinema in the 1930s, I consulted *The Cinema Yearbook of Japan 1936–37* and profited from discussions with Naoki Yamamoto and Aaron Gerow. I also found references to Japanese film in French periodicals such as *Pour Vous* 462 (September 23, 1937).

15. To fill this niche the journal *Close Up* proudly subtitled itself "*the only magazine devoted to films as an art*." It regularly surveyed developments and notable films from Asia, the Soviet Union, and Europe. Tellingly *Close Up* was based in Switzerland, a multilingual non-nation; more telling, it was founded in 1927 at the tail end of the international avant-garde and did not survive long in the sound era, failing in 1933.

16. Roger Leenhardt, "Le Cinéma, art national," *Esprit* 65 (February 1938), reprinted in Leenhardt, *Chroniques de cinéma* (Paris: L'Etoile, 1986), 57–60.

17. Leenhardt, *Chroniques du cinéma*, 58.

18. Dudley Andrew and Steven Ungar, *Popular Front Paris and the Poetics of Culture* (Cambridge, MA: Harvard University Press), Chapter 3 "*Esprit* in the Arena of Extremist Politics" and "Conclusion as Forecast."

19. Even in the United States, by the late 1960s foreign films played on 9 percent of all screens in the country.

20. From the start, festivals, and Cannes foremost among them, were also crucial markets in the high capitalism that Hollywood stands for. Thomas Elsaesser is the latest scholar to keep a dual-perspective in mind, that of business and that of art (or critique). He terms it "mutual interference." See Thomas Elsaesser, *European Cinema: Face to Face with Hollywood* (Amsterdam: Amsterdam University Press, 2005), 126.

21. An unforeseen consequence was that festivals encouraged producers or cultural commissions from out-of-the-way places to initiate or enhance a daring project, gambling on the lottery of a major prize. For better or worse festivals generate as well as discover what they show. *Rashomon* appeared in Venice in 1951 as a total surprise, a discovery made by an intuitive festival scout. But many of the subsequent exports from Japan were produced with Venice in mind. Daiei studios specialized in rather high-budget self-exoticism, aimed at foreign critics. They counted on a rebound effect to improve indigenous box-office receipts. Intent on capturing attention at festivals, Japanese producers were tempted to experiment with extremes of what some consider a kitsch aestheticism.

22. While Gilles Deleuze famously developed Bazin's belief in a completely new phase of cinema coinciding with the war, Jacques Rancière is skeptical. See his *Film Fables* (Oxford: Berg, 2006), Chapter 7.

23. André Bazin, "Le Festival de Cannes 1946," in *Le Cinéma de l'occupation et de la résistance* (Paris: 10/18, 1975), 166–72, and Georges Charensol, "Cinéma américain, cinéma européen," *Formes et Couleurs*, no. 6 (1946).

24. Jacques Rivette, "Mizoguchi viewed from here," *Cahiers du Cinéma*, no. 81 (March 1958), reprinted in Jim Hillier, ed., *Cahiers du Cinéma: The 1950s* (Cambridge, MA: Harvard University Press, 1985), 264.

25. Paul Willemen, "For a Comparative Film Studies," *Inter-Asia Cultural Studies*, 6, no. 1 (2005): 103.

26. In André Bazin, *Cinéma 53 à travers le monde* (Paris: Cerf, 1954), 174.

27. I am reporting the high-minded rhetoric on the international critical front; but behind the scenes international trade deals were capitalizing on a growing appetite for things Japanese. At the same time, the pure Japanese culture pictured by the jidei-geki had to compete with a blossoming Japanese popular culture including musical comedies and teenage films employing Hollywood motifs and style, featuring homegrown actors effectively "designed" to imitate the long-legged stars of foreign films. On the elongation of legs, changing of eyes, and so on, see Michael Raine, "Youth, Body, and Subjectivity in the Japanese Cinema, 1955–60." PhD dissertation (University of Iowa, 2002), 109–31.

28. See Michael Raine, "Masumura Yasuzo's *Giants and Toys*," in *Japanese Cinema: Texts and Contexts*, ed. Alistair Phillips and Julian Stringer (New York: Routledge and American Film Institute, 2007).

29. Jean-Paul Sartre, "Orphée noir," in *Anthologie de la nouvelle poésie nègre et malgache*, ed. L. Senghor (Paris: Presses Universitaires de France, 1948). Translated into English by S.W. Allen as *Black Orpheus* (Paris: Présence Africaine, 1976).

30. See Robert Young, Introduction, in *White Mythologies: Writing History and the West* (London: Routledge, 1990). A more pointed expression of this dilemma can be found in Nelson Maldonado-Torres, "The Topology of Being and the Geopolitics of Knowledge: Modernity, Empire, Coloniality," *CITY* 8, no.1 (2004): 29–56.

31. I say "nearly everyone," because in 1954 Masaichi Nagata (Mizoguchi's producer) launched an annual Asian film festival, the showcase for what would soon become the Asian Film Producers' Federation (members including Japan, Taiwan, South Korea, Malaysia, Hong Kong, Philippines, and Thailand). The festival took place in a different country every year, and permitted filmmakers to measure their own work or aspirations against what others were doing in the region. One or two co-productions were initiated. See Kinnia Yau Shuk-ting, "Shaws' Japanese Collaboration and Competition as Seen through the Asian Film Festival Evolution," in *The Shaw Screen; A Preliminary Study* (Hong Kong Film Archive, 2003), 279–91.

32. The Art Theater Guild (ATG) was not quite "independent." On the one side it received partial financing from Toho which treated it as a kind of lab; on the other side, its key director Kashiko Kawakita, wife of the man who produced *Nippon* and *The New Earth* before the war, led a partly European life, connecting the ATG and directors like Oshima to developments in (and funding from) Europe. The ATG would outlast 1970, putting more hopes in documentary than in experimental features. See Roland Domenig, "Anticipation of Freedom: The ATG and Japanese Independent Cinema,"

Midnight Eye, June 26, 2004, www.midnighteye.com/features/art-theatre-guild.shtml

33. Serge Daney, *La Rampe: Cahiers critique 1970–1982* (Paris: Cahiers du Cinéma, 1983), 157.

34. See also Serge Daney, "Cinéphile en voyage," in *Persévérance* (Paris: POL, 1994), 117ff.

35. Marijke de Valck, "Film Festivals: History and Theory of a European Phenomenon that Became a Global Network." PhD dissertation, University of Amsterdam, 2006.

36. Rey Chow, *Primitive Passions: Visuality, Sexuality, Ethnography, and Contemporary Chinese Cinema* (New York: Columbia University Press, 1995).

37. Jean-Loup Passek, "Yugoslavian cinema." Catalog of the Centre Pompidou, Paris (April–July 1986).

38. The film's Serbian title, however, translates literally as "A House for Hanging."

39. *Treasure Island* is the title of a 1993 Taiwanese film by Chen Kuo-fu.

40. Ni Zhen, *Memoirs from the Beijing Film Academy: The Genesis of China's Fifth Generation*, trans. Chris Berry (Durham, NC: Duke University Press, 2002).

41. Angelo Restivo, *The Cinema of Economic Miracles: Visuality and Modernization in the Italian Art Film* (Durham, NC: Duke University Press, 2002).

42. Peggy Chiao and Chen Kuo-fu made their remarks in the panel "The Global Reception of Taiwanese Cinema" at the conference Double Vision: New Taiwanese Cinema, held at Yale University, November 1, 2003. Chen translated my own *Major Film Theories* into Chinese in 1984.

43. Already in 1986 a collective of filmmakers and critics had issued a manifesto, explicitly in the manner of the Oberhausen Manifesto of 1965, pressing the industry to strive for quality art that would capture local audiences as a rebound effect from success abroad. The film's victory at Venice vindicated this, and it came despite the fact that the Chinese managed to keep the Taiwan flag from being displayed. The seven person jury included Jin Xie, the prominent third generation director of *Woman Basketball Player #5*.

44. Geoffrey Gilmore, head programmer for years at Sundance, confirmed my intuition about this in Pusan, Korea, October 2005.

45. De Valck, "Film Festivals," 176.

46. Hollywood's marketing divisions have shamelessly bought favorable critical reviews, for they play on the fact that a critic's stature rises when his or her blurb appears as part of a film's advertising, whether in print media, on posters, or on a DVD box. The critic's newspaper or journal in turn profits from the exposure, encouraging five-star reviews. Beyond this are the junkets to premieres and press conferences with which studios have been known to tempt critics.

47. This missed rendezvous may reference the one in *Jules et Jim* when Jim leaves a café just minutes before Catherine arrives, thereby changing their lives, and the movie, forever.

48. Emmanuel Burdeau made this point in *Cahiers du Cinéma*, June 2004.

49. Lim Giong played in Hou Hsiou-Hsien's *The Puppetmaster*, and then composed the scores for two more of his films.

50. Serge Daney, *L'Exercise, a été profitable, monsieur* (Paris: POL, 1993).

vector, flow,

zone

towards a history

of cinematic *translatio*

n a t a š a   ď u r o v i č o v á

> *noise is inscribed from the start within the panoply of power.*
> *Equivalent to the articulation of space, [noise] indicates the limits*
> *of territory and the ways to make oneself heard within it, how to*
> *survive by drawing one's sustenance from it.*
>
> Jacques Attali, *Noise*[1]

cinema as place, space, soundscape

Under any definition, one of the essential features of globalization is the
proliferation of channels of communication. It is more and more common
in every aspect of our lives that spatio-temporalities mismatched in scale
and speed are placed abruptly next to one another, made to speak *to*, or *at*,
one another—both literally and metaphorically.

Built as it was on the paired desires to bring the distant closer and to make
the proximate strange enough to be worth seeing, cinema was a superb
workshop for such perceptual mismatches: the taking of photographic
pictures from their provenance in a precise, nameable locality ("*l'arrivée d'un*

train en gare de La Ciotat") and the showing of that place as if it were distant, by juxtaposing the familiar image in projection with places much more distant yet. This fundamental premise obtained beyond the genres of *vues* and *actualités*, where the transport of one place to another was announced forthrightly. For the concern with "origin"—with the precise siting and accurate belonging of these all-too-circulable images—almost immediately also played itself out in legal and trade disputes about films' material ownership: of patents, prints, or intellectual property. The complementary attraction of the moving image was that it also rendered one's own place strange, foreign even—Shanghai for the audiences in Shanghai, Beograd for Beogradians—when inserted into a nickelodeon projection sequence alongside Paris, Moscow, or New Delhi.

What in the literary application of modernism was known as irony, that is, double vision, found its equivalent in cinema's capacity to get a spectator to see his or her self as an Other even while seeing the other as a variant of one's self. In this process of splitting-and-displacement cinema helped feed the "specter of comparison," the decentering and comparative enterprise through which a multitude of places progressively entered into structures of relationships on a world-encompassing spatial grid, a conceptual map under-girding the universalizing impulse of modernity. The grid joined cinema to other media, newspapers in particular, which had been preparing this ground in the preceding century. By inviting questions such as "Where is this happening?", "Where am I situated with relation to what I am seeing?" or "Is what happens over there the same as what happens over here?", motion pictures implicated the viewer's experience within a vectorized grid of spatial relations, an orientational system implicitly related to a mappable space.[2]

This orienting and emplacing aspect of cinema's reality effect was offset, and dialectically countered, by the surging popularity of fiction film, a mode in which diegesis offers a more enclosed, discrete, and spatio-temporally separated space than that of the frontal cinema of attractions. Within less than a decade of cinema's beginnings, this increasingly dominant any-space of fiction was being put in the service of the paradigm of the national, and in this sense again grounded, respatialized—though now ideologically and legally under the sign of the state. This nationalizing turn has been seen as a rhetorical strategy in the battle for control of markets—a battle which acquired a more explicitly political goal in the course of World War I.[3]

Reframing this historical period from a more generalized media-oriented perspective, Jean-Michel Frodon has argued that the growth of cinematic fiction from World War I on was a direct function of cinema as an optimal machine for projecting an idealized collective self-image of a unified national body, with an attendant capacity to provide what he terms a *projection nationale* (meaning both "a national projection" and "a nation's projection").[4] In a thesis that explicitly matches the scale of cinematic projection to the Andersonian template of a print-based "imagined community," Frodon proposes that cinema provides an optimal representational scale for the level of a nation-state—a scale asserting itself even more clearly with the standardization of synchronized sound coincident with national borders. As the post-Cold War proliferation of the Herderian ideal of single-ethnic-state provides so many examples of, it is still today nearly impossible to imagine a state unless it can cast its own cinematic *projection nationale*: think cinema in re-emergent post-1989 countries like Ukraine, Serbia, or Kazakhstan.[5]

Whether issuing from within the image as part of the mise-en-scene, from between the images as intertitles, or later synchronized to appear from within the diegesis as dialogue, the fact of language with its inescapable drag-line to a particular location posed a fundamental challenge to a medium indebted at once to photographic capture of a space and to movement, mobility, displacement. It is in the alignment *and* realignment of the vectorized, deictic, triangulated lines of both projected photography and language—secured by pointing back to a place of origin in a recognizable world, as well as forward to a point of focus and comprehension—that we can begin to search for the transnational space cinema has opened up. This tenuous experiential accuracy is one reason why films in Esperanto are so patently unthinkable, in the absence of Esperanto-land where such films could have been shot.

As Frodon argues, well before synchronous sound appeared in late 1920s so as to tie image to place via sound in a tighter phenomenological bond, many nation-states had already been actively drafting cinematic production for "national service." Considered as part of an arsenal for conducting what could be termed territorial proxy wars, movies were tapped both for their commercial potential and as a proof of the formal uniqueness of a national culture. Every film-producing country, no matter what size, debated ways to secure its own territory against cultural intrusions from outside even while simultaneously aiming to expand—culturally for the most part— across its borders to other countries, whether contiguous or more distant. This was as much the case for minor producers like Poland or Argentina as it was for imperial powers, new (United States, USSR) or old (France).

Such "national projection" was generally the cultural ideal and goal on the side of the *making* of films, that is, on the part of the artists and producers (as well as politicians in a position to support, and be supported by, the discourse of national creativity). But this ideal was viewed as the inverse, as a constraint, from the reception end of the institutional spectrum. Exhibitors, and very often film critics, placed rather as great if not greater value on international flow of culture. In stark contra-distinction to the situation in the vertically integrated United States, distributors and theatre owners thus made up a potential fifth column of national film trade, in particular in many European countries.[6] Such stance made sense: much like during the ubiquitous 1920s debates about movies as agents of

Americanization, as soon as theatres were wired for sound they instantly became linguistic heterotopias, sites of geopolitical scale-jumping, turning into spaces where differently scaled and differently distant cultures came to directly confront—"speak to"—one another in previously unknown ways. "We recall the film about India," write two French critics about the transition period, "where appeared [. . .] Rabindranath Tagore, reciting a poem celebrating his land. One did not understand a word but one sensed oneself to be in the presence of Homeros."[7] The trope of Babel was everywhere. Movie theatres could thus be perceived at best as cosmopolitan sites of cultural and linguistic border-crossing or, more threateningly, as porous walls preparing ground for border-breaking, possibly followed by political annexation. Hence the tales about street riots in Paris, Prague, Milan, or in border cities like Breslau or Strasbourg, at the mere sound of certain kinds of foreign dialogue in local theatres.[8] Put differently, these sometimes provoked and even apocryphal narratives signal the incomplete fit between the "projection nationale" and the material conditions of international film trade, where the zone of the transnational opens.

It is thus a true paradox that it was the dominant aesthetic model of Hollywood film sound—a simulation of the effect of liveness, presence, for-me-ness—that put extra wind in the sails of many national cinemas.[9] In contradistinction to the few experiments in supra-national sound montage by such committed formal experimenters as Walter Ruttman, Eisenstein/Alexandrov, or Luis Buñuel, this model of fiction film was predicated on the congruence of the diegesis, the acoustic space of the movie theatre, and the designated national space outside it. Touring Europe with *The Jazz Singer*, Al Jolson would appear on stage after the screening and exhort the enthusiastic audiences in Stockholm or Berlin to demand their own Jolson, in their own language. Beyond its communicative content, speech in the wired theatre thus functioned pragmatically, as a shifter, drawing each (urban) audience's attention to their own situatedness vis-à-vis the film projected. Live on stage, Jolson would highlight the gap between a "me" speaking American English, and a "you" who "ain't heard nothin' yet!" (in German, Swedish, French), thereby placing the point of synchronized sound production and that of speech reception onto a shared geopolitical grid, splaying the gap between "there" and "here" in the service of closing it as soon as possible, presumably with the help of a Western Electric sound system.[10]

This "hereness," emphasis on presence, compensated for the fundamental technological separateness—and thus separability, non-identity—of voice and speaking body. Freed from its corporeal *hyle* into unbounded air, disembodied voice had, after all, until then been the chief advantage of radio and gramophone, sound cinema's main commercial competitors. Within the media system as a whole, then, sound cinema's unique attraction was that it offered to reattach the disembodied voice to an "audible" body, making the massively amplified speech seem to issue from a particular person's mouth and lungs, and thus from an identifiable point, to "home" it.[11] Outside the designated zones of transmission and thus comprehension, speech became, instead, pure noise. This metamorphosis was submitted to a virtuoso analysis of physics and politics of space in *Kameradschaft* (1931) by G.W. Pabst, of communication and electrical systems in Jean Duvivier's *Allo, Berlin? Ici Paris!* (1932), and reprised as a melodrama of displaced labor in Chaplin's *Modern Times* (1936).

In sum: the transition to synchronized sound put the cinematic institution everywhere into a double set of contradictions vis-à-vis the nation-state, at once reinforcing *and* undoing it. If we focus our attention on *production*, sound *film* reinforced the condition of the national because it attached cinema more firmly to traditional forms written culture, lent itself to strengthening the forces of protectionism and heightened enthusiasm for national forms of mass culture. Sound *cinema*, meanwhile, was evolving in the opposite direction, toward maximizing international circulation because of the increased cost of wiring and patents, and thus toward greater international interdependency. Considered on the other hand as an *experience*, movies struggled to sustain their appeal derived from their expansiveness and mobility, let us call it their unboundedness (whether spatial or social), even while the success of the mainstream sound film was fundamentally tied to its ability to provide an experience of for-me-ness, to reinforce the self as a central and stable perceptual fulcrum. This dual set of institutional counter-tensions formed the baseline condition of cinema as ever more reflective of, and enmeshed in, a transnational scale of space—a scale characterized by a simultaneous dependence on and transcendence of the nation-state.[12]

translatio

The key prerequisite for breaking up the film traffic gridlock erupting when the mobile medium of moving pictures became obliged to fit itself to the scale of a national language was to find adequate protocols of linguistic transfer. Had this been a strictly semantic challenge, a matter merely of supplying the functional equivalent of the source language in a target language and then "somehow" attaching it to the image track, "translation" would be an adequate term.[13] As it almost immediately became apparent, however, an equally important factor determining and guiding the protocols of linguistic transfer would be the political economy of translation, that is, the mix of economic and political factors deploying language to regulate much more than the path to comprehensibility. The challenge of translation evolved almost immediately into a gearbox of power through which cinematic flows were regulated, and legitimized; as I will show below, the distinction between what made up a dominant or a minor cinematic flow could be reinforced or inverted by decisions made under the rubric of "translation." As the protocols for linguistic transfer were being set, let us say between 1928 and 1933, every element in the decision to translate a film (which language, what procedure, where to execute it, under what set of rules) immediately became a matter of a specific set of transnational power relationships, and in many cases subject to explicitly political negotiations.

Rather than using the term "translation," which foregrounds the process and so implicitly stresses the final purpose of semantic equivalence, identity or parity, I will therefore borrow an older, and more culturally weighed term, the Latin *translatio*. Excised from the couplet *translatio studii/translatio imperii*, which in pre-modern historical understanding asserted that transfer of classical learning and transfer of political power were companion processes legitimizing each other, the term *translatio* is here meant to signal a widened description of the translation process. Extending beyond semantics so as to include the social and political ground-rules of text transfer from one to another set of cultural circumstances, it is explicitly attentive to the non-identity, asymmetry, or unevenness of power relationships in which all translation is inevitably implicated.[14]

Viewed through this wider lens, cinematic translation protocols are distinctly not, as is often claimed, a direct function of spontaneous audience preference, or of transparent market choices.[15] Rather, these protocols make up the pathways through which (state-)national cultures may not only *control and contain* but also *share in and coattail on* the benefits of international film trade, that is, do at the same time the hegemonic work of the expanding film culture and the counter-hegemonic work of boosting its own/site-specific culture. Thus when, in 1929 and in 1941 respectively, the Italian and then the Spanish governments ruled to dub all imported films to secure their "national air space" against linguistic intruders even while profiting from the imports' ideological, entertainment, and tax revenue benefits, they involved themselves in a discursive strategy of appropriation-via-translation. The strategies set during the totalitarian rule continued and continue to influence these domestic media industries, and to an extent their wider media landscapes, to the present day. Godard, in voice-over in his *Histoire du cinéma*, muses for instance on the debt of Italian neorealism to the mobility of cinematographers free from recoding equipment thanks to the standard of post-synchronization, a direct legacy of dubbing. Conversely, the small Swedish film industry responded at the start of the 1930s to the cheaper and thus pervasive subtitled films by heightening the gap between the cosmopolitan imports and the local culture, creating in the interstices of the dual linguistic register (experienced in every movie theatre where a subtitled film was shown), a subcategory of comedies grounded in regional dialect so distinct that its difference against more distant cultures became a political value in and of itself.[16]

Cinematic *translatio* is the epitome of the dilemma the process of translating always poses: on one hand, every film culture benefits from receiving *and* absorbing new elements through translation, which enliven it and bring it into a homeostatic relationship to other systems. On the other, each transport into another target culture (say, the export of a French film into Armenia, or of a Hindi film into the United States) competes for finite space and attention, altering the balance in the transnational ecosystem that encompasses all cinema. As Michael Cronin puts it in his analysis of the recto-verso relationship of translation to globalization: "translation is never a benign process . . . and it is misleading to present it as such: [it] is both a predator and a deliverer, enemy and friend."[17]

Contra a cultural imperialism thesis which assumes that expansion always entails absorption and leveling, the dynamic framework of *translatio*, superimposed over film circulation patterns, should instead draw attention to synoptic and asymmetrical relations, to flows, shifting networks and strategic alliances among modes of cinematic activity—transnational configurations all. Viewed systemically, the *translatio* factor is a necessary though not sufficient condition for cinema's globalization. Viewed historically, each concrete set of practices (which vary not only country to country but also in time, including—as I will show—technological time) articulates a set of multivalent relationships between a "stronger" and "weaker" film culture, and thus creates various force fields in the interchange between films' production and reception. The aim of redefining the pervasive and inescapable work of cinematic translation as a field of *translatio* is to draw attention to the politics of these uneven flows of exchange, and further, to argue that translation should be studied as an integral layer of spatial figuration, superimposed onto and hovering over both the cinematic institution *and* the representational field of the screen in which specific emergent transnational formations then can become apparent. On this definition, the interference of *translatio* can range from the zero-degree of unchallenged cultural for-me-ness in the case of a domestic film played in a domestic setting (shadowed by its latent spectral complement, the remake, whose job is frequently to displace the "foreign" prototype) through the vast middle field of films seen, more or less well, via the scrim of a linguistic supplement (accents, dubbing, subtitling, paraphrasing) to the growing number of polylingual films where the insufficiency of *any* supplement—and thus the failure of the orienting vector of language—is the dramatic heart of the film: think *Babel* (United States, 2006). In the final analysis, *no* film is *not* subject to the basic condition of *translatio*.

96

language, state, scale

How cinema's acoustic representational space was arranged for the spectator's benefit varied in different national spaces. To paraphrase the Yiddish joke ("a language is a dialect with an army"), a language is a dialect with a national cinema. The assorted ground rules of *translatio*, worked out in the gearbox of the mobile/global and the site-specific/local elements of the cinematic apparatus, emerged during the key 1929–33 period within the matrices of international patent and trade laws and domestic legislation, and have had a remarkable longevity, changing only very slowly, mainly since the late 1990s. The themes that emerge in the study of this phase are questions of hierarchy (what languages are translated at all; and, when they are, into what format), questions of commodification (is the production of language a form of labor, or is it part of the "raw material" attached to the terrain where that language is spoken—a claim underlying nationalist discourses), and questions of organization (what part of the production apparatus should be mobilized to supplement a film with its translation).

In contrast to the choices confronting smaller national cinemas, Hollywood's favored for-me-ness was a sound aesthetic conceived for a market and an industry predicated on economies of scale; the standardization of live stage shows that Warner Brothers undertook in the form of sound-on-disc film shorts would have, after all, not been either necessary or possible had their national circuit covered a smaller country and thus a smaller market. In a different, more modular conception of synchronized sound on the other hand, voice and image were combined in a space explicitly conceived as synthetic, composed for the benefit of the receiving audience. Thus, the first public screening featuring the German Tri-Ergon system of sound-on-film recording offered the feature *Ich küsse ihre Hand, Madame!*, in which the image of the popular star Harry Liedtke was synchronized with the much-admired voice of the equally popular singer Richard Tauber, as if aiming for some kind of entertainer *über*-persona—a scheme fundamentally counterintuitive in the Hollywood liveness paradigm.[18]

Audiences in other parts of the world were—still are—"homed" in acoustic spaces constituted, that is, sound-mixed, somewhat differently yet. Ranging from the politically homogenized "Tuscan" dialect, post-synchronized to float equidistantly above all Italian moviegoers (a result of policies established during the Fascist state's project of leveling every type of regional difference), through the enduring Japanese and Thai options of the live benshi/lecturer formats, to the Bollywood mix-and-match voice track devised in the late 1950s and carried through to India's burgeoning intranational dubbing scene today—all these models of filmgoing experience were constructed so as to tolerate a wider range of acoustic spaces than the classical "for-me-ness" of Hollywood.[19] In that sense the preconditions for translation remain a part of their aesthetic palette. Marvin d'Lugo demonstrates the dynamic nature of this process in the Spanish-language field in Chapter 8 of this volume.

But the limits and constraints of an acoustic "national projection" played itself out especially as efforts to determine the proper matching of language and scale. Would translation have to correspond to the scale of a state, or could a linguistic imagined community instead be matched to that of demographics, sometimes in conflict with political boundaries?[20] In 1930, the

US Department of Commerce, wrestling with this key export problem for its members, divided Europe into three types of "markets" based on estimates to which they might accept film imports (as versions, as dubbed dialogues or with subtitles) in a regional rather than the national language. (This transposition of cultural geography into economics anticipates the issue of region codes for DVD, an issue to which we will return in closing.) The challenge of the moment was whether a German-dialogue version of, say, a MGM film could also be released in theatres in Hungary or Czechoslovakia, on the assumption that a significant portion of local viewers would understand it without translation. Similarly, was there a Spanish dialect "compromise" that would satisfy at once the peninsular, the assorted Latin-American and the Filipino audiences? Could an American film be screened untranslated in a Paris theatre, given that Anglophone tourists would prefer it over the same US studio's French version screened in another theatre nearby? And, by extension, at what point did a French film first need to be translated into Arabic when screened in an upscale theatre in Cairo? Beirut? If Mandarin was to be the official language of China's nascent sound cinema, what of the state's rejection of the Cantonese- and Hokkien-speaking Hong Kong and Taiwanese audiences?[21]

The problems of proper scale matching persist today: can Disney screen its French dub in Quebec or must it provide a Québécois interpretation of the French translation? Can a British or an Australian film qualify for the "Foreign" category of the Academy Awards? And most recently, can a French film have English-language dialogue?[22] As a direct reaction to the threat of such linguistically threaded trade competition (and in full congruence with Mussolini's nationalist film policies) the Venice Film Festival asserted itself from its very beginning in 1932 as a *translatio*-free zone, refusing to accept any versions or any translated films, whether dubbed or subtitled.[23]

translatio *without translation: versions and polylinguals*

The most eccentric manifestation of the asymmetrical and uneven process of matching geopolitical scale and language were multiple-language versions (MLVs), films conceived and executed by a producer in one country so as to simulate the product of another national cinematography by shooting it in the language of, and with the performers from, that country.[24] For better part of the 1930s, the United States, many European, and especially the German studios, reproduced some of their successful films as MLVs, either in their home studios with imported actors (e.g. the German-language version of a Czech-language original, shot in a studio in Prague), or abroad, shot on location in the designated country with local actors (e.g. a French film shot in Hungary to produce a "Hungarian" film), simulating a national product. In the format of MLVs the process of *translatio* thus conjured forth a composite space that couldn't be read out as any "real" geopolitical space—a world completely populated by Italian- or French-speaking cowboys and settlers traversing the American West (*Il gran sentiero, La piste des gèants* (1931), two of the five versions of Fox's *The Big Trail*), or a Berlin full of working-class women and men speaking French to each other (*À moi le jour, à toi la nuit*, UFA's French version of *Ich bei Tag und Du bei Nacht*, 1932), or Marseille in which a romantic drama involving a local café owner's son and his girlfriend transpires entirely in Swedish, or in German (*Längtan till havet* and *Zum goldenen Anker*, the Swedish and German versions of *Marius*, Paramount, 1931). Neither bland no-spaces of transit and anomie, nor either the anonymous "great white sets" of the Deco era's cosmopolitan fantasies, these radically unthinkable spaces of the versions (qualitatively different from the same film dubbed into language y or z) were more like actualizations of cinema's virtual transnational core, the counterfactual worlds of *translatio*.[25]

That was one option. The second readily available strategy through which early sound cinema could supersede the all-too-limiting *projection nationale* were polyglot films whose dialogue track mixed a variety of languages, and whose plots dramatized the terms of cinema's inherent formal and economic transnationality. Built on substantive linguistic splitting—around the parity of several languages—these films create an ad-hoc imagined community, whether of permanent migrants or of provisional "rootless cosmopolitans," in which affiliation by mother tongue is the first rule that must be broken. Internally, with their space at once smaller than a nation (since only people in that particular polylingual group are fully addressed) and larger than one (because two or three linguistic populations are claimed), such films forthrightly break with the policed acoustic and communicative space of the nation-state.[26] The classic instances of the polyglot aesthetic are the already-mentioned *Kamoradschaft* and *Hallo? Berlin? Ici Paris!* aka *Hallo, halo! Hier spricht Berlin!*, to which could be added Renoir's *La Grande Illusion* (1937) or Godard's notorious *Le Mépris* (1964). In the first, the film's core theme—the undermining of national borders in the name of international solidarity—plays out in a labyrinthine coal mine under the German-French border as it first burns, then descends into complete darkness: all communication is quickly reduced, first to staccato speech, to the sounds of shouting, then to basic material noise, with space reduced simply to what its acoustics reveal. In the second, a monolingual French and ditto German switchboard operator test their romantic attachment via the communicative limits of telephone wires which eventually turn pure signal into speech. For Renoir, the linguistic abilities of the characters as well as of the viewer are among the narrative's major motivational elements. And Godard evokes the basic condition of Babelic polyglossia—the crisscrossing and clashing of languages, idioms, and accompanying modalities of thought as present on an international film set—as they spiral toward a final disaster at the site of production: death by pervasive miscommunication.

Or take for instance the stratification of the French-Moroccan co-production of *Le Grand voyage* (2005). Its natural audience—the film's imagined community—is comprised first off by those mirroring the story's protagonist: bilingual immigrants living in the interstice where the Francophone and the (Maghrebi) Arabic-speaking world coexist (which under this description would include France alongside Morocco, Algeria, Tunis, perhaps Lebanon and Chad). Further, the audience is widened in its sphere to countries with substantial populations of variously Arabic speakers, from Syria through Iraq and Saudi Arabia to Malaysia (brought into ecumenical conversation during the climactic *hajj* in Mecca), as well as Francophones everywhere, ultimately opening out to the rest of the world, the none-of-the-aboves, for whom the melodrama of the son and the father unable or perhaps unwilling to communicate in each other's language is reduced to the level of pantomime with sound, subtended by the homogenizing subtitles, which in this context obstruct rather than clarify the plot's unfolding.

Even in the United States, a country self-proclaimedly averse to linguistic diversity within its mainstream culture, a number of recent films have constructed a narrative space in the communicative gap between characters speaking standard American English and those speaking a Native American language (*Dead Man, Dancing with Wolves, Windtalkers, The New World*), a variety of Spanishes (*Babel, Hidalgo, Spanglish*), or more recently, Japanese (*Letters from Iwo Jima*). In these "true polylinguals" the confrontation of languages is extensive enough so that some form of translation (usually subtitles) is required to make sense of the story.[27] These narratives differ in a fundamental sense from the safe monolingual for-me-ness taken for granted in a mall theatre (broadly defined), including films like *Trouble in Paradise* (1932), *Lost in Translation* (2003), or *The Interpreter* (2005). In these, alien speech is subject to what Christoph Wahl has termed "postcarding," an acoustic flashing of the spectator with a brief sample of a more or less exotic language, dramatized asymmetrically enough to preempt further need for actual translation because whatever is said can be readily inferred, or else paraphrased by a diegetic character, indirectly reaffirming the film's dominant linguistic centering in for-me-ness.[28]

Given that the plots of such linguistically hybrid cinema are inevitably tied to global movement in some form—travel, war, migration—the polyglot films (which, Wahl and others think, now constitute an emergent genre) seem like the very allegory of transnationality. And that is, of course, what they are: representations of a world in which crossing a borderline of some sort or sharing air space, however defined, with a stranger—the basic condition of alienation—is modernity's most pervasive dramatic material.[29] Yet an allegory is not interchangeable with the real material conditions of cinema—which should be identified on a level constitutive of the cinematic institution as a whole. Every film, polylingual or not, is always a manifestation of *translatio*.

In the vast cinematic middle field, for most film audiences of the world, watching movies does not entail either being seamlessly "homed," immersed in a familiar acoustic and cultural 'scape of one's own (national) cinema *or* signing up for the estrangement experience of the manifestly foreign, as in the narrative space of a polyglot plot. With the general exception of (North) American and Japanese audiences, plus certain regional audiences in India, a majority of the world's audiences has for sustained periods taken in its movies encrusted with a thin but distinct coating of difference, that is, supplemented by an additional layer of graphic or acoustic matter comprising the inevitable residue of the two standard methods of translation, dubbing, and subtitling.

On one disciplinary front this layer has been extensively studied in the audiovisual subfield of translation studies, largely highlighting aspects of textuality. Its principal object of analysis is the language supplement (for example, matters of linguistic comprehension, semantic protocols of translation, politics of word choice, translation's work of censorship). More recently, it has also been approached in the framework of general semiotic theory, as a significant stratum of acoustic or graphic data, and viewed as a problem of reference (questions of transcription), from a cognitive/sensory perspective (for example, as a problem of legibility, measurement, orientation). This second approach is above all attentive to the acoustic and photographic supports of speech within a media context.[30] As proposed here, the approach via *translatio* would draw on notions from both these theoretical orientations, and propose a revisionist account of film history in which the pervasive linguistic displacement and the accompanying media transposition foreground mainstream narrative films in its non-identical form, attending to their circulation, transport or transfer rather than only to their ideal textual form.

Each of the main translation procedures, dubbing and subtitling, have a separate history in most nation-states (one that covers the cultural and industrial protocols in which each was deployed as long as films were basically produced for main projection in a movie theatre, let us say until the mid-1980s). Tracking it should involve, first of all, the stitching together each (national) cinema's strategic as well as formal relationship to those it imports from and exports to, but also its connections with other media, the broader public sphere, trade laws and fundamental geopolitical concerns. Attending to the weft and warp of a transnational history of world cinema, the study of *translatio* as a network would unfold alongside other lines of transnational mapping, such as genre and stardom.[31]

Dubbing first. The process called dubbing evolved in a tight sequence of technological, technical, political and formal trial-and-errors, becoming by 1933 a viable and relatively accessible procedure.[32] The fraught pathways to its acceptance and the strong feelings it provoked en route—Jean Renoir famously said that if cinema existed in the Middle Ages, dubbers would be burned at stake as witches—attest to what we might think of as its *pharmakon*-like status, both an indispensable remedy for death by commercial atrophy and a latent box-office poison within the cinematic apparatus. Damn if you dub, damn if you don't.

The wholesale imposition of dubbing in a number of countries in the 1930s, most of them in Europe, was a result of explicitly political decisions. In blocking out the sound of foreign tongues (most importantly the languages of the two successfully expanding empires, the United States and Germany), dubbing provided an "acoustic roof" over the native soil, a linguistic barricade whether against the encroaching Babel of generalized modernity or against regional political expansion. This was the position first of the Italian and later of the Spanish governments, which mandated dubbing in respectively 1929 and 1941; Germany achieved a comparable protectionist effect through an exponentially growing number of trade, racial and nationalist restrictions. A number of other countries, including France, Switzerland, and Czechoslovakia, followed instead a more differentiated "divide-and-conquer" strategy which allowed both dubbing and subtitling but closely regulated the conditions under which each method was to be deployed. The regulations bore in particular on internal geopolitical divisions within these nation-states, so that the sound of the problematic foreign (sometimes minority) language remained quarantined inside well-defined areas or social strata.[33]

But while a dubbed dialogue track strove to graft a symbiotic relationship between a local cinema's aura of spectatorial intimacy (its for-me-ness, let us say) onto imports, it also lessened the "home-game" advantage for the domestic film producers. To make up for this lost competitive edge of linguistic uniqueness, some European states—following a legislative prototype set up by the French Ministry of Education—stepped in with complementary regulations. Protectionist, but politically far from the pathological nationalisms of Italy and Germany, France in 1931 instead legislated a policy dictating a ratio between films released with subtitles (*version originale*) in a dozen or so *art et essai* theatres in Paris and a few key cities, and dubbed prints (*version française*), mandated for the bulk of the provincial theatres. This law also stipulated that the work of dubbing must occur on French territory, and that dubbing artists must be named in credits on par with other performers and craftsmen—a strategy subsequently emulated in other countries.[34]

Not only did this forthrightly political decision open up a door to a viable and professional and eventually star-driven voice casting, something which ultimately led, for instance, to the Disney franchise's glocal fortunes since the early 1980s.[35] More generally, once the nation-state staked out a direct interest in the film imports, dubbed films shifted jurisdiction from straight imports and became reconfigured into a "compromise formation," a multinational product aggregating two cultures and two industries. As far as the Hollywood studios were concerned, this meant that a film's translation was no longer primarily the assignment of their foreign departments (usually located on the East Coast), as during the silent era. With the translated soundtrack subject to legal control in the country where it was produced (by the local distributor), national censorship and intellectual property laws could apply to it directly, even when at cross-purposes with that of the original.[36] As a product, in turn, the dubbed film was the creation of craft and talent (actors, labs, studio technicians) normally working for the domestic industry. A fifth column cultural industry of sorts, the potentially "subversive" dubbed imports generated tax revenue and entertained domestic audiences even while becoming contained, visibly tethered to local use via the bit of the native voice and national (cultural) politics. At times, with a domestic film industry undergoing a crisis—itself possibly caused by imports—the ancillary industry of dubbing could thus paradoxically remain something of a placeholder for a "national cinematography." This has for instance been the case for the very small post-1993 Slovak film industry, helped along by ancillary revenues from film and television dubbing in the wake of the disintegration of the state-supported national cinematography of Czechoslovakia (whose dubbing studios had traditionally employed top of the line technicians and actors). To a different extent, dubbing has fulfilled a similar place-holding role in Iran during certain crisis periods, as well as in the post-Soviet Ukraine.[37] It is at the heart of the historiographic project of *translatio* that this model of "cinema-as-compromise–solution" remains a blind spot in the still-impermeable American cinema scene.

As an alternative to dubbing, subtitles, while cheaper and fairly readily supplied, were from the beginning seen as a second best method of translation. For one, integrating them into the image posed technical problems quite distinct from the old routine of intertitles (it took several years to find a way to imprint the celluloid strip with a stabile and sharp line of text at the lower edge of the frame).[38] Mainly, however, the need for continuous and fairly rapid reading—as contrasted to the more leisurely and regulable pattern of reading intertitles—reattached cinema, with a vengeance, to the problematic institution of generalized literacy. The lower cost of subtitling over and against dubbed films (averaging 15–20 percent) made them an overdetermined choice for distribution in "small markets"—but not unless this advantage to the distributor was complemented by high levels of education. This was the case for instance in Scandinavia, the Netherlands, and Czechoslovakia but not necessarily elsewhere: between the two world wars illiteracy rates were around 30 percent in Poland, and much higher in other "markets" like Turkey, where the relationship to traditional forms of writing was rapidly changing in the swirl of general modernization.[39]

On the side of reception, subtitled films thus came charged with the burden of "education," or other dues to their share of cultural capital. In

France the subtitled releases (*versions originales*) were legally the sole prerogative of the small and urban *art et essai* circuit; in the discourse of the period their reading was rapidly construed as a form of connoisseurship (of voice, of language, of the soundtrack), that is, of cinephilia.[40] But reading reframed as "work" could as easily be equalized with "not-entertainment," so that subtitles then could be deployed as a barrier protecting the domestic film industry operating in a zero-degree translation zone.

This was the case, for instance, in Mexico where subtitling—that is prohibition on films dubbed into Spanish (in a stance inverse to that of Spain, which tied its mandated dubbing to import quotas)—was mandated in 1949, and has until recently been used as an active, if often challenged, protectionist measure for the domestic film industry.[41] Arabic-speaking countries, too, have traditionally favored subtitles in movie theatres over dubbing, and not just for the important reason of maximizing a relatively wide-and-thin-spread theatre market (the unified "middle-Arabic" written text being, much like the Chinese script, more widely comprehensible than the many regional Arabic spoken vernaculars). According to one claim, the additional semio-cognitive barrier of the writing supplement helped to preserve a psychological gap between the imports (especially from Hollywood) and the regional audiences, said to prefer avoiding the culturally distasteful synthetic world arising from "Western" characters "speaking" Arabic; alternatively, subtitling makes it much easier to edit out culturally and politically offensive formulations and expressions. Cinema's perceptual amalgam is contrasted to television programming, more intimate and socially conservative (especially when imported from Latin America), dubbed for the region's television channels alongside the standard protocol for children's programming and animated films.[42] The ultimate case in point of subtitling deployed as deterrent against external competition is, of course, the United States, where the vaunted toxicity of subtitles (on par with dubbing) has historically been brandished as one of the—if not *the*—main argument against film imports *tout court*.[43]

Yet once it has been assumed, this cognitive "burden" of reading can be put to quite dynamic uses, and even refracted in two inverse directions, as two recent examples from Russia show. Having accepted the graphic overlay supporting the subtitles as a formal ingredient indispensable for the international circulation of his films, Timur Bekhmambetov, the director of the extremely successful and highly CGI-driven Russian fantasy film pair *The Night Watch/The Day Watch*, broke with the premise that the text ribbon at the lower edge of the frame should constitute a quasi-invisible supplement to the soundtrack. As if taking a cue from the silent period's repertoire of intertitle techniques, the English subtitles here occasionally cease to pretend not to exist and burst forth well inside the frame's playing field, floating across the image, bleeding and undulating as if affected by the raw force of the uncanny pervading the diegesis, fairly shouting for attention in an

Althusserian hailing: "You, yes you Anglophone viewers, you *are* being given special geopolitical treatment here! Enjoy it, already!" Leaving the theatre, the viewers may wonder whether the same privileged graphic treatment was afforded to their French or Japanese counterparts.[44]

An opposite direction is taken by *Russian Arc* (2003), Alexander Sokurov's tour de force survey of Russian history in the form of a 90-minute single-shot passage through the Hermitage. Plotted as a polylogue between visible and invisible characters belonging to different historical eras and meandering through the palace's endless Resnais-ian halls, the film lays its Russian dialogue track in a pattern so acoustically and thus ontologically complicated—who is it who is speaking? when? who can hear? who is listening? Who is eavesdropping?—that the drama of point-of-audition is accessible only to speakers of Russian who can follow it as it plays out. For while subtitles are provided, and mark the different levels of the voices graphemically, through italics, the constantly forward-moving camera competes for the viewer's undivided attention to the flow of time. Dubbing, however, would have in this case been about as useful as dubbing an opera. Making itself untranslatable—in a heteroglossic rather than polyglossic manner—Sokurov's film thus enacts a kind of "for Russian speakers only" triage through a spectator's (un-)pleasure. In the process the film tips its hand regarding its core running theme, the entrenched historical stand-off between "Russia" and "Europe"—a theme which then spilled over into the release history of the film itself, in conflicts about its co-production status with Sokurov's German cinematographer, its festival credits, etc.[45]

As with *Night Watch*, the point here is not to debate the merits of individual subtitling strategies or their execution, but rather to understand what vectors of aesthetic as well as political positioning are supplemented and perhaps supplanted in the phase of translation, and what this does to the visibility of a film on a global scale.

translatio *in a zero-degree zone*

Some historical research exists on the attempts of the various European film industries in their efforts to reach US screens and audiences in different phases of the silent period. The patterns and strategies of the export of US films worldwide have of course been amply documented.[46] The international flow *into* the United States after sound, however, has largely been studied through the prism of aesthetic influence, attentive especially to craft and talent immigrating to Hollywood from Europe. Yet during the first decade of sound the ground rules for what counted as "a foreign film" in the United States underwent a period of intense fluctuation: after the silent high-culture spectaculars such as *Metropolis* (screened in urban theatres known as sure-seaters), there were renewed efforts to reverse the one-way flow of exports. Imports returned, garnering quite a bit of popular success by 1931, floated by lively English-language musicals like *The Congress Dances* (UFA's English-language version of *Der Kongress tanzt*) or *Zwei Herzen in* 3/4 *Takt* (released as *Two Hearts in Waltz Time*), UFA's carefully repackaged Jannings/Dietrich vehicle MLV *The Blue Angel*, or Paramount-Joinville's tango films with Gardel (discussed in Chapter 8 by Marvin d'Lugo). Imported films were also attractive to the various ethnic communities across the United States, for whom translation was, precisely, to be avoided. Estimating from the number of foreign films listed as exhibited in the United States in *Film Daily Yearbook* for 1932–34, this early wave of foreign films appeared to be somewhat successful.[47]

Yet gradually, in this interwar decade, imports—both as ethnic programming, as versions and as translated films—were displaced by remakes proper (defined as selling/purchasing the right to reproduce the film in its entirety, from script to elements of mise-en-scene) and replaced versions (where the "remake" is owned by the same producer), becoming a Trojan horse of Hollywood's monolingualism. All elements of otherness— linguistic, cultural, formal—were eliminated in the machine of what is now referred to as the classical system.[48] By the end of the decade a de facto blockade on translated films prevailed in the United States. Reappearing after World War II, in the swirl around the Paramount Decrees and carried by the wave of neorealism, film imports had a resurgence in the United States inside a new crop of independent "art cinemas," but by then their fundamental ghettoization inside the "non-entertainment" quadrant was— and still continues to be—taken as a given. Nonetheless the logic of *translatio* operated within mainstream US cinema for roughly a decade, in the 1960s, as the temporary shrinking of the US domestic market reconfigured the boundaries of for-me-ness itself. The runaway productions relocated especially to Italy and Spain, countries with a long-standing tradition of post-synchronization, and produced films with a heavily over-lay(ere)d soundtrack, in consistently accented or dubbed, always audibly post-synchronized English of performers "matted" into spaghetti (or paëlla) westerns, or equally distinctly "unAmerican" historicals *à la El Cid*.[49]

It took almost half a century after the dismantling of the vertically integrated industry to make a first serious crack in the "English-only" barrier erected around the mass moviegoing protocol in the United States: in 2002 the composite-Chinese soundtrack of *Crouching Tiger, Hidden Dragon* (CTHD) was the first non-English dialogue to penetrate the hitherto inaccessible acoustic space of the American mall multiplexes.[50] That offensive had been carefully planned in pre-production focus groups, established not only to find out how to adapt the *wuxia* genre to American teenagers' taste, but also to determine whether the presence of subtitles could be made acceptable for mainstream US distribution. The green light came from the first generation whose reading skills had been honed by the continuous "breaking news" creep-line and stock market ticker at the lower edge of their television screens, and by perceptual multitasking at their PC terminals.[51]

We can hardly speak of a wave of film imports enlivening US mall theatres in the wake of *CTHD:* "Language is destiny in the American market," regretted in familiar fashion an article about the failure of subsequent film imports to repeat Ang's and Schamus's feat.[52] Yet the movements comprising globalization are as multidirectional as they are unavoidable. For we can now point to a significant presence of "the foreign" in the persistently fortressed US film market—once, that is, that space's boundaries have been digitally rearticulated. Its economic structure first modified by the 1980s' VHS revolution, this field has since the mid-1990s or so been rescaled both internally—via the configuration of software and miniaturized screens ranging from DVD players to PDAs—and externally, by redrawing the parameters of a *projection nationale*. At the US local Blockbuster video store, "Foreign" is now, for better and worse, a genre-like category alongside "Drama" or "Sci-Fi," a recalibration still largely unthinkable in the US theatrical distribution and exhibition system, where the alignment "foreign=translation=art" for better part of the twentieth century succeeded in establishing a negative borderline of visibility for the world's movies.

translatio in the age of digital transfer

space/region/zone/edition: rescaling the image world

Metonymically intertwined with transport in its material, aura-laden sense, "translation" meant in the Middle Ages the process of carrying over, transporting, a bone of a saint from one place of rest to another.[53] There is a parallel here with the status of translation in film history, fundamentally affected by the material weighing-down of celluloid-based cinema. The dual structure of simultaneous identity (the film as a title, its bookkeeping entry, its tax or screening visa number) and non-identity (the film prints, vastly multiplied, variously translated and titled, numerously duplicated, screened, scratched, patched, archived, or lost) is the opaque area in which the process, labor, and impact of translation were largely obscured.

Unmoored from real estate and from its heavy stock, from the collective and anonymous experience born in the triangle of projector/screen/ loudspeakers, its once-celluloid reels miniaturized and digitally remediated, the basic unit of 'a film' is now redefined to include an entire secondary para-textual environment including scores of subtitled and/or dubbed audio data.[54] And beyond the portable disk as such, with the promise of all film history available just an internet terminal and a credit card number away, digitized cinema has become mobile to the nth degree, a meta-medium aspiring toward—to borrow the term Dudley Andrew coins in Chapter 4 in this volume—a *décalage*-free utopia of global simultaneity, perpetual availability and ubiquitous access.[55]

The detachment from a fixed viewing location has been accompanied by a representational verso: the drift away from indexicality, the generalized acknowledgement that "cinema" is gradually less a medium of ontological contract with physical reality, of images taken, and more that of special effects, that is, of images made. The global transport of images having, since the late 1990s, increased by an order of magnitude, the vector of "here/there," the pleasure of seeing a place—either one's own or else a distant one—on which so much of cinema's commerce has depended, has been reconfigured by the increasingly flaunted possibility that the space has been digitally manipulated. Often the "proof" of photographic contact with the physical space is instead supplied in the form of the para-textual material (the "Making of . . ." bonus materials, where traditional documentary conventions persist). While national labels have retained their function (a moviegoer still chooses to see—or to avoid—an "American," or a "Korean," or a "Bollywood," or a "French" film), in these geographically indeterminate and synthetically produced or enhanced landscapes and/or characters, space can increasingly be perceived as a design rendered three-dimensional by software rather than a photographically "recorded" rendition of a pro-filmic place. Sound in general, and language in particular then becomes even more important for bestowing physical properties onto the graphics. Properly remixed, dialogue, sound effects and reverb then read out as dimensionality and as orientational ground secured though language ("Where are we supposed to infer we are?"), upgrading space into place. Digitized cinema, capable of near-infinite and near-instantaneous global circulation, thus depends on adequate sound track, including language track, even more than photo-cinema did. For it would now theoretically be possible to wrap every new release in an envelope of sound that would seamlessly locate, 'home' it in any geopolitical space where a DVD can be played, to the point where the film's provenance could 'vanish': *A Series of Unfortunate Events* could as easily seem to be 'from' Argentina as 'from' Turkey or Canada.

But while promoting and depending on flows, global trade can only generate profit if it also sustains and regulates barriers, lines of differentiation. Cinematic *translatio* participates in this regulatory system by prorating a film's local and the global elements through formulas that vary by place, time and politics. What considerations do then go into the making of the gearbox of *translatio* in the deterritorialized digital cinema—or, to put it differently, how is the relationship of space, place and language recalibrated in the digital technology? We will next be following the global film market expansion, and the regulation of that expansion, through two registers: that of language as data, and that of the structures on which such conversion—such translation-- is predicated, namely the proprietary constraints of intellectual property and patents.

By definition, a patent is, after all, meant to limit circulation. But in contrast to the forked pathways that arose, for instance, out of the separately evolving technologies of projection at key historical moments (such as the Western Electric and Tobis Klang sound film patents wars at the start of the sound era, or the television reception standards PAL, SECAM, and NSTC, kept incompatible by the political divisions of the Cold War era), most of the world's DVDs and their players are based on a shared and common patent and technology of recording and storage.[56] A few years ago this global standard was supplemented with additional features whose sole function was to reduce the device's interchangeability in order, as it were, to add geopolitical unevenness to the near-instantaneous distribution flow made possible by the digital infrastructure. The obstruction was achieved by devising a set of codes that require a match "key" between a disc's and a player's system to run the movie, and which were made licensable. In counter-distinction to encryption, which aims to prevent unrestricted peer-to-peer copying, this "digital rights management scheme" thus operates by tethering a disc to a particular kind of player, which is, in turn, tethered to a precisely delimited geopolitical space.

The plan for this rearticulation of DVD cinema's global space was developed in the mid-1990s by the blandly titled DVD Forum, a Tokyo-based international consortium of 200-plus equipment manufacturers and media producers. Its chief purpose is to control the readily portable and near-infinitely reproducible data stored in DVD form through ever-evolving modes of encryption and code redesign.[57] A "security consultant" for the film industry (as well as for makers of other types of commercial software), the consortium aims to optimize profits through "windowing," a schedule of staggered release dates in contiguous zones, itself a variant of the traditional film print distribution strategy of "run-clearance-zones," previously applied especially *within* the boundaries of one country. Upgraded to the scale of the "geopolitical whole"—the world, as it were—this scheme parses the imagined totality of space and time into eight regions: the continental land mass divided into six variously assembled geographical aggregates (see Figure 5.1), a zone reserved for the mobile/open no-space of "air- and sea-faring vessels," and a zone described sometimes as "other," and sometimes as "future"—a virtual domain reserved for DVD players specially secured through always-changing encoding.[58]

If, in the traditional variant of the moving picture experience, one enters the black box of a movie theatre for two hours of centered experience, the process is fundamentally different when situating oneself to watch a DVD. For the process of slipping a disc into the small black box of the DVD player tacitly entails logging into a global digital *dispositif* and thereby placing oneself onto a global positioning system—cardinalizing oneself via a technical device, to borrow Bernard Stiegler's term.[59] Failure to sign on to this

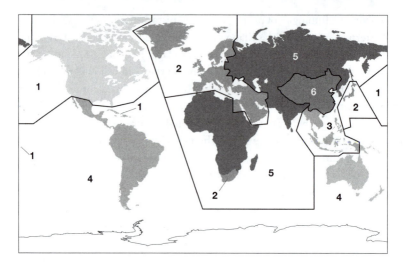

Figure 5.1

The world map according to the DVD region code

grid—by inserting a DVD from a "disallowed" region—prompts not "nothing" (i.e. absence of signal) but rather a prohibition message (including a little open-palmed hand, a universal rejection icon). This built-in spatial constraint is signaled only by a digit on the back of the DVD's packaging; the map actually showing the limits of the zone system (Figure 5.1) is generally not shown on the packaging but must be looked up separately online (and indeed does not appear on the site of the DVD Forum). While the number, and the term "region" that goes with it, thus imply the distribution of the code as a geopolitical arrangement—the key six zones are drawn up as coincident with boundaries of political states—it is not apparent what criteria have been used either to set the scale, or to draw the borders of, a given "region": demographics? politics? culture? communication systems?

The one legend that invites some "reading out," that is, some orientation in the system of numbered regions encoded in the *dispositif*, is the DVD's language array, generally provided on the box. Logically, each zone might be mirrored by the list of appropriate (official) languages spoken in the region, and through which a spectator would be cued in, "homed," within the region-space: thus, English and French for Region 1 (North America), English, Spanish, Portuguese and French for Region 4 (Central and South Americas plus Australasia), and so on.

Yet empirically, judging from dozens of sites and packagings where this function is supplied, an equation between a region's list of countries and the language array of the DVDs is at best approximate. Thus, most Region 1 DVDs sold in the United States include alongside English (sometimes present as both audio track and as subtitles, as distinct from closed captions) and the Canada-compliant French (again, subtitles or dub), also Spanish (either as a dub or as subtitles); though the entire area south of the US-Mexican border falls technically into Region 4, the presence of Spanish surely reflects the demographic and commercial realities within the officially monolingual United States (Toby Miller's Chapter 7 in this volume studies precisely the dynamics and importance of this transnational audience). A title released as a Region 2 DVD can go from no translation at all—a zero-degree/domestic edition of one of the two dozen or so national cinematographies encompassed in that region—to an array coincident with but not exhaustive of the region. Thus the "Special Edition" for a Region 2 release of the US-produced *Fargo* provides subtitles in French, Spanish, Dutch, Croatian, Portuguese, Greek, Czech, Hungarian, and Polish but no German or Italian dub/audio track, nor any number of other languages spoken in the states in Region 2 (e.g. Slovak, Turkish, Lithuanian, Arabic, Afrikaans, or Japanese).[60] Such incompletely matched correspondences between the DVD region as a trade entity and a geopolitical entity seem to be the norm. The translation scheme presents itself as local and ad hoc; an investigation of each decision and case—what we next will consider under the term localization—would add up to a bottom-up study of digital cinema's transnational dimension, its *translatio*.

But alongside these two pseudo-spatial grids of a DVD's geographical circulation—of code-defined regions, and of (sub-)regions signaled by language—a third, let us call it "vertical," grid comprises a DVD's full nexus of *translatio*. This dimension is signaled in the language of interface to the platform that allows the viewer to execute the set-up itself ("open," "loading," "resume"), to execute navigation on the disc itself ("menu," "chapter selection"), and may include the "extras" ancillary to the feature itself (bonus materials, voice-over commentaries, and so on). Even while from the point of view of programming all these materials have a different status, given that they all are "secondary" materials, a decision has nonetheless always to be made whether, and how, to translate them.

From the vantage point of cinema this sort of material counts as liminal terrain, corresponding at most to the language used in a film's credit sequence, a para-text largely inhabited by proper names and commonly not subject to translation at all (only when watching a film from a culture with a different alphabet does one become conscious of the difference such margin can make). But because we are concerned with media transfer, the translatorial treatment of this quasi-trivial component draws attention to an additional set of processes involved in a film's remediation—for remediation includes, after all, the alignment of fundamental differences in procedures.[61] In being reformatted to DVD, that is, remediated, the data file formerly known as a film is also equipped with a graphic user interface (GUI) featuring commands that allow a viewer to scan, stop, enhance etc. the image and sound data flow. This process includes what is known as "localization"—meaning the wholesale procedure of

111

adapting data to "local environments/standards"—and can be glossed as a technical counterpart of verbal translation. While translation, an *inter-linguistic* procedure, operates between a source and a target language, localization is an *inter-semiotic* process of transcoding that includes revising, as needed, the standard code, local operating requirements (e.g. PAL conversion), as well as the more conventionally legible semiotic materials of the application, including but not limited to script, icons, language tags, and language.[62]

Put otherwise, the difference we are considering here is that between the work of translating say a novel from Polish to Portuguese (or, *mutatis mutandis,* a Polish film for a Portuguese audience), and the work of releasing a new version of a software in dozens of new markets—"local environments"— worldwide at the same time (blockbuster-style, we might add): in a true translatorial paradox of non-identity, then, "localization" is the procedure that allows the release of data on a global scale. However, this scale must here be conceived not through references to a *geographic* territory but rather *discursively,* by virtue of the existence of any alternative, concurrent, "environments"—whether linguistic, social or technological. For as we saw in our close reading of the DVD box legend, "global" is in this sense not a spatial but a virtual "totality." Defined tautologically, we could say that localization is what happens when, for whatever reason (technological, cultural, economic), a new *edition* is needed, *and* when this process of upgrading or adaptation to the new environment strives to erase all orientation marks that signal it as having a provenance in some other environment. Such marks of difference would include the full gamut of semiotic matter, ranging from basic programming code through graphics, alphabets and other symbolic codes in the interface that might signal to the user that he or she is a disallowed "other," and conversely also acknowledge that the material on the screen "comes from somewhere."

In translation theory such a vehemently domesticating approach is known as "functional equivalent translation." Its goal is that all traces of the source text's provenance *somewhere,* not to mention the work of translation itself, should be erased so that the text reads as if entirely local, originating "from here"—a literary equivalent of a national cinema's constitutive and reassuring for-me-ness. When, in short, viewers in another country can watch, point, and click their way through the entire gamut of materials and functions of a DVD without ever being confronted by any trace of the foreign or otherwise incomprehensible material they cannot access—an alien menu description or a disallowed command—the work of localization has been successful.[63] Putting this peculiar work of "deep-adaptation" in media-historical retrospect, we could say that the multiple-language versions of the early 1930s were, exactly, films localized *avant la lettre*: "rolling out" a new edition of a new MS Windows is the corresponding process to Paramount preparing thirteen versions of *Television* (1930), from translating the screenplay through adjusting allusions and elements of mise-en-scene and casting 13 sets of new actors, to generating publicity material which would make it appear as if the American-gone-transnational studio miraculously delivered a "true" German or Romanian or Portuguese or film.

Precisely this effect is at the heart of the massive localization work undertaken in advance of simultaneous global release of a blockbuster DVD, such as *Lord of the Rings*. To this purpose Time Warner outsourced the production of twenty-five different release versions of the DVD edition, remastered in PAL and SECAM, reformatted into five region zones and translated into twenty-one language versions (with the film itself in some cases available both dubbed and subtitled), often supplemented in turn with "local content," meaning material available only to spectators spatialized by language.[64]

It is in this sense, then, that the DVD player, the remote, and the menu can be jointly operated as a global positioning system of sorts in the virtual transnational space implied in each edition—a space in which viewers then situate themselves via a selection or combination of languages from the available offering. As an individual spectator points-and-clicks the remote and select a linguistic vantage vis-à-vis the digitally encased space of the film, he or she may ponder what we could call a cognitive anti-map. In surveying the three-grid language array (of original sound, of available format of translation, of available commands and GUI), what underlying political formation might aggregate, say, the speakers of Chinese, Russian, Arabic, and Dutch listed together on the menu? And what is the imaginary space— virtual imaginary community—of such an "anti-map?"

Granted, this imaginary mapping is perhaps conceivable only by the film equivalent of "netizens"—digital cinema's trackers and inhabitants. But how much analytic attention such a schematization of geopolitics through language does provide can nonetheless be glimpsed from the feedback loop of the World Wide Web. Proliferating online are not only a growing number of sites with commentaries and evaluations of the merits of a given film translation, but also sites offering bit torrent downloads of film subtitles in a truly vast—if not (unlike the Jesus Film project) exactly global—range of languages. More creatively yet, a plethora of linguistic variations on dubbing and subtitling of borrowed images circulates on YouTube, where images, sounds, and words are traded in a geopolitical free-for-all. These specialized epiphenomena of the global attest to the wish, perhaps even need, to carve out local pathways through the transnational *combinatoire* of digital cinema, new routings of the audiovisual that are vectorized so as to become, at least in potential, as personal and as denationalized as traditional cinephilia.

113

notes

1. Jacques Attali, *Noise: The Political Economy of Music* (Minneapolis, MN: University of Minnesota Press, 1984), 6.

2. On the relationship between geographic visibility, maps and cinema, see for instance Sam Rohdie, *Promised Lands: Cinema, Geography, Modernism* (London: British Film Institute, 2001), 1–19. For a theory of how local belonging integrated itself in worldwide discursive structures through institutions of bound and unbound seriality, see Benedict Anderson, *The Spectre of Comparison: Nationalism, Southeast Asia and the World* (London: Verso, 1998), Chapter 1.

3. Richard Abel, *The Red Rooster Scare: Making Cinema American, 1900–1910* (Berkeley, CA: University of California Press, 1999). More generally, forms of international and colonial circulation of early cinema are investigated through a variety of approaches in Roland Cosandey and François Albera, eds. *Cinéma sans frontières 1896–1918 / Images across Borders* (Lausanne: Payot, 1995).

4. Jean-Michel Frodon, *La Projection nationale: cinéma et nation* (Paris : Odile Jacob, 1998), Introduction.

5. Mette Hjort has made a strong case for "small nation cinema" as a qualitatively distinct formation in the context of globalization. See her *Small Nation, Global Cinema: The New Danish Cinema* (Minneapolis, MN: University of Minnesota Press, 2005), and Mette Hjort and Duncan Petrie, eds. *The Cinema of Small Nations* (Bloomington, IN: Indiana University Press, 2007).

6. In each case the strength of the fifth column varied depending on the structure of theatre ownership. On France, see especially Martine Danan, "From Nationalism to Globalization: France's Challenges to Hollywood's Hegemony." PhD thesis, Michigan Technological University, 1994.

7. Maurice Bardèche and Robert Brasillach, *Historie du cinéma: le cinéma parlant* (Paris: André Martel, 1954), 16 (my translation).

8. See for instance Sheila Skaff, "Intertitles and Language Conflict in Bydgoszcz, El Paso and Juarez, 1908–1920," paper presented at the meeting of the Society for Cinema and Media Studies, Chicago, IL, March 2007. Also Sheila Skaff, *Through the Looking Glass: Cinema in Poland, 1896–1939* (Athens, OH: Ohio University Press, forthcoming).

9. On the impact of the Hollywood sound model outside the United States, see Charles O'Brien, *Cinema's Conversion to Sound: Technology and Film Style in France and the US* (Bloomington, IN: Indiana University Press, 2005). The term "for-me-ness" is a coinage for a sound design effect in which the auditor always hears optimally, regardless of the narrational arrangement of the image. See Rick Altman, "Afterword," in Altman, ed. *Sound Theory/Sound Practice* (New York: Routledge, 1992), 250.

10. For an allegorical reading of synchronized sound's "liveness," see Thomas Elsaesser, "Going Live: Body and Voice in Early Sound Cinema," in *Le Son en perspective / New Perspectives in Sound Studies*, ed. Dominique Nasta and Didier Huvelle (Berlin: Peter Lang, 2004), 155–68. For *Jazz Singer* on a Swedish stage with live performers, see Jan Reinholds, *Filmindustri 1900–1975* (Lerum, Sweden: Reinholds Text & Förlag, no date), 76.

11. This argument is elaborated in Nataša Ďurovičová, "Local Ghosts: Dubbing Bodies in Early Sound Cinema," in *Il film e i suoi multipli / Film and its Multiples*, ed. Anna Antonini, IX Convegno Internazionale di Studi sul Cinema (Forum: Udine, 2003), 83–98. Reprinted in *Moveast 9* (2003), http://epa.oszk.hu/00300/00375/00001/durovicova.htm

12. A contemporary analysis of opportunities for the US film industry in this set of counter-tensions appears in Howard T. Lewis, *The Motion Picture Industry* (New York: Van Nostrand, 1933), Chapter XIII. For the Euro-American perspective on this tension, see Victoria de Grazia, "Mass Culture and

Sovereignty: The American Challenge to European Cinemas, 1920–1960," *Journal of Modern History* 61, no. 1 (1989): 53–87. Walter Benjamin seizes upon this contradiction—which he links to the crisis of fascism—when he points out that, despite the apparent nationalization (and thus "auratization") of the new talkies, the cinematic system itself, the industry at large, is driven toward international concentration by the capital of international electrical firms. See Benjamin, "Work of Art in the Age of Mechanical Reproduction," in *Illuminations*, ed. and introd. Hannah Arendt, trans. Harry Zorn (New York: Schocken, 1969), note 9.

13. The purest instance of this mode of "functional" translation could be demonstrated in a project called "The Jesus Film," coordinated by an evangelical missionary group based in the United States. Its visual component, a two-hour filmic account of the life of Jesus, has been either dubbed or narrated into nearly 900 languages, with some 200 more to go. The language versions range from full blown (if very artless) dubbing into major world languages to a voice-over narration in minor tribal languages provided by missionaries to that area. For the film, the account of the project and the full list of languages deployed, go to www.jesusfilm.org. Since the film is hermetically enclosed within its own distribution and exhibition system, the translations are not subject to any of the institutional features that characterize filmic *translatio*. This project has come to my attention thanks to Johanna Poses, who discusses it at length in her original MA thesis "Your Own Personal Jesus? Translation Strategies in the Jesus Biopic" (University of Amsterdam, 2005).

14. In the early Middle Ages *translatio studii*, the undertaking of translating canonic texts from Latin into vernacular, was a strategy of legitimization, that is, an attempt to ally the contender rising to power with the preceding cultural or ideological authority (of Rome) and thus gain ideological legitimacy, having already won the military contest (*translatio imperii*). The term's best known usage is in Ernst Robert Curtius, *European Literature and the Latin Middle Ages* (Princeton, NJ: Princeton University Press, 1953/1990). In other words, the main goal of *translatio* is to appropriate and thus incorporate the dominant culture's texts so as to strengthen one's own via the imported elements rather to try to dominate or suppress it. For a contemporary use of this trope see for instance Zrinka Stahuljak: "An Epistemology of Tension Translation and Multiculturalism," *The Translator* 10, no. 1 (2004): 33–59. Ella Shohat and Robert Stam, "The Cinema after Babel: Language, Difference, Power," *Screen* 26, nos. 3–4 (1985): 35–58, remains a cornerstone essay on the politics of language and translation in cinema.

15. For an interesting discussion of audience preferences contra cultural political decisions in this regard, see Miika Blinn, "The Dubbing Standard: Its History and Efficiency Implications for Film Distributors in the German Film Market," IME Working Papers on Intellectual Property Rights, no. 57, Dynamics of Institutions and Markets in Europe, www.dime-eu.org/files/active/0/WP57-IPR.pdf

16. See for instance Leif Furhammar, *Från skapelsen till Edvard Persson* (Mt Pleasant, Stockholm: Wahlström & Widstrand, 1970).

17. Michael Cronin, *Translation and Globalization* (New York: Routledge, 2004), 142.

18. See Klaus Kreimeier, *Die UFA Story: Geschichte eines Filmkonzerns* (Munich: Hanser, 1992), 216.

19. For the linguistic work of Italian cinema, see Sergio Raffaelli, *La lingua filmata: didascalie e dialoghi nel cinema* (Florence, Italy: Le lettere, 1992). For Indian

cinema, see Ashish Rajadhyaksha and Paul Willemen, eds., *Encyclopaedia of Indian Cinema* (London: British Film Institute and Oxford University Press, 1999), 9–11. For Thailand, see Dome Sukvong, " 'A oriente del sole, a occidente della luna': il cinema muto in Tailandia / East of the Sun, West of the Moon: A Region in Memory," www.cinetecadelfriuli.org/gcm/previous_editions/edizione2003/Thai.html

20. A survey of laws regulating dominant and minority languages in current EU media is in a study commissioned by the Organization for Security and Cooperation in Europe, "Minority Language-Related Broadcasting and Legislation in the OSCE," www.stanhopecentre.org/2007/index.php?option=com_content&task= view&id=34&Itemid=39

21. For the US overview, see Kristin Thompson, *Exporting Entertainment: America in the World Film Market, 1907–1934* (London: British Film Institute, 1985), 160. For the matter of US Spanish-language versions in the Philippines, see Guillermo Gómez Rivera, "The Truth about the Spanish Language in the Philippines," http://filipinokastila.tripod.com/truth.html (accessed May 21, 2007). For the question of Chinese dialects, see Sheldon Hsiao-peng Lu, "Dialect and Modernity in 21st Century Sinophone Cinema," *Jump Cut*, no. 49 (Spring 2007) http://ejumpcut.org/archive/jc49.2007/Lu/text.html

22. The official website devoted to Quebec dubbing is www.doublage.qc.ca. On the AMPAS category "Foreign," see John Mowitt, "The Hollywood Sound Tract," in *Subtitles: On the Foreignness of Film*, ed. Atom Egoyan and Ian Balfour (Cambridge, MA: MIT Press, 2005), 381–400. On uses of English in current French cinema, see Martine Danan, "National and Post-National French Cinema," in *Theorising National Cinema*, eds. Paul Willemen and Valentina Vitali (London: British Film Institute, 2006), 177.

23. *Variety*, September 6, 1932, 11.

24. The literature on the subject has burgeoned. Among important research sources are Mario Quargnolo, *La parola ripudiata: L'incredibile storia dei film stranieri in Italia nei primi anni del sonoro* (Gemona, Italy: La cineteca del Friuli, 1986); Juan B. Heinink and Robert G. Dickson, *Cita en Hollywood: antología de las películas norteamericanas habladas en castellano* (Bilbao: Mensajero, 1990); and Harry Waldman, *Paramount in Paris: 300 Films Produced at the Joinville Studios, 1930–33, with Credits and Biographies* (Metuchen, NJ: Scarecrow, 1998). Recent publications devoted to the topic of versions include three special issues of the journal *Cinema & Cie* (no. 4, Spring 2004; no. 6, Spring 2005; no.7, Fall 2005), and Jan Distelmeyer, ed., *Babylon in FilmEuropa: Mehrsprachen-Versionen der 1930er Jahre* (Munich: edition text + kritik, 2006).

25. For a superb discussion, see Anna Sofia Rossholm, "Film, Theatre and Translation of the Local: *Marius* in Sweden," in her *Reproducing Languages, Translating Bodies: Approaches to Speech, Translation and Cultural Identity in Early European Sound Film* (Stockholm: Almkvist & Wiksell, 2006), 144–60. After World War II, co-productions, in particular in Europe, stepped into this role—simulating a national product by way of retaining an element of "for-me-ness" (usually a plot turn, a star and a linguistic trace) as well as by way of their tax definition, guaranteeing the film's cultural reach beyond the borders of the co-originating state. For a historical discussion, with a focus on translation, see Mark Betz, "The Name above the (Sub)Title: Internationalism, Coproduction, and Polyglot European Art Cinema." *Camera Obscura 46*, no. 16.1 (2001): 1–44.

26. Christoph Wahl, "Discovering a Genre: The Polyglot Film," *CinemaScope* 1 (2005), www.madadayo.it/Cinemascope_archive/cinema-scope.net/index_

n1.html. For a fuller treatment see his monograph, *Das Sprechen des Spielfilms* (Trier, Germany: Wissenschaftlicher Verlag, 2005). A different model of cinema that breaks with the national paradigm is outlined in Hamid Naficy, *An Accented Cinema: Exilic and Diasporic Filmmaking* (Princeton, NJ: Princeton University Press, 2001). Where Wahl sees cinema's wholesale response to globalization, Naficy's accent on individual accent, as it were, stresses, rather, authorial uniqueness which refracts the pervasive modern condition of deterritorialization with a formal and personal signature.

27. The extreme version of this occurs in Mel Gibson's two grandiose historical projects concerned with forms of Christian empire-building. In exactly the opposite direction of the infinitely translatable Jesus Film project (see note no. 13), with the choice of a dead language serving as a kind of negative *lingua franca*, both *The Passion of the Christ* (2004) with its Aramaic and Latin dialogues, and *Apocalypto* (2006, spoken in Yucatec Maya) destroy the "for-me-ness" for most all contemporary audience, so as to vector/align the spectator (pseudo-) historically rather than geographically. Thus, in a roundtable discussion about *Passion*'s potential anti-Semitism, the few remaining Aramaic-speakers in northern Lebanon were invoked as the film's "imagined community." See Laure Goodstein, "*Passion* Disturbs a Panel of Religious Leaders," *New York Times*, February 25, 2004.

28. See Wahl "Discovering a Genre."

29. For a discussion of the ethics of the hierarchies involved in the translation of such films, with some interesting Canadian examples, see John Kristian Sanaker, "Les Indoublables: Pour une éthique de la représentation langagière au cinéma," *Glottopol* 12 (May 2008): 147–60, www.univ-rouen.fr/dyalang/glottopol.

30. The textualist approach dominates the large body of work devoted to screen translation in translation studies. For a regularly updated survey, see a bibliography compiled by Jan Ivarsson at www.transedit.se/Bibliography.htm. By far the most sophisticated instance of a media-theory-informed approach to film translation as media transfer is that of Rossholm, *Reproducing Languages, Translating Bodies: Approaches to Speech, Translation and Cultural Identity in Early European Sound Film* (Stockholm: Almkvist & Wiksell, 2006). The locus classicus of this entire topic remains Shohat and Stam, "The Cinema after Babel."

31. A somewhat comparable historiographic enterprise is Franco Moretti, *Atlas of the European Novel 1800–1900* (New York: Verso, 1998), and one attempt at writing a non-aggregate history of world cinema, in Gian Franco Brunetti, ed. *Storia del cinema mondiale* vols. I–IV (Torino, Italy: Einaudi, 1999–2001).

32. For a detailed technological and industrial survey of early dubbing see Ďurovičová, "Local Ghosts."

33. For Italy, see for instance Raffaelli, *La lingua filmata*. For Spain, see Diego Galán, "El doblaje obligatorio" http://cvc.cervantes.es/obref/anuario/anuario_03/galan/p04.htm. For France, see Paul Léglise, *Histoire de la politique du cinéma français: Le cinéma et la IIIeme république* (Paris: Pierre Lherminier 1977). For Germany, see for instance Wolfgang Becker, *Film und Herrschaft: Organisationsprinzipen und Organisationsstrukturen der nationalsozialistischen Filmpropaganda* (Berlin: Volker Spiess, 1973), 26–31, and passim.

34. Danan, "From Nationalism to Globalization," Chapter II.

35. Pavel Skopal, "Kolem světa v 32 jazycích. Lví král a strategie lokální globalizace." *Iluminace* no. 2 (2005): 31–49.

36. For a recent example, see Doreen Carvajal, "French Dubbers Complain of Pressure to Water Down Scripts," *International Herald Tribune*, January 21, 2007.

37. In the Czechoslovak industry the first wave of uprooting of this local stake of the voice—and in that sense the institutional decline of "star dubbing"—came in with the loss of the state monopoly brought about by the arrival of VHS technology in the late 1970s. See Miroslav Hůrka, *Když se řekne zvukový film* ... (Prague: Český Filmový Ústav, 1991) and Ivan Žáček, "Český film—chorobopis", *Iluminace*, no. 2 (2005): 51–80. On Slovakia, see Braňo Hronec, "Slovenskeho dabingu bude na Markíze menej," http://medialne.etrend.sk/televizia/clanok.php?clanok=1451. An evaluation of this highly professional dubbing style appears in Mark Abé Nornes, *Cinema Babel: Translating Global Cinema* (Minneapolis, MN: University of Minnesota Press, 2007). On Ukraine, see Taras Shevchenko, "Constitutional Court Obliges to Dub all Films in Ukrainian," http://merlin.obs.coe.int/iris/2008/3/ article29.en.html. On the intermittently important role of dubbing for the Iranian film industry, see Hamid Naficy, "Dubbing, Doubling, Duping," *Pages*, no. 4 (July 2005): 113–17, www.pagesmagazine.net/2006/article.php?ma_id=7830018.

38. A good basic overview of the history, technology and literature related to subtitling is the site www.transedit.se/, maintained by Jan Ivarsson.

39. Another key factor in literacy can be found in the graphemic reforms linked to modernization of traditional cultures, for example in Turkey (which switched from Arabic to Latin alphabet in 1924), the cyrillization of previously Arabic-alphabet Central Asian communities as they became absorbed into the USSR, or simplification movements in Korea and China around the turn of the twentieth century. For an overview see Robert Frederick Arnove and Harvey Graff, eds. *National Literacy Campaigns: Historical and Comparative Perspectives* (New York: Plenum Press, 1987).

40. The subtitle read as a gateway to a fundamental stance of formal estrangement, that is, to art, is the underlying organizing principle of Atom Egoyan and Ian Balfour's imaginatively edited *Subtitles*. Centering as they do on traditional aesthetic concepts such as faithfulness—and by extension for instance matters of copyright—the concerns of subtitlers overlap here with those of literary translators. A widely cited argument challenging the standard procedure of producing experientially and formally transparent subtitling is Abé Mark Nornes, "For an Abusive Subtitling," in *The Translation Studies Reader*, 2nd ed, ed. Lawrence Venuti (New York: Routledge, 2004), 447–69.

41. See for instance Jennifer Liu, "A New Golden Age for the Silver Screen," *Revista* (Fall 2001), www.drclas.harvard.edu/revista/issues/view/10; Luis de la Calle, "Innovación y creatividad de película para el desarrollo," *El Semanario*, December 4, 2007, www.elsemanario.com.mx/news/news_display .php?story_id=194.

42. Ramez Maluf, "A Potential Untapped? Why Dubbing Has Not Caught on in the Arab World," *Transnational Broadcasting Studies* 15 (Fall 2005), www.tbsjournal.com/Archives/Fall05/Maluf.html; Mohammad Y. Gamal, "Egypt's Audiovisual Translation Scene," *Arab Media and Society* (May 2008), www.arabmediasociety.com/?article=675.

43. See for instance Ramona Curry, " 'A Rebel Lion Breaks Out': (Re)parsing the 1960s U.S Film Critical Discourse about Dubbing vs. Subtitling," conference paper, Society for Cinema and Media Studies, Chicago, IL, March 2007.

44. The Region 1 editions of the DVD of *Night Watch* vary—one has the graphic

subtitles, one does not. See http://horrortalk.com/reviews/NightWatch/NightWatch.htm.

45. See the uncredited interview with Sokurov on the website devoted to the film: www.sokurov.spb.ru/island_en/feature_films/russkyi_kovcheg/mnp_ark.html.

46. On imports to the United States during the later silent period, see Anthony Guzman, "The Exhibition and Reception of European Films in the United States during the 1920s." PhD dissertation, University of California at Los Angeles, 1993; on the earlier period, see Abel, *The Red Rooster Scare*. On US exports, see Thompson, *Exporting Entertainment America*. For an author-centered approach to entering the US film market and industry, see Irène Bessière and Roger Odin, eds. *Les Européens dans le cinéma américain: Émigration et exil* (Paris: Presses Sorbonne Nouvelle, 2004).

47. For an assessment see Max Goldberg, "Presentation of Foreign Pictures in US Market," in *Film Daily Yearbook 1932* (New York: Film Daily, 1933), 533.

48. Among sturdy examples of classical-system-compliant duplication are the couplets *Intermezzo* (Sweden 1936) / *Intermezzo* (USA, 1937) and *Pepé le Moko* (France, 1937) / *Algiers* (USA, 1938), cases where the remake stands "in the stead of" the original by virtue of their extreme proximity.

49. See *The American Film Institute Catalog of Motion Pictures Produced in the United States Feature Films, 1961–1970* (Berkeley, CA: University of California Press, 1997).

50. Hong Kong martial arts films, the one imported genre with some record of wide US distribution, were shown dubbed, predominantly in inner-city independent theatres. For an interesting discussion of US imports of recent martial arts films as directly tied to the dilemmas of translation, see Erich Kuersten, "*Shaolin Soccer*, Miramax and the Question of Subtitles," *Pop Matters*, May 23, 2003, www.popmatters.com/film/features/030522-shaolin-soccer.shtml.

51. James Schamus, personal communication, May 2002, Chicago, IL. For a more theoretical take on the composite effect of the stock-market creepline in the televisual image, see Eric Cazdyn, "A New Line of Geometry," in *Subtitles*, ed. Egoyan and Balfour, 403–19.

52. Anthony Kaufman, "Is Foreign Film the New Endangered Species?" *The New York Times*, January 22, 2006.

53. Cronin *Translation and globalization*, 8.

54. A standard DVD is capable of storing eight different soundtracks (original + seven dubbeds) and thirty-two different subtitles. Yves Gambier and Henrik Gottlieb, eds. *(Multi)Media Translations* (Amsterdam: Benjamins, 2001), xiii.

55. Almost, that is. At the present 12 percent of all the films in the IMDB have been digitized.

56. On the early sound film patents, see Wolfgang Mühl-Benninghaus, *Das Ringen um den Tonfilm: Strategie der Elektro- and der Filmindustrie in den 20er und 30er Jahren* (Düsseldorf: Droste, 1999), Chapters 2 and 6. For the differences in TV standards see http://en.wikipedia.org/wiki/SECAMDVD technology. For DVD technology see http://en.wikipedia.org/wiki/Dvd.

57. See the organization's website www. dvdforum. org. The legally oblique nexus of DVD technology and access is discussed in Brian Hu, "Closed Borders and Open Secrets: Regional Lockout, the Film Industry, and Code-Free DVD Players: A Review of Multi-region Accessibility on the Philips 642 DVD player." *Mediascapes* (Spring 2006), www.tft.ucla.edu/mediascape/Spring06_ ClosedBordersAndOpenSecrets.html.

58. According to Wikipedia, "region 7" is an encryption secured for special uses such as distribution to MPAA pre-screeners, usually in a dedicated player. See Wikipedia entry "DVD_region code," http://en.wikipedia.org/wiki/DVD_region_codes [sic].

59. The instance here is only a tangential point to mark a link to Stiegler's intriguing overarching thesis, which charts globalization as an ongoing historical process of involuntary and permanent reinscription of local or individual techniques of memory (time) and orientation (space), ultimately determining the subject's capacity for sustained thought, into technologies of global transmission. See Bernard Stiegler, "Our Ailing Educational Institutions: The Global Mnemotechnical System," *Culture Machine* 5 (2003), http://culturemachine.tees.ac.uk/Cmach/Backissues/j005/Articles/Stiegler. htm, a translation, by Stefan Herbrechter, of Chapter 4 of *La Technique et le temps*, vol. 3, *Le Temps du cinéma* (Paris: Galilée, 2001).

60. See www.dvdbeaver.com/film/DVDCompare6/fargo.htm. On issues of translation and DVD compatibility, see also Matthew Kayahara, "The Digital Revolution: DVD Technology and the Possibilities for Audio-Visual Translation," *Journal of Specialized Translation* 3 (2005), www.jostrans.org/issue03/issue03_toc.php.

61. One gloss of remediation is:

> If we want to describe what new media does to old media with a single term, "mapping" is a good candidate. Software allows us to remap old media objects into new structures—turning media into "meta-media" [...] In contrast to media, meta-media acquires three new properties. First, with software, data can be translated into another domain—time into 2D space, 2D image into 3D space, sound into 2D image, and so on [...] Second, media objects can be manipulated using GUI (Graphical User Interface) techniques such as: move, transform, zoom, multiple views, filter, summarize [...] And third, media objects can now be "processed" using standard techniques of computerized data processing; search, sort, replace, etc. media objects can now be "processed."
>
> (Lev Manovich, "Understanding Meta-Media" *CTheoryNet* www.ctheory.net/articles.aspx?id=493#_edn1#_edn1)

62. For an example of what the work of transcoding such process entails, see Mozilla's collective/open localization project at www.mozilla.org/projects/l10n/. For an interesting discussion of the distinction between attending to the level of code as opposed to that of the interface, see Jay David Bolter, "Remediation and the Language of New Media," *Northern Lights* 5, no. 1 (2008): 25–37, www.intellectbooks.co.uk/journalarticles.php?issn=1601829X&v=5&i=1&d=10.1386/nl.5.1.25_1

63. A perfect gage of the "depth" of this process is whether the translation has reached the hidden functions a DVD sometimes includes—extras, or in-jokes known as "Easter eggs," embedded deep in the interface as a kind of contractual reward for the "DVD-phile" spectator.

64. For an account of the procedure itself, see "Výroba evropských verzí sběratelské verze DVD 'Pán prstenů—Návrat krále' v Čechách," www.jcsoft.cz/fantasy/viewnews.asp?id=528. For one fuller analysis of the release strategies and reception of *LOTR*, see for instance Sven Jöckel, *Der Herr der Ringe im Film: Event Movie, postmoderne Ästhetik, aktive Rezeption* (Munich: Reinhard-Fischer, 2005).

nataša ďurovičová

cinema as

transnational

exchange

chinese cinema

and transnational

film studies

y i n g j i n   z h a n g

Since the late 1980s, scholars have become more and more aware that the national cinema paradigm does not adequately respond to contemporary issues in film studies and film practices. Admittedly, even the concept of "national cinema" itself has proven to be far from unproblematic, and many scholars have advocated a shift from national cinema to "the national" of a cinema—a shift that allows for diversity and flexibility rather than unity and fixity, as previously conceived. However, as the forces of transnationalism assume increasing magnitude in the era of globalization, the national as a new critical concept continues to be unstable, and its conceptual space is constantly criss-crossed by other discourses and practices variously described as "international," "multinational," "postnational," "paranational" and, last but not least, "transnational."

This chapter attempts to reconceptualize Chinese cinema in relation to the shifting problematics of national cinema and transnational film studies, in both theoretical and historical contexts. In terms of theory, we can no longer pretend to ignore glaring gaps and blind spots in film history previously covered up or glossed over by the national cinema paradigm.

In terms of history, we must revisit the existing framework of film historiography and reevaluate certain disjunctures or ruptures in a century of Chinese film production, distribution, exhibition, and consumption. This combined theoretical-historical perspective seeks to better comprehend Chinese cinema at a juncture when it has evidently outgrown the national cinema parameters and has emerged as a significant force in world cinema in the era of globalization and transnationalism.

reproblematizing national cinema

Since the late 1980s, critics of national cinema in the West (which here includes Australia, Europe, and North America) have identified a number of problems in previous film scholarship and have worked toward a paradigmatic shift from unity (a myth of national consensus) to diversity (several cinemas within a nation-state), from self-identity (a cinema defined against Hollywood) to self-othering (a nation's internal heterogeneity), from text (auteurist studies) to context (cultural history, political economy), from elitist (great intellectual minds) to popular (mass audience), from production (studio-centered) to financing, distribution, and exhibition (process-oriented). In a seminal book on French cinema that subsequently launched an influential national cinemas series from Routledge in the mid-1990s, Susan Hayward questions two standard film historiographical approaches, those of the "great" auteurs and of film movements. For her, both approaches pay narrow attention to "moments of exception and not the 'global' picture" and place a national cinema in "the province of high art" rather than popular culture,[1] thereby necessitating a synchronic and diachronic filling of the gaps between select auteurs and movements.

Indeed, Gerald Mast, one of the early proponents of the auteurist approach, had this comparison to offer in the mid-1970s: "Just as the history of the novel is, to some extent, a catalogue of important novels and the history of drama a catalogue of important plays, the history of film as an art revolves around important films."[2] For Mast, film art is undoubtedly the most reliable textual source from which a scholar is entitled to study what he calls "the great film minds" in the history of cinema. Not surprisingly, at a time when auteurism prevailed in film studies, the emphasis on "great" auteurs came hand in hand with the emphasis on "pivotal" film movements, the latter seeking to identify like-minded auteurs in groups, generations, and nations. As Andrew Higson observes of British film history, a select series of relatively self-contained quality film movements are recognized and assigned the responsibility of "carrying forward the banner of national cinema."[3] On a larger scale, writes Stephen Crofts, "such cinema 'movements' occupy a key position in conventional histories of world cinema, whose historiography is not only nationalist but also elitist in its search for the 'best' films."[4]

Both auteur and movement approaches prevalent in national cinema studies involve a selective appropriation of history and tradition—what Higson calls "the myth of consensus"—as well as significant degrees of amnesia or pretended ignorance of other contemporaneous types of identity and belonging, "which have always criss-crossed the body of the nation, and which often cross national boundaries too."[5] To supplement the typical strategy of a self-identity defined against Hollywood or another national cinema, Higson recommends an inward-looking process, whereby a national cinema is conceptualized in relation to the existing national, political, economic, and cultural identities and traditions.[6] Writing of Australian cinema, Tom O'Regan urges national cinema scholars to take on "multiple and diverse points of view" because, for him, "[n]ational writing is that critical practice which thoroughly establishes and routinely works through the heteroclite nature of cinema."[7]

Higson's and O'Regan's attempts at internally "othering" national cinemas bear the imprints of the multiculturalism debate during the 1990s, but an outstanding result of the shift from unity to diversity is a critical realization that, even within a nation-state, "there is no single cinema that is *the* national cinema, but several [national cinemas]."[8] This paradigmatic shift is most evident in Crofts' taxonomy, from seven categories of national cinema in 1993 to eight varieties of nation-state cinema production in 1997. Albeit still in need of further elaboration, Crofts' new proposal "to write of states and nation-state cinemas rather than nations and national cinemas" foregrounds a recent consensus regarding the sheer heterogeneity and incommensurability among nations, states, and national cinemas.[9] To quote O'Regan: "At some time or other most national cinemas are not coterminous with their nation states."[10]

The recent shift to diversity and heterogeneity has benefited directly from a gradual expansion of the field of critical investigation beyond textual exegesis. As early as 1985, Steve McIntyre called for redirecting

> attention away from concern for exact theoretical explication of progressiveness (or whatever) supposedly immanent in texts, towards a historically and culturally specific analysis ... of production and consumption, audience composition, problems of reference, and so forth.[11]

Higson followed in 1989 with

> an argument that the parameters of a national cinema should be drawn at the site of consumption as much as at the site of production of films; an argument, in other words, that focuses on the activity of national audiences and the conditions under which they make sense of and use the films they watch.[12]

Crofts concurred in 1993 with a recommendation that "Study of any national cinema should include distribution and exhibition as well as production within the nation-state."[13]

The new emphasis on exhibition and consumption has engendered new visions as well as new problematics. Pierre Sorlin, for instance, rewrites the history of Italian national cinema in terms of generations of filmgoers, but the undeniable fact that, historically, a national audience watches domestic *and* foreign films has provoked a debate on what exactly counts as "national" in film consumption.[14] John Hill warns against Higson's argument in his essay, "The Issue of National Cinema and British Film Production," in which he states that "The problem . . . is that it appears to lead to the conclusion that Hollywood films are in fact a part of the British national cinema because these are the films which are primarily used and consumed by British national audiences."[15] What Hill wants to preserve in the exhibition sector of a national cinema, then, is an unambiguous distinction between national (or domestic) productions and those from Hollywood or other national cinemas.[16]

Obviously, recent attempts at problematizing national cinema have fundamentally destabilized—if not yet collapsed—this bounded, highly territorialized concept, making it impossible to function as an essentialist, unitary, all-encompassing category of analysis. "National cinemas," O'Regan suggests, "are identified as a relational term—a set of processes rather than an essence,"[17] and this shift of emphasis from essence to *process* explains the increasing frequency in the use of "the national" in national cinema studies. Hayward, for one, draws attention to this mutually enforcing process: "cinema speaks the national and the national speaks of the cinema." Being "relational" in a *continuum* stretching from the local to the regional and global (more on this continuum later), the national has found in cinema a powerful means of enunciation, but inevitably, such enunciations change in response to evolving socio-political and cultural processes. Two key words have surfaced to describe the ongoing process, "fluctuating" and "unfinished": a national cinema cannot but be "historically fluctuating" simply because "the underlying process is *dynamic* and perpetually *unfinished*."[18]

reconceptualizing chinese cinema

As a national cinema, Chinese cinema is both "fluctuating" and "unfinished." It is fluctuating because of its unstable geopolitical and geocultural constitution in China's fractured landscapes of nationhood; it is unfinished because of its historical ruptures of regime change and its periodic movement of border crossing and self-fashioning. As is well known by now, "Chinese cinema" has unstable boundaries and may simultaneously refer to pre-1949 cinema based in Shanghai, mainland cinema of the People's Republic (1949 to present), Taiwan cinema, Hong Kong cinema, and even Chinese diasporic cinema (for example, works by directors like Ang Lee). With its structural multiplicity and instability, Chinese cinema is "a messy affair . . . [and] is fundamentally dispersed," to borrow O'Regan's characterization of Australian cinema,[19] and I have further emphasized that Chinese cinema is dispersed "historically, politically, territorially, culturally, ethnically, and linguisticially."[20]

Given its dispersed nature, it is debatable whether "Chinese cinema" could be adequately replaced by "Chinese-language cinema" (*huayu dianying*), as Sheldon Lu and Emilie Yeh have proposed. The new term first surfaced in the early 1990s when scholars in Taiwan and Hong Kong (e.g., Lee Tain-dow and William Tay) attempted to bypass the limiting territorial imagination of "Chinese [nation-state] cinema" (*Zhongguo dianying*) and looked for an alternative, flexible conceptualization similar to that of "Cultural China" or "Greater China."[21] While the advantage of "Chinese-language cinema" in foregrounding differences of regional dialects and in challenging—if not transcending—the singular nation-state model is surely undeniable, its narrow *linguistic* emphasis is by no means sufficient to capture the rich varieties of geopolitics, regionalism, and ethnicity in Chinese cinema. To say the least, "Chinese-language cinema" is helplessly inadequate (or even self-contradictory) when used to reference a certain kind of commercially successful films from mainland China, Taiwan, and Hong Kong, such as *The Big Shot's Funeral* (dir. Feng Xiaogang, 2001), *Double Vision* (dir. Chen Kuo-fu, 2002), and *Silver Hawk* (dir. Jingle Ma, 2004), which intentionally deploy extensive English dialogue in a mixture of "global *mélange*" and employ a multinational cast in order to expand international viewership beyond an established base of Chinese-language audiences.[22]

Rather than privileging *language*, a reconceptualization of the national in Chinese cinema as multiple *discursive projects* is a more productive way to go. Inspired by the recent problematization of national cinema and by Judith Butler's theory of enunciation,[23] Chris Berry advances an argument in favor of "recasting national cinema as a multiplicity of projects, authored by different individuals, groups, and institutions with various purposes."[24] Apart from multiplicity as its obvious strength, a major attraction of this recast model of national cinema is its *flexibility* of both project articulation and participation alliance: the national—being "fluctuating" and "unfinished"—is historically articulated by different projects and different participants, and the makeup of such participation changes over time as different individuals, groups, and institutions negotiate their positions and form or dissolve their alliances. As Berry suggests, sometimes the nation articulated in a cinematic project may not be accommodated by the modern, unified nation-state model, and sometime it may exceed it.[25] In other words, the boundaries of a cinema and a nation or state may not—and do not have to—fit perfectly, and a long history of such imperfect fits (especially in Hong Kong and Taiwan) has resulted in the current "messy" and "dispersed" nature of Chinese cinema(s), with or without a plural designation.

Thinking in terms of a multiplicity of projects, we can delineate at least three significant shifts in Chinese cinema that may or may not parallel what have happened in other national cinema studies as summarized above: first, from conventional scholarship of great auteurs and movements to an exploration of alternative practices previously downgraded or excluded in Chinese film history; second, from thematic, ideological analysis of individual films to what might be broadly termed "industry research,"[26] including various aspects of film production, distribution, exhibition, and consumption; third, from a narrow concern with national cinema per se to a transnational reconceptualization of cinematic projects on a continuum stretching from the local through the national to the regional and the global.

Like its European counterparts, Chinese cinema has been studied extensively in terms of auteurs and film movements. Among favorite subjects are three "avant-garde" movements of the 1980s—the fifth generation in mainland China (e.g., Chen Kaige, Tian Zhuangzhuang, and Zhang Yimou), the Hong Kong new wave (e.g., Tsui Hark, Stanley Kwan, Wong Kar-wai), and new Taiwan cinema (e.g., Hou Hsiao-hsien, Edward Yang, Tsai Ming-liang)—and all three of them have received close textual scrutiny.[27] The left-wing (or leftist) film movement, which dominates scholarship in Chinese, has likewise received two book-length treatments in English,[28] while a more subtle differentiation of cinematic nationalisms (e.g., industrial nationalism, class nationalism, traditionalist nationalism, colonial and anti-colonial nationalism) is used to structure a more balanced survey of pre-1949 mainland Chinese cinema.[29]

Needless to say, leftist film of the 1930s and the new waves of the 1980s represent but two high points (or "golden ages" as some have preferred) in Chinese film history. It is crucial to keep in mind, however, that neither were they the *only* cinematic projects of the national during their time, and nor were they instantly absorbable into dominant ideological and commercial realms. More often than not, these retrospectively glorified movements appeared first as *alternative practices* that constituted disjunctures or ruptures in Chinese film history. For instance, ideologically, new Taiwan cinema questioned the nation-state formation under the Kuomintang (KMT) regime and released a repressed memory of Japanese colonialization (nostalgically reinterpreted as more benevolent than KMT). The "island nation" imagined in new Taiwan cinema was thus placed squarely at odds with state policies, in particular the language policy that excluded or discouraged the use of Taiwanese dialect before the mid-1980s, but ironically new Taiwan cinema would find itself congenial to the new political project of the national (e.g., de-sinicization), implemented by the pro-independence

DPP (Democratic Progressive Party) after it gained power in the 1990s. Its ideological trajectory from alternative to mainstream notwithstanding, new Taiwan cinema was accused (mostly by old-fashioned film critics) of being responsible for the deterioration and eventual bankrupcy of Taiwan film industry after the late 1980s.[30]

A similar trajectory from periphery to center can be located in the career of fifth generation directors, whose emergence in the mid-1980s signified first and foremost a rupture between the dominant system of socialist filmmaking and an emergent form of post-socialist filmmaking. But ironically, in economic terms, this rupture was made possible precisely by the socialist state apparatuses, without whose financial support the fifth generation's early dissenting films, such as *Yellow Earth* (dir. Chen Kaige, 1984) and *Red Sorghum* (dir. Zhang Yimou, 1987), might not have been produced in the first place. In a further ironic twist, the withdrawal of state funding in the early 1990s engendered yet another rupture in post-socialist filmmaking, this time forcing the sixth generation directors (for example, Wang Xiaoshuai, Zhang Yuan) into independent, underground, or "outlawed" production outside the purview of state ideological apparatuses, resulting on the one hand in routine official bans at home and on the other in high-profile international awards overseas.

Going further back in history, the leftist film movement emerged as yet another rupture—this time between two major waves of commercial filmmaking in the 1920s and 1940s—and it would not have gained such momentum without several distinct transnational factors. Behind a characteristically nationalist, patriotic posture, young leftist filmmakers borrowed ideologically from Marxist vocabulary (e.g., "imperialism," "capitalism," "class," etc.), aspired aesthetically to international modernisms (e.g., Hollywood genres, German expressionism, Art Deco design), and depended financially on a transregional, intranational integration of resources from Beijing, Shanghai, and Hong Kong. Luo Mingyou's Lianhua company was instrumental to the rise of leftist cinema, but his transnational connection to Hollywood via his distribution and exhibition network in Beijing and northeast China, his transregional co-dependence on Hong Kong financing, and his initiatives to establish overseas Lianhua branches in Singapore and the United States were typically ignored in film historiography in favor of his expedient slogan of "reviving domestic cinema" (*fuxing guopian*) in 1930. A careful look into Luo's industry practices may reveal other dimensions of his transnational ambition, as well as reasons behind his failure to sustain a national cinema movement.

To reexamine Chinese film history from the perspective of *industry research*, we have realized that several previously canonized auteurs and movements might appear originally as disjunctures and ruptures, which were subsequently rewritten as representative of national cinema at the expense of mainstream film practices, most of them commercial in nature.

If Chinese cinema is measured in terms of what audiences actually watch, leftist films and new waves become *exceptions* rather than norms, and what previous official historiography brushes aside as "frivolous" commercial fares (e.g., martial-arts films) were in reality part of the economic force that drove the development of Chinese cinema across national borders. What is significant for industry research is that waves of commercial filmmaking (for example, in Shanghai of the mid- to late 1920s, in Hong Kong of the 1950s and 1960s, and in Taiwan in the 1960s and 1970s) occurred precisely during times when cross-regional, transnational resources were mobilized from disparate geopolitical territories, which extended from mainland China, Hong Kong, Taiwan to South East Asia (as in the Shaw Brothers and Cathay) and even the United States (as in the case of the Cantonese company Grandview).

A pressing problem for industry research is that, at present time, the field is ill prepared theoretically and methodologically to cope with issues of production, distribution, exhibition, and reception. Audience study is perhaps the least developed branch of Chinese film studies, and market analysis is only starting to attract serious attention (Rosen; Wang; Zhu). In spite of a growing number of Chinese publications on the rapidly changing film market in the age of globalization and the World Trade Organization (WTO), scholars have yet to learn how to interpret changes in a more meaningful and proactive way than merely stating box office and related market statistics (Zhang Fengzhu et al.; Meng Jian et al.). To chase the mechanical pendulum swing from one extreme point of aesthetic criticism (dominant in China during the 1980s) to another extreme of market euphoria (of intensifying attraction since the new millennium) might bring about more problems than solutions, for the simple reason that a slogan like "dancing with capital" (*yu ziben gongwu*) could very likely reduce scholars to trend-followers (or worse, dutiful industry consultants) rather than independent thinkers.[31] Behind an enthusiastic celebration of transnational market successes (most of them co-productions with multinational corporations based in Hong Kong and the United States) may hide a motivation fundamentally national or even nationalist in nature (for example, a view that China has shed its "Third World" image and is joining the ranks of developing countries).

130

refashioning transnational studies

To avoid being carried away by the present-day all-powerful forces of transnational capitalism and its complicit regional, national, and local institutions, we must keep transnationalism in a proper *historical* perspective. True, as Alan William asserts, "In the beginning, the cinema appeared to be the first truly global, transnational medium, for this simple reason: it had no, or very little, language."[32] The absence of verbal language seems to foreground what Martine Danan calls a "prenational" stage of development when cinema attracted audiences with astonishing visual images and corporeal sensations.[33] This "prenational" stage, for which the term "Chinese-language film" makes little sense, also proved to be transnational at the levels of image making and industry operation. Typical acts and mannerisms of Chaplin, for instance, were duly incorporated into Chinese film comedy, a genre traditionally thought to be indigenous in its audience appeal, and early Chinese producers relied heavily on American and Japanese technicians, especially during the transition to sound in the early 1930s. The pioneering work of foreign technical crews in early Chinese cinema (a subject so far largely ignored) illustrates Higson's observation: "Cinema was from the outset a matter of transnational cooperation, and filmmakers have been itinerant."[34] Indeed, the fact that since the mid-1980s, Chinese filmmakers (for example, Jackie Chan, Ang Lee, John Woo) have been particularly itinerant and frequently traveled between Asia and North America may make it tempting to entertain a vision of "postnational cinema," as Danan does for French cinema. Nonetheless, the linear—if not teleological—logic implicit in Danan's model does little justice to the immense complexity of Chinese film history.

Instead of following a neatly charted temporal progression from prenational through national to postnational, I find it more illuminating to conceive of the national in a *spatial* continuum stretching from the local to the global. Alan Williams distinguishes three types of contemporary commercial narrative cinema. The first type is the capital-intensive, increasingly faceless "global cinema" of the related "action film" genres; the second type is the medium-budget "national" production designed for a home audience; and the third type is "the low-budget, film-festival-oriented 'art,' 'independent,' or 'auteur' cinema . . . [which] may properly be termed 'international' . . . [in that] these films function, in part, as armchair travel experiences for the global couch-potato class."[35]

In the landscape of transnational Chinese filmmaking, Jackie Chan and John Woo indisputably belong to the category of action-filled "global cinema," and Zhang Yimou seeks to join their ranks by launching such high-budget martial-arts films like *Hero* (2002) and *House of Flying Daggers* (2004), both released commercially in the United States. In the middle spectrum of "national" production, Feng Xiaogang's New Year's comedies (*hesui pian*), such as *Cell Phone* (2003) and *World Without Thieves* (2004), function very much like what Eric Rentschler describes as "the post-wall cinema of consensus" in Germany, which has lost the critical edge of new German Cinema and seeks, instead, "to entertain, rather than instruct, and explore trivial rather than deep conflicts, typically by means of conventions associated with popular genres and tastes."[36] Feng Xiaogang may be criticized for catering to popular tastes and peddling fantasies of wish-fulfillment, but he prides himself in commanding a loyal domestic following.

In comparison with high-budget and medium-budget productions, low-budget independent or underground filmmaking constitutes the most exciting area in contemporary Chinese cinema. As evident in Jia Zhangke's *Xiao Wu* (1997) and *The World* (2004), the national is deliberately marginalized or suspended in this third type of filmmaking so as to foreground new tensions of the local (for example, hinterland small towns, migrant communities in globalized cities) and the global (for example, Western commodities, global tourist landmarks).

Recent Chinese independent filmmaking may confirm Higson's argument that "the contingent communities that cinema imagines are much more likely to be either local or transnational than national,"[37] but it is too early—and too irresponsible—to dismiss the national altogether in Chinese film studies. While it is true that, as cinematic project, the national may have conceded much ground to the local and the global in the current phase of transnational Chinese cinema, the very fact that independent or underground Chinese "auteurs" like Jia Zhangke are "discovered" and honored at international film festivals as "representatives" or "spokespersons" for China and Chinese culture suffices to indicate the *persistence of the national* on a global scale. Indeed, the term "transnationalism" betrays such inevitable grounding in the national, and a combination of various prefixes—from "trans," "inter," "intra," and "multi" to "pre," "post," and "para"—only testifies to the centrality of the national in refashioning film studies.[38]

In response to Sheldon Lu's 1997 statement that "The study of *national* cinemas must then transform into *transnational* film studies,"[39] Chris Berry and Mary Farquhar pose three questions that deserve further elaboration:[40]

- What does "transnational" mean and what is at stake in placing the study of Chinese cinema and the national within a transnational framework?
- What happens to "national cinema" in this new conceptual environment?
- What does it mean to think about "transnational film studies" as an academic field?

First, in addition to conceptualizing the transnational in the Chinese case as a higher, potentially homogenizing, symbolically centripetal order as in "Greater China" or "Cultural China," Berry and Farquhar recommend approaching it as "a larger arena connecting differences, so that a variety of regional, national, and local specificities impact upon each other in various types of relations ranging from synergy to contest."[41] Historically, Chinese cinema has always articulated such specificities, and the new transnational framework must not seek out cases of homogeneity only while neglecting those of heterogeneity and contestation. As a matter of fact, a different kind of homology may take shape if heterogeneities are examined in a transnational framework, and this is exactly the case of similar ideological and industrial practices adopted by state-controlled cinemas during the 1950s and 1960s—socialist cinema on the mainland and Mandarin cinema in Taiwan.

Second, conceived of as a multiplicity of cinematic projects, Chinese cinema provides rich resources for studying recurring patterns and modes of articulation—patterns that emerge more clearly from a transnational perspective than from a narrow focus on national identity and auteurist style. Similar to what I advocate as a *site-oriented approach* to transnationalism,[42] Berry and Farquhar concentrate on film *genres* as sites of intersections where patterns of cinematic articulation are formed and transformed across a wide spectrum of temporalities, spacialities, thematics, and ideologies in China and Chinese diasporas. As distinctive Chinese genres, opera (*xiqu*) and martial arts (*wuxia*) receive their close scrutiny, and contesting examples of the respectively "national" are gathered from Shanghai *yingxi* (shadowplays of the 1920s), Taiwanese *gezaixi* (regional operatic plays, the mainstay of Taiwanese dialect filmmaking of the 1950s and 1960s), Hong Kong *huangmeixi* (yellow plum tunes popular in the territory and South East Asia during the 1950s and 1960s), revolutionary *yangbanxi* (model plays of Peking opera and ballet during the 1960s and 1970s), as well as iconic figures such as Bruce Lee, Jackie Chan, and Jet Li. In the rubric of "vernacular modernism" theorized by Miriam Hansen, a different type of transnational investigation of martial arts films (Bao; Z. Zhang) has yielded insights into an intriguing network of intranational, transnational discourses and practices, from the late Qing Chinese fascination with the magic science of flying ("body in the air") to the 1920s debate on nativist historicism and the transfiguration "from Pearl White to White Rose Woo" in the screen image of Chinese *nüxia* (female knight-errant).

Third, given its historical and geopolitical complexity, Berry and Farquhar believe that "Chinese cinemas can stand as key sites in the intellectual shift to cinema and the national, and also be part of the urgently needed attack on Eurocentrism in English-language film studies as that field also becomes transnational."[43] The logic of site-oriented investigation entails that film studies must be refashioned as transnational studies not just by linking multifarious sites of production, distribution, exhibition, and consumption across the globe (for such projects have been pursued previously, especially in terms of international relations and the division of labor), but also by interrogating its own location and positionality in the production and dissemination of knowledge in film history and film theory. As cinema continues to serve as a powerful means of articulating the inequality of power relationships and the increasing unevenness of human experiences across the globe, film studies cannot but become transnational studies.

1. Susan Haywood, *French National Cinema* (London: Routledge, 1993), xi, 7.
2. Gerald Mast, *A Short History of the Movies*, 2nd ed (Indianapolis, IN: Bobbs-Merrill, 1976), 2.
3. Andrew Higson, *Waving the Flag: Constructing a National Cinema in Britain* (Oxford: Oxford University Press, 1995), 22.
4. Stephen Crofts, "Reconceptualizing National Cinema/s," *Quarterly Review of Film and Video* 14, no. 3 (1993): 49–67, 62.
5. Higson, *Waving the Flag*, 273–74.
6. Andrew Higson, "The Concept of National Cinema," *Screen* 30, no. 4 (1989): 36–46, 42.
7. Tom O'Regan, *Australian National Cinema* (London: Routledge, 1996), 3.
8. Hayward, *French National Cinema*, 14.
9. For a discussion of this, see Stephen Crofts, "Reconceptualizing National Cinema/s," *Quarterly Review of Film and Video* 14, no. 3 (1993): 49–67, and Crofts, "Concepts of National Cinema," in *The Oxford Guide to Film Studies*, ed. John Hill and Pamela Church Gibson (Oxford: Oxford University Press, 1998), 385–94, 386.
10. O'Regan, *Australian National Cinema*, 71.
11. Steve McIntyre, "National Film Cultures: Politics and Peripheries," *Screen* 26, no. 1 (1985): 66–76, 67.
12. Higson, "The Concept of National Cinema," 36.
13. Crofts, "Reconceptualizing National Cinema/s," 61.
14. Pierre Sorlin, *Italian National Cinema 1896–1996* (London: Routledge, 1996).
15. John Hill, "The Issue of National Cinema and British Film Production," in *New Questions of British Cinema*, ed. Duncan Petrie (London: British Film Institute, 1992), 10–21, 14.
16. The debate between Hill and Higson, however, has much more to do with British film policy regarding national cinema production than with the exhibition and consumption of Hollywood films. For discussions of cultural protection, see also Andrew Higson, "The Limiting Imagination of National Cinema," in *Cinema and Nation*, ed. Mette Hjort and Scott MacKenzie (London: Routledge, 2000); Ian Jarvie, "National Cinema: A Theoretical Assessment," in *Cinema and Nation*, ed. Hjort and MacKenzie.
17. O'Regan, *Australian National Cinema*, 5.
18. See Hayward, *French National Cinema*, x and 16; see also Alan Williams, ed. *Film and Nationalism* (Brunswick, NJ: Rutgers University Press, 2002), 6.
19. O'Regan, *Australian National Cinema*, 2.
20. Yingjin Zhang, *Screening China: Critical Interventions, Cinematic Reconfigurations, and the Transnational Imaginary in Contemporary Chinese Cinema* (Ann Arbor, MI: Center for Chinese Studies, University of Michigan, 2002), 3.
21. Sheldon Hsiao-peng Lu and Emilie Yueh-yu Yeh, eds. *Chinese-Language Film: Historiography, Poetics, Politics* (Honolulu, HI: University of Hawaii Press, 2005), 1–24.
22. Columbia Asia was involved in co-producing both *The Big Shot's Funeral* and *Double Vision*, two top-grossers in China and Taiwan, respectively. The cast of *The Big Shot's Funeral* includes Donald Sutherland (United States), Ge You (China), and Rosamund Kwan (Hong Kong). For an analysis of "global *mélange*" in recent Taiwan film production, see Y. Zhang, *Screening China*, 299–305.

23. Judith Butler, *Excitable Speech: A Politics of the Performative* (London: Routledge, 1997).

24. Chris Berry, "If China Can Say No, Can China Make Movies? Or, Do Movies Make China? Rethinking National Cinema and National Agency," *Boundary 2* 25, no. 3 (1998): 129–50, 132.

25. Ibid., 148.

26. Y. Zhang, *Screening China*, 95–96.

27. See Rey Chow, *Primitive Passions: Visuality, Sexuality, Ethnography, and Contemporary Chinese Cinema* (New York: Columbia University Press, 1995); Tonglin Lu, *Confronting Modernity in the Cinemas of Taiwan and Mainland China* (New York: Cambridge University Press, 2002); Kwok-kan Tam and Wimal Dissanayake, *New Chinese Cinema* (Hong Kong: Oxford University Press, 1998); Emilie Yueh-yu Yeh and Darrell W. Davis, *Taiwan Film Directors: A Treasure Island* (New York: Columbia University Press, 2004).

28. Laikwan Pang, *Building a New China in Cinema: The Chinese Left-Wing Cinema Movement, 1932–1937* (Lanham, MD: Rowman & Littlefield, 2002); Vivian Shen, *The Origins of Left-wing Cinema in China, 1932–37* (New York: Routledge, 2005).

29. Jubin Hu, *Projecting a Nation: Chinese National Cinema before 1949* (Hong Kong: Hong Kong University Press, 2003).

30. Y. Zhang, *Screening China*, 244–49.

31. "Dancing with capital" is a catch phrase Huang Shixian, a retired professor from Beijing Film Academy, frequently used in conference talks in China and the United States.

32. Williams, *Film and Nationalism*, 1.

33. Martine Danan, "From a 'Prenational' to a 'Postnational' French Cinema," *Film History* 8, no. 1 (1996): 72–84.

34. Andrew Higson, "The Limiting Imagination of National Cinema," in *Cinema and Nation*, ed. Hjort and MacKenzie, 67.

35. Williams, *Film and Nationalism*, 19.

36. Eric Rentschler, quoted in Hjort and MacKenzie, "Introduction," in *Cinema and Nation*, ed. Hjort and Mackenzie, 13. See also Eric Rentschler, "From New German Cinema to the Post-Wall Cinema of Consensus," in *Cinema and Nation*, ed. Hjort and MacKenzie, 260–77.

37. Higson, "The Limiting Imagination of National Cinema," 73.

38. For the term "multinational," see Paul Willemen's statement: "The economic facts of cinematic life dictate that an industrially viable cinema shall be multinational": Willemen, *Looks and Frictions: Essays in Cultural Studies and Film Theory* (London: British Film Institute, 1994), 212. For the term "paranational," see Susan Hayward's intriguing explication ("Framing National Cinema," in *Cinema and Nation*, ed. Hjort and MacKenzie, 99–100):

> Hollywood's *para*-nationalism is pathologic—"*para*" in the sense of its internal nationalist discursive practices ("near"),—"*para*" in the sense of its proto-colonialist practices ("beyond"). "*Para*" in the sense that, both near and beyond, its nationalism is abnormal and defective … Hollywood's ability only to reflect itself to itself, to repeat its discourses inter- and extra-nationally, is both its strength and its weakness … It denies and senses its own alienation—it repeats its own "success formulas" and buys up, to remake (American-style), the successes of other national cinemas.

One recent Hollywood trend is precisely to purchase the rights of Asian commercial hits (especially in the genres of action and horror), delay or deny their exhibition in North America, and remake them "American-style" to flaunt Hollywood's borrowed innovation.

39. Sheldon Hsiao-peng Lu, ed. *Transnational Chinese Cinemas: Identity, Nationhood, Gender* (Honolulu, HI: University of Hawaii Press, 1997), 25.

40. Chris Berry and Mary Farquhar, *China on Screen: Cinema and Nation* (New York: Columbia University Press, 2005), 4–13.

41. Ibid., 5.

42. This site-oriented approach is mentioned in pages 39–41 of my 2002 work, Y. Zhang, *Screening China: Critical Interventions, Cinematic Reconfigurations, and the Transnational Imaginary in Contemporary Chinese Cinema*. It derives from James Hay's proposal for

    a way of discussing film as a social practice that begins by considering how social relations are spatially organized—through sites of production and consumption—and how film is practiced from and across particular sites and always in relation to other sites. (216)

43. Berry and Farquhar, *China on Screen*, 14.

national cinema

abroad

the new international

division of cultural labor,

from production to viewing

t o b y   m i l l e r

Film studies in the United States, Britain, and their white-settler colonies (Canada, Aotearoa/New Zealand, Israel, and Australia) is condemned to near-irrelevancy in the public sphere of popular criticism, state and commercial policy, and social-movement critique. The common-sense rationalities of consumer sovereignty engage journalists, filmmakers, and most people who express opinions on the topic. They subscribe to the view that films and film industries succeed or fail through pure market dynamics—audiences like them and pay for them, or they do not. Film studies' mistake was to set up a series of *nostra* early on about what counted as knowledge, then police the borders. A standard disciplinary tactic, such rent-seeking conduct is effective as a form of gatekeeping, but ineffective as a means of dialogue. Two forms of theory predominate as a consequence. One analyzes cinema texts, the other cinema audiences. Understanding texts means either apolitical formalism or ideology critique that deploys a hermeneutics of suspicion via counter-indicative interpretation. The individual close reading remains hegemonic, along with its concatenation into impressionistic generic claims. No one seems to undertake content analysis, which provides a systematic means of establishing patterns across texts and genres. Understanding audiences means using psychoanalysis (with no technical training and no empirical back-up other than autobiography) or cognitivism (with no technical training and no empirical back-up other than reciting research done by others). No one seems to use focus groups or undertake ethnography, other than staring at their children. Analyzing other issues (the division of labor and screen distribution, for instance) somehow or other is not deemed theoretical. The dominant *données* barely need rehearsal, but Table 7.1 illustrates the binary of film studies' good and bad objects.

When it comes to national cinemas, Anglo-restricted scholarship does reach out a little. Questions of cultural policy are addressed, and the result appears to transcend the normal science of film theory's silent, patrolling parent, literary studies. But once systems of subvention by the state are explained, the fan within the analyst takes over, and we are in for an academic version of coffee-table film rankings, with stylistics and social movements standing in for old-fashioned, populist aesthetic evaluation. Along the way, we are treated to ringing denunciations of cultural imperialism as outmoded and wrongheaded, although globalization and neoclassical shibboleths about consumer choice driving screen success are not wholeheartedly endorsed, for all the interpretative power imaginatively ascribed to audiences.

Conversely, my concern here takes off from the collaborative projects that have produced *Globalisation and Sport, Global Hollywood, Cultural Policy, Critical Cultural Policy Studies, Global Hollywood 2*, and a special issue of *Social Semiotics*—the culmination of two decades' research and publication.[1] Those volumes sought to blend political economy with cultural studies in a mixture of theoretical and empirical engagements, indicating that the New International Division of Cultural Labor (NICL) is at the core of culture-industry success. In the *Global Hollywood* books in particular, we wanted to remagnetize the study of Hollywood beyond its twin poles of film theory and business history. We believed that theories of spectatorship, form, and style had not had an impact on film reviewers, or influenced public policy

Table 7.1

Film studies' good and bad objects

Good Object	Bad Object
Psychoanalysis central	Psychology unsubtle
Spectatorship sexy	Audience unimportant
Archive acceptable	Laboratory *louche*
Criticism canonical	Ethnography extraneous
Auteur interesting	Wonk wearisome
Textual analysis alpha	Content analysis crude

in any way we could discern. Nor had business history engaged with critical areas for progressives, such as labor, copyright, the military, and other aspects of the state. Theories of cultural imperialism had been consigned to recycling without consideration of their meaningfulness around the world. In short, a vast amount of work had to be done to demonstrate the realities: massive US state subvention, the audience as an object of surveillance rather than a broker of tastes, and the NICL as the key to Hollywood's dominance. Policy work, political economy, ethnography, movement activism, and the social-science archive were crucial to that effort, which adopted hysterisis as its lodestone so that overlapping causes and sites could be understood. That necessitated both macro- and micro- scales, and foci on:

- the global, where capitalism is ordered
- the national, where ideology is determined, and
- the local, where productive and interpretative work are done.

That meant in turn engaging the labor process of making meaning, the material relations that describe a cultural text's life through script development, pre-production, production, post-production, marketing, distribution, exhibition, and reception. Film remained at the apex of that process semiotically, but not financially, as shown in Figure 7.1.

Within this pyramid lies the dynamizing force of work, part of the centrifugal and centripetal forces that may simultaneously and contradictorily favor both core and periphery growth. Labor is the place where we find what Hortense Powdermaker called "the realities of the power struggle all along the assembly line of creation."[2] Film is directly and indirectly a site of origin for these other forms, and has the most venerable status, so it is at

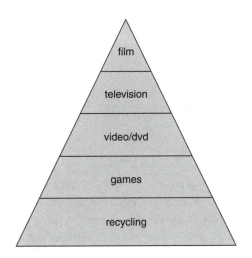

Figure 7.1

The screen pyramid

the top. Video, DVD and television have the most popularity, and games the most revenue, so they come next, and broaden out the diagram. Recycling is at the bottom, with the newest stature and potentially greatest socio-economic effect, as film stock from movies is reinvented as polyester, and metals are retrieved from computers and televisions. As you may be aware, pre-teen Chinese girls pick away, without protection of any kind, at discarded television sets and computers from the First World to find these precious metals, then dump the remains in landfills. The metals are sold to recyclers, who do not use landfills or labor in the First World because of environmental and industrial legislation prohibiting the destruction to soil and water, and harm to workers that are caused by the chemicals and gases in these dangerous machines.[3] They are part of what happens to "national cinemas."

In turn, international organizations were key actors in our analysis, as shown in Figure 7.2.

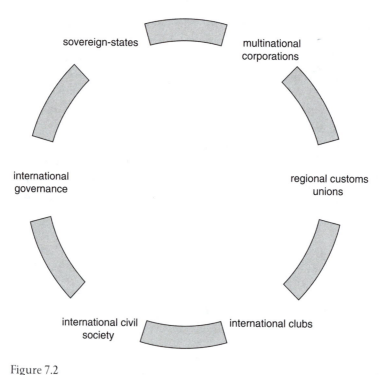

sovereign-states

multinational
corporations

international
governance

regional customs
unions

international civil
society

international clubs

Figure 7.2
The institutional circle

Historically, the best critical political economy and cultural studies have worked through the imbrication of power and signification at all points on the cultural continuum. Graham Murdock puts the task well:

> Critical political economy is at its strongest in explaining
> who gets to speak to whom[,] and what forms these

symbolic encounters take in the major spaces of public culture. But cultural studies, at its best, has much of value to say about . . . how discourse and imagery are organized in complex and shifting patterns of meaning[,] and how these meanings are reproduced, negotiated, and struggled over in the flow and flux of everyday life.[4]

In heeding that guidance, this chapter makes a case for the centrality of time and space to film theory, specifically to the career of Mexican cinema in the United States. I propose alternatives to contemporary mainstream film theory from political economy and media anthropology, seeking to blend economic and ethnographic insights with textual analysis in an account of the distribution of a national cinema beyond its borders. To do that, I borrow from several sources, notably Roger Chartier, Bruno Latour, and Néstor García Canclini.

Their methods offer a radical historicization of cultural context, supplementing the examination of textual properties and spectatorial processes with an account of *occasionality* that details the conditions under which texts are made, circulated, received, interpreted, and criticized. The life of any popular or praised text is a passage across space and time, a life remade again and again by institutions, discourses, and practices of distribution and reception. Cultural historian Chartier proposes a tripartite approach to textual analysis, namely reconstruction of "the diversity of older readings from their sparse and multiple traces"; a focus on "the text itself, the object that conveys it, and the act that grasps it"; and an identification of "the strategies by which authors and publishers tried to impose an orthodoxy or a prescribed reading on the text."[5] This grid from the new cultural history turns away from reflectionism and formalism. In a similar vein to Chartier's work, there is much to be gained from the use of actor-network theory in following the career of globally circulating media, as per the way Latour and his followers treat cars, missiles, trains, and enzymes. This was my method when I wrote a snowball and web-based study of *The Avengers* and its reception a decade ago, and I found it helpful.[6] Latour seeks to allocate equal and overlapping significance to natural phenomena, social forces, and texts in the analysis of contemporary life. Just as objects of scientific knowledge only come to us in hybrid forms that are coevally affected by social power and textual meaning, so the latter two domains are themselves affected by the natural world.[7] García Canclini seeks a way through the tired and tiring morass of Yanqui multicultural discourse towards interculturalism, which transcends the national-policy borders of the multicultural, and is supple enough to permit site-specific encounters and an understanding of culture that transcends US ethnic politics and pluralism. He demonstrates that accounts of global markets must engage with three key factors. First, the paradox that globalization in fact deglobalizes, in that its dynamic and impact are not only about mobility and exchange, but also disconnectedness and exclusion. Second, minorities no longer primarily exist within nations— rather, they emerge at transnational levels, especially with massive migration by people who share a language and continue to communicate, work, and consume through it. Third, demographic minorities may not form cultural minorities, because majoritarian elites in one nation may dispatch their culture to countries where they are an ethnic minority.[8] This again makes sense as guidance for tracking the life of the commodity sign. Because texts accrete and attenuate meanings on their travels as they rub up against, trope, and are troped by other fictional and social texts, we must consider all the shifts and shocks that characterize their existence as cultural commodities, their ongoing renewal as the temporary "property" of varied, productive workers and publics, and the abiding "property" of businesspeople.

There are good examples to follow from beyond film studies' well-worn hallways and citational police. Jeff Himpele has traced the life of films in La Paz, Bolivia, from their debuts at the elite theater in the city *centro* to their voyages up the surrounding canyon walls, where they play at various popular movies houses frequented by Aymara immigrants and families. All the while, pirated video copies multiply and circulate. Using interviews with distributors and theater owners, Himpele demonstrates how print quality and exhibition map onto Bolivian social structure, with increases in altitude corresponding to indigenous identity and social rank. Distribution and exhibition in La Paz form a "spatializing practice," delineating difference and constructing social imaginaries ingrained in colonial, race, and class hierarchies. Certain genres of film become associated with imagined zones of people. Each zone gets access to "new" releases at different times, depending on its perceived social, political, and economic status.[9] Although official distribution itineraries can be undermined by the proliferation of pirated videocassettes, early access to new releases is only one component of cultural capital. There is a certain status in renting from the commercial video store, just as there is prestige associated with which movie theater one attends. Himpele's willingness to follow both dominant and subaltern circulation practices is significant. He neither valorizes pirates for upsetting structural inequalities, nor focuses on ideology as a one-way, uncontested process. His methodology, marked by an expanded category of "appropriate" research sites, accounts for the negotiations that take place between industry power and consumer practice—"how" a text accretes and abandons meaning in its travels.

Political-economic and ethnographic approaches that "follow the thing" bring attention to media texts and commodities as they change their meaning and value depending on where and when they are viewed and consumed. For example, there was controversy and even violence among exiled audiences in 1990 when their image of Iran was challenged during a festival devoted to post-revolutionary cinema at the University of California,

Los Angeles. And diasporic Vietnamese in southern California picketed a video store for fifty-three days in 1999 because its owner, Truong Van Tran, had displayed a picture of Ho Chi Minh in his Little Saigon shop.[10] Combining the political-economic with the ethnographic can bring attention to audiovisual practices that are rarely included in common paradigms of national, postcolonial, or Third Cinema. When we are told a national cinema exists, for example, does that mean it is produced in a particular country or that it is the cinema mostly watched in that country or that it is the cinema seen in theatres versus "films" viewed on television or computers? For instance, the Nigerian screen industry has been growing since the early 1990s. It is a US$45-million-a-year business of four hundred low-budget narratives, a blend of supernatural horror and *telenovela*-influenced melodrama that addresses the economic challenges of an emergent cosmopolitanism. The local industry, Nollywood,[11] produces "films" on video, with no state sponsorship. It is shaping the media culture of Anglophone and, increasingly, Francophone Africa. In Ghana and Kenya, especially, production companies are imitating the Nigerian model.[12] Of course, multinational capital is also present. British American Tobacco handed out cigarettes in Nigeria as part of its 2002 "Rothmans Experience It Cinema Tour," which also offered viewers theatrical facilities far beyond the norm and new Hollywood action adventure. Similarly dangerous reuse projects to those in China also thrive.[13]

The other force dominating Nigerian screen culture is Bollywood. Brian Larkin's research on the global reach of Hindi film shows that it rivals and even marginalizes Hollywood in Nigeria, offering a "third space" between Islamic tradition and Western modernity that exerts a powerful influence over Hausa popular culture. One would be hard pressed to find Nollywood or Bollywood representing "African cinema" at international festivals or embassy screenings. Their popularity raises questions not only about what constitutes African cinema but also about the limitations of models that fail to recognize the regional power and influence of locally produced popular forms. Larkin points out the difficulty of this research within existing disciplinary hierarchies:

> the popularity of Indian films in Africa has fallen into the interstices of academic analysis, as the Indian texts do not fit with studies of African cinema; the African audience is ignored in the growing work on Indian film; the films are too non-Western for Euro-American-dominated media studies, and anthropologists are only beginning to theorise the social importance of media.[14]

But alongside the interculturalism of which García Canclini speaks, and the traces of meaning that Chartier uncovers, these studies amply illustrate that each time a text undergoes a material transformation, it necessitates another conceptualization beyond "national cinema," much like the car parts, rockets, and microbes that Latour and his group study.

mexican cinema in *gringolandia*

This chapter turns now to the travels, travails, and reception of Mexican cinema in the United States. To do so, I traverse the following terrain: the nature of the Latino population in the United States, and its incarnations by marketing; distribution; exhibition; festivals; television; video/DVD; and the Internet—working through the pyramid and the cycles identified above. There are case studies of *Y tu mamá también* and *Amores perros*, along with Cinema Tropical and Latin American Video Archives.[15]

marketing

Latinos comprise 15 percent of the US moviegoing public. The average Latino attends 9.9 movies each year, as opposed to 8.1 films for white, non-Hispanic Americans and 7.6 films for African Americans, and Latinos are six times more likely to watch films with Latino themes and stars. The fastest growing group of cinemagoers in the United States, they spend the most money at concession stands in movie theaters and watch the most television. Nevertheless, Latinos have just 5 percent of roles in Hollywood cinema. This is especially invidious given the hidden value of Mexican labor in service industries that support Hollywood cultures of both production and daily life.[16]

Latinos have historically been neglected in the psychographic research that US marketers assiduously generate about other spectators, such as preferred days and times of theatrical attendance and correlations between gender, genre, and popcorn consumption. The traditional assumption is that recent arrivals in the United States watch imported films, and later generations prefer Hollywood. But some analysts suggest that many new arrivals from Mexico come from the popular classes, and have not frequented movie theaters at home for economic reasons. They are not targeted as a film audience in the United States, something especially important because the new Mexican cinema is aimed at the cosmopolitan urban middle class; it resonates with international youth culture rather than the traditional Arcadian utopias of official Mexican culture.[17] The idea of a unitary Latino audience is especially unmanageable for capital, because so many people are recent arrivals from modern nation-states, unlike the majority of US citizens, and have varying attitudes to language retention and use. Their high aggregate numbers are complicated once the term "Latino" is broken down by dominant language, region of origin, region of domicile, nationality, race, and class. Unlike any other prominent language in the United States, Spanish is a native tongue in a vast array of other countries, mostly in the same hemisphere.

As Arlene Dávila points out, Latino "abundance" does not simplify promotion of Latin American culture in general. The United States now has over eighty Latino advertising agencies and branches of multinationals dedicated to deciphering and managing "their" audience. Because of struggles since the 1960s by minority activists, and responses by the US government, the categories "Latino" and "Hispanic" now encompass people with heritage from Mexico, Puerto Rico, Central America, and the Hispanic Caribbean. And because Mexico has been the dominant provider of Spanish-language TV (SLTV) in the United States, it is seen both as the "natural" Latino source of drama and news, and as an unreasonably powerful, even dominant, visual and linguistic influence. Dávila quotes the common complaint that "English TV takes you all around the world, but Spanish TV keeps you in Mexico." Some expatriate Mexicans even fear that the images of Mexicanness on US television promote stereotypes among both *hispanohablantes* and *angloparlantes*, and there is evidence of annoyance among other Latinos that Mexicans stand in for them in much advertising.[18]

The Spanish news agency, EFE, notes that "Hollywood just doesn't know how to address itself to this bilingual audience." Disney's 2000 Spanish-language version of *The Emperor's New Groove* failed with Spanish-speaking audiences in the United States, who went to see the English version instead.[19] Director Gregory Nava is skeptical of Hollywood producers' commitment to the Latino audience: "one thing fails and they think the audience isn't there . . . [they] are interested, but they're very frightened. Nobody is willing to make a long-term commitment."[20] In the words of the Univisión TV network: "La industria de Hollywood continúa buscando la llave al mercado hispano, una lucrativa meta dado que esta comunidad es, proportional-mente, la mayor audiencia cinematográfica del pais" (the Hollywood industry continues searching for the key to the Latino market, a lucrative one given that the community is proportionally the biggest film audience in the country).[21] Meanwhile, the Mexico-USA Committee to promote the film industry, which meets periodically so that industry mavens across the border can converse, looks at issues such as copyright protection, co-production, and the availability of Mexican cinema in the United States.[22] The code for making and selling Spanish-language cinema in the United States has not been broken.

145

distribution

Distributors advertise, promote, and dispatch movies, as well as negotiate how long they play, charging exhibitors a percentage of box-office profits—often as much as 40 percent, in addition to 25 percent in fees for sales to TV networks, and 30–40 percent to cable. They use what is euphemistically called "creative accounting" to conceal these profits from foreign organizations that are due a share of revenue. In the United States, movie studios operate vertically integrated networks of distribution to control access to audiences, and utilize a massive domestic TV market to ensure returns on investment, even from their multiple failures in theatrical exhibition.[23]

The risks for outsiders are added to by New York City's thriving extra-legal film-duplication industry, and operators like a Californian company that was discovered in 2002 illegally distributing Mexican films. It took between US$30,000 and $45,000 in revenue per month. Conversely, the major studios ensure that co-productions elsewhere remain under their financial control—so when Columbia TriStar co-produced *Sin ton ni Sonia* by committing 20 percent of funds, it also secured local and international distribution. Time Warner owns the rights to a considerable amount of historic Mexican film, which it has acquired by purchasing properties from local copyright holders, while Sony Corporation's Columbia Pictures has control of Cantinflas' *oeuvre*.[24]

US distributors evaluate art-house/non-English-language movies in terms of cast,[25] reviews (principally from the *New York Times*, the *Los Angeles Times, Variety*, and *Hollywood Reporter*) and festival success (notably Sundance, Cannes, Berlin, Venice, New York, and Toronto). When distributors pick up a film, producers need to ensure effective cross-collateralization and promotion and a favorable deal with exhibitors. There may also be some value in saturation marketing, where theaters in a region heavily populated by Latinos are rented out for the release of Spanish-language films, which can then be promoted locally. This is known as "four-walling." Specialty distributors, however, mostly use a method called platforming—releasing prints in three to five key theaters in Los Angeles, New York, and San Francisco to build awareness via newspaper reviews prior to release in other cities. This has been the traditional conduit for Latin American cinema, relying on English-language advertising and word-of-mouth in both languages. Foreign-film distributors are faced with the additional problem of what to emphasize in trailers—usually the only publicity they can afford apart from small notices in newspapers. Miramax trailers, for example, tended to hide the fact when its movies were not in English, even in art-house circuits, while Fox TV in Los Angeles refused to air commercials for *Cronos* because they were in Spanish. Barriers to the distribution of foreign films in the United States also include the cost of subtitling and dubbing.[26]

146

exhibition

There were Spanish-language exhibition circuits from the first major expansion of US film theaters in 1910. By the advent of sound films in the late 1920s, several million Mexicans were living in the south-west of the United States, from Texas to California. They provided a crucial audience for Hollywood's brief experiment with foreign-language versions of its English-language features, which stimulated Spanish-language film theaters in San Francisco, Denver, Dallas, Laredo, Los Angeles, San Antonio, and small towns throughout Texas. In major cities, art-house theaters also opened at this time, frequently showing Spanish-language material. During the *época de oro*, those theaters showcased Mexican art and life to the US-based Spanish-speaking population, keeping cultures of origin, language, and values visible and audible at a time when pressures to assimilate linguistically were high and Hollywood did not represent their experience. But even Mexican film was frequently mediated institutionally through Hollywood. For example, when *Rancho Grande* was released in the United States in 1936 with English subtitles, the majority of its revenue went to United Artists.[27]

The East Coast influx of Puerto Ricans in the 1940s and 1950s stimulated a significant market for Mexican film in New York City. By 1950, 300 theaters nationwide were devoted exclusively to Spanish-language films, and a hundred more featured them once or twice a week. It has been suggested that 700 screens showed Spanish-language films between the 1940s and the 1960s. In the 1960s, after the *época de oro* declined and SLTV emerged, the number of US theaters dedicated to Mexican cinema dropped. Columbia Pictures maintained a Spanish Theatrical Division into the late 1970s, when it was sold to Televicine. At that time 450 US theaters showed Spanish-language cinema, with annual revenue of US$45 million, though precise figures are difficult to ascertain. Most of the hundred or so Mexican films released each year were screened in the United States, and Mexico actually had a favorable balance of world film trade in the late 1970s. But the numbers went into rapid decline from that time, with films circulating on rented, sold, and illegal videos, television, and art-houses. During the early 1980s, the key exhibitor Pacific Metropolitan switched from screening Spanish to English-language films. By 1987, US audiences for Mexican cinema were at 50 percent of their high point, and ten years later, Mexico exported only US$100,000-worth of features to the United States. Places like the Mission District in San Francisco saw Latino audiences turn towards Hollywood and multiplex luxury. The remaining Spanish-language theatres were boarded up then renovated as clubs or parking structures with the late 1990s dot-com boom, when many Latino families left the area entirely in the face of a gentrification that excluded them.[28]

At times, the art-house, subtitled circuit has been a successful outlet for Mexican cinema since the loss of dedicated exhibition. For instance, *Como agua para chocolate* took nearly US$20 million in seven months in theaters in 1992. Its distributor, Miramax, built from an initial release in just two cinemas to target the art-house audience's familiarity with magical realism, while convincing Mexican restaurants to recreate the film's cuisine as a prelude to wider exposure. But for the most part, the art-house circuit has neglected Latin America.[29]

The noted producer Moctesuma Esparza announced his intention in 1999 to start a Maya Cinema chain of ten to twenty mostly Spanish-language

147

theaters featuring imported films and nachos and horchatas as well as popcorn, but by the end of 2005 few were open, while Cine Acción in San Francisco launched a Latino cinema space at the Brava Theater and 2002 marked Los Angeles' first multiplexes dedicated to Spanish-language cinema—which nearly shut down in 2005 due to financial difficulties.[30]

toby miller

---

case study

Amores perros (*AP*) and *Y tu mamá también* (*YTMT*) have been the most successful Mexican film exports since the late 1990s. Their appeal across ethnicity inside the United States has suggested another "golden" opportunity for Mexican cinema, the latest of several false dawns for the industry's export trade. Independent distributors and sales agents such as Strand Releasing, IFC Films, Lions Gate, Cowboy Booking, Sony Pictures Classics, and Good Machine Intl. immediately invested in Latin American imports.

Numerous US critics listed *AP* among their favorite films of 2001. It was nominated for Best Foreign Film at the Oscars (the first time a Mexican movie had been selected in a quarter of a century) and the Golden Globes, and won the American Film Institute's Audience Award, the Boston Society of Film Critics and Chicago Film Critics Association Best Foreign Language Film Awards, the National Board of Review Best Foreign Language Film, the Chicago International Film Festival's Audience Choice Award, an MTV Movie Award, and Outstanding Foreign Film in the American Latino Media Arts Awards. The film grossed US$5.4 million in the United States and was on 187 screens, where over a million people saw it—very good figures for an import (a Hollywood hit may reach 3,000 screens). The success was attributed by the distributor, Lions Gate, to genre and the rejection of indexical Mexican locales. Guillermo del Toro suggests this was important domestically, not just abroad: "The foreign market that Mexican cinema has conquered is Mexico." This was in keeping with director Alejandro González Iñarritu's wish to make an international story about city living, and producer Marta Sosa's dictum that filmmakers focus on their audience. At the same time, *AP* was criticized by key figures in Mexican popular culture, notably Televisa's vice-president of programming, Luis de Llano, who derided "street language that directors think makes the movie more hip and modern," but which he regarded as ill-advised mimicry of the United States. For other observers, this tendency was a welcome byproduct of the era's neoliberalism, part of "a certain Free Trade Area of the Americas . . . sensibility."

YTMT debuted in the United States at ¡*Accion!: cine mexicano actual*, organized by New York's Guggenheim Museum, the Mexican Cultural Institute, and Cinema Tropical. There were concerns that its unrated status (a consequence of sexual content that meant no one under 18 could attend) would diminish theatrical appeal. But IFC Films, a subsidiary of the Cablevision cable company that started in 2000 and was connected to Bravo and the Independent Film Channel, bought the rights in what may have been its last effort to stay in business. Initially, *YTMT* was distributed to art-houses and areas with high proportions of Mexicans, while promotions targeted SLTV and patrons of Mexican restaurants. It quickly expanded to Anglo venues via cross-promotion with IFC's affiliated art-cinema cable stations. US$3 million was spent on marketing. IFC managed to get Salma Hayek, who is a fantasy-object in the film, to promote it in the United States, toured the film with the director Alfonso Cuarón and the male stars, purchased radio and TV commercials, and used a grass-roots campaign of stickers, postcards, and posters. IFC spokesperson Bob Berney says "the film broke away from the foreign-language market and showed that a Spanish-language film is not a foreign-language [movie] in the United States. The film became a crossover mainstream film with all the major theater chains wanting to play it." *YTMT* brought in US$13.62 million within the United States. It was nominated for an Oscar for Best Screenplay, a Grammy for the soundtrack, and a Golden Globe for Best Foreign Language Film, and gained prizes at the Fort Lauderdale International Film Festival, Santa Fe Film Festival, and the Independent Spirit Awards, Gay & Lesbian Alliance Against Defamation and Glitter Awards, as well as winning the Best Foreign Language or Foreign Film Awards of the Las Vegas Film Critics Society, Boston Society of Film Critics, Dallas-Fort-Worth Film Critics Association, Seattle Film Critics, Southeastern Film Critics Association, Los Angeles Film Critics Association, Broadcast Film Critics Association, San Francisco Film Critics Circle, Satellite, National Society of Film Critics, Online Film Critics Society, Political Film Society, New York Film Critics Circle, and Florida Film Critics Circle.[31]

festivals

Several important film festivals dedicated to Latin American cinema have recently emerged in the United States. They vary between highly professional and more community-oriented events, and their articulation of foreign films to US distributors has been inconsistent. Cine Estudiantil in San Diego was established in 1994, and was renamed Centro Cultural de La Raza's San Diego/Baja California Latino Film Festival (or Cine) in 1998. The Cine Sol Latino Film Festival in Harlingen, Texas began in 1993, the East Los Angeles Chicano Film Festival in 1995, and the Los Angeles International Latino Film Festival (sponsored by the city's Cultural Affairs Department and the *Los Angeles Times*, in search of both readers and civic legitimacy, no doubt) in 1997. The latter draws over 15,000 spectators a year. Other major centers include the Brazilian Film Festival of Miami, the CineSol Latino Film Festival in South Texas, the New York International Latino Film Festival, the Latino Film Festival of the San Francisco Bay Area, the Pan-Cultural Film Festival in Houston, the San Antonio CineFestival (the oldest, born in 1977, and linked to the Guadalupe Cultural Arts Center's year-round film exhibition), the Miami Latino Film Festival, the Providence Festival of New Latin American Film, the Chicago Latino Film Festival (which plans to generate a state-of-the-art arts facility under the aegis of the International Latino Cultural Center), the Havana Film Festival of New York, and the Cambridge Latino Film Festival.[32]

Attracting distributors even to large Latino-film festivals has been difficult in the past, but the recent emergence of these festivals in major Latino population centers indicates a belated appreciation of Latinos as both intellectual film-watchers and potential consumers with discrete needs. Since the 2000 Census results, more and more distributors have been careful to turn out. In 2002, the marketing company TSE Sports & Entertainment announced an Hispanic Film Festival Circuit that would tour the most successful titles from Latino festivals across the United States. The strategy was to offer national advertisers a level of exposure that unlinked city-based events could not.[33]

Non-ethnically or regionally specific festivals are also important. Examples include the New York Film Festival, New Directors New Films, the New York Lesbian and Gay Film Festival, and the Human Rights Watch International Festival. The Smithsonian Institution's National Museum of the American Indian has an annual Native American Film and Video Festival, and the New York Museum of Modern Art has also held major Latin American events.[34]

---

case study

Cinema Tropical provides an interesting variation on distribution and festival practice. It receives support from the New York State Council on the Arts, the Mexican Cultural Institute of New York, the US/Mexico Fund for Culture, Latin American Video Archives, the New York Consulates of Argentina and Chile, and an alcohol company, in a partnership between private sponsors, state and non-governmental organizations, and Latin American governments. Cinema Tropical has weekly screenings at Two Boots Pioneer Theater, an art-house independent linked to a small downtown New York pizza chain, and the Americas Society, while its summer programs revolve around *Cine Móvil* in various parks across the city. There are other collaborations with the New York International Latino Film Festival, Queens Theater in the Park, and El Museo del Barrio. Similar seasons exist in San Diego via the Media Arts Center's four-month Mexican film program.[35] LaCinemaFe began in 2001 as another showcase for Latin American film in New York. Again, the identity of its sponsors is important. They include the *Hoy* newspaper, a hotel, the Mexican Cultural Institute of New York, Continental Airlines, alcoholic beverages, Univisión, a hair salon, and various others—a combination of Latino-oriented companies and firms that market to the entire US population. It signifies the presence of both direct and indirect commercial links to the community, and the potential for non-Latino audiences, as well. By 2005, it had expanded to cover ten US cities and included a special feature: "Mexican Films Made by Gringos."[36]

television

Since the 1920s, the commercial broadcast media have targeted Latinos, from the halcyon days of ethnic radio and relays from Mexico. The first Spanish-language television network began broadcasting in Texas in 1961. The size of Mexico's domestic market and its production capacity have been dominant factors in SLTV since that time. For once costs are cleared and popularity created in Mexico, programming can be used in the United States.[37]

In 1992, the AC Nielsen Company created an Hispanic-American Television Index to measure the SLTV audience, funded by Telemundo and Univisión. It revealed that approximately 69 percent of Latinos watched English-language television *only*, with the audience for SLTV hence representing 4 percent of all US viewers. National advertisers have not historically supported SLTV in great numbers, allocating just 1.7 percent of their total expenditure to SLTV. But since the 2000 Census, both Nielsen and other leading commercial research firms, such as Arbitron, have focused on developing new instruments for measuring Latino tastes and practices. The two networks have amassed commercial sales of close to a billion dollars annually, a much higher rate of increase than the major English-language networks.[38]

Ana M. López suggests that the SLTV networks "have sustained a certain retrograde vision of the Mexican cinema," with films from *la época de oro* displayed as "frozen icons" of an industry no longer worth supporting. US Latino audiences are said to interpret these texts as "chic kitsch," while the exploitation cinema of the 1980s and 1990s (*lucha libre* and *vaqueros*) is regarded as "fodder for the *recien llegados* [recent arrivals]" until they learn English. Univisión is the dominant SLTV network, with 70 percent of the Latino audience. It has twenty-six stations, thirty-two affiliates, a cable network, and an internet portal, and is valued at US$6.8 billion. It rarely screens recent

151

Mexican movies, nor does its subsidiary TeleFutura, although Univisión buys films from Televisa in a contract that lasts until 2017. Univisión's website on cinema is almost entirely dedicated to Hollywood. TV Azteca's Azteca America in Visalia is working with Pappas Telecasting to create a new US network. It is unclear how cinema will fit in. Florida-based Telemundo, which NBC purchased for US$1.98 billion, has 20 percent of the Latino audience watching its ten-station, nine-affiliate cable network. Telemundo has started a new youth network, mun2, which publicizes mainstream movies. The Hispanic Television Network, which began operations in 1999, has fourteen owned or affiliated stations and focuses on Mexican material, including 400 movies. HBO Latino/en Español is a subsidiary of the most successful cable network in the United States. It is expensive for audiences to receive, as it is a premium service, and mostly offers subtitled Hollywood films, with an occasional Latin-American feature in Spanish. Showtime, another premium cable channel, held a Latino Filmmaker Showcase in 2000. The Sundance cable TV channel dedicates August each year to Arte Latino, which is articulated with the Sundance Institute's showcase of Latino cinema at its annual festival. And by 2006, the major *angloparlantes* broadcast networks had all announced their intention to program *novelas*.[39]

video/dvd

About 33 percent of Latinos select equal numbers of mainstream and Spanish-language titles, and 63 percent select English-language movies only. This is important because even though a film's profitability should really be measured through each site of screening, theatrical revenue is dominant when decisions are made in Hollywood about further production. After its first month in theaters, *Selena* had taken US$30 million at the box office, with 85 percent of the audience Latino, but the second month generated only an additional US$3.8 million. In a promotional letter to the Latino community, the producer and director appealed for support of the film in theaters, noting that "Video sales don't count on the most important bottom line— box office receipts." Most Hollywood films are now released in Spanish on DVD. In the television market, Paramount makes Spanish-language videos of its Nickelodeon children's series, and Buena Vista Home entertainment promotes Disney texts in Spanish-language versions. Disney sold its first Spanish-language interactive video games in 2001. Meanwhile, Ground Zero Entertainment developed a Latino film division with the express purpose of making and releasing movies direct to video.[40]

Of course, video/DVD is also important as an alternative and archival venue. The National Latino Communications Center (NLCC) is a media arts and production non-profit concern. Its Educational Media wing has a video-distribution service whose NLCC Video Collection serves both domestic and educational audiences with documentaries, independents, classic films, and short subjects, though its main work is for public broadcasting. Other concerns, such as New York's Videoteca del Sur, are motivated less by historical archivism or profit than by the desire to correct political inequalities and unequal cultural exchange. Mexican films from the past are available on video from a variety of sources, including the Agrasánchez Archives, a for-profit system begun by the noted producer Rogelio Agrasánchez, Sr. and continued by his son. It archives and transfers to video hundreds of Mexican films and also sells memorabilia. Mexican film of the 1950s has a cult audience in video stores as well. Similar businesses that cater to film buffs of Mexican cinema in search of video material for US-based audiences, without necessarily being based there, have included Laguna Films, Compañía Oxxo, the JPR Record Club, Spanish Multimedia, PicPal, Meridian Video, Son Cubano, Facets Video, Alfa Films, One World Films, and Libros Sin Fronteras. Companies may also specialize in kitsch genres that have become cults, such as Mexican horror films of the 1950s and 1960s (for example, Aztec Pit of Blood, Creepy Classics Video, Trash Palace, and Video Screams) while Blackboard Entertainment in California offers Spanish-language educational video.[41]

---

case study

The Latin American Video Archives (LAVA) had an online database and ordering service to enable professors and others to locate rare films in video form, in addition to maintaining its own archive of several thousand titles and a film distribution and subtitling service. In keeping with its non-profit, educational mission, LAVA received funding from charitable foundations and local government. A project of the International Media Resources Exchange, the Rockefeller and MacArthur Foundations commenced a program of ongoing support to the Latin American screen in 1991. It was crucial, as was the US-Mexico Fund. LAVA used its expensive subtitling equipment as a service rather than to gain revenue, and relied on academic labor to do most translating. In turn, the majority of its sales were to academic institutions, either through libraries or departments of anthropology, history, or Spanish and Portuguese. Both commercial features and documentaries were important parts of their holdings. LAVA promoted its work via a website and email newsletters, but closed its actual and virtual doors at the end of 2005—one more story in the history of small-scale distribution.[42]

Just 12 percent of Latinos prefer Spanish-language to English-language sites, with 25 percent favoring bilingual services—similar proportions to other media, while 73 percent of English-speaking Latinos are online.[43] Catalan research discloses that 68 percent of the world's websites were in English and 3 percent in Spanish in 2000. Latino-oriented Internet media services doubled in 1999, at the high point of the dot-com boom. Several large US concerns targeted both US- and Latin American-based audiences through Spanish-language subsidiaries, such as Yahoo! En Español, Time Warner's Latin America, and Microsoft's MSN T1. Procter and Gamble, the consumer company that produces many US TV soap operas, formerly put out *Avanzado*, a bilingual online magazine and search engine, through the yupi.com portal, which was targeted at Latinos. Owned by TELMEX and Microsoft, the YupiMSN site was localized to cover different segments of the Latino audience across the Western hemisphere as yupimsn.com, alongside latinosmsn.com, which focused on Hollywood, although its TV section was cosmopolitan. Twentieth Century Fox Entertainment began FoxHomeEnEspanol in 2002, the first Hollywood studio site in the United States designed for Spanish-language spectators. It was short-lived.[44]

conclusion

Most approaches to Mexican film have simply not considered its life in major Mexican population centers—within contemporary Mexico or Aztlan. But it is vital to address the who and what and how of Mexicanness in all its locations if one is to speak credibly of Mexican cultural institutions. This may seem a special case, but consider the work adumbrated earlier on Bolivia and Nigeria. I do not suggest jettisoning texts, or existing forms of analysis, which are extremely valuable as particular tools. I *do* propose pluralizing and complicating texts—understanding them as moments that spin their own tales of travel and uptake, as essentially unstable entities that change their very composition as they move across time and space. When it comes to key questions of meaning—what gets produced and circulated, and how it signifies—I have turned to a political-economic ethnography/ethnographic political economy to supplement the New International Division of Cultural Labor focus of earlier projects. When it comes to the world of "national cinema," the implication is that both terms of the couplet must be problematized—but not in an armchair-theoreticist way—rather through a nimble materialist history that pays heed to the specifics of time and space as they wreak havoc on the definition and career of "film." The Mexican example makes the case compellingly, as it both questions the borders that divide and describe peoples and the technology that carries screen culture.

notes

1. Toby Miller et al., *Globalisation and Sport: Playing the World* (London: Sage, 2001); Toby Miller et al., *Global Hollywood* (London: British Film Institute, 2001); Justin Lewis and Toby Miller, eds. *Critical Cultural Policy Studies: A Reader* (Malden, MA: Blackwell, 2003); Toby Miller et al., *Global Hollywood 2* (London: British Film Institute, 2005); Toby Miller and George Yúdice, *Cultural Policy* (London: Sage, 2002); Richard Maxwell and Toby Miller, eds. "Cultural Labor," special issue, *Social Semiotics* 15, no. 3 (2005).
2. Hortense Powdermaker, *Stranger and Friend: The Way of an Anthropologist* (London: Secker & Warburg, 1967), 217.
3. Michael Mallory, "The Cutting Room," *Los Angeles Times*, February 17, 2003; Basel Action Network and Silicon Valley Toxics Coalition, *Exporting Harm: The High-Tech Trashing of Asia* (Seattle, WA: Basel Action Network, 2002).
4. Graham Murdock, "Across the Great Divide: Cultural Analysis and the Condition of Democracy," *Critical Studies in Mass Communication* 12, no. 1 (1995): 89–95, p. 94.
5. Roger Chartier, "Texts, Printings, Readings," in *The New Cultural History*, ed. Lynn Hunt (Berkeley, CA: University of California Press, 1989), 157, 161–63, 166.
6. Toby Miller, *The Avengers* (London: British Film Institute, 1997).
7. Bruno Latour, *We Have Never Been Modern*, trans. Catherine Porter (Cambridge, MA: Harvard University Press, 1993), 5–6.
8. Néstor García Canclini, *Diferentes, desiguales y desconectados: Mapas de la interculturalidad* (Barcelona: Gedisa, 2004), 195.
9. Jeff Himpele, "Film Distribution as Media: Mapping Difference in the Bolivian Cinemascape," *Visual Anthropology Review* 12, no. 1 (1996): 47–66.
10. Hamid Naficy, *The Making of Exile Cultures: Iranian Television in Los Angeles* (Minneapolis, MN: University of Minnesota Press, 1993); Elena Shore, "Ho Chi Minh Protests," *Pacific News Service*, 2004.
11. Ironically, the description was coined in *Gringolandia* but is now begrudgingly embraced in the South.
12. Jonathan Haynes, ed. *Nigerian Video Film* (Athens, OH: Ohio University Press, 2000); Brian Larkin, "Indian Films and Nigerian Lovers: Media and the Creation of Parallel Modernities," *The Anthropology of Globalization: A Reader*, ed. Jonathan Xavier Inda and Renato Rosaldo (Malden, MA: Blackwell, 2001), 350–78; Brian Larkin, "Report on Nollywood Rising Conference." Unpublished paper, 2005.
13. James Bates, "Warner Douses Smoking Promo," *Los Angeles Times*, March 5, 2003; Basel Action Network, *The Digital Dump: Exporting Re-use and Abuse to Africa* (Seattle, WA: Basel Action Network, 2005).
14. Larkin, "Indian Films and Nigerian Lovers," 353.
15. This section draws in part on work done for the Instituto Mexican de Cinématografía with Néstor García Canclini, Enrique Sánchez-Ruiz, and Ana Rosas Mantecón.
16. Rocio Ayuso, "Hollywood Seeks Key to Spanish-Language Market for Films," *Agencia EFE S. A.*, April 4, 2002; Nicholas Fonseca, "Beyond Borders," *Entertainment Weekly*, April 26, 2002, 26; "Hollywood a la caza de los hispanos," *Univision.com*, www.univision.com/channel/40ent/images/; Omar Gonzalez, "Cine '98—A Step Toward *Cine Revolución*," *In Motion Magazine*, 1998, www.inmotionmagazine.com/omarg.html; Nielsen Media Research, *Household Viewing: Average Viewing Per Week*, 2002, www.nielsenmedia.

com/ethnicmeasure/hispanic-american/weekly_HH_viewing.html; Nick Madigan, "H'wood Neglecting Latino Auds, SAG Sez," *Variety.com*, May 5, 1999, www.variety.com/index.asp?layout=print_story&articleid= VR1117500026&categoryid=18; "All-Time Box Office," Motion Picture Association of America Press Release, March 7, 2000; Chon A. Noriega, "Making a Difference," *Politics and Culture* 2, no. 1 (2002) http://laurel .conncoll.edu/politicsandculture; Carlos Fresneda, "Latinos en Hollywood: el 'boom' de los tópicos," *El Mundo*, April 8, 2002; B. Ruby Rich, "Mexico at the Multiplex," *The Nation*, May 14, 2001, 34–36.

17. *Latino Media News*, February 2000, http://members.aol.com/aavila9999/ feb2000.html; Aparna Pande, "Latino Film Marketing: Forging Ahead Boldly or Blindly?," *MarketingProfs.com*, 2001, www.MarketingProfs.com; Todd Llano, "How Hispanic Films Make it to the Big Screen," *Hispanic* 8, no. 6 (1995): 22–25, p. 22; Lewis Beale, "A New Kind of Mexican Revolution Hits the Screen," *New York Times*, November 4, 2001, 31.

18. Arlene Dávila, *Latinos Inc.: The Marketing and Making of a People* (Berkeley, CA: University of California Press, 2001), 1–2, 197–99; John Sinclair, *Latin American Television: A Global View* (Oxford: Oxford University Press, 1999), 116; Frank G. Perez, "Effectively Targeting Hispanics in the Southwest: Views from Public Relations Professionals in a Border City," *Public Relations Quarterly* 47, no. 1 (2002): 18–21.

19. "Fracasa el estreno ultimo del filme Disney en Español para Hispanos," *EFE S.A.*, January 9, 2001.

20. Quoted in Fonseca, "Beyond Borders," 27.

21. Fresneda, "Latinos en Hollywood."

22. Patricia Ornelas Vargas, "Movie Mexico!" *Film Journal International* (July 2000): 148–9; "Movie Mexico!" *Film Journal International* (December 2001): 85–86.

23. Colin Hoskins, Stuart McFadyen and Adam Finn, *Global Television and Film: An Introduction to the Economics of the Business* (Oxford: Clarendon Press, 1997), 57; Bill Daniels, David Leedy, and Steven D. Sills, *Movie Money: Understanding Hollywood's (Creative) Accounting Practices* (Los Angeles, CA: Silman-James Press, 1998), 86, 104; Fred Goldberg, *Motion Picture Marketing and Distribution: Getting Movies to a Theatre Near You* (Boston, MA: Focal Press, 1991), 5; Miller et al., *Global Hollywood 2*.

24. Ayuso, "Hollywood Seeks Key"; "*Columbia TriStar* co-produce con México," *Estacion Central*, 2002, www.estacioncentral.com/cine/cinemexicano/ mexican.htm; David W. McIntosh, "The Rise and Fall of Mexican Cinema in the Twentieth Century: From the Production of a Revolutionary National Imaginary to the Consumption of Globalized Cultural Industrial Products." Unpublished manuscript, not dated: 10; Meg James, "Sony Wins Rights to Cantinflas' Works," *Los Angeles Times*, June 14, 2002, C1.

25. Art-house cinema in the United States generally refers to non-Hollywood, often foreign films, mostly shown at independently owned theaters or in universities, with a focus on narrative rather than action, sometimes linked to the *avant-garde*, frequently not in English, and historically appealing to a highly educated white audience. See Kenneth P. Adler, "Art Films and Eggheads," *Studies in Public Communication* 2 (1959): 7–15; Todd Bayma, "Art World Culture and Institutional Choices: The Case of Experimental Film," *Sociological Quarterly* 36, no. 1 (1995): 79–95; Ronald J. Faber, Thomas C. O'Guinn, and Andrew P. Hardy, "Art Films in the Suburbs: A Comparison of Popular and Art Film Audiences," in *Current Research in Film: Audiences, Economics, and Law*, Vol. 4, ed. Bruce A. Austin (Norwood, NJ: Ablex, 1988),

toby miller

45–53; Joshua Gamson, "The Organizational Shaping of Collective Identity: The Case of Lesbian and Gay Film Festivals in New York," *Sociological Forum* 11, no. 2 (1996): 231–61; Jim Lane, "The History of Alternative Film Exhibition and the Social Construction of Taste," *Film and History* 24, nos. 3–4 (1994): 4–5; Steve Neale, "Art Cinema as Institution," *Screen* 22, no. 1 (1981): 11–40.

26. Peter Henné, "Worldly Distributors," *Film Journal International* (November 2001): 142; Enrique Puente, "Latin Universe." Paper for Fifth Congress of the Americas, Puebla, Mexico, 2001; Enrique Sánchez-Ruiz, "Globalization, Cultural Industries, and Free Trade: The Mexican Audiovisual Sector in the NAFTA Age," in *Continental Order? Integrating North America for Cybercapitalism*, ed. Vincent Mosco and Dan Schiller (Lanham, MD: Rowman & Littlefield, 2001), 107; Tiuu Lukk, *Movie Marketing: Opening the Picture and Giving it Legs* (Los Angeles, CA: Silman-James Press, 1997), 118–19, 138–39; Daniels, Leedy, and Sills, *Movie Money*, 94, 91; Elisabetta Brunella, "Old-World Moviegoing: Theatrical Distribution of European Films in the United States," *Film Journal International* (March 2001): 28–32; Pande, "Latino Film Marketing."

27. Douglas Gomery, *Shared Pleasures: A History of Movie Presentation in the United States* (Madison, WI: University of Wisconsin Press, 1992), 171, 177, 179; Ana M. López, "A Cinema for the Continent," in *The Mexican Cinema Project*, ed. Chon A. Noriega and Steven Ricci (Los Angeles, CA: University of California, Los Angeles Film and Television Archive, 1994), 8.

28. Carl J. Mora, *Mexican Cinema: Reflections of a Society 1896–1980* (Berkeley, CA: University of California Press, 1982), 245, 140; Hilary E. MacGregor, "Latino Movie Theater Chain Promised," *Los Angeles Times*, September 1, 1999, 1; David Maciel, "Los desarraigados: Los chicanos vistos por el cine Mexican," in *México Estados Unidos: Encuentros y desencuentros en el cine*, eds. Ignacio Durán, Iván Trujillo, and Mónica Verea (Mexico: Universidad Nacional Autónoma de México/Consejo Nacional para la Cultura y las Artes/Instituto Mexicano de Cinematografía, 1996), 166–67; Douglas Gomery, personal communication, 2002; Sánchez-Ruiz, "Globalization, Cultural Industries, and Free Trade," 94, 101; Puente, "Latin Universe"; Nissa Torrents, "Mexican Cinema Comes Alive," in *Mediating Two Worlds: Cinematic Encounters in the Americas*, eds. John King, Ana M. López, and Manuel Alvarado (London: British Film Institute, 1993), 224; Sean Logan, "Cine Mexicano," *Prism* (October 1995).

29. Chon A. Noriega, "Mexican Cinema in the United States: Introduction to the Essays," in *The Mexican Cinema Project*, ed. Chon A. Noriega and Steven Ricci (Los Angeles, CA: University of California, Los Angeles Film and Television Archive, 1994), 3; Sandra Hernandez, "Latin Beat," *LA Weekly*, October 2–8, 1998; Harmony H. Wu, "Eating the Nation: Selling *Like Water for Chocolate* in the USA." Paper for Latin American Studies Association conference, Guadalajara, Mexico, April 17–19, 1997; Lorenza Munoz, "A Start-Up's Tough Spanish Lessons," *Los Angeles Times*, March 19, 2000, 19; Henné, "Worldly Distributors."

30. MacGregor, "Latino Movie Theatre Chain Promised."; Karen Schwartzman, "Alternative Distrib'n Efforts Bear Fruit," *Daily Variety*, May 15, 2002, A11; Fresneda, "Latinos en Hollywood"; Ricky B. Sisk, "Luces, Camara, Accion," *Urban Spectrum* 16, no. 2 (2002), www.urbanspectrum.net/fea.cinema.html.

31. Schwartzman, "Alternative Distrib'n Efforts Bear Fruit"; Camila Castellanos, "Get Your Tickets Now!" *Business Mexico*, August 1, 2001; Gabriel Sama, "Latin American Films See Domestic, US Revival," *Wall Street Journal*, March 22, 2002, C11A; Paul Constance, "Lights, Camera, Revival,"

IDBAmérica (December 2001), www.iadb.org/idbamerica/English/NOV01E/ nov01e2.html; Eugene Hernandez, " 'Y Tu Mama' Hits it Big," *IndieWIRE*, April 9, 2002, www.indiewire.com/film/biz/biz_020409_briefs.html; quoted in Beale, "A New Kind of Mexican Revolution," 31; Castellanos, "Get your Tickets Now!"; Simeon Tegel, " '*Perros*' Fetches Profit for Estudio," *Variety*, 26 March–1 April, 2001, 142, 144; Alberto Fuguet, "Magical Neoliberalism," *Foreign Policy*, no. 125 (2001): 66–73; "México cosmopolita," 2002; Sama, "Latin American Films See Domestic, US Revival"; Sharon Waxman, "Filmmaker's Road Picture Steers Him Back to his Roots," *Washington Post*, May 4, 2002, C1; Rene Rodriguez, "A New Wave in Mexican Cinema?" *Houston Chronicle*, April 14, 2002, 11; Patricia Thomson, "IFC Films: The Business of Synergy," *Independent Film and Video Monthly* (March 2002), 38; E. Hernandez, " 'Y Tu Mama' Hits it Big"; David Bloom, "Inside Moves: Yo, 'Mama'." *Variety.com*, May 19, 2002, www.variety.com/index.asp?layout= print_story&articleid= VR1117864076&categoryid=13; Loretta Munoz, "How Do You Say 'Breakout'?" *Los Angeles Times*, April 19, 2002, F1; Ayuso, "Hollywood Seeks Key"; Fonseca, "Beyond Borders," 27; *Variety Box Office*, June 10–16 (2002): 10.

32. Chon A. Noriega, *Shot in America: Television, the State, and the Rise of Chicano Cinema* (Minneapolis, MN: University of Minnesota Press, 2000), 237 n. 56; Lorenza Munoz, "Introducing 70 Films from Latin Quarters," *Los Angeles Times*, October 1, 1999, F2; Latin Film Network, 2002, www.latinfilmnetwork.com/ festivals.htm; "Dificultades de distribución," *Diario de Yucatán*, June 21, 2001; "*Estudio México* planea distribución en EU," *Estacion Central* (2002), www.estacioncentral.com/cine/cinemexicano/mexican.htm; Schwartzman, "Alternative Distrib'n Efforts Bear Fruit."

33. S. Hernandez, "Latin Beat"; Justino Aguila, "Supply and Demand Rearrange Video Shelves," *San Francisco Chronicle*, September 16, 2001, 36; Lauren Horwitch, "Hispanic Film Fest Circuit Hits the Road," *Variety.com*, June 9, 2002, www.variety.com/index.asp?layout=print_story&articleid=VR1117868225& categoryid=1236.

34. Noriega, "Making a Difference."

35. Schwartzman, "Alternative Distrib'n Efforts Bear Fruit."

36. LaCinemaFe, Latin American Cinema Festival of New York, 2001, lacinemacafe.com; Alberto Armendáriz, "Abandaran en EU al cine Latinoamericano," *Reforma* 22 (August 2005): 2E.

37. Sinclair, *Latin American Television*, 92, 97; Cable TV Ad Bureau Multicultural Resource Center, *Information, Insight and Strategies to Achieve Greater Advertising Effectiveness in Today's Diverse Markets*, 2002, www.cabletvadbureau.com/ MMRC/.

38. Noriega, *Shot in America*, 169; Mari Castañeda Paredes, "The Reorganization of Spanish-Language Media Marketing," in *Continental Order? Integrating North America for Cybercapitalism*, ed. Vincent Mosco and Dan Schiller (Lanham, MD: Rowman & Littlefield, 2001), 124; Sinclair, *Latin American Television*, 92, 94, 96; Joan Raymond, "¿Tienen Numeros?," *American Demographics* 24, no. 3 (2002): 22–25; Stuart Elliott, "Hispanic Networks Hone an Edge in a Race for TV Ad Dollars," *New York Times*, May 30, 2002, C7.

39. López, "A Cinema for the Continent," 11; Beale, "A New Kind of Mexican Revolution," 32; Univision, *Cine* (2002), www.univision.com/cont; "Univision, AOL Seek Hispanics," *Houston Chronicle*, December 14, 2001, 3; "Hispanic-American TV Booms," *Broadcasting and Cable*, May 20, 2002, 29; Castellanos, "Get your Tickets Now!"; Frank del Olmo, "English Isn't a Second Language on TV," *Los Angeles Times*, January 20, 2002, M5; "Hispanic-

American TV Booms"; Cable TV Ad Bureau Multicultural Resource Center, *Targeted Networks, Specialized Programming Blocks and Culturally Relevant Promotions*, 2002, www.cabletvadbureau.com?MMRC/programming_ mun2.html; Nancy Coltun Webster, "Network Eyes Mexican Viewers," *Advertising Age*, August 14 (2000): 16; Aguila, "Supply and Demand"; HBO Latino, "Film Schedule en mayo," 2002, www.hbolatino.com/peliculas/; Michelle Chase, Interview, 30 May, 2002; *Latino Media News*, February 2000; "Sundance Channel Showcases 'Arte Latino' Cinema," *La Voz de Colorado*, August 23, 2000, 11; Fresneda, "Latinos en Hollywood."

40. Dan Bennett, "Video en Español," *Video Store* 23, no. 42 (2001): 22–23; Madigan, "H'wood Neglecting Latino Auds"; Alex Avila, "Taken for a Ride: Hispanic Filmmakers Experience the Ups and Downs of Hollywood and Ask, 'What's Next?'," *Hispanic* 10, no. 6 (1997): 35; Joan Villa, "Retailers, Studios Increasingly Eye Hispanic Market," *Video Store*, April 7–13 (2002): 12; "Disney Games in Spanish," *Video Business*, 8 January, 2001, 6; Jennifer Netherby, "Latin at Ground Zero," *Video Business*, 5 November, 2001, 23.

41. Noriega, *Shot in America*, 182–83; Agrasánchez Film Archives, "History of the Archives," 2002, www.agrasfilms.com/nav4/archives.htm; Aguila, "Supply and Demand"; Bennett, "Video en Español."

42. Latin American Video Archives, 2002, www.lavavideo.org; *Update* 2, no. 2 (1998); Chase, Interview.

43. Cable TV Ad Bureau Multicultural Resource Center, *Targeted Networks*; Collin Brink, "US Hispanic Internet Users: Thinking in Spanish and Surfing in English," *EMarketer*, February 26, 2001, www.emarketer.com/analysis/edemographics/2010227_edemo.html; Pew Internet & American Life Project, *Hispanics and the Internet* (Washington, DC: Pew Internet & American Life Project, 2001); Andy Vuong, "Latino 'Net Use Up; Latino Sites Down," *Denver Post*, July 26, 2001, C1; Pew Internet & American Life Project, 2006, www.pewinternet.org/trends.asp#demographics.

44. Brink, "US Hispanic Internet Users"; Paredes, "The Reorganization of Spanish-Language Media Marketing," 121, 129; Kate Fitzgerald, "Seeking Entree to Hispanic Doorways," *Advertising Age*, February 11, 2002, S6; Yupi.com, *Entretenimiento*, 2002, www.yupimsn.com/entretenimiento/cine/verano2002?; "Hollywood.com Launches Spanish-Language Sites in Mexico and Argentina," *Hollywood.com* 2002, www.hollywood.com/about_us/pressrelease/id/469081.

aural identity,

genealogies of

sound technologies,

and hispanic

transnationality

on screen

marvin d'lugo

"where do the singers come from?": translation, migration, modernization

> *Mama, I want to know where do the singers come from? Are they from Havana or Santiago?*[1]

The popular Cuban song *El son de la loma* (*The Song from the Hill*) begins with the question, "¿De dónde son los cantantes? (Where do the singers come from?) metaphorically bringing into focus questions of origins of popular cultural forms and their circulation through a variety of sound technologies, including motion pictures. A characteristically Cuban musical form, the *son* blends African rhythms and Spanish melodies. *Son de la loma* was popularized on radio and phonograph recordings by the famed Cuban *sonero* Trio Matamoros during the "golden age" of Cuban music in the 1930s, quickly becoming a musical standard throughout the Spanish-speaking Caribbean. As such, the song serves as a representative example of the transfer and transformation of "traditional, collective creativity, commonly called 'folklore,' to the domain of the mass media, the 'mass culture' of technical reproduction and industrial commercialization."[2] Given its hybrid origins in African Cuban culture, and its subsequent circulation, *Son de la loma* suggests a version of what Walter Benjamin termed the "afterlife of the work of art." Writing about the social significance of translation, Benjamin asserted:

> The important works of world literature never find their chosen translators at the time of their origin, their translation marks their stage of continued life. The idea of life and afterlife in works of art should be regarded with an entirely unmetaphoric objectivity.[3]

Indeed, over the years *Son de la loma* underwent a series of such translations in ways that illuminate our appreciation of the particular status of aural traditions in the shaping of Latin American cultural identity. After its initial period of mass-circulation through recordings and radio, the lyrics resurfaced in the title of Severo Sarduy's novel *De dónde son los cantantes* (1967) as it reshaped the song's question into a parody of Cuban literary constructions of national identity. Interestingly, the novel, written in France by the self-exiled Cuban writer, benefited from the "boom" of Latin American fiction in the 1960s, indirectly bringing the original song into a broader pan-Hispanic cultural circuit far beyond its original Cuban and Caribbean origins. In 1976, Cuban filmmaker Luis Felipe Bernaza made a documentary that took as its title that now familiar question, *Where Do the Singers Come From?* as if to reaffirm the narrower "national" roots of Cuban music through a cinematic examination of the history of the Cuban *sonero* tradition. Aimed at celebrating through Cuba's revolutionary state-orchestrated cinema "music of certain popular authentic values,"[4] the film, in fact, worked as an implicitly political response to Sarduy's appropriation of the song's initial question. Such varied appropriations of a traditional melody are indeed "translations" in the sense that Benjamin uses the word. They transpose popular cultural traditions into new contexts, radically reforming the meanings of the original, yet anchoring the new version within the genealogy of the original "text."

In essential ways the genealogical lines traced by *Son de la loma* condense the broad and complex processes within which musical sounds migrate across media and even geographic boundaries in Latin American culture, ambivalently affirming the nostalgia for lost traditions and, paradoxically, circulating those ideas through media that are themselves the very agents of the modernization that sparks such nostalgia for the past. One of the underlying questions that such a musical genealogy poses is the privileging of the nexus between popular aural culture and the expansion of sound cinema in the region.

As an exaggerated and commercialized form of popular culture, the Latin American movie musical in all its variations constitutes a kind of *Volkgeist*, closely identified with, and yet often reacting against, the modernization and increasing urbanization of Latin American society. Ángel Rama has, in fact, argued, the musical forms which will be identified with the Latin American movie musical, traced their roots to the great migrations from rural to urban spaces during the first three decades of the twentieth century: "The living popular culture of the moment was . . . the vital, vulgar culture of the urban masses. [It] drew on rural folk traditions as the natural matrix of their own creativity."[5] Other cultural historians, such as Jesus Martin-Barbero, Carlos Monsiváis, and Néstor García Canclini, have expanded Rama's view, underscoring the ambivalent ways in which urban culture, through the agency of sound technology—phonograph recordings, radio and sound motion picture—reworked pre-urban folkloric traditions into popular memory. Speaking of the appeal of US Latino music, Juan Flores observes "the paradoxical inversion of geographical location and cultural belonging" for immigrant Latin American populations in the United States as the feeling for "home" and community is affirmed with the strongest emphasis from a distance when there is an uncertainty as to place.[6]

Implied in any discussion of cultural modernization in Latin America is, as Monsiváis contends, the process of social and cultural migrations, not only from rural to urban spaces, but also from traditionalist cultural positions to newer emerging class and gender identities, finally from traditional class-bound conceptions to more hybrid notions of culture.[7] "Moving to the city" historically involved a transformation in personal outlook for immigrants as the result of their uprooting and their entrance into a newly emerging mass culture.[8] Communication technologies mediated that transformation, enabling peasants to renegotiate their former lifestyles within the newly reshaped spaces of the city.[9] In part, that renegotiation involved the nostalgic evocations of values of the rural culture that had been lost by the modernization process. Folkloric and popular music, such as the Argentine tango, the Cuban *son* and the Mexican bolero, often expressed that displacement process as nostalgia for the places and times of the past and, beginning in the 1920s, became a common cultural trope circulated by the expanding technology of radio.[10]

Martín-Barbero describes the web of aural variations provided by radio in Argentina, where soap operas developed, in Mexico where traditional music such as the ranchera songs were heard, and Brazil, where the musical traditions of the huge black population serves to transform recently arrived urban populations into national mass audiences.[11] The migration of popular aural culture from rural to urban, eventually to regional communities beyond national borders also parallels the growing interconnectedness of the sound technologies that made such aural migrations possible. We see this strikingly in the case of cinema where, despite the rootedness of Latin American motion picture production within "national" spaces, since the early 1930s, the international circulation of films helped to forge a substantive Latin American transnational cinema.[12] The distribution of Spanish-language musical films determined by markets that defied political boundaries further contributed to the formation of a transnational Hispanic audience whose cultural outlook was no longer shaped exclusively by national themes and interests.

The first record company in Latin America had been set up in Mexico in 1925 by the Venezuelan impresario Eduardo Baptista. Previously, records had been imported from the United States. In order to consolidate the growing transnational market, his and other music companies "required products that could easily cross national borders and consolidate a market position through Latin America."[13] During this same period, the companion sound technology of radio transmission was gaining broadly defined audiences. In Argentina, the live transmission of the Firpo-Dempsey boxing match in 1923 brought the medium its first major audience. A year later, the first regular broadcast of soccer matches was begun.[14] At first, audiences' preferences for "live events" limited the appeal of broadcast recordings to local performers, with radio stations presenting such performances either from their studios or from the stage of local theaters. The connection with motion pictures was made when popular singers, such as Carlos Gardel, began recording songs based on the musical scores that accompanied silent films.[15]

Referring to the impact of radio on Latin American popular culture, Martín-Barbero claims that "radio reorganizes the universe of oral cultures through a precise mediation of written and musical texts."[16] That claim may be expanded to describe the effect of the relation among sound media generally wherein a truly popular Latin American imaginary of modernity was formed during this crucial period through the cinematic circulation of popular music—tango, bolero, and ranchero songs—that had previously been specifically identified with local popular culture.[17] Martín-Barbero acknowledges the particular privilege of the cinematic institution in this process when he observes the impact of popular singers such as Jorge Negrete and movie idols like Cantinflas and María Félix: "Here was where the traces of the first project of modernity could be recognized, made from imagination, feeling, and hence, identity."[18]

Through the power of expanding radio signals as well as the transportability of phonograph recordings, the auditory discourse of nostalgia itself circulated across the region. For Monsiváis, what had previously been local musical sounds now became part of a deterritorialized communal aural tradition.[19] This circulation of music, in turn, worked to weaken national borders as film historians have suggested,[20] bringing into focus the beginnings of an aural bonding of a Hispanic transnational community taking shape around the mediatized discourse of folkloric music. This is a historical instance of what John Mowitt more generally describes as the social stabilization of "the practices of listening"[21] with which, more than questions of technology, those of social reception of music become critical. Extending

Walter Benjamin's thesis in "The Work of Art in the Age of Mechanical Reproduction," Mowitt argues that, like the reproducibility of images that displace the "aura" of the work of art, the reproducibility of music has its own series of social effects and displacements. The technologies of sound reproduction imply, for Mowitt, "a social order confirmed within the contemporary structure of listening." Quoting the writings of music theorist Jacques Attali, he affirms that music is a tool for "the creation and consolidation of a community."[22]

Mowitt situates a properly subjective faculty—that of hearing/ listening—deep within social processes. Following Benjamin's argument, he acknowledges the popular status of cinema as the confirmation of the saturation of modern reality by equipment.[23] Listening is dependent upon memory and thus gives social significance to the reproductive technologies that organize memories through the repetition and reinforcement of sounds.[24] Sound recording, radio, later televisual representations are thus refigured in Mowitt's argument as parts of a continuum that reinforces rather than competes for the subjective attention of the listener. Conceptually, the model of the aural community that Mowitt proposes, combined with the historical amalgamation of sound technologies in Latin America, sets the stage for our consideration of the historical practices of musical cinema in Latin America as they contribute to the forging of a Hispanic "transnation" of listeners.

The term "transnation" is here used as a shorthand for reference to the emergence of a deterritorialized population formed through migration and built on the recognition of common cultural bonds, including language and social customs. Unlike "globalization," a term which in Latin American contexts often carries the baggage of cultural hierarchies and political prejudices,[25] the "transnation" affirms the individual's desire for identification with an expansive imagined community of shared cultural remembrances "not structured by the logic of the state."[26] For Puerto Rican cultural theorist Juan Flores, the dynamics of Hispanic diasporic culture in the Caribbean leads to the growing visibility of a contemporary delocalized Hispanic "transnation" in the United States through the popular musical expressions that unite this disparate community. As that transnation gains demographic and political prominence in the mainland United States, Flores observes the emergence of the social consciousness and cultural expression of this new geopolitical reality burst forth in the late 1960s and early 1970s, "surely the watershed years in the construction of a new language of Latino identity."[27]

Hispanic migration culture to and within the Americas, even of the political bent Flores describes, has deep roots that predate twentieth-century Latin American population shifts. The demographic history of the region was of course defined by the racial mixing of European with native American populations, accompanied by colonial migrations which, over centuries, imposed cultural norms as well as the progressive exchange of cultural products and people understood under the general rubric of migration culture.[28] Walter Mignolo traces some of the political back-story of the transnation which he sees

> emerg[ing] from the imperial conflict between Spain and the United States, in the nineteenth century, which has generated the physical borders of Mexico and the United States, but also the metaphorical borders as enacted in the histories of Cuba/United States, Puerto Rico/United States that basically define the configuration of Latino/as in this country.[29]

Crucial to such transnational cultural mappings are two parallel processes: the implied narratives of migration, both as the literal movement of people from rural to urban spaces and across borders and the metaphoric expansion of cultural styles and outlook that transcend national borders aided by the unification process of language itself. The Spanish language, for Mignolo, is not simply the imagined patrimony of the national state, but on the contrary, the agency through which common, transnational outlooks are achieved.[30]

In the mediatization of the Spanish language through sound technologies, sound cinema becomes an attractive vehicle of nostalgic aural identification and its antithesis, cultural modernization. Precisely through the prodigious regional circulation of staged musical films, with popular entertainment at a low price of admission, audiences were able to hear the sounds that they recognized as part of their own cultural heritage, and to imagine these sounds to be those of a common cultural identity in ways that often refigured the imagery associated with local culture with a broader sense of a transnational Hispanic community. The emerging Latin American star system did much to personalize the mechanisms of audience identification with these musical sounds. The development of what I will call aural identity emerged through the chain of transformations, hybridizations and the general deterritorialization of songs and musical rhythms during the crucial first two decades of the sound period, which needs to be historicized within the broader contours of the politics and aesthetics of identity construction that subsequently characterizes Latin American mass media.

the film hispano

The appropriate point of origin of that paradigm of aural identification is located beyond the region and precipitated through the advent of sound cinema and its impact on the Hollywood film industry. Fearing the loss of its lucrative Latin American market, Hollywood studios conjured up an early mass-media construction of an all-purpose Spanish-language audience not differentiated by region, culture or even differences of accent. Discussing the US movie industry's vulnerability in the face of the real menace of potent European national cinemas during the transition to sound, Alan Williams hypothesizes that

> recorded speech, as opposed to written titles, fatally introduced an element of cultural and social specificity into narrative film that simply hadn't been there before . . . Once this happened, the cultural and social sensitivities of different audiences would have become vastly easier to disturb, since film stories with spoken dialogue took place in a world more solidly grounded in the experience of everyday life—as opposed to fantasies about it.[31]

Hollywood's efforts to retain its overseas markets by developing multiple-language productions is often relegated to a footnote in the broader history of US cinema's transition to sound.[32] Yet, from the perspective of the development of Latin American film industries, these early efforts are important in that they crystallized the geopolitical tensions that eventually shaped the rise of national sound cinemas in the region. Erasing the borders of cultural specificities, of different ethnic and racial identities, even denying the uniqueness of local accents, Hollywood conceived of a Hispanic transnation merely as a marketing strategy, that is, as a homogenized regional community of cultural consumers.

The films that were produced by the Hollywood studios were generally received with disdain in Latin America and rightly perceived as an impostor "Hispanic" cinema. Hollywood's effort, however, did provoke the first coordinated pan-Hispanic reaction and the first ever gathering by the representatives of Spanish-language cinema from Spain and Spanish America (government officials, producers) to explore a collective response to Hollywood. The Primer Congreso de Cinematografía Hispanoamericana, which convened in Madrid in October of 1931, was ostensibly motivated by what its participants saw as the provocation of Hollywood's imposter Spanish-speaking cinema. The producers of these *films hispanos*, as they were called in the Spanish-language press, would contract actors from different Spanish-speaking countries with no regard to their accents. Film casts reflected a random mixing of Castilian versus Latin American accents for actors which led many to label the *films hispanos* a "war of accents."[33] The group that convened in Madrid well understood that what was at stake was more than ethnic or national pride. The *film hispano* concocted by Hollywood carried with it a commercial threat. Spanish-language cinema was struggling not just to achieve some abstract notion of distinctive cultural identity. It was fighting for its very economic survival against the hegemonic re-encroachment of Hollywood's industrial and commercial leviathan.

The "war of the accents" seems all but dissipated in the development of a certain type of *film hispano* within which musical numbers appeared to mask the multiple errors of speech and even inappropriate typecasting of spoken films. These films diverged from the pattern described as multiple-language version films,[34] in that they were not usually remakes of English-language films but rather films designed to play up regional Hispanic cultural stereotypes. It is thus useful to underscore a distinction that is seldom made in non-Hispanic film circles about the *films hispanos*, between the spoken films and the emergence of musical film, the latter constructed *around, by* and *for* the musical numbers. Following on the already proven commercial success of Jolson's *The Jazz Singer*, the idea of a musicalized sound cinema suggested a form of address that might avoid the pitfalls of perceived cultural and linguistic inauthenticity that plagued other expressions of Hollywood's Spanish-language film productions.

From the start of the sound period, the musical comedy genre posed special problems for Latin American distribution. When the MGM musical *Broadway Melody* (1929) was shown in Buenos Aires, it was presented in English with "explanatory captions," subtitles in Spanish on the lower portion of the screen.[35] The film turned out to be a commercial success, largely due to its novelty as a "talking and singing picture." Audiences soon tired of the novelty, however, and demanded musicals sung and spoken in Spanish. Indeed, of all the Hollywood genre films distributed in Latin America in the first decades of the sound era, the musical was the one most roundly and consistently rejected by Latin American audiences.[36] Early efforts by Hollywood to capitalize on the Jolson model by making Spanish-language musicals, most notably Xavier Cugat's ill-fated *Charros, gauchos y manolas* (*Cowboys, Gauchos and Manolas*, 1930), failed, largely because, while such films claimed the attractiveness of the musical, they fell short of delivering the glamour of the star system that had so effectively shaped national and international markets in the silent period. As well, like the non-musical *films hispanos*, they lacked the aura of cultural authenticity.

The achievement of that goal was at last realized in a series of *films hispanos* starring the Argentine tango singer, Carlos Gardel, that circulated during the early 1930s with impressive success throughout the Spanish-speaking world, including the US audiences. Though designed for the purpose of maintaining Paramount's Spanish-language market, the Gardel films soon had the unintended consequence of actualizing a regional transnational market of films made *by* Latin Americans that challenged Hollywood's market control. Gardel's Paramount films need to be seen, however, not merely as the imitative formula of hegemonic Hollywood movies. They reflect what Paranaguá sees as a life-size laboratory for Latin American film productions as they borrowed from Hollywood's own self-imitation process which literally "translated" US mainstream motion pictures into internationally marketable products.[37] What is significant in this regard is that the very idea of a Hispanic transnational cinema derives first from an industrial and marketing model in which the idea of the transnation is understood as a market, not a cultural entity. As such, Hollywood's *films hispanos* gave early impetus to a regional transnational genre of Latin American cinema by providing it with both the concept of a market and also the musical basis of aural identification. The Gardel phenomenon, which initially dwarfed many of these local efforts in both their production values and commercial success, is instructive not only for its value in charting the genealogy of a particular Hispanic transnational star, but, as well, for the way in which it brings into focus the mass mediation of popular cultural forms that would shape transnational cinema throughout the region in the coming decades.

the gardel phenomenon and transnational sound in the 1930s

Gardel appeared from various perspectives to be the Spanish-language Jolson,[38] an apt analogy since, like Jolson, he came to sound cinema with an already-established celebrity persona. Just as Warner Brothers created the cinematic Jolson through its promotion of *The Jazz Singer*, so too, the cinematic Gardel was really the invention of Paramount Pictures as it exploited and expanded the dense network of repetitive aural culture that live performances, sound recordings, and radio had forged around Gardel and other popular singers. Latin American cultural commentators like to emphasize Gardel's mythic or legendary status, the broad appeal of his biography which involved a rags-to-riches scenario of a poor boy from the slums whose talent led him to embody the sophisticated high culture.[39] The singer's exceptionalism, however, probably did not lie in any intrinsic aspects of the star's biography or magnetism, nor even his singing voice, but in the accumulation of elements that helped shape and mobilize the Gardelian aural and visual discourse.[40]

Like Jolson, and Paramount's first effort at a transnational singing star, Maurice Chevalier, Gardel's movie successes were preceded by his successful music hall career as a charismatic singer. After a debut as a cabaret singer, Gardel joined José Razzano in 1917 to form a musical duet that performed tangos in a Buenos Aires movie theater in the intervals between silent film screenings. The Gardel-Razzano performances were so popular with local audiences that the baritone was contracted by Max Glücksman, an Austrian-born businessman and owner of the recently established Argentine recording label Nacional-Odeón. Gardel's subsequent triumph as a recording artist for Columbia, Victor, and Odeón, with a recorded repertory that would eventually number close to 800 songs, reinforced the tango as a form of popular musical expression identified primarily, but not exclusively, with the urban culture of Buenos Aires.

During the critical decade of the 1920s, Glücksman, as a multimedia impresario, would serve as an influential bridge figure for Gardel and the diffusion of the tango through the singer's recording, radio and eventual cinematic performance. In 1922 Glücksman set up an experimental radio broadcasting station in Buenos Aires called TFF Radio Grand Splendid. The station, located in the same Buenos Aires building as the movie theater of the same name, which Glücksman owned, would transmit live performances from the theater.[41] Over time, a group of musical performers would obtain recording contracts and their voices would become part of the expanding tango repertory. By the mid-1920s, and following the pattern common around the world, the critical synergy between performance, recording and broadcasting was well established in Argentina as radio and theater reinforced the appeal of cinema for increasing numbers of Argentines.[42]

Gardel made his radio debut on Glücksman's Radio Splendid in 1924 and the next year embarked on the first of a series of successful European tours. He appeared to large and enthusiastic audiences in Madrid, Barcelona, and Paris. On one of these tours to France in 1929 he was contracted by Paramount to appear in several sound films that were specifically tailored to play on his already established celebrity persona. This was also about the time Maurice Chevalier was "discovered" in Paris by Irving Thalberg and embarked on his own cinematic "conquest of America."[43] The Paramount strategy was by now apparent: to find rivals to Warner Brothers' star property, Al Jolson. With such strong parallels to Jolson's career and image, Gardel must have seemed to Paramount an ideal candidate for the role.

To some degree the Gardel films may be seen simply as Spanish-language imitations of a recognizable Hollywood musical genre. Unlike the Busby Berkeley-choreographed cinema that was increasingly Hollywood's evolving pattern, as Paranaguá argues, Gardel reinforces a formula in which the singer and his performance become the central elements.[44] In this, Gardel's films frequently follow a cinematic-narrative formula identified with Jolson, that is, as a self-conscious stage performance in the middle of the filmic action that recalls for audiences "the 'documentary' impact of a radio broadcast . . . offering the sort of 'almost documentary presentations' of musical hall performance."[45] Beyond these features, Gardel's exceptionalism is built on the way in which, as a lyricist, an authentic musical "author," he intervened in and transformed the historical trajectory of the tango, presenting new lyrics, modifying the themes which modify in his repertory now include a strong element of nostalgia.[46]

The cycle of nine feature-length films Gardel shot in Paris and New York between 1931 and 1935 were not adaptations from English-language Hollywood productions but films written and produced expressly as vehicles for Gardel. Although all but one of these was a full-length feature, according to Nataša Ďurovičová, these films fall into a category more structurally akin to Paramount's serially produced shorts, "Paramount on Parade," which were made to supplement US-made films for the local audiences in a local language.[47]

Gardel's first four films, though arguably of negligible artistic merit, were popular commercial successes. Owing to the singer's own growing popularity, even in the United States, marked by his broadcast on NBC radio in 1933, they were followed by five more films shot at Paramount's New York sound studio during 1934 and 1935.[48] A sign of Gardel's commercial growing attractiveness may be noted in Paramount's willingness, even after the company's bankruptcy in late 1933, to renegotiate his contract in order to involve his own recently-established production company, Éxito's Spanish Pictures, partly financed by Western Electric, with the agreement for Paramount to distribute his films.[49] Under this new arrangement, Gardel appeared in *Cuesta abajo* (*Down Hill*, 1934), *El tango en Broadway* (*The Tango on Broadway*, 1934), *El día que me quiera* (*The Day You Love Me*, 1935), *Tango Bar* (1935), and *Cazadores de estrellas* (*Star Hunters*, 1934–35). The last of these, perhaps the least well known of the series, may ultimately be the most significant in that it reveals the special status of Gardel in the constellation of Paramount's production-marketing plans. It is a film more commonly identified by its English distribution title *The Big Broadcast of 1936*, but actually shot in 1935 for distribution the next year. Gardel appears in a cameo musical number for the Latin American distribution copy and is billed along with Bing Crosby, Jack Oakie, and Ethel Merman. Clearly, the Argentine singer had achieved a transcendence that is perhaps best understood by comparing his transnational status with that of *the other* Paramount international singer, Maurice Chevalier, whom Gardel personally considered to be his professional model.[50]

Cazadores clearly demonstrated that in Gardel, both Paramount and the transnational genre of the *film hispano* had at last found a superstar of the stature of Hollywood's constellation. To be sure, other Hispanic stars of national note had been involved in the *film hispano* projects: the Spaniards Catalina Bárcena and Rosita Díaz Jimeno, the Argentines Mona Maris and Imperio Argentina, and the Mexican Rosita Moreno. What was different in Gardel's case and that of his potential rival, the Mexican José Mojica, was that these were singers, not actors. It was song and music, not the spoken language that bridged the national and regional gap.

Given the commercial logic of the *film hispano* form, Gardel's characters and songs, many of which were written by the singer in collaboration with lyricist Alfredo La Pera, negotiated the local and a wider appeal, unrivaled even by the tango films being shot in Buenos Aires during the early 1930s. The characters embodied some of Gardel's persona and the lyrics used a measure of *lunfardo*, the Buenos Aires argot, but were still comprehensible to a larger Spanish-speaking audience both in Latin America and Spain. The tango repertory Gardel developed worked through a thematic core with a broader appeal. The most striking feature of the Gardel films for tango history was the singer's development of a series of lyrics that appeared to modify the previous lines of development of tango music and verse.[51] Unlike the earlier conventions of the tango, these new songs had a plot and exploited the popular trope of nostalgia ballad: it told a story of loneliness, misfortune, and nostalgia for people and times past, topics that would become staples of the tango lyrical repertory.[52] This quality is perhaps never more in evidence than in one of the Gardelian classics, "*Volver*," from *El día que me quieras*, arguably his most accomplished film. The lyrics speak to sentiments that must have seemed to many a symbolic expression of economic realities of migration, the disaffection from the city and lost loves that formed the back story of the intensified urbanization of Latin American society of the period. The "return" of the lyrics' refrain underscored the urban audience's sense of separation from home culture and a simpler pre-urban past, and the heartfelt desire to "go back." Built on a viable non-imposter star system, the Gardel films successfully combined a highly legible local culture as embodied in the tango tradition that, paradoxically, becomes the locus of aural identification for an increasingly deterritorialized Hispanic world community.

refining the transnational model: mexican ranchera film

The Gardel musical formula had proven a far more successful market model for the maintenance of Hollywood's Spanish-speaking market than had been the multiple-language versions. Historians have often noted how that formula hybridized into a variety of popular Latin American musical film genres within a period of only a few years in the mid-1930s. Besides Argentine tango films, the Brazilian *chanchada*, which combined popular music— especially sambas—dance, and parodic comedy,[53] and the Mexican ranchera film were products of the same period. Of these regionally inflected variants of the Hollywood movie musical, perhaps no single film proved more successful internationally during the decade than Fernando de Fuentes's *Allá en el Rancho Grande* (*Over at the Big Ranch*, 1936), a Mexican work that attained a spectacular commercial success throughout the Spanish-speaking world. In all ways, *Rancho* was unlike the look and sound of Gardel's tango films, for this was a shamelessly folkloric musical that built on the Mexican tradition of rural comedy and song. Yet, it paralleled the broad acceptance of the Gardel films throughout Latin America, Spain, and even in the United States,[54] by the way it proposed a musicalized version of nostalgia for recognizable cultural stereotypes. Indeed, *Rancho*'s plot, characters, and themes tapped into the anxiety in the face of an ever-increasing urbanization of culture which, like Gardel's songs, recirculated across national borders through radio.

The argument has been cogently made that Mexican national cinema was born of a strong "musical vocation,"[55] that is, the twin power of melodrama and the ranchera tradition, *Santa* (Antonio Moreno, 1931) and *Allá en el Rancho Grande*, two early commercial successes of Mexican cinema.[56]

171

In both instances these are traditions that parallel developments of Hollywood genres (melodrama and singing cowboy films) although the local flavor of the Mexican version was, as Monsiváis claims, "protected" by exaggeration and excess, the only resources available given the lack of budget for Hispanic film productions.[57] It is useful to recall that, strictly speaking, melodrama, even in the silent period, was itself a musical genre,[58] with music often picking up the ineffable sentiments of characters and, in both theater and later silent cinema, externalizing these heightened emotions in ways that musicalize the narrative. Even though excess is one of the hallmarks of the melodramatic mode, Mexican melodrama hispanized that mode by bringing this excess to new extremes by emphasizing the intense musicalization of emotions.

At the heart of *Rancho* is a clear mark of cultural and political conservatism. Fernando de Fuentes makes a film that breaks with his own previous politically engaged cinema (*El prisioner trece; El compadre Mendoza; Vámonos con Pancho Villa*) through a melodramatic glorification of a pre-modern Arcadian fantasy which, as Emilio García Riera maintains, served for Mexico's bourgeoisie as a response to the anxiety of Mexican president Lázaro Cardenas's socialist policies of land reform, nationalization of the oil reserves and the formation of labor unions.[59] Though the film's action is clearly set in 1922 and later in the 1930s, its depiction of the idealized good ranch owner who cares for and is revered by his peons is a utopian rewriting of the historical epoch that preceded the Revolution of 1910. Here, as in so many of the film's imitators, nostalgia is paired with the melodramatic. Julianne Burton-Carvajal calls the film "a reactionary fantasy of a return to a patriarchal Eden of pre-Revolutionary simplicity, order and innocence, far from the threats of urbanization and other incursions of modernity."[60]

This traditionalist patriarchal theme, in fact, harks back to a pan-Hispanic narrative that had been the inspiration of Argentine and Spanish silent films (*Nobleza gaucha* (*Gaucho Chivalry*, 1915); *Nobleza baturra* (*Rustic Chivalry*, 1925, 1936)). Florián Rey's 1936 remake of his own popular Spanish silent film, which itself was a clear remake of the Argentine source, premiered in Mexico just months before the scripting of *Rancho Grande*. Indications are that de Fuentes saw the Rey film and consciously imitated aspects of the atavistic honor code in his plot. In this reactionary mold, the work of traditionalist ideology is carried out through the series of musical numbers that "stage" patriarchal values and prompt the real audience's nostalgia for an imagined lost time. What is most striking about this genealogical strain is its cinematic circulation across borders. Acknowledging a broad transnational audience, the film's hybrid sources and international success reflect in striking ways the cultural traditions of exchange within Hispanic culture that belies nationalist rivalries between Hispanic countries. De Fuentes's film operates as a pastiche of the familiar, a feature that seemed to endear it all the more to audiences as it synthesized a variety of cultural formulas. As in Florián

Rey's film, the plot recalls the medieval tradition of the *derecho de pernado* ("right of first night"), the landowner's privilege. Musically, the film draws from rural song traditions, even using as its title a popular song that by 1936 was already an old standard in Mexico. As well, it relies on patterns of cultural stereotyping, even including the hoary Mexican hat dance, the *jarabe tapatío*.

The reactionary essence and clichéd detailed of *Rancho* are not at all accidental. In an effort to garner a domestic market in the face of Mexican cinema's economic collapse before the onslaught of Hollywood's films,[61] de Fuentes evokes an imaginary time and place that rhapsodized the bucolic, rural past. From the opening shots of the hacienda in 1922, set against the backdrop of Gabriel Figueroa's postcard imagery of billowing clouds, the film not only ignores the present, but also idealizes the patriarchal past. In its insistence on the attractiveness of a rustic paradise insistently expressed through popular song, the film seemed to acknowledge the off-screen tension between the rural and the urban expressed through the competing popularity of Mexican bolero music and the more culturally conservative ranchera music as these vied for radio audiences from the mid-1930s onward.[62]

In terms of the film's echoing of popular tastes in recorded and broadcast music, it is worth noting the star presence of Tito Guízar, a well-known and attractive singer of the day, who had lived in New York and had built a career in New York radio, singing Mexican ballads in the person of *El charro alegre* (*The Happy Cowboy*).[63] It would be Guízar, in fact, who convinced de Fuentes to change the original title for the film from "Cruz," the heroine's name, to *Allá en el Rancho Grande*, based on the centrality of the well-known song to the plot.

Fitting with its conservative ideological message is the film's abundance of clichéd cultural customs and "local flavor" that were so sorely lacking in the Gardel films. Cockfights, mariachi singers, folkloric dances, and a series of subplots built around picturesque characters, such as comic sidekicks and uppity maids add a conspicuous humorous dimension to the film. Eduardo de la Vega Alfaro notes the theatrical origins of the film in the *teatro de revista*, musical reviews of the 1920s. The dialogue of secondary characters is marked by a highly stylized Mexican Spanish that is both stagey and also humorous.[64] This hybridity of textual sources served to reinforce the cultural specificity of a Spanish-language tradition, even as it appeared to imitate the singing-cowboy genre universalized by Hollywood. De la Vega Alfaro sees some of the importance of the film's innovative use of Mexican folklore and popular music: "de Fuentes's film presented the Mexican national identity in a positive light, whilst also reflecting positively on all of Latin America which, of course, resembled Mexico in social composition and culture."[65] Ana López similarly notes that paradox wherein the cultural specificity of this film and other Mexican films should have limited the transnational circulation of Mexican cinema yet actually contributed to that transnational Hispanic appeal: "The Mexican cinema's obsessive reworking of national characteristics was profoundly appealing to other nations that were perhaps less archetypically defined, less powerful and/or less visible."[66]

The attractiveness of *Rancho Grande*'s national and folkloric elements was also aided by the development of radio in Mexico, especially Emilio Azcárraga's radio XEW in Mexico City, which reinforced many of the ideological and cultural patterns that helped circulate the identificatory musical sounds of Mexican cinema.[67] A series of laws promulgated between 1932 and 1936 required that at least 25 percent of the music played on Mexican radio stations consist of "typically Mexican" songs.[68] Azcárraga's 200 kilowatt XEW, the most powerful radio signal in Latin America at the time, which could be received as far away as Havana, was partially owned by RCA. "Ranchera music, though frequently sad, was set in the warmth, sunlight, and comfort of northern Mexico in some impossibly prosperous past."[69] The musical tradition that comes into play through de Fuentes's film, like the Gardel phenomenon that preceded it, is one built upon the refiguring of an already-established cultural stereotype that emphasizes a nostalgic experience. Identified with the charisma of its singers and rooted in a seemingly personal nostalgic theme—amorous love and love of the land—its status as a movie discourse is reinforced by the echo of its circulation through the mass-media technology of radio.

Rancho Grande was initially more popular internationally than in Mexico, first for Spanish-speaking audiences living in the United States and only subsequently for Mexican and Latin American audiences. The reaction in Spain, though years after the film had become a hit in Latin America and won Mexico its first international film awards at the Venice Film Festival, proved equally enticing. Marina Díaz López conjectures that the extra-textual combination of a recollection of a simple past at a time of contemporary strife, with a heavy textual emphasis on the well-established music tradition that had been reinforced through other sound media, stabilized and universalized the genre within the Spanish-speaking world (28). Thanks to the extraordinary success of *Rancho Grande* and its imitators—nearly twenty within the first two years of the film's release—by the decade's end, Mexican cinema became the principal Hispanic export film industry, creating a dynamic of cultural exchange with Spanish America without precedent.

the competitive politics of cultural identification in the 1940s

The 1940s marked a curious and contradictory new chapter in the ongoing competition between Hollywood and Latin American film industries. Just as the Mexican ranchera musical was flourishing throughout the region, Hollywood studios revived its own Hispanic musical vogue of the early 1930s (*Flying Down to Rio*, etc.) as a "pan-American" genre in a series of films that coincided with and exploited the Roosevelt administration's "Good Neighbor" policy. Exotic yet inviting Latin American settings and music were highlighted in such films as *Down Argentine Way* (Irving Cummings, 1940), *Weekend in Havana* (Walter Lang, 1941) and *The Gang's All Here* (Busby Berkeley, 1943). In Hollywood's version of Latin American ethnography, the Portuguese-speaking Brazilian bombshell, Carmen Miranda, served as a stand-in for the prototypical Latin American, reviving the argument that Hollywood was insensitive to regional cultural difference.[70]

Hollywood's Latin American vogue found very little enthusiasm among Latin America audiences since home-grown productions boasted stars who could really speak and sing in Spanish. The decade of the 1940s, in fact, witnessed the broader diffusion of the transnational Hispanic musical as a "native" genre, mirroring and yet competing with Hollywood's musical forms. While Hollywood's formula was largely built on a touristy depiction of colorful Latin American stereotypes, the Latin American mode of address to its film audiences was through the nostalgic and sentimental appeal of the Latin "difference." We may see this, for instance in the movie career of Pedro Infante, who had been performing on Mexican radio since the mid-1930s. Infante made his screen debut as a singing cowboy in Juan José Segura's *Cuando habla en corazón* (*When the Heart Speaks*, 1943), a blatant imitation of *Rancho Grande*. By the decade's end, he would be the most internationally acclaimed of ranchera singers, in many ways a Hispanic superstar of the transnational appeal of Gardel. Part of the cultural stereotype employed by Infante and the other major singing cowboy of Mexican cinema of the period, Jorge Negrete, was that, besides riding and singing, as did Gene Autry and other Hollywood cowboys, they both cultivated an off-screen persona as womanizers and often mirrored that role in the characters they played. Interestingly, in these film plots, their seductive powers were often linked to their singing performance. Affirming Latin masculine traits and the force of patriarchal culture, these figures embodied the ranchera tradition's ideological investment in a nostalgia mode that repudiated the modernity of urban and particularly US culture.

By the 1940s, the Mexican film industry had become the Mecca of this transnational Latin American film industry. The country was a cultural and political "buffer" between the United States and Latin America. With the US efforts to destabilize the film industry of the Nazi-sympathizing Argentine regime, Mexican cinema enjoyed a major infusion of US industrial capital for its own technological modernization, thus converting it during World War II into a crucial "space in between." That is, Mexican films translated North American modernity into a Hispanic idiom, while enacting the Good Neighbor policy through varied film plots.[71] Given the appeal of Mexican films for hemispheric export, and the collapse of competition from Europe, most notably Spain, which had just gone through a devastating civil war that destroyed earlier efforts at a transnational film industry, Mexican cinema was able to maintain a strong industrial and financial base. Geopolitics and industrial power thereby helped encourage a symbolic migration of Latin American music to Mexico through a form of talent transfer hitherto unseen in the Hispanic world. As Ana López notes:

> Mexican cinema became the great musical equalizer, regularly featuring and absorbing popular Latin American rhythms and performers: Argentine tangos (via Libertad Lamarque), Cuban rumbas (Ninón Sevilla, María Antonia Pons, Blanquita Amaro), sones (Rita Montaner), and later mambos, cha cha chas, and even sambas.[72]

As a result, according to López, "Mexican cinema outside the ranchera genre posited Latin American music and dance as general markers of a "Latinness" increasingly dissociated from any national specificity."[73]

Again, it was radio that first picked up this cinematic trope and recirculated it across borders. Monsiváis sees radio, cinema, and sound recordings becoming complementary expressions of the same transnational aural identity during this period:

> Technology is fundamental to this process. The film and radio industries provide songs with landscapes that last. And radio, that most persuasive of media, chooses the voices and styles to be privileged, especially from 1930 onwards, after the establishment of the XEW radio station empire.[74]

It was not the ranchera song, however, so deeply rooted in a Mexican cultural imaginary, but the hybridized bolero, that facilitated the development of the decade's transnational musical sound. As Monsiváis argues, before it became an industry, the bolero "was a matter of collective creation."[75] Ethnomusicologists trace the diverse genealogy of the genre from its Spanish origins to its transformation into a Cuban musical and dance form, finally to its appropriation within Mexican cinema and radio.[76]

The rise of the bolero coincided historically with the emergence of sound-based technologies of mass media. The "golden age" of bolero music, 1930–60, nearly perfectly coincides with the *época de oro* of Mexico's export film industry. As well, that epoch is marked by the emergence of Agustín Lara and concludes with the international careers of the trio Los Panchos, whose formulation of the Mexican bolero style was inherited from Lara and who, like Lara, first came to prominence in Mexico through their performances on XEW. Los Panchos appeared in sixteen films during the 1940s and 1950s.

In the first two decades since its founding in 1929, XEW forged a role as the regional arbiter of popular musical tastes. Its impact reached its zenith in the early 1940s, precisely at the moment in which Mexico became the dynamo promoting and circulating transnational popular-cultural formulas on screen and on the airwaves. Film and radio disseminated the bolero and, as Monsiváis argues, contributed to the end of the isolationism of local cultures by proposing a "new sensibility" (romanticism in the age of technology), dictating through the two sound media the "rules of popular sounds."[77]

As well, the bolero is insistently identified with urban culture and therefore modernity. Both Lara's music and the composer himself were destined to become a ubiquitous presence in mass media, especially with his own weekly radio program, *La hora íntima* (*The Intimate Hour*), on Mexico's XEW, "the voice of Latin America from Mexico," as it proclaimed itself.[78] Radio had helped forge the bolero as a popular musical form increasingly identified with lower-class tastes and mores.[79] Cinema, however, worked as a bridge to transcend both class and region as films addressed an increasingly wider transnational audience. The quintessential expression of the bolero on screen was the so-called fichera film, which Eduardo de la Vega Alfaro labels "brothel-cabaret melodramas."[80] These Mexican films of the late 1940s are often identified by film and cultural historians with the modernization project of the government of Miguel Alemán (1946–52). Through their melodramatic discourse, fichera films reflected the rise of urban culture and the breakdown of traditional social values as presumed by the *Mexico profundo* of the ranchera tradition. The association of dance and dancehall with prostitution was no accident. It was viewed as embodying the broader social impact of modernization in Mexico and throughout Latin America and, among other things, the changing status of women and their embrace of new social and economic freedom.[81] In Ismael Rodríguez's *Nosotros, los pobres* (*We, the Poor*, 1947) and Alberto Gout's *Aventurera* (*Adventuress*, 1949), the cabaret narratives reinscribed the migration from rural areas to the city. *Nosotros los pobres*, by some accounts the most popular Mexican film of the 1940s, is Pedro Infante's first film to be set in an urban space. Implicitly, it poses the narrative of urban migration, while the story of the protagonist's sister as a prostitute makes clear links to the cabaret tradition.[82]

The fichera genre depicted urban settings as a new transnational "cosmopolitan" space that contrasted sharply with the ranchera mise-en-scene of rural traditionalism. In one characteristic film of the period, Emilio "Indio" Fernández's *Salón México* (1948), the formal and emotionally restrained Mexican danzón, performed by light-skinned women, is juxtaposed with the more sensuous rumbas and other African Cuban dance numbers performed by dark-skinned women. The film's heroine, Mercedes, played by the Argentine-born Marga López, seems to fit easily into a narrative in which ethnic and national origins are subservient to the pan-Latin melodramatic scenarios of song, dance and story. Such hybridity of music and performers, while generally underscoring the modernizing effects of human migration, also mirrors the Mexican film industry's transnational market ambitions as it stages the narrative of modernization through the mise-en-scene of the cabaret.

Nowhere is this utopian transnational communal space more in evidence than in Alberto Gout's *Aventurera*, a work often singled out as the most extreme version of the cultural excess that distinguished the cabaret film. The transnational elements are strikingly present in the Cuban-born rumbera star, Ninón Sevilla, here playing a girl from the provinces who winds up as a dance hall performer singing to the accompaniment of the Cuban orchestra of Dámaso Pérez Prado. The film's musicalized melodrama not only recirculates the Mexican bolero to wider film audiences but also includes an eclectic repertory of musical genres with notable transnational markets. For instance, the bolero trio Los Panchos, whose popularity as recording artists and performers had already established them in the United States and Latin America, sings sentimental boleros that contrast with an elaborately staged and raucous samba, a version of "Chiquita Banana" that is a clear imitation of Carmen Miranda, who, by this point, was Hollywood's version of the pan-Hispanic singing bombshell. In this way *Aventurera* self-consciously inscribes the competitive discourses of Hollywood and Latin American musical performances within the same filmic space. Indeed, rather than a neocolonial imitation of Hollywood's Latin musicals, as some have characterized the film, the version of the cabaret proposed by Gout appears as an unbounded imagined space in which coherent linear narratives are discarded and national borders dissolve. Such a film addresses the Hispanic audience by playing another imposter Latin American style.

The nature of the textual imposture that guides *Aventurera* returns us to the tension of markets and audiences shaped around cultural marks of identity. As with Argentine tango cinema, the ranchera and bolero-cabaret traditions utilize cultural circuits of multimedia address to an audience that transcended the national borders. Through their audience's collectivized memory of the sounds of a shared cultural identity, the Latin American musical of the period entered a distinctly Latin American version of modernity. Its patterns continually flirted with the imposter "other," continually marking a form of nostalgia for an idealized past.

178

the political afterlife of popular latin american musical traditions

Carlos Monsiváis begins his 1997 essay on the history of the bolero with what he calls a "postmodern prologue" in which he evokes a moment in Pedro

Almodóvar's Spanish melodrama, *Tacones lejanos* (*High Heels*, 1993) in which Marisa Paredes as a torch singer returning to Madrid from a long sojourn in Mexico, makes her triumphant return to the Spanish stage by singing Agustín Lara's *Piensa en mí* (*Think of Me*). For Monsiváis, the moment is intended to underscore the temporal displacements that are woven into the cinematic-musical conjuncture at the heart of the bolero and of Latin American musical cinema generally: "we know immediately: the bolero has become the essence of the past—not of the real past, not even of the idealized past, but of everything that was before Progress destroyed sentimentalism ('cursilería')."[83]

His observations may well have been inspired by a series of films of the 1980s and early 1990s that not only recycled the Latin American melodies that had built that earlier transnational cinematic-musical discourse but which dramatize within their plotting and stories the central narrative of aural migration. Fernando Solanas's French-Argentine co-production, *Tangos: el exilio de Gardel* (1986), set entirely in Paris, opens up a new wave of tango cinema that recalls the past as a way of reshaping contemporary Argentine and Latin American politics. The neo-tango craze is eventually picked up in another international co-production, Carlos Saura's *Tango* (1997), a film whose Argentine-Spanish-Italian funding suggests the extent of this transnational genre. In Mexico, María Novarro's *Danzón* (1991) evokes a new feminist cinema that is rooted in the shadows of the fichera film's dance hall in which the heroine's pursuit of a dance partner inevitably becomes a broader nostalgic exploration of musical and cultural origins for Mexicans who, over recent decades, have come to see themselves as a largely urbanized nation. Saura's countryman, Pedro Almodóvar, brings ever wider audiences to rediscover the bolero as a new version of transnational Hispanic cultural identity, now closely tied to a gay sensibility. In Almodóvar's filmography, in fact, Latin American boleros sung by Lucho Gatica, Chavela Vargas, Lola Beltrán, and La Lupe, precede the Augustín Lara song Monsiváis describes. Notably, in the Spanish filmmaker's appropriations of Latin American song, music becomes the pervasive strategy through which protagonists reshape their emotional and even social identity. That extraterritorial use of Latin American songs refigures the transnational trajectory Latin America's musical past of some forty years earlier and gives evidence of the broader aural identification that belies that tradition. At the same time, as Almodóvar's cinema reflects, it becomes an essential part of the postmodern aesthetic made all the more politically pressing in the face of encroaching globalization.[84]

What is striking about these "translations" of musicalized Hispanic cinema in recent decades is their insistent linkage to the cluster of musical motifs identified with urbanization and modernity into what García Canclini now terms Latin American postmodern identities.[85] In the face of globalized market culture, with its denigration of communities on the margins as cheap labor, this resurgence of older cultural formulas responds to political forces much deeper than mere artistic style. For contemporary Hispanic filmmakers, those now-classic musical tropes become a lingua franca through which filmmakers attempt to address a geographically diverse imagined community of Latinos. This form of musicalized cinema (as opposed to the Hollywood genre of the "movie musical") foment in audiences a sense of cultural affiliation, expressing through the symbolic migrations of sounds and images from the nostalgic and sentimental past a newly emerging political sense of the Hispanic community that resists homogenization by multinational commercial interests.

As the previous discussion suggests, a cluster of transnational meanings has privileged certain types of Latin American music and has been used precisely in that slipzone between political action and cultural solidarity. In the wake of the multiple economic crises and social instability that plagued the region and decimated the once stable "natural" audiences of Latin American cinema in the 1980s,[86] the appeal of the musical sounds of a transnational identity is rekindled in a series of films that effectively refigure the musical genealogies of the early sound decades in new contexts. The exotic music of the tropics is recaptured in a work of artistic preservation in Wim Wenders and Ry Cooter's *Buena Vista Social Club* which, far from fossilizing African Cuban jazz, has had the effect of promoting a similar migration of sounds of identity through a series of other diasporic Caribbean-based musical documentaries. These include Fernando Trueba's *Calle 54* (1993), Alex Wolfe's *Santo Domingo Blues: Los tígueres de la bachata* (2004), and, among fiction films, Benito Zambrano's Spanish-Cuban-French co-production, *Havana Blues* (2005).

To some degree these films, not unlike their 1930s predecessors, are works of nostalgic recuperation. They evoke the disembodied past as a form of reassurance in the face of profound cultural and economic displacement. It would easy to dismiss these productions, therefore, as efforts to exploit marketing strategies, not unlike the original *films hispanos*. At the same time, they express a deeper problematic within which the consumption of popular culture operates as a dynamic activity that reaffirms an otherwise fragmented and dispersed cultural identity. In its contemporary resurgence, the special privilege of musicalized cinema does not lie in the cinematic medium's appropriation of the sounds of the transnational Hispanic identity, but rather, conversely, the Hispanic transnational community's embrace of cinema's construction of identity, "its artistic, folkloric, and media narratives that shapes it [as these] are realized and transformed within sociohistorical conditions that cannot be reduced to their mise-en-scene."[87] As the cliché has it, musicalized cinema becomes the eyes and ears of newly emerging cultural and political identities.

Beginning in the early sound era, with the transformation of musical folklore into the product of mass media, cinema came to occupy a crucial space of circulation that enabled its move within national borders and also across the transnational space that traced the routes of Hispanic migration culture. Precisely because of its status as mass media and mass culture, musical cinema has been able to evolve through a mode of address that ultimately proves ideal for the articulation of the Hispanic transnational communal identity in the continual process of transformation and adjustment to modernity.

notes

1. The lyrics of the song derive from anonymous Cuban folkloric sources:

   Mamá yo quiero saber
   ¿De dónde son los cantantes?
   Que los encuentro galantes
   y los quiero conocer
   Son sus trobas fascinantes que me las quiero aprender

   ¿De dónde serán? Ay mamá
   ¿Serán de La Habana?
   ¿Serán de Santiago
   Tierra Soberana?

   (Mama, I want to know
   Where do the singers come from?
   I find them gallant and I want to meet them.
   Their songs are fascinating and I want to learn them.
   Where could they be from? Ay, Mama!
   Could they be from Havana?
   Could they be from the sovereign land of Santiago?)

2. Juan Flores, *From Bomba to Hip-Hop: Puerto Rican Culture and Latino Identity* (New York: Columbia University Press, 2000), 17.
3. Walter Benjamin, *Illuminations: Essays and Reflections*, ed. and introd. Hannah Arendt, trans. Harry Zohn (New York: Schocken, 1969), 71.
4. Michael Chanan, *The Cuban Image* (London: British Film Institute, 1985), 264.
5. Ángel Rama, *The Lettered City*, ed. and trans. John Charles Chasteen (Durham, NC: Duke University Press, 1996), 103.
6. Flores, *From Bomba to Hip-Hop*, 52–53.
7. Carlos Monsiváis, *Aires de familia* (Barcelona: Anagrama, 2000), 155–61.
8. Rama, *The Lettered City*, 79.
9. Jesús Martín-Barbero, *De los medios a las mediaciones: comunicación, cultura y hegemonía* (Mexico: G. Gili, 1987), 171.
10. Noël Valis has examined an identical linkage between the geographic displacement producing nostalgia in the continuing rural exodus in Spain that associated with absence and loss and that elides with notions of home and homeland. This is a process that begins in the nineteenth century: "Nostalgia intensified when more and more people moved from their villages to cities, losing that topographical, sense-oriented identification with the particular landscapes of their lives." See Noël Valis, *The Culture of Cursilería: Bad Taste, Kitsch and Class in Modern Spain* (Durham, NC: Duke University Press, 2002), 207.

181

11. Martín-Barbero, *De los medios a las mediaciones*, 186–89.

12. Paulo Antonio Paranaguá, "The Sound Era in Latin America," in *Latin American Visions: Catalogue* (Philadelphia, PA: The Neighborhood Film/Video Project of International House, 1989), 13–19, p. 15.

13. Vanessa Knights, "Modernity, Modernization and Melodrama: The Bolero in Mexico in the 1930s and 1940s," in *Contemporary Latin American Cultural Studies*, eds. Stephen Hart and Richard Young (London: Arnold, 2003), 127–39, p. 129.

14. Jorge Finkielman, *The Film Industry in Argentina* (Jefferson, NC: McFarland Press, 2004), 109.

15. Ibid., 117–18.

16. Martín-Barbero, *De los medios a las mediaciones*, 64–65.

17. The stabilization of commercially viable sound cinema by the end of the 1920s was the result of extensive corporate investments in both Europe and the US that involved the amalgamation of sound-era technologies including the radio and the record industries. See Gleason L. Archer, *History of Radio to 1926* (New York: Arno Press and *New York Times*, 1971), 233–39; also Charles O'Brien, *Cinema's Conversion to Sound: Technology and Film Style in France and the US* (Bloomington, IN: Indiana University Press, 2005), 28.

18. Martín-Barbero, *De los medios a las mediaciones*, 65.

19. Monsiváis, *Aires de familia*, 192.

20. Ana M. López, "Of Rhythms and Borders," in *Everynight Life: Culture and Dance in Latin/o America*, ed. Celeste Fraser Delgado and José Esteban Muñoz (Durham, NC: Duke University Press, 1997), 310–11.

21. John Mowitt, "The Sound of Music in the Era of its Electronic Reproducibility," in *Music and Society: The Politics of Composition, Performance and Reception*, ed. Richard Leppert and Susan McClary (Cambridge: Cambridge University Press, 1987), 173–97, p. 178.

22. Ibid., 179.

23. Ibid., 185.

24. Ibid., 183.

25. Néstor García Canclini, *La globalización imaginada* (Mexico: Paidós Mexicana, 1999), 31–32.

26. Néstor García Canclini, *Consumers and Citizens: Globalization and Multicultural Conflicts* (Minneapolis, MN: University of Minnesota Press, 2001), 29.

27. Flores, *From Bomba to Hip-Hop*, 201.

28. Lluís Bonet and Albert de Gregorio, "La industria cultural española en América Latina," in *Las industrias culturales en la integración latinoamericana*, ed. Néstor García-Canclini and Carlos Moncloa (Mexico: Grijalbo, 1999), 87–128, p. 87.

29. Walter Mignolo, *Local Histories/Global Designs: Coloniality, Subaltern Knowledges, and Border Thinking* (Princeton, NJ: Princeton University Press, 2000), 67.

30. Ibid., 219.

31. Alan Williams, "Historical and Theoretical Issues Related to the Coming of Recorded Sound to the Cinema," in *Sound Theory Sound Practice*, ed. Rick Altman (New York: Routledge, 1992), 126–37, p. 136.

32. See, for instance, John King, *Magical Reels: A History of Cinema in Latin America* (London: Verso, 1990), 31–32; Paulo Antonio Paranaguá, "América Latina busca su imagen," *Historia general del cine*, Vol. 10 (Madrid: Cátedra Signo e imagen, 1996), 205–393, pp. 216–22.

33. Agustín Sánchez Vidal, *El cine de Florián Rey* (Zaragoza, Spain: Caja de Ahorros La Inmaculada, 1991), 148.

34. Ginette Vincendeau. "Hollywood Babel: The Coming of Sound and the Multiple-Language Version," in *"Film Europe" and "Film America": Cinema, Commerce and Cultural Exchange 1920–1939* (Exeter, UK: University of Exeter Press, 1999), 207–24, pp. 208–10.

35. Finkielman, *The Film Industry in Argentina*, 131.

36. Monsiváis, *Aires de familia*, 61.

37. Paranaguá, "América Latina busca su imagen," 222.

38. Simon Collier, "Carlos Gardel and the Cinema," in *The Garden of Forking Paths: Argentine Cinema*, ed. John King and Nissa Torrents (London: British Film Institute, 1988), 16.

39. Donald S. Castro, "Popular Culture as a Source for the Historian: Why Carlos Gardel?" in *Studies in Latin American Popular Culture* 5 (1986): 144–62, p. 151.

40. Gardel's status as the foremost international interpreter of the tango, however, did set him apart from the situation of his two closest and relevant rivals or models, Al Jolson and Maurice Chevalier, in that his presence, besides being that of an entertainer, was also as a socio-cultural icon identified with a cluster of identifiable cultural scenarios that included machismo, social marginalization and a nostalgia for home and mother that resonated for audiences throughout the Spanish-speaking world. See Castro, "Popular Culture as a Source for the Historian."

41. Paulo Antonio Paranaguá notes that the use of "national" music at film screenings in Argentina began around 1924 with the inclusion of well-known musicians in the program who would perform between screenings of silent films. As he contends: "The audience frequented theaters as much for the music as for the images." See Paranaguá, "The Sound Era in Latin America," 13–19.

42. Finkielman, *The Film Industry in Argentina*, 112–13.

43. Martin Barnier, *Des films français made in Hollywood: Les versions multiples 1929–1935* (Paris: L'Harmattan, 2004), 58.

44. Paranaguá, "América Latina busca su imagen," 222.

45. O'Brien, *Cinema's Conversion to Sound*, 72.

46. Castro, "Popular Culture as a Source for the Historian," 145–49.

47. Nataša Ďurovičová, "Paramount und das homöostatische Moment: MLV-Produktion in Joinville," in *Babylon in Europa: Mehrsprachen-Versionen der 1930en Jahre*, ed. Jan Distelmeyer (Munich: text+kritik, 2006), 65–78, p. 71.

48. Luciano Monteagudo and Verónica Bucich, *Carlos Gardel y el primer cine sonoro argentino* (Huesca, Spain: Filmoteca de Andalucía, Chicago Latino Film Festival y Festival de Cine de Huesca, 2001), 31.

49. Collier, "Carlos Gardel and the Cinema," 18.

50. Ibid., 21.

51. Finkielman, *The Film Industry in Argentina*, 117.

52. Monteagudo and Bucich, *Carlos Gardel y el primer cine sonoro argentino*, 90.

53. López, "Of Rhythms and Borders," 321.

54. Its New York run occasioned the first-ever subtitling of a Mexican film into English. See Marina Díaz López, "La comedia ranchera como género musical," in *Cinémas Amérique Latine* 8 (2000), 27–40.

55. Juan Antonio Brennan, "La música cinematográfica," in *Cinémas Amérique Latine* 8 (2000), 21.

56. It is worth noting in this context that even *Santa*, an urban melodrama set in a Mexico City brothel, contained a geographically diverse set of musical numbers, including the title bolero, by Mexican composer Agustín Lara, an American-style foxtrot, and even a Spanish flamenco dance number.

57. Monsiváis, *Aires de familia*, 61.

58. Rick Altman, *Silent Film Sound* (New York: Columbia University Press, 2004), 36.

59. Emilio García Riera, *Historia documental del cine mexicano*, Vol. I: 1929–37 (Guadalajara, Mexico: Universidad de Guadalajara, 1992), 130–31.

60. Julianne Burton-Carvajal, "Mexican Melodramas of Patriarchy: Specificity of a Transcultural Form," in *Framing Latin American Cinema: Contemporary Critical Perspectives*, ed. Ann Marie Stock, trans. Ambrosio Fornet (Minneapolis, MN: University of Minnesota Press, 1997), 211.

61. García Riera, *Historia documental del cine mexicano*, 212–13.

62. Anne Rubenstein, "Bodies, Cities, Cinema: Pedro Infantes' Death as Political Spectacle," in *Fragments of a Golden Age: The Politics of Culture in Mexico Since 1940*, ed. Gilbert Joseph, Anne Rubenstein, and Eric Zolov (Durham, NC: Duke University Press, 2001), 210.

63. Díaz López, "La comedia ranchera como género musical," 30.

64. Eduardo de la Vega Alvaro, "Allá en el Rancho Grande, Over There on the Big Ranch," in *The Cinema of Latin America*, ed. Alberto Elena and Marina Díaz López (London: Wallflower Press, 2002), 25–33, p. 31.

65. Ibid., 32.

66. Ana M. López, "A Cinema for the Continent," in *The Mexican Cinema Project*. ed. Chon A. Noriega and Steven Ricci (Los Angeles, CA: UCLA Film and Television Archives, 1994), 8.

67. Rubenstein, "Bodies, Cities, Cinema," 210.

68. Anne Rubenstein, "Mass Media and Popular Culture in the Post-revolutionary Era," in *The Oxford History of Mexico*, ed. Michael C. Meyer and William H. Beezley (Oxford: Oxford University Press, 2000), 637–70, p. 646.

69. Rubenstein, "Bodies, Cities, Cinema," 210.

70. Some studios, such as Twentieth Century Fox, seemed to have learned the lesson of the *films hispanos* since it made a point of dubbing its *Mark of Zorro* (1940) in six Spanish regional accents for Mexican, Chilean, Venezuelan, Cuban and Castilian audiences. See Luis Reyes and Peter Rubie, *Hispanics in Hollywood: A Celebration of 100 Years in Film and Television* (Los Angeles, CA: Lone Eagle, 2000), 19.

71. Enrique Krauze, *Mexico: Biography of Power*, trans. Hank Heifitz (New York: Harper Perennial, 1997), 520.

72. López, "Of Rhythms and Borders," 324.

73. Ibid., 324–25.

74. Carlos Monsiváis, *Mexican Postcard* (London: Verso, 1997), 190.

75. Ibid., 173.

76. Knights, "Modernity, Modernization and Melodrama," 128–29.

77. Monsiváis, *Aires de familia*, 215.

78. Monsiváis, *Mexican Postcard*, 190.

79. Knights, "Modernity, Modernization and Melodrama," 133.

80. Eduardo de la Vega Alvaro, "Aventurera," in *Tierra en trance: el cine latinoamericano en 100 películas*, ed. Alberto Elena and Marina Díaz López (Madrid: Alianza, 1999), 101.

81. Joanne Hershfield, *Mexican Cinema/Mexican Women 1940–1950* (Tucson, AZ: University of Arizona Press, 1996), 100.

82. Knights, "Modernity, Modernization and Melodrama," 135.

83. Monsiváis, *Mexican Postcard*, 167.

84. Interestingly, Almodóvar's most recent film, *Volver* (*To Return*, 2006) takes its

title from the Gardel tango and recontextualizes that song as a Spanish flamenco *bullería* rendition, which evokes the continuity between Gardel's Latin American past and Spanish aural culture built on the popularity of Latin American songs on radio.

85. García Canclini, *Consumers and Citizens*, 28–29.
86. According to Octavio Getino, between 1979 and 1989, through the advent of new technologies (video, satellite, cable), as well as intensified economic and social instabilities, Latin American cinema witnessed the loss of half of its domestic and regional market. See Octavio Getino, *La tercera mirada: Panorama del audiovisual latinoamericano* (Buenos Aires: Paidós, 1996), 150.
87. García Canclini, *Consumers and Citizens*, 96.

how movies

move

n i n e

(between hong kong

and bulawayo, between

screen and stage . . .)

l e s l e y   s t e r n

once upon a time in africa

Let us begin in Africa.

Bulawayo, Zimbabwe, 1995:

> That's what we watched a lot in our community hall—
> kung fu, kung fu, kung fu. And that's the only thing that
> was not taught in the townships. And then we asked
> ourselves: what should we do? Oh but Cont, you been
> learning karate from these Rhodesian masters and now
> they've left for South Africa, so why don't you introduce
> some classes, do karate with the children. And so I started
> with one child, two or three, and it grew to four or five,
> and by 1980 there were fifty-six of these children . . . [one
> day we had to relinquish our rehearsal space to a drama
> group, and we told ourselves . . .]. So we know karate,
> and if this man teaches us acting then we can join the

two and make our own kung fu films. So that's how we
started.

(Cont Mhlanga telling the story of how

his performance group, Amakhosi, began in the

early 1980s, but with its origins in the 1970s[1])

Mombasa, Kenya, the 1970s:

> We live over here in Pandya House, a tenement building with
> shops and offices below. Over here is the Regal Cinema
> which exclusively plays American shoot-'em-ups, Italian
> spaghetti shoot-'em-ups, and Chinese Kung-Fu-'em-ups...
> In this theater Eastwood is badass, McQueen is cool, Bronson
> is tough, and Bruce Lee can kick all their asses. Shane and
> Shaft and Superfly and Cleopatra Jones.

(Shishir Kurup, a Los Angeles-based Asian American

performance artist, in the opening of

his performance piece "in Between Space"[2])

Dar es Salaam, Tanzania—a memory of what it was like in the 1970s:

> Bruce Lee's *Enter the Dragon* (1973) generated a passion for
> kung fu among urban South Asian-Tanzanian youth.
> Popular song lyrics like "Everybody was kung fu fighting,"
> posters of Bruce Lee on the streets of Dar es Salaam, the
> fetish for the nunchaku and black-cloth Maoist shoes,
> the speedy martial movements of beachside wrestling
> matches, side kicks, and one-finger push-ups—all were
> extravagantly popular. The Mao suits worn by groups of
> railway technicians from China and North Korea brought
> to Tanzania during the '70s—and worn by Lee as well
> carried a certain chic for local Asian youth. Images of
> Jim Kelly, Fred Williamson, Tamara Dobson, Pam Grier,
> Grace Jones, and Richard Roundtree also circulated as
> representations of "America" or the "West."

(May Joseph, in her book *Nomadic Identities*[3])

Let us begin in Africa. These opening voices all evoke a zone of intersection,
a realm where various cultural movements and modes criss cross: the
cinematic and popular culture, film and theater, fashion and performance,
Hollywood and kung fu, karate and pedagogy, Hong Kong and Africa. None
of these voices speaks from or for African cinema, but all of them are
concerned with the cinema in Africa. All of them gesture towards ways in
which an "other" cinema—specifically kung fu—is deployed in the shaping
of a local public sphere. Bulawayo will be my focus in this chapter. But I
begin more generally in Africa—a continent, a region—both in order to

situate Bulawayo within a larger context than the nation (though smaller than the global), and to signal that what follows will be grounded less in the question of influence and cinematic migration (the influence of Hong Kong action cinema on localized film cultures all over the globe, say), and more on the question of what a particular community, shaped by and in response to a particular history, has done with cinema, specifically Hong Kong action cinema.

In Bulawayo, the second largest city in Zimbabwe (a country in sub-Saharan Africa, adjoining South Africa, Mozambique, Zambia, and Botswana) the appropriation and transmutation of kung fu cinema took a quite specific direction, materializing in the development of a very distinctive, extraordinarily vibrant, mode of African township theater. The catalyst for this movement was a group called Amakhosi, whose members, inspired by kung fu movies which they saw as children and teenagers in the township community halls (in the 1970s, while a guerrilla war of liberation was being waged) learned karate, formed a theater group in the 1980s and incorporated karate and kung fu techniques into their productions. They came to national prominence with a series of politically contentious and fearlessly outspoken plays, calling into question practices and policies of the newly independent government headed by Robert Mugabe. They are still active today.

This chapter has at once a narrow focus, and a broad speculative sweep. It asks: how do movies move? This question is doubly inflected. On the one hand it has to do with the geopolitical: not only with how films circulate, how they are exported and imported, distributed and exhibited, but also with how they move over time (or how their meanings change over time and according to location—where and how they are viewed). On the other hand, it has to do with the aesthetic: about the affective dimension, the capacity of films to move their viewers on a sensory and emotive level.

off the map: searching for the afterlife of movies

Sometimes movies move off the map, both in terms of film studies and in terms of destinations which fall through the net of globalism (primarily because they do not participate in a visible, or measurable, circuit of trade). What happens to films in those shadowy nether regions? Regions where there is no film culture in the sense commonly accepted in the West, no industry, no tangible spin-offs from spectatorship such as reviews, blogs, fan clubs. Regions where, nevertheless, certain globally mobile films or genres resonate with aspects of local culture, enabling fertile transformative practices. These transformative practices might mean a radical remaking of films in the process of which the films themselves appear to reach a dead end, or to disappear off the map. However, although the films do not feed into local *film* cultures, they do intersect with other aspects of the local culture and survive as a kind of ghostly imprint. It is this afterlife of the movies that captures my interest, an interest focused less on the global mobility of films (specifically Hong Kong action cinema), and more on the fertility of the encounter generated in "local" places (in this instance, Bulawayo).[4]

However, the question of the relationship between "global mobility" and "local fertility" cannot be solved simply by inverting the hierarchical relation between the two terms. We need to tackle some of the more difficult questions about the historical conditions that provide for a *resonance*, which make for *fertile ground* and enable certain effects to take root. And in doing this we encounter further questions. How, for instance, do we attend to the particularities of the local without abstracting the object of scrutiny from a larger confluence of cultural, political and aesthetic influences? How can we retain the theoretical dimension of my doubly inflected cinematic "movement" without heading into a cul de sac of vacuous generalization (as in a poetics of kung fu that simply describes the affective dimension, and posits this as the cause of global appeal)?[5] It is only through a critical engagement with particular sites of encounter and mediation between the filmic and the social that the double inflection of cinematic movement can be adequately apprehended, and that the "transnational" can be realized as a useful critical tool.

But how do we ascertain at what scale to pitch our analysis, in such a way that we can illuminate something about the particularity of the social, and about the way films, in a more general sense, move? How do we situate the movement of film in a geopolitical framework of multiple scales and coordinates? How do we apprehend the domestic and parochial ghosts of history that intercept the smooth passage of films around the globe? Underpinning this network of queries (anxieties?) is a curiosity about how we are to understand and describe the formation of alternative public spheres (and film's role therein) in an era characterized as transnational. To pursue this curiosity, I shall suggest, entails detailed attention to how films may circulate, and indeed might be articulated (differently) in social spaces outside the cinema, and outside the rubric of film studies. By this I mean to suggest a way of coming at the subject obliquely, from the margins of film studies, from the shadowy paths traced out by ethnography, local history, political science, cultural studies.[6] Treading circuitously we might begin to approach those places in the South, places in the Second and Third Worlds, where films may have little economic life but where they enjoy an "afterlife" with rich cultural ramifications.

moving between: between bulawayo and hong kong

Bulawayo and Hong Kong: two places, two imaginary cities, two metonyms for kung fu. Imaginative, that is, in that they exist for each other in a phantasmatic or fictive guise. But they are also real cities, historically and geographically located. It is in this space between history and imaginative possibility, as well as in geographical space, that the relation unfolds. How did these kung fu movies reach Southern Africa, and why did they so seize the imagination of Amakhosi? What are the connections between two former British colonies with such vastly different histories of urbanization and modernization? Is the connection primarily aesthetic, to be traced in performance codes as they move from one medium to another, from film to theater? Can an influence be traced in the importation of ideas from the movies into quotidian practices of township life? Or does the answer lie in a more banal and pragmatic response to cultural dumping? In exploring these questions, this chapter will zigzag backward and forward between Hong Kong and Bulawayo.

Hong Kong action cinema has exhibited an extraordinary transnational reach, and at least since the 1970s these films have circulated in a variety of places ranging from China towns and ethnic communities all over the United States to many cities in South East Asia, India, Latin America, Africa, and elsewhere. It constitutes a very interesting case study, as evidenced in a burgeoning field of scholarship, for investigating questions about world cinema, about the category of the "popular" and "international." Since its 1970s peregrinations Hong Kong cinema has become a critical site, a name, for investigating the intersections (and, crucially the uneven exchanges) between the local and global, the national, the international and the transnational. But little work has been done on the reception of kung fu in places like Mexico and Africa.[7]

I begin in Africa, but Africa is a big place, and although I have thus far used the term rhetorically it will become necessary to differentiate locales. I will be concerned with a very specific instance of how a particular genre—kung fu, and more generally Hong Kong action cinema—was seized upon as an imaginative tool and instrumentalized as the cornerstone of a cultural and political project in Bulawayo. But underlying the issue of How is the question of Why. Why, when kung fu was so popular and ubiquitous across African cities in the 1970s, why does it acquire such a distinctive imprint in Bulawayo and not elsewhere, in particular not elsewhere in Zimbabwe, a country fraught by war (during the 1970s) and the transitions to a newly independent state (in the early 1980s)? What is it that is specific, rather than general, about the trajectory of appropriation and transformation of cinematic tropes into a performative and social/ideological praxis located outside cinema? By looking, albeit sketchily, at the history of Bulawayo, precolonial as well as colonial and postcolonial, I will try to excavate the preconditions for the reception of Bruce Lee, Jackie Chan and others, and to speculate on why and how this cinema inspired a political and ethical practice related to the building of a township infrastructure.

My general question, simply, is this: what do people in particular places, configured by very specific historical and social circumstances, do with films, and what are the preconditions for receptive and transformative practices? The particular instance of Amakhosi, a performance and cultural group situated in Bulawayo, offers an answer that brings together the political, the aesthetic and the ethical in such a way as to tell us something about some of the ways that films move, not simply from one place to another, one center of national cinema, say, to another, but how films move through the fabric of daily life, how they are *acted upon*, appropriated and woven into localized quotidian lives. This essay, then, is a kind of genealogy, excavating traces of Hong Kong cinema that fruitfully conjoined with local impulses.

so that's how we started

In the opening quote Cont Mhlanga talks about Amakhosi's early aspirations to make kung fu films. Well, they never did get around to making their own kung fu movies. The infrastructure and capital was nowhere in sight. But they did develop—in dialogue as it were with the martial arts films they so adored—an extraordinarily vibrant performance culture. This is how it began: a group of friends, young men and women who were mostly at school in the 1970s during the last decade of white colonial rule in Rhodesia, and either at school or working in factories in the early 1980s, inspired by the movies seen in their community hall, conspired to learn karate (in their appropriation conflating, like others elsewhere, kung fu and karate, which would have made poor Bruce Lee weep tears of blood).[8] Blacks were not officially prohibited from entering white movie theaters as in apartheid South Africa, but they were unofficially prohibited, not the least by ticket pricing, and it was in the township community halls that they saw movies (in 16mm and later video). During the 1970s there was a liberation war fought in Rhodesia against the white colonial regime by two black liberation armies, attached to the two main black political parties: ZANU (Zimbabwe African National Union), whose members came primarily from the central region of the country, Mashonaland, where the capital Harare, is situated, and ZAPU (Zimbabwe African People's Union), based primarily in the southern region of the country, Matabeleland, whose regional capital is Bulawayo (although party affiliation crossed ethnic lines). In 1980 the war ended (with the defeat of the white Rhodesian army), there was an election and ZANU, under the leadership of Robert Mugabe, was voted into power.

For about a decade (the 1980s) Zimbabwe appeared to be a great success story: an apparently stable socialist government effectively negotiating the transition from colonialism to liberation, deftly combining state monopolies in some areas with a retention of colonial capital and industrial infrastructure in others. But for the Ndebele (people living in Matabeleland)

1980 simply ushered in another decade of continuing violence. The Mugabe government unleashed a reign of terror against Matabeleland (where ZAPU, now a party of potential opposition, was located). Although presented as skirmishes initiated by Ndebele "dissidents," in fact the government carried out systematic political atrocities throughout the area; thousands were tortured, massacred and disappeared (many to be found later in mass graves).[9] In Bulawayo, the capital of the region, marginalization from the center and central government, located in Harare, was made manifest in a considerable reduction of municipal funding (and diminished access to international aid), at a time of drought and the devastating effects of the AIDS pandemic.

Cont Mhlanga speaks of karate initially being deployed as a community tool, teaching the children, providing occupation and training. The friends formed a karate group calling themselves Amakhosi (which means "the royals"—an attempt to pay tribute to all of the traditional kingdoms; it is also the name of a Johannesburg soccer team). But after Mhlanga and his friends had seen some visiting actors from South Africa they had the idea of writing localized kung fu plays. Mhlanga wrote and directed the first plays, which soon mutated into sophisticated agit prop incorporating karate, kung fu moves copied from the movies, singing and dancing—traditional and contemporary—and biting political satire. Imagine Brecht meets Jackie Chan meets ingoma dance meets *Dirty Dancing*, and you will begin to get the picture of the kind of theater. The original members of Amakhosi formed a tight working collective: all tasks rotated and were not gender-specific, from administration to cooking. Each day began with a formal karate class. Amakhosi, however, was not just a theater group, they aspired to form a cultural center, to convert a place into a space in the De Certeau sense (a location of imaginative possibility), to provide a nucleus for the formation of a new alternative public sphere in post-independent Bulawayo.

Why kung fu? One response is to diminish the question of influence by pointing out that these films were dumped on the Second and Third Worlds, the people in community halls had little choice, and simply made creative use of what was served up. This response foregrounds reception, reading, and local cultural praxis but downplays any relation between genre and aesthetics; in this scenario B-grade westerns or James Bond movies (which indeed enjoyed popularity in Bulawayo) could have fulfilled the same function; there is nothing specific about Hong Kong kung fu. A quite different response downplays the local and elevates the global, simultaneously arguing the pertinence and specificity of Hong Kong kung fu. Here, there is a logic to the dispersal of Hong Kong cinema all over the globe in the 1970s. This cinema (Hong Kong action flicks, let us say, including not only kung fu but also sword movies, and various martial arts) circulated, it is argued, because it crossed national boundaries and spoke in an international language. A 1999 book *City on Fire: Hong Kong Cinema* begins with the claim that "Hong Kong filmmakers helped set the style for a cinema that fits the globalization age—full of action with high body counts and minimum dialogue, thus universally translatable."[10]

If we want to really grapple with this question—why kung fu?—and if we want to be able to situate the particular instance of Bulawayo and also understand why it resonates in a variety of places across the globe in terms that flesh out a notion of "the universally translatable" and accord some agency to reception in diverse communities, then we need to understand something about the particular history of Hong Kong cinema as a transnational phenomenon produced and distributed under the changing logics of late capitalism.

films "full of sex and ghosts and monsters"

Hong Kong is a small nation which has forged a cinematic identity out of a long series of negotiations around its relation to mainland China and the rest of South East Asia. Today of course it is visible to the world in ways that are historically unprecedented for "national" cinemas outside Hollywood, and, as epitomized in a film like *Crouching Tiger, Hidden Dragon* (Ang Lee, 2000), Hong Kong martial arts cinema, in its capacity to attract transnational capital and talent and its success in penetrating world markets, appears as an exemplary model of the transnational. It is tempting to navigate a teleological tale which moves from the national to the transnational (from a national industry model shaped by state and corporate capital to the transnational, secured by a dominant paradigm of finance capital), and simultaneously attends to the evolution and transmutation of a genre, broadly speaking the *wuxia* or martial arts film. In fact the range of emerging historical research and theoretical debate on Chinese cinema(s), indicates something other than a teleology which terminates in a collapsing of the post and transnational. On the contrary, as Yingjin Zhang puts it in Chapter 6 in this volume, it is a national cinema both "fluctuating" and "unfinished."

My interest is in Hong Kong action cinema's transnational migrations in an era prior to the supposedly postmodern global one we now inhabit, particularly in the penetration of the 1970s (and later) Hong Kong action cinema into an international market that is not generally thought of as "the West". Stephen Teo has postulated a distinction between "late transnationalism" (beginning in earnest in the 1970s, and following through to the present day) and an "early transnationalism" (the 1920s and 1930s). The early period is marked by the production of films that are addressed and exported to a diasporic Chinese audience, and consequently "informed by the concept of abstract China as a 'diasporic imaginary'." Although "late transnationalism" stretches from the 1970s to the present time, there are marked discontinuities between then and now. Teo argues that the martial arts cinema of the early 1970s (representing the first international push in terms of marketing) was "presented on its own terms to the West. In contrast, the 'globalized postmodernism' of today, as exemplified by *Crouching Tiger, Hidden Dragon* presents a martial arts cinema in terms of the internationalized aesthetics of art cinema."[11] His distinction is useful, but if we skew the focus to markets outside the established trade routes of the global economy, and beyond a diasporic Chinese audience, then we might find that people who constitute(d) those markets do not exactly meet the films on their own terms, but also set the terms of appropriation themselves. In order to grasp the resonances which allow for creative readings, remakings and appropriations, it is necessary to hopscotch sideways for a moment, to chart sketchily some of the maneuvers entertained by Hong Kong cinema in its relation to "Chinese cinema" and to South East Asia and the Second and Third Worlds.

Hong Kong cinema has always been immersed in struggles around the intersection of foreign and domestic, in negotiations over the national, over language (Cantonese and Mandarin), and in forays into the transnational. Always, because of its small domestic market, it has had to look to foreign markets, to input from off-shore capital, and a complicated orchestration of the film studios with various subsidiaries and satellite companies. Against this background (though other cultural factors feed into the mix) the martial arts film, with a history stretching back long before the 1970s (and epitomized by the long-running Wong Fei-hung series), is a hybrid genre, informed by a range of influences.

If the martial arts films of the 1970s were derided in the West as chopsocky trash and "oriental confections,"[12] this was not the first time Hong Kong filmmakers had endured derision. In the period between 1937 and 1940, as argued by Poshek Fu in *Between Shanghai and Hong Kong: The Politics of Chinese Cinemas*, when Hong Kong enjoyed "a golden age" of cinema, became a regional center of dialect cinema and strengthened its hold on the Chinese diasporic audience, it also came under increasing pressure from the racial regime of British colonialism and the cultural hegemony of China-centered nationalism.[13] In 1939 Hong Kong filmmakers stood accused by their Chinese compatriots of producing escapism, movies "filled with such grotesque subjects as sex, ghosts and monsters."[14] The transition to critical acclaim began with the Hong Kong New Wave in the 1980s but the kung fu decade—the 1970s—was pivotal in terms of transition.

To understand how the 1970s became the kung fu decade, and to grasp both the national and transnational significance of this, requires some charting not only of the production of kung fu movies but also their export and overseas circulation. It has, however, always been difficult to research the economics and movements of Hong Kong films because Hong Kong companies have not been required to reveal many details of their corporate structure and financial matters. Moreover, researchers have been much more interested in the more obvious, and most likely more lucrative, circulation of Hong Films in Asia, in the Chinese diaspora worldwide and in the United States. Nevertheless it is possible to sketch a plausible picture.[15] The first boom period for Hong Kong cinema was in the 1950s and 1960s. In the 1950s Shaw Brothers and MP and GI, the two major companies, were substantially financed by South East Asian capital,[16] and also exported films to an expanding overseas market though still dominated by Asian countries. Raymond Chow joined the Shaw organization in 1958 and left in 1970 to form a new company, Golden Harvest, partly financed initially by Thai and Taiwanese investors. From early on he had studios and theaters in a number of countries, and diversified into both satellite film companies and various branches of the entertainment business including home video, satellite broadcasting, radio and amusement parks. In the early 1970s local production fell and for various reasons the South East Asian market contracted and so the need to expand internationally became more urgent. It was the success of Bruce Lee that changed the direction of the Hong Kong film industry.

The kung fu phenomenon, heralded by the Bruce Lee vehicle, *Enter the Dragon*, seemed to burst from nowhere onto the world scene in 1973. But only if we consider the United States to be the world. This was the first film made by Lee in the United States and it was a huge success. But in fact Lee had already made two films with Golden Harvest in Hong Kong, *The Big Boss* (1971) and *Fist of Fury* (1972), which were huge international hits (though not in the mainstream US market). It was *Enter the Dragon*, a co-production between Warner Bros and Golden Harvest, that launched kung fu into a larger international arena. Between 1971 and 1973 it was estimated that about 300 kung fu films were produced primarily for the international market, some of which were never released in Hong Kong, and the overseas market grew from over twenty countries in the early 1970s to over eighty within a few years.

> The kung fu boom was driven by the studios themselves. Shaw Brothers and Golden Harvest saturated the international market with kung fu films in a deliberate move to open up new markets as the traditional South East Asian market appeared to shrink.[17]

But soon the boom was over. Bruce Lee died in 1973, and the kung fu wave of popularity receded, not to be revived until the late 1970s with the rise of Lee's successor, Jackie Chan.

Stephen Teo has argued that the kung fu films set the tone for the modernization of Hong Kong cinema itself, reflecting the dynamic qualities of Hong Kong society, and exerting a populist appeal.[18] Paradoxically, it seems that this very specificity of locale—the dynamic qualities of Hong Kong Society, modernity, populism—particularly as incarnated by Bruce Lee, provided the preconditions for international popularity.

Elsewhere Teo has written that "No other figure in Hong Kong cinema has done as much to bring East and West together in a common sharing of culture as Bruce Lee in his short lifetime."[19] Most scholarship has focused on Lee's appeal to diasporic Chinese audiences in South East Asian countries, and to African American and cult audiences in the United States. Scholars tend to converge in their delineation of Lee's persona as crystallized in certain modernist qualities—abstraction (of place), neutrality (of language), populism (appealing transnationally to urban working classes and oppressed ethnic groups). Much is made of the racial pride and anti-colonialist views of Lee's heroic working-class persona pounding the shit out of an assortment of foreigners, bosses, authority figures. He possesses no skill but martial arts and a simple moral code, expresses dignity in the face of oppressors and exploiters, defends the weak, champions the truth. Bill Brown has referred to his "generic ethnicity,"[20] Teo has identified "an abstract kind of cultural nationalism,"[21] expressing ethnic pride in the idea of "Chineseness," and Aihwa Ong has suggested that the films, as part of an "ethnic moral economy" are primarily directed towards a Chinese diasporic audience, providing an avenue of "flexible citizenship."[22] Denise Khor, in her dissertation "The Geographies of Film Spectatorship: Bruce Lee in Transnational and Ethnic Studies Perspective," extends this argument about the lack of precise locality, and generic ethnicity, to give an overview of the popularity with African American audiences.[23]

Within the above accounts there are three factors that are somewhat buried and which I want to bring to the surface. To some extent they are buried by me, it must be admitted, in so far as I have emphasized a commonality and underplayed the extent to which these writers might individually engage with the "buried" factors. As this chapter unfolds I hope to weave a connection between the three questions, or rather, to foreground their essentially braided status. These are the factors: first, if the bubble burst and there was something of a lacuna between Bruce Lee and Jackie Chan, if fewer kung fu films were being made and were internationally successful, then how exactly were the films kept alive in the Chinese diaspora and elsewhere? Box office figures alone can tell us only so much. Second, how do the aesthetics of kung fu play into transnational popularity, and how does this dimension intersect with the populism? Third, what about the other axis—the North-South?

the b circuit

Paul Willemen, in "Action Cinema, Labour Power and the Video Market," points out that although it was well into the 1980s before the production sector in the United States registered the presence of Hong Kong-style martial arts films, its distribution-exhibition sector quickly incorporated cheaply acquired films from Hong Kong, Taiwan, and Japan into its exploitation sub-cinema sector.[24] It is also highly conceivable that the Hong Kong majors, through their subsidiaries and dispersal into the entertainment sector, including video rentals, kept the supply going and the fever alive. But the intricacies of the journey of these films through the United States needs further research. Even more research waits to be done on the journey of these films through the Second and Third World, though we can speculate with some degree of accuracy I think. We can speculate that the films frequently slipped out of the domain of Hong Kong ownership, were transferred either into transnational distribution companies, or more likely local entrepreneurs in places like Africa, Mexico, and India.

S.V. Srinivas has elaborated on the "B circuit" in India, the "final frontier" of the film industry, beyond which there is no market:

> the vast segment of the film industry that comprises of hundreds of small distribution companies (often dealing with re-runs, soft-porn films, cheap imports, films dubbed from other languages etc.) and run down cinema halls in cities (the legendary Lighthouse in Abids, Hyderabad, which is now closed, for example) as well as small towns. Characterized by low levels of investment, this segment is witness to repeated interventions by both distributors and exhibitors which result in the de-standardization of a film's status as an industrial product. Another distinction of the B circuit is its questionable legality: condemned prints, uncensored films, censored films with sexually explicit interpolations, and prints whose rights have lapsed are to be found circulating here.[25]

We can extrapolate from the Indian example to other colonial situations where the B circuit was formed out of a combination of "cultural dumping" and a response to demand. "Cultural dumping" refers to the saturation of the periphery by those at the center of the global cultural marketplace, so that the distinctiveness of the periphery and local cultures is reduced. In general terms, it is a kind of short-hand for the cocacolanization of the world. But more specifically, it refers to the Third World as recipient of leftovers, of commodities that have almost exhausted their commodity status; it is a practice, as Karin Barber has put it, "akin to the dumping of expired drugs and non-functional buses."[26] Ulf Hannerz has said:

197

> The cost of taking old Western movies, soap serials, or skin flicks (choosing only examples from the screen) to their final resting place in the Third World is so low that whatever income they generate is almost pure profit: probably an unanticipated addition to whatever they earned in the markets for which they were actually produced.[27]

In fact, such profits as are earned quite probably never make their way back to the origins of production and original circuits of distribution. Local or trans-African (or trans-Indian, or trans-Latin American companies) would most likely have bought either the prints or the rights, or they would be bootlegged, and their exhibition would have been, in the colonial context anyway, monitored by the state. Certainly entrepreneurial exploitation succeeds in constituting audiences, but many communities were/are, through practices of viewing, appropriation and remaking, defining themselves as audiences in a social space. In colonial Rhodesia the state would have had a large part in the control of movies and conditions of screening. And certainly the practice of cultural dumping would have been significant, and continued after independence and through the 1980s (somewhat modified with the advent of video).

But when talking of "dumping" it is important to distinguish between different kinds of commodities. The dumping of drugs and genetically modified (GM) foods in postcolonial Africa (tied in with the bestowing of aid) by the First World needs to be distinguished from cultural commodities, which still partake of the same economy but might be used in much more diverse and creative ways (how do you use GM foods creatively?). In looking at the movement of kung fu through the Third World it is wise to be alert to the social worlds around the movies, to local forms of popular culture, and thus to the resonances which provide fertile ground for resurrection, which galvanize these exhausted commodities into a new life, an unanticipated after-life. In Bulawayo, particularly in the oldest township like Makokoba where Amakhosi lived, the people had some say in the running of the community halls and clubs during the colonial era, and the social life around the bioscope was lively, meshing into the fabric of quotidian life and popular culture.

It is not just because they are physical and universally translatable that these movies encounter fertile ground, nor can their felicitous reception be explained as a simple pragmatic reaction to dumping. A number of factors converge, some to do with the market (not least, the push into non-Asian markets), and some less easily defined. Srinivas concludes his article "Hong Kong Action Film in the Indian B Circuit," by remarking

> As for the Hong Kong Action film, is there something intrinsic to the martial arts and action films that account for their phenomenal career in the B circuit? Surely. The linkages between these (and other "low") genres and B circuits across the globe are no doubt being investigated by other scholars even as I write this.[28]

My chapter is a tentative contribution to this field of inquiry, fairly speculative and based on a very localized example. However, I would maintain that it is always the presence of a strong and locally inflected popular culture that initially provides the fertile ground.[29] Generally there is a convergence of local or indigenous aspects of popular culture with at least two kung fu characteristics: stylized violence incorporating acrobatic skill, and black humor. Sometimes the stylization resonates with actual violence, and sometimes the acrobatic component resonates with local popular traditions of dance, martial arts, performance. At the risk of essentializing and homogenizing the whole of the South let me bite the bullet or pull some punches and say that there is a kind of droll humor, often tinged with satire and self-mockery, exhibited as a reaction to (political) adversity in countries outside the First World, which might illuminate the east-south axis of the kung fu migration and the resonance of these movies in places with cultural and political experiences in many ways different from the Chinese. Similarly the conjunction of economic poverty and lively culture illuminates why these movies do not necessarily translate into other movies but might be subjected to different kinds of remaking and a diversity of after-lives. Before looking in detail at the Bulawayo example, and in order to get more of a sense of the transnational inflections of the kung fu phenomenon I am going to take a short detour—to Ghana, and Mexico, via painted flour sacks and Shaolin tennis shoes.

painted flour sacks made in ghana and shaolin tennis shoes made in mexico

From the mid-1980s through the mid-1990s in Ghana there was a thriving traveling film—or, more accurately, video cassette—culture. Entrepreneurs would travel, often by bus, through rural areas with all the accoutrements of exhibition—television monitor, video recorder, gas generator—and set up makeshift theaters for movie marathons that would last three or four days. The screenings, which included Indian, Hong Kong, and African cinema along with Hollywood, would be advertised by large posters, hand-painted with oil-based paints on two split and sewn-together flour sacks (and later locally purchased canvas). These posters certainly bear some relation to the movies they describe and promote but they are less interesting as subservient "descriptions" and more interesting as gorgeous, graphically rich renderings of the relation between movies and a popular imaginary. These posters came to the attention of the West through an exhibition in Los Angeles by the collector Ernie Wolfe (and have subsequently been exhibited in many US museums) and are memorialized in the book *Extreme Canvas: Hand Painted Movie Posters from Ghana*. In that book Deidre Evans-Pritchard writes:

> In West Africa, movies provide entertainment but they also resonate with the realities of local lives . . . These movies are fantastical but they are close to the proverbial bone . . . West Africans may have ended up with B-movies that we no

199

longer wanted over here, but in exchange they gave us the sack cloth commercial art posters that they no longer needed over there. One wonders, who got the better deal?[30]

Well, therein lies, no doubt, a twisty tale, but the example gives us a form of remaking where the movies themselves acquire an after-life which itself mutates and multiplies, as it travels.

China and Mexico: the transnational connection between these two places is woven in many historically intricate threads, but the one I shall pluck is kung fu. A stray thread at that, suggesting a work of future unraveling rather than a formulated thesis, a thread leading to some musings on the migration of kung fu through the fabric of Mexican popular culture. These musings are prompted by a recent art work, *Wong Fei Hungs*, produced in Tijuana by Torolab (Raúl Cárdenas-Osuna), and exhibited in Paris. The installation pivots around a conceit, or traveling trope, generated out of juxtaposing a Chinese legendary icon (the Shaolin kung fu master, Wong Fei Hung) and a Mexican legendary icon (the Virgin of Guadalupe). The poetically inscribed (but economically underpinned) bridge between the two is realized in a series of tennis shoes, called collectively *Wong Fei Hungs*. At first they look like any old tennis shoes, except for the gorgeous colors, primarily red and orange, the colors of the kung fu master. Then you look more closely at the streamlined design and the inset logos, and the names, such as Fuerza Ancestral (Ancestral Strength) and Baile de Leon (Lion Dance). Each shoe carries a graceful black logo, a small silhouette of Wong Fei Hung in classic pose, at once dancer and warrior. In addition each shoe carries its own images and logos, such as the Virgin, "Made in Mexico," the lion dance, an image of Stephen Chow in *Shaolin Soccer*.

Why a shoe and a holy virgin? Before answering this, let us backtrack a moment, to sketch briefly and in broad strokes the popularity of kung fu in Mexico. The reasons for this popularity are, as always, mixed, but to understand how Mexico provided fertile ground we would be wise to look to local manifestations of popular culture. Just as the capoeira developed in Brazil, so Mexico evolved its own form of martial arts, epitomized in masked wrestling, or *lucha libre*. And it is the *lucha libre* that provides us with a nodal affinity. On one level the history of this form is recent, dating back to the 1930s when a promoter brought some US wrestlers to Mexico. But a distinctive Mexican style soon developed. It was more graceful and athletic than the North American version, and also drew upon indigenous traditions, particularly in the masks which echoed images from Meso American and Olmec cultures. The stylized mask of the great champion *El Santo* (The Saint) alluded to the famous Olmec jaguar face, surviving in various stone statues and figurines. This mask, whatever its origins may be, clearly resonates with other, particularly Asian cultural forms, such as the Japanese Kabuki and Peking opera, not to mention US comic book heroes.

And *lucha libre* connects, as well, to karate and certain kung fu schools: in all these martial arts use of the closed fist is forbidden and so the chop becomes a natural option.

It is *El Santo* himself who embodies and enacts the link between martial arts and the movies in a heterogeneous Mexican style, which can be seen to incorporate and remake kung fu.

Santo was a phenomenally successful luchador when he entered movies in the late 1950s, and when a Santo comic book was initiated, turning him into an icon of Mexican popular culture. His first two movie titles mimicked the *lucha libre* format: *Santo contra el Cerebro del Mal* (*Saint against the Brain of Evil*, 1958) and *Santo contra los Hombres Infernales* (*Saint against the Infernal Men*, 1958).[31] In his 1962 Mexican film *El Santo contra las mujeres vampiro* (in the atrociously dubbed US version, *El Santo* inexplicably becomes *Samson*) the vampire women were in fact kung fu practitioners, also adept in wrestling moves. The Mexican habit of combining horror and kung fu was appropriated by the extraordinary collaboration between Hammer Films and Shaw Brothers Studios, *Legend of the Seven Golden Vampires*, shot in Hong Kong in 1974 with a large number of great martial artists and actors. In the Mexican title kung fu was foregrounded: *Kung-Fu Y Los Siete Vampiros de Oro*.[32]

Why a shoe and a holy virgin? Despite appallingly low wages and wretched conditions, Mexico has, in recent years, as part of the transnational merry-go-round been losing garment assembly jobs to Central America, call centers to Argentina, data processing to India, and electronics manufacture to China. But Mexican national pride was dealt a devastating blow recently with the revelation that it has lost something even more precious to China. Figurines and images of the most beloved (and most domestic) icon of the republic—the Virgin of Guadalupe—are now being manufactured in China. Images and icons of this brown Virgin (Mexico's contribution to the Catholic church) are found in almost every home in the country, and have a national significance often almost detached from their religious function.

Speaking of manufacture, and export, and iconic commodities, what is an iconically Chinese product? Something akin to the Virgin of Guadalupe which has made its way into the inner core of Chinese culture? Asking himself this question Cárdenas came up with the Feiyue martial arts shoe, marketed as "The #1 shoe choice for Shaolin monks and masters!" (on Amazon.com) but now worn in China by kids playing in a courtyard, crowds in the street, professors in universities, museum curators. China is the biggest tennis shoe producer in the world, supplying Nike, Adidas, Converse, Reebok to name a few. Mexico cannot compete, but it is possible to cast a ripple into the pool, to provoke reflection on this newly configured transnational market. So Torolab went looking for the figure that would link the spirit of the Shaolin soul to ideals of popular culture, and who better than the legendary Wong Fei Hung? It is time to redirect the transmission, says Cárdenas, to play the game in such a way that a shoe becomes not only a tool to pay homage to a popular and historical icon from China, but also a means of reversing the transmission, of sending shoes made in Mexico, bearing the image of the Virgin of Guadalupe, less a religious icon than an icon of the inequality in Third World countries, and the unevenness of transnational commerce.[33]

violence and memory[34]

Kung fu movies arrive and travel through Africa like Shaolin tennis shoes. In Bulawayo, I contend, the conjunction of pedagogy (what we might, in short-hand refer to as the *Shaolin* dimension) and performance in the martial arts films found a felicitous reception. In adapting the films to theater Amakhosi and their followers acted on the films and acted out, learning from the cinema in order to transform the social.

But to fully understand why this phenomenon arose in the city of Bulawayo (and not in Harare, for instance) means to understand the way the past resonates, is heeded, resisted, appropriated in the practices of everyday cultural life today, as well as in the mediated nuances of theatrical practice.[35] The phenomenon actively urges attention to the way in which the past is played out via a range of registers and levels, and to the way in which the local is articulated in relation to a variety of relatively global formations. In terms of charting a genealogy two distinct possibilities present themselves. One is situated within a paradigm of war and violence, the other within a paradigm of peace and civic organization.

The first approach (grounded in history but parlayed into popular perception and myth) would see Amakhosi as descendants of a warrior nation, of the great Zulu king Mzilikazi who, in precolonial times (around 1840), invaded and violently established his rule in the area now known as Matabeleland. His warriors were called the Amandebele, the people of the long shields (hence the name Ndebele). Mzilikazi's son Lobengula, who founded the first Bulawayo, "Place of Slaughter," fought gloriously and with some success against the colonial forces before being defeated (in 1893) but, it is argued, never reconciled and never relinquished resistance. In this approach Amakhosi's appropriation of kung fu would be attributed to their (largely ethnic) attraction to, and facility for, the "martial" component of the martial arts.

The second approach, based on an historical interpretation which emphasizes the rapidity with which the Ndebele kingdom in Zimbabwe established a civil order in the 1840s, and which stresses a tradition (precolonial and colonial) in which outsiders and migrants were peacefully assimilated into Ndebele society,[36] would see Amakhosi as representative of a larger cultural movement, engaged in a project to build a civic community. In this approach the martial arts influence could be measured in their success not only in developing a new theatrical form, but in the building of

"Township Square," the cultural center situated symbolically between the old colonial town and the oldest of the townships—Makokoba and Mzilikazi.

In fact it is not an either/or question. Surely it is the case that Amakhosi and Bulawayo, today, are shaped by a history that stretches back to the precolonial era, a history in which questions of state and nation have been ever present, ever contentious. But that history, like their current practice, is politically inflected in ways that cannot be reduced to the ethnic.

Colonial Bulawayo was built on the destruction of an earlier Bulawayo, King Lobengula's settlement, the original stronghold of the Ndebele nation. As the economic heartland was ripped out of the country by the British invaders people were dispossessed not only of their land but also of livelihoods. After 1893 many Ndebele men were forced into wage labor in Bulawayo where they often took up permanent residency (whereas the townships in Harare were characterized more by itinerant labor, workers maintaining a primary affiliation to their rural homes). The first African township (which became Makakoba) came into being in 1894. One of the consequences of this was rapid urbanization, a more intense process of modernization than in Salisbury (the colonial name for Harare), the development of a modern proletarian political movement, and political investment in urban governance. It was in Bulawayo that the earliest independent African schools in Central Africa were located, where there was a much stronger trade union movement than in Salisbury and where most political leaders came from in the 1930s. Most of the early nationalist leaders (in the 1950s and 1960s) also came from Matabeleland. But just as important as the trade unions in shaping the identity of Bulawayo was the cultural sphere. This process was helped by a marginally more liberal white administrative class in Bulawayo than in Salisbury, and somewhat more enlightened town planners who emphasized home ownership, and leisure activities that would produce self-respecting and well-behaved natives. In the face of a white controlled municipality the people of the Bulawayo townships struggled for participation and a stake in shaping the city's cultural life. This cultural life was reflected in a range of quotidian organizations—child care, women's groups, sports associations, particularly soccer and boxing (boxing was the one arena where the African Associations retained total control), music, dancing.[37] The community halls served as venues both for meetings and for visiting artists from South Africa (Bulawayo being relatively close to the border), for music and dance events and film screenings (there were few cinemas in the city, expensive and white dominated). Formal schooling was more restricted than in Harare (both because there were far fewer missions and because of less government funding), although this seems to have actually raised the stakes for the people to seize for themselves as much as possible the processes of modernity. Libraries were a particular focus of organization, and art activities. And then there were the beer halls, sites of carousing and wild inventive dancing, and the major source of income for the municipality.[38]

Let us fast forward to the early 1980s when Amakhosi forms. Township theater emerged after liberation, but during a traumatic postwar period, and also, for the people of Bulawayo and Matabeleland, against a background of continuing violence. In Bulawayo there is a strong perception that after Independence authority for the control of the beer halls and concomitant control of the funds was redirected to central government and away from the municipality, and that the consequence was a lack of subsidized support for preschool and sports facilities, libraries, youth and women's groups, leisure and cultural activities. Locals suddenly found that although they were apparently being accorded a greater degree of participation in the running of the townships, in practice they had less control. Schools were collapsing, unemployment was high, and the war, under a different guise, was continuing in Matabeleland. It is in this context that Amakhosi developed (and in its wake a proliferation of theater groups), espousing an ethos of theatrical practice that incorporated community and cultural production, aiming to constitute anew and shape the public sphere.

aesthetics

Aesthetics and universality are often hitched together, either implicitly in the discursive voice of festive postmodern globalism, or explicitly in the snooty disparaging voice of high minded cultural critique that positions aesthetics as the handmaiden of depoliticized art. Hong Kong action cinema might well be taken to exemplify this conjunction of aesthetics and universality. While commercial popularity in the 1970s seemed to translate directly into critical disdain, the genre dubbed as "chop-socky," nowadays the situation is different. The presence and influence of Hong Kong cinema is ubiquitous, and this ubiquity or international popularity is often ascribed to some generalized notion of aesthetics (and retrospectively mapped onto the chop-socky confections).

Let me rehearse some of the positions outlined earlier, as they acquire a slightly different inflection when perceived through the lens of the aesthetic. From *City on Fire*, a phrase very representative of its time: "Hong Kong filmmakers helped set the style for a cinema that fits the globalization age—full of action with high body counts and minimum dialogue, thus universally translatable."[39] In her introduction to the excellent anthology, tellingly titled *At Full Speed: Hong Kong Cinema in a Borderless World*, Esther C.M. Yau writes, "Hong Kong movies both anticipate and register the impact of speed in the era of immediate global access."[40] Stephen Teo distinguishes between the martial arts cinema of the 1970s, presented on its own terms to the West, and that of today, presented in the guise of a new "*internationalized aesthetics* of art cinema."[41] David Bordwell, on the other hand, sees a continuity from the 1970s to today; he emphasizes the aesthetics of popular entertainment, encapsulating the popular success of this cinema in the phrase, "*aesthetics in action.*" "After you walk out of the best Hong Kong action movies you are charged up, you feel that you can do anything," he writes, and then asks a crucial question: "How can mere movies create such feelings?"[42] To understand how, to understand the relation between feelings, sensations, performance and film language it is crucial to explore this question in precisely the kind of meticulous detail that he does. Nevertheless I remain rather grumpily begrudging. I understand that the "you" who walks out of the best Hong Kong action movies is a rhetorical "you," but still I want to multiply that "you" as we do in Australia—"hey yous what yous up to?"—to draw into the picture the "yous" who walk out of *shonky* Hong Kong movies feeling high, the "yous" who are not moved in the same way, or who are moved to different kinds of action, the "yous" in the American South and metropolitan centers in the United States who watched Hong Kong martial arts films in the 1970s in double bills with blaxploitation flix, the female "yous" who got a buzz from watching women in action, the John Woo cult "yous," the "yous" who watched the matinee slot on television dedicated to kung fu, the young French avant-garde filmmaking "yous,"[43] the diasporic Chinese "yous" in Chinatowns all over the world. And here and now the township "yous" in Bulawayo.

So, we need a more nuanced account. But it is not just a matter of nuance, nor simply a matter of multiplication (multiply the audiences, genders, ethnic identities, modes of pleasure . . .), the easy response of a certain righteous version of cultural studies to film studies' theorizing. Actually I believe that if we want to understand the transnational popularity of these movies then Bordwell's attempt to think through some relation between the popular and the aesthetic is a good start. The problem for me resides in a constricted notion of the aesthetic posed by a cognitive framework.

> Popular cinema . . . is deliberately designed to cross cultural boundaries. Reliance on pictures and music rather than on words, appeal to cross-cultural emotions, easily learned conventions of style and story, and redundancy at many levels all help films travel outside their immediate context. That audiences all over the world enjoy Hong Kong movies illustrates the transcultural power of popular cinema.[44]

This assumes an unmediated and invariable transmission between the feelings of the film and the feelings of a viewer, it assumes that an analysis of the components of film form will yield an adequate account of how the feelings of the film are transmitted to a standardized transnational viewer.

I would rather, in discussing the relation between aesthetics and transnational popularity, emphasize the *potential* and *capacities* of film to *move*, to move spectators and in turn, to *be moved*, that is to be acted upon, to mutate over time (not just in the moment of screening) and across space (not just the space, say, between Hong Kong and Bulawayo, but the space of the community hall where the films are viewed and the townships where soccer and boxing are popular, where acrobatic forms are built into all sorts of dances, traditional and contemporary, indigenous and Western). The popular does not have to be underpinned by an automatic pairing of the aesthetic and the universal. To understand how the aesthetic capacity of a cinematic movement is inflected locally it might be useful to look to local formations of popular culture. This is the key that can move us from abstract, or formalized aesthetics to a viable version of aesthetics in action.

The capacity of this cinema to engage and mobilize diverse communities (from Indian fan clubs to the French avant-garde to theater workers in the Bulawayo townships) does suggest a certain aesthetic potential, aesthetic here signifying work on the senses. On the whole, Hong Kong action cinema is bodily, or indexical, though the bodies we speak of are filmic bodies, decomposed and recomposed.[45] We might say that there is a particular conjunction of the bodily, the technological and the phantasmatic. Two terms set the parameters for this cinema: body and movement. It is important to stress the bodily dimension of this cinema, not in order to argue for identification (what usually differentiates narrative from abstract cinema), but in order to understand the phantasmatic and affective capacities as related to the bodily. Let us say that the cinematic body possesses motility, the "capability or power of moving,"[46] it is agentive, the mover has the capacity to originate movement, it has agency but not intentionality. The technological apparatus also possesses motility, and Hong Kong action cinema exercises this capacity by crystallizing and generating energy. Think of the characteristics we associate with this highly kinetic cinema: rapidly changing camera angles, collision editing for action sequences, changing film speeds, close ups of bullets and punches, frenetic pacing, choreographed fight scenes, Bordwell's "pause-burst-pause" pattern like meter in music,[47] trampoline and wire work enabling bodies to leap, somersault, dive and fly through the air. Movement *on* the body also inaugurates movement *through* bodies, both filmic and extra-filmic. The viewer is never, in cinema, simply a repository, an end point, a destination for a message. The viewer—I, you, we—is implicated in a circuit of affects, in a dialectical dance of movement and stillness, posture and motion. Serge Daney argues that the situation in which people are rendered immobile before moving images in a state of "blocked vision" (as Pascal Bonitzer once referred to it) enables them to see all sorts of things. He evokes

> immobile people who become sensitive to the mobility of the
> world, to all types of mobility, the mobility of fictions (ahead
> to happier tomorrows and various other dreams), bodily

mobility (dance, action), material and mental movements (dialectical and logical games).[48]

Hong Kong cinema provides a possibility of transformation: the technological work produces a cathexis of energy in filmic bodies, renders these bodies as extra-daily and initiates a circuit in which energy *moves* from the screen through the people watching, producing a sensation of *movement*, of transformation. The affective force of the films has the capacity to energize quotidian bodies, so that they are experienced as extra-daily. This is of course phantasmatic. Which is not to say it is an illusion; the affect is somatic, experienced physiologically, as well as emotionally, but the sensation of extra-daily (the feeling that you can do anything) is fantastic. The wildly differing ways in which these fantasies might be inflected, and acted on or acted out, can only be understood by looking at the circumstances of reception (deciphering the shadows of history and formations of culture that pertain).

Among the myriad ways in which the fantasmatic sensation of extra-daily bodiness might be inflected there is the fantasy of flying. The defiance of gravity that is fundamental to this fantasy is a defiance of bodily restraints. Paradoxically, a very bodily cinema possesses the capacity to provoke out-of-body sensations, instantiated as imaginative leaps outside the logic of local quotidian reality. The fantasy of flying is not a modern fantasy, but it is a fantasy superbly mobilized and even cathected, let us say, by the modernist potential of cinema (Leonardo and Gravida lead, via Freud, to the cinema), and woven into the *Wuxia* film since early days (and foreshadowed by the late Qing Chinese fascination with the magic science of flying).[49] To escape the body, our grounding in material reality, to fantasize flying: is this escapism? Yes, it seems to me it is indeed the marvelous escapist potential of the cinema and Hong Kong action cinema epitomizes this tendency, enables it if you like. It helps us to understand its capacity *to move*, aesthetically, its affective force, and its capacity to *move* geographically.

But if, in film theory, we stop here—at the point of identifying transnational potentialities—then we fail to register film as a public and performative medium engaging technology and multiple viewers. To identify this escapist potential is one thing it seems to me; to try to understand how it might be instantiated for different viewers in different places is something quite different, a task which requires more patience and more pragmatism and more ethnographic sensibility. What is interesting is precisely the diverse ways in which fantasies of flying, or the aesthetics of transubstantiation, might well be tapped and mobilized during the process of viewing, in a crossing and transference between psychic and somatic, personal and social, public and private, past and present. This escapist fantasy par excellence, this fantasy of escaping the gravity of the body, possesses the power to generate imaginative projections, the power to imagine different modes of being, different forms of psychic and social engagement.

It is conceivable that this fantasy of flying, or to put it in more mundane terms, this fantasy of escaping the strictures of the quotidian body, appealed to people in the townships at a time of heightened struggle against the colonial state, followed by the oppression experienced under the new postcolonial state. Equal to the escapist dimension was surely the additional aesthetic resonance of kung fu cinema with so many aspects of their own popular culture—dance, swing, jazz, music, praise poems, spirit possession, soccer, the performative aspect of rituals, religious and secular. However, the sources of the appeal and the directions of its appropriation are not just aesthetic. Rather, we have to understand how the kung fu movies— particularly those of Bruce Lee and later Jackie Chan, but also the whole Shaolin tradition—inspired an ethical form of action.

ethics

Many martial arts, not least kung fu, incorporate an element of the ethical in the sense of work on the self. A dedicated training of the body is seen as inseparable from character training. Concentration, focus, meditation, mental agility, the discipline of routine exercise, are all seen as prerequisites for action, for physical prowess. Inner focus or spiritual cathexis enables economic and efficient combat. There is also, however, a social dimension to this ethical work. Meaghan Morris has a wonderful essay called "Learning from Bruce Lee" in which she argues that in so far as the Shaolin tradition of training finds its way into martial arts films, especially Bruce Lee vehicles, these films are all training films.

> [T]he training film offers more than a spectacle of fabulously
> self-made bodies acting out their masochistic reshaping
> routines. It also frames and moralizes this spectacle as a
> pedagogical experience. Training films give us lessons in
> using aesthetics—understood as practical discipline, "the
> study of the mind and emotions in relation to the sense of
> beauty"—to overcome personal and social adversity.[50]

She pays particular attention to the Bruce Lee biography, *Dragon: The Bruce Lee Story* (1993), describing the scene where Linda and Bruce watch *Breakfast at Tiffany's* and encounter Mickey Rooney's gross rendering of Mr. Yunioshi, as "a rhythmically exact little story about people being differently 'moved'."[51] "The point of a pragmatic aesthetic pedagogy," she writes, describing what is virtually a cliché of martial arts movies, "is always to shape a socially responsive as well as physically capable self that can handle new experience."[52]

Amakhosi began as a karate club in 1980, under the leadership of Cont Mhlanga. One of the key inspirations for the formation of the group was the kung fu films seen in their community halls in the 1970s and on into the 1980s. Although they saw a wide mish-mash of martial arts films (particularly though not exclusively from Hong Kong) the key influences they cite are Bruce Lee and Jackie Chan. The members of Amakhosi grew up surrounded by a culture of violence, and Independence did not bring relief; on the contrary 1980 ushered in a new era of violence and massacre for the Matabele. Amakhosi was formed at a time when the municipal infrastructure of the city of Bulawayo was definitively collapsing. Revenue from the beer halls which had traditionally been ploughed back into the municipality seemed not to materialize under the Mugabe government, and the promise of increased central funding for education, health, and other amenities proved empty.

Kung fu, particularly as exemplified by Bruce Lee, is "fighting without fighting."[53] It means fighting with an open or empty fist, fighting without weapons. The fantasy element is also underscored by pragmatism: "skill is achievable, a result of fitness and training."[54] It is achievable for characters within the diegeses but also for viewers. There is a kind of breath-taking wizardry about kung fu aesthetics, and this Amakhosi believed they could master. And they did. They did it through training, apprenticeship, dedication to an ideal, believing not only that they could transform their own bodies (and minds) but also that they could imagine and bring into being a new and different sociality, based on strength not violence. In other words they followed the Bruce Lee example. And Jackie Chan. Though I have not given much attention to Chan in this chapter, he is an important influence: for his skill, very much for his performative humor, and his own legend (being apprenticed as a child to a Peking opera troupe). Amakhosi slowly evolved from a karate club into a theater group, along the way giving up on the goal of making movies. The main and ostensible reason for this was indisputably financial. Why then, we might usefully ask, did Mhlanga not start a karate club or kung fu fan club, as in the Indian examples Srinivas talks about? To answer this we have to look to the local and to the specific conditions of reception. I believe that the ethical aspirations of the group to intervene in and shape the culture of the city determined the turn to theater and training.

Amakhosi formed a mixed collective of men and women, the original core group numbering about fifteen. This was very unusual in Zimbabwe (and indeed in Bruce Lee and Jackie Chan movies!) where women who were involved in theater were considered "loose" and easy targets for abuse.[55] Apart from a commitment to gender equality there was an underlying pragmatism: everyone in the townships knew who the Amakhosi women were because of their visibility on stage, and no one would ever dare to mess with them; they could hold their heads high and walk through the streets alone, day or night. The issue of women in theater was thematized in the Amakhosi play *Stitsha*, first performed in 1991 and subsequently incorporated as a key play in the repertoire, a play characterized by satire, humor, and scenes of wild dancing and highly acrobatic stage fighting. From the beginning Amakhosi trained children and young people, initially in karate, but eventually in a full two-year program of theatrical arts and cultural administration.

In the first decade Amakhosi trained first in the small yards of members' homes, and then in a small office space downtown, but they would rehearse twice a week at Stanley Square, an open square in Makakoba township. Anyone could come and people came in droves, were invited to offer criticism and take part in discussion. This was part of an evolving practice aimed at creating a public sphere that would grow in the space evacuated by the government. Cont Mhlanga has said, "in order to create an ethical culture you need to have a sound infrastructure."[56] The colonial administration had put in place a township infrastructure, and with independence came the opportunity for the postcolonial state to modify that structure and institute new directions and democratic participation. When this did not happen in Bulawayo Mhlanga and Amakhosi developed a series of initiatives. They envisaged an environment where, among other things, training would be offered to unemployed children and young people, where visiting artists from other parts of Africa and overseas could perform, where rehearsal space could be provided for musicians, where eventually video production could be developed, where discussion and forums and soccer matches could be held. A cultural center was indeed built in the latter half of the 1990s on a symbolic site. It now includes, as well as the above, an amphitheater and music facilities.

Agility was not something that the young Amakhosi needed in the early 1980s. They had grown up in the townships in tough times, and it is indeed this context that made for fertile ground in terms of an encounter with kung fu. However, what kung fu, and then karate offered was the possibility of actualizing this agility, through training and discipline. Disciplined training meant a refinement of intertwined physical and political agility. Amakhosi were prepared to fight, but to do this with an "open fist," to speak out about politics (on the level of the national and the local, often calling into question the shibboleths of nationalism, and tackling issues which at least in the early days were not publicly voiced, like AIDS) through their plays and through the way they lived their lives. This is where ethics and aesthetics intermesh. I use "ethics" partly in the commonly understood sense of wanting to promote ethico-political ideals such as gender equality, but I also use the term to denote a work of *ascesis*, in the Foucauldian sense. In the face of adversity and political violence Amakhosi, like their kung fu heroes, have been committed to an ideal of self-discipline which entails an attempt to harness and shape energies and impulses. This commitment is grounded in practices of pedagogy, an engagement with the larger Bulawayo township community, an integration of professional and quotidian life.

Through such agility (even though karate is no longer central to their practice), Amakhosi survives in a tough climate, despite continued and fearless criticism of the government, both in their plays and in social commentary. Since the mid-1990s, but particularly since 2001, Mugabe has become one of the worst dictators on the African continent. In May 2006, Mhlanga was arrested for creating "civil disobedience." He was released on condition that he "brings in all the actors in the play for questioning" as well as scripts; he was ordered not to interact with non-governmental organizations like Crisis International, and to desist from the "staging of supposedly political and subversive plays at Amakhosi Centre." Mhlanga declared publicly that he had no intention of following these orders: "We live through making and staging plays. It's our profession and that's what we do and will continue to do. The play will be shown at the centre no matter what these guys [security agents] say."[57] Thousands, throughout Zimbabwe (especially members of the opposition Movement for Democratic Change (MDC) but also particularly the poor and dispossessed who have little recourse to publicity), have been less lucky. People have been disappeared, arrested without trial, tortured, had their homes burned to the ground, homeless people have been bussed into the wilderness and dumped.

Many of the young people I met in 1996 when they were training at Amakhosi are now writing and directing plays, musical theater, opera. Some have been overseas to extend their training, where they have also offered training to others. A number are homeless and starving (following the so-called massive slum clearances by the government), many are no longer alive (the AIDS pandemic in Africa is ruthlessly democratic, it spares none; moreover, medical resources throughout the country are exhausted, so any illness is potentially lethal).

Amakhosi amazingly survives, but this is not an entirely triumphalist tale. They are under threat, as much as anything from the appalling poverty that is consuming the country. This is Africa, it is off the map . . .

let us end in africa

Let us end in Africa where images from the screen migrate into the social. In this chapter I have moved backwards and forwards between Hong Kong and Bulawayo, tracking a particular trajectory in the transnational movement of kung fu cinema. But it is in Bulawayo that I end, here where the films are subjected to remaking, not as cinema but as something else. We might call that something else theater or we might call it a way of life. I have used the cinema as a way to burrow back into quotidian lives shaped against histories of violence and civic renewal, to explore, in this instance, how movies make sense and how people make sense of movies (how they move and are moved) within a public sphere. One of the utilities of the notion of the transnational may be located in the impulse not simply to produce knowledge *about* local situations and cultures, but to explore how knowledge and inventive cultural practices are produced locally, to examine how those things we call films mutate, how images from the screen migrate and contribute to the forging of new sensibilities and socialities.

This chapter is dedicated to the memory of Mackay Tickeys—comedian, stage warrior, friend and Amakhosi original—who died June 16, 2006.

acknowledgments

An early version of this chapter was presented at the "Cinema as Vernacular Modernism Symposium," the University of Chicago, May 17–18, 2002. I am grateful for the invitation and for comments and suggestions provided by participants at that event. Thanks also to Nataša Ďurovičová and Jeffrey Minson for their helpful suggestions.

notes

1. In my short video, "An Introduction to Bulawayo Township Theatre," 1995.
2. May Joseph, *Nomadic Identities: The Performance of Citizenship* (Minneapolis, MN: University of Minnesota Press, 1999), 49.
3. Ibid., 53.
4. Although there is no film industry as such in Zimbabwe and not many feature films have been made (in Harare), in fact there have been some interesting productions, both in film and video, as well as interesting modes of distribution. However, my focus in this chapter is not on film production, but on the "imprint" of films elsewhere in the culture.
5. Much excellent work has recently been done on the affective potentialities of
   Hong Kong action cinema. See, for instance, some of the excellent articles in *Hong Kong Connections: Transnational Imagination in Action Cinema* such as "The Secrets of Movement: The Influence of Hong Kong Action Cinema Upon the Contemporary French Avant-Garde," by Nicole Brenez (163–173; 310–11), and "At the Edge of the Cut: An Encounter with the Hong Kong Style in Contemporary Action Cinema," by Adrian Martin (175–88; 311–12). See *Hong Kong Connections: Transnational Imagination in Action Cinema*, ed. Meaghan Morris, Siu Leung Li, and Chan Ching-kiu (Durham and Hong Kong: Duke University Press and Hong Kong University Press, 2005).
6. Film studies seems to have isolated itself somewhat from debates in other disciplines about scale, scale conceived of as a geopolitical issue of urgency imbricating disciplinary questions, both of methodology and theory. See for instance Jean Comaroff and John Comaroff, "Ethnography on an Awkward Scale: Postcolonial Anthropology and the Violence of Abstraction," *Ethnography* 4, no. 2 (2003): 147–79. Thanks to Ariana Hernandez for drawing my attention to this article, and for other helpful insights.
7. In a seminal collection of writings on African Popular Culture, published in 1997, Karin Barber noted that the anthology did not include much attention to "the reception and circulation of imported cultural forms such

as Kung Fu." Karin Barber, ed. *Readings in African Popular Culture* (Bloomington, IN: Indiana University Press, 1997), 7.

8. Although Lee was very concerned to prove that Chinese martial arts were superior to Japanese karate (and a streak of Japan-phobia runs through his films) in fact the brand of kung fu he himself developed, *Jeet Kune Do* or "The Art of Intercepting the Fist," has similarities to karate particularly in its efficiency and economy.

9. The atrocities of this period have been extensively documented. See, as representative, Richard Werbner, "In Memory: A Heritage of War in Southwestern Zimbabwe," in *Society in Zimbabwe's Liberation War*, ed. Ngwabi Bhebe and Terence Ranger (Harare: University of Zimbabwe Publications, 1995), 192–205; Catholic Commission for Justice and Peace/Legal Resources Foundation, *Breaking the Silence, Building True Peace: A Report on the Disturbances in Matabeleland and the Midlands, 1980–1988* (Harare: Catholic Commission for Justice and Peace/Legal Resources Foundation, 1997); Lawyers Committee for Human Rights (LCHR), *Zimbabwe: Wages of War* (New York: LCHR, 1986); E.P. Makambe, *Marginalising the Human Rights Campaign: The Dissident Factor and the Politics of Violence in Zimbabwe, 1980–87* (Lesotho: Institute of Southern African Studies, 1992).

10. John Lent, "Foreword," in *City on Fire: Hong Kong Cinema*, ed. Lisa Odham Stokes and Michael Hoover (London: Verso, 1999), ix.

11. Stephen Teo, "*Wuxia* Redux: *Crouching Tiger, Hidden Dragon* as a Model of Late Transnational Production," in *Hong Kong Connections*, ed. Morris, Li, and Ching-kiu.

12. The phrase "oriental confections" appeared in a 1973 *Variety Review*.

13. Poshek Fu, *Between Shanghai and Hong Kong: The Politics of Chinese Cinemas* (Stanford, CA: Stanford University Press, 2003), 91.

14. Ibid., 70.

15. See Steve Fore, "Golden Harvest Films and the Hong Kong Movie Industry in the Realm of Globalization," *Velvet Light Trap*, (Fall 1994): 40–59; Grace L.K. Leung and Joseph M. Chan, "The Hong Kong Cinema and its Overseas Market: A Historical Review, 1950–1995," in *Hong Kong Cinema Retrospective: Fifty Years of Electric Shadows* (Hong Kong: The 21st Hong Kong International Film Festival, 1997), 143–49; Poshek Fu, "Going Global: A Cultural History of the Shaw Brothers Studio, 1960–1970," in *Hong Kong Cinema Retrospective: Border Crossings in Hong Kong Cinema*, ed. Law Kar (Hong Kong: The 24th Hong Kong International Film Festival, 2000), 43–51.

16. Leung and Chan, "The Hong Kong Cinema and its Overseas Market," 144.

17. Stephen Teo, "The 1970s: Movement and Transition," in *The Cinema of Hong Kong: History, Arts, Identity*, ed. Poshek Fu and David Desser (New York: Cambridge University Press, 2000), 104.

18. Ibid., 99–100.

19. Stephen Teo, *Hong Kong Cinema: The Extra Dimension* (London: British Film Institute, 1997), 110.

20. Bill Brown, "Global Bodies/Postnationalities: Charles Johnson's Consumer Culture," *Representations* 58 (Spring 1997): 24–48, 33.

21. Teo, "The 1970s," 97.

22. Aihwa Ong, *Flexible Citizenship: The Cultural Logics of Transnationality* (Durham, NC: Duke University Press, 1999), 164.

23. Denise Khor, "The Geographies of Film Spectatorship: Bruce Lee in Transnational and Ethnic Studies Perspective." Master's thesis, University of California at San Diego, 2003). See also Vijay Prashad, *Everybody Was*

Kung Fu Fighting: Afro-Asian Connections and the Myth of Cultural Purity (Boston, MA: Beacon Press, 2001).

24. Paul Willemen, "Action Cinema, Labour Power and the Video Market," in *Hong Kong Connections*, ed. Morris, Li, and Ching-kiu, 223–47, 315–17, p. 235.

25. S.V. Srinivas, "Film Culture, Politics and Industry," *Seminar*, no. 525 (May 2003): 47–51, p. 49, www.india-seminar.com/2003/525/525%20s.v.%20srinivas. htm. See also S.V. Srinivas, "Hong Kong Action Film in the Indian B Circuit," *Inter-Asia Cultural Studies* 4, no. 1 (2003): 40–62, www.sephis.org/pdf/ srinivas3.pdf; S.V. Srinivas, "Hong Kong Action Film and the Career of the Telugu Mass Hero," in *Hong Kong Connections*, ed. Morris, Li, and Ching-kiu, 111–23, 302–05.

26. Karin Barber, "Popular Arts in Africa," *African Studies Review* 30, no. 3 (1987): 25.

27. Ulf Hannerz, *Cultural Complexity: Studies in the Social Organization of Meaning* (New York: Columbia University Press, 1992), 235.

28. Srinivas, "Hong Kong Action Film in the Indian B Circuit."

29. In mapping the field of African popular culture Karin Barber has written,

> We should not, then, take the "traditional"/"elite" ("modern", "Westernized") division that demarcates the field of African culture in so many discourses at face value. Rather we should read it as an indication of something else that it cannot accommodate: the shifting, mobile, elusive space of the "popular", which is in fact continuous with both the "traditional" and "the modern" categories and which deconstructs all the oppositions which sustain the binary paradigm.
>
> (Barber, *Readings in African Popular Culture*, 8)

Manthia Diawara has often argued that the cinema in Africa, rather than "African Cinema" (largely an art cinema defined by auteurs) should look to forms of popular culture. For instance:

> it may be that the filmmakers in other parts of Africa [than Nigeria] should generate a more popular form of cinema looking at existing popular spectacles such as theatre, wrestling matches, song and dance. Both Nigerian and Ghanaian.
>
> (Manthia Diawara, "The Present Situation of the Film Industry in Anglophone Africa." Reprinted from "African Cinema: Politics and Culture," in *African Experiences of Cinema*, ed. Imruh Bakari and Mbye Cham (London: British Film Institute, 1996), 109)

See also the film, *Aristotle's Plot* (1996, directed by Jean-Pierre Bekolo, Zimbabwe/Cameroon, 71 min.), the BFI's African contribution to the Centenary of Cinema series, in which the cast of characters have names such as Policeman, Bruce Lee, Cinema, Essomba Tourneur.

30. Ernie Wolfe, ed. *Extreme Canvas: Hand Painted Movie Posters from Ghana* (New York: Dilettante Press and Kesho Press, 2000), 49. Thanks to Jim Schamus for drawing my attention to this book.

31. Both films were released in 1958, and directed by Joselito Rodríguez. Filming

lesley stern

was done in Cuba, and ended just the day before Fidel Castro entered Havana and declared the victory of the revolution, www.luchavavoom.com/ luchadores.html

32. See the DVD review by Phil Chandler on www.dvdcult.com/ rev_7Vamps.htm.

33. In discussion. My thanks to Raúl Cárdenas-Osuna both for giving me background material to his project and for many exchanges about kung-fu and the Mexican connection.

34. I borrow this phrase from the title of a book that begins: "Our book is called *Violence and Memory* because violence has so powerfully shaped history and memory of the past in Matabeleland." See Jocelyn Alexander, JoAnn McGregor, and Terence Ranger, *Violence and Memory: One Hundred Years in the "Dark Forests" of Matabeleland, Zimbabwe* (Oxford: James Curry, 2000).

35. Most published material (and there is not a great deal) on theater in Zimbabwe does not address this question directly, and needs to be read symptomatically. See David Kerr, with Stephen Chifunyise, "Southern Africa," in *A History of Theatre in Africa*, ed. Martin Banham (Cambridge: Cambridge University Press, 2004), 265–311, p. 300. See also Stephen Chifunyise, "Trends in Zimbabwean Theatre Since 1980," in *Politics and Performance: Theatre, Poetry and Song in Southern Africa*, ed. Liz Gunner (Johannesburg: Witwatersrand University Press, 1995), 55–73. In a raucous discussion of *Workshop Negative* at the University of Zimbabwe in 1987 Chifunyise, then representing the government's Department of Youth and Culture, accused the play of misrepresenting Zimbabwe's history. For a different perspective, see Preben Kaarsholm, "Mental Colonisation or Catharsis? Theatre, Democracy and Cultural Struggle from Rhodesia to Zimbabwe," in *Politics and Performance: Theatre, Poetry and Song in Southern Africa*, ed. Liz Gunner (Johannesburg: Witwatersrand University Press, 1995), 224–51.

36. Following Cobbing's famous intervention in his dissertation: Julian Cobbing, "The Ndebele under the Khumalos, 1820–96." PhD dissertation, University of Lancaster, 1976.

37. See Terence Ranger, "Pugilism and Pathology: African Boxing and the Black Urban Experience in Southern Rhodesia," in *Sport in Africa: Essays in Social History*, ed. William J. Baker and James Mangan (New York: Africana Publishing, 1987), 196–213; Preben Kaarsholm, "Si Ye Pambile—Which Way Forward? Urban Development, Culture and Politics in Bulawayo," in *Sites of Struggle: Essays in Zimbabwe's Urban History*, ed. Brian Raftopoulos and Yoshikuni Tsuneo (Harare: Weaver Press, 1999), 227–56.

38. As was the case in a number of colonial sub-Saharan African cities.

39. Lent, "Foreword," ix.

40. Esther C.M. Yau, ed., *At Full Speed: Hong Kong Cinema in a Borderless World* (Minneapolis, MN: University of Minnesota Press, 2001), 5.

41. Teo, "*Wuxia* Redux," my emphasis.

42. David Bordwell, "Aesthetics in Action: *Kungfu*, Gunplay, and Cinematic Expressivity," in *At Full Speed*, ed. Yau, 73, my emphasis. See also his book with the telling title *Planet Hong Kong: Popular Cinema and the Art of Entertainment* (Cambridge, MA: Harvard University Press, 2000).

43. As in Nicole Brenez's marvelous account: Brenez, "The Secrets of Movement."

44. Bordwell, *Planet Hong Kong*, xi–xii.

45. As Brenez points out, the cinema in France was invented as a technique for

decomposing movement (Brenez, "The Secrets of Movement," 165), and she goes on to examine the way in which Hong Kong action cinema has provided a liberating lever for French experimental cinema to reconstruct the problem of movement.

46. Oxford English Dictionary.
47. Bordwell, "Aesthetics in Action," 82.
48. Serge Daney, "From Movies to Moving," *Documenta Documents*, no. 2 (1996): 76–79, p. 77.
49. See Zhen Zhang, "The Anarchic Body Language of the Martial Arts Film," in *An Amorous History of the Silver Screen: Shanghai Cinema, 1896–1937* (Chicago, IL: University of Chicago Press, 2005), 199–243; 387–97.
50. Meaghan Morris, "Learning from Bruce Lee: Pedagogy and Political Correctness in Martial Arts Cinema," in *Keyframes: Popular Cinema and Cultural Studies*, ed. Matthew Tinkcom and Amy Villarejo (London: Routledge, 2001), 171–86, 176.
51. Ibid., 180.
52. Ibid., 179. Her perspective differs somewhat from that of Stuart Kaminsky and Yvonne Tasker. See Stuart M. Kaminsky, "Kung Fu Film as Ghetto Myth," in *Movies as Artifacts*, ed. Michael T. Marsden, John G. Nachbar, and Sam L. Grogg Jr. (Chicago, IL: Nelson-Hall, 1982), 137–45; Yvonne Tasker, *Spectacular Bodies: Gender, Genre and the Action Cinema* (London: Routledge, 1993).
53. Marilyn Mintz, *The Martial Arts Films* (North Clarendon, VT: Charles E. Tuttle, 1983), 74.
54. Stephen Teo, "The True Way of the Dragon: The Films of Bruce Lee," in *Overseas Chinese Figures in Cinema* (Hong Kong: Urban Council, 1992). Cited by Siu Leung Li, "The Myth Continues: Cinematic Kung Fu in Modernity," in *Hong Kong Connections*, ed. Morris, Li, and Ching-kiu, 60.
55. Moreblessings Chitauro, Caleb Dube, and Liz Gunner, "Song, Story and Nation: Women as Singers and Actresses in Zimbabwe," in *Politics and Performance: Theatre, Poetry and Song in Southern Africa*, ed. Liz Gunner (Johannesburg: Witwatersrand University Press, 1995), 111–38.
56. A series of personal interviews since 1994.
57. *The Standard* newspaper, May 14, 2006. www.the standard.co.zw.

the new paradoxes

of black

africa's cinemas

o l i v i e r   b a r l e t

Despite the shrinking spaces for its exhibition, and despite accusations of disconnect from its public, Africa's Francophone cinema is in search of a new aesthetic in an effort to leave the margin where it had confined itself.

the perennial matter of audiences

The catalogue for "Africa Remix," the major exhibition of contemporary African art that traveled between Düsseldorf, London, Paris and Tokyo from July 2004 to July 2006, contains an interesting essay by Manthia Diawara, a professor at New York University, entitled "L'Autoreprésentation dans le cinéma africain."[1] Evoking the critique of neocolonialism and imperialism Ousmane Sembène developed via a Brechtian aesthetic, Diawara argues that the French Cooperation has attempted to counter that aesthetic by privileging an anthropological aesthetic instead. Accordingly, the backing given to Francophone cinema in Africa can thus be seen as a trap laid out for the filmmakers to get them to produce a reassuring primitive image of Africa that reflects the West's vision of the continent. It is in the portraitist photography of a Seydou Keïta or a Malick Sidibé, as well as in Nigerian home video that Diawara sees the aspirations of the African middle class, which thus appeal more directly to an African audience: "This aesthetic choice differs radically from the intentions of the Francophone cinema, which only addresses the Europeans [. . .] Because it is a product of mass consumption, cinema can't afford to ignore its audiences," he adds.[2] The debate is recurrent but becoming exacerbated today, boosted by the growth of identity politics, triggered in turn by the increasing violence with which the Western countries reject immigrants, both inside and outside their borders.

What the filmmakers are accused of is treason. They are thus caught in the middle. While the Westerners expect of them an "authentic Africanness" of the ethnographic variety to deign to be interested in their films, the Africans demand another kind of "authentic Africanness," one that would meet their expectations of a positive representation of themselves.

But let us consider the photos of the portraitists Manthia Diawara mentions: with the help of a variety of objects and attitudes their subjects have made use of identifiable signs of their social ambitions found precisely in films and magazines offering a "modern" Western world. One only need consult the *Afriphoto* book on Malick Sidibé, co-published by *Africultures* and *Editions Filigranes*: sun shades, flares, underwear, straightened hair, cigarettes at the mouth, transistor radios, sporty poses . . . One can certainly claim that this is all about appropriation, about a playful subversiveness combined with a desire for progress, but is it not also an instance of a rampant globalization at play through the fascination with consumer objects evoking another world?

Kids in jeans do not aspire to wearing *boubous*. Addressing an African audience does not mean having to return to some cultural authenticity. Like everywhere else, people dream of consuming more and of the good life. With the exception of short films, which are most often produced under the auspices of audiovisual training schemes (Dakar, Yaoundé, Ouagadougou, Accra) and which follow in their predecessors' footsteps by taking on social problems, films shot on video—all over the place and not just in Nigeria—most often offer tales of social mobility and over-formatted comedies of manner set in bourgeois interiors. The triumphs of this popular cinema, which is taking over from the *telenovelas*, are similar to the success of Indian cinema in Africa or else in the Middle East and South East Asia. The post-1992 emergence of Nigerian video-cinema, which has been well received by the local public and which today constitutes a bona fide film industry, is everywhere in Africa, and especially among the young up-and-coming video filmmakers, taken as an instance of home-based development, no longer in need of external financing (and thus able to avoid the shaping force of the North's expectations). With more than 1,200 features produced in 2004, Lagos is beating Bombay! But Nollywood's displacement of Bollywood will not change the situation: no matter how much its exports increase, Nigerian video film will not make African cinema shine any more brightly around the globe. Despite some rare exceptions, it is characterized by the same self-perpetuating formula as Indian films. These super-codified films retell endlessly, and at top speed, the same stories without generating the myths and utopias needed to bring people together and help them build their future. Ghana is a case in point: while its film production came to a halt with Kwaw Ansah's last films, and the graduates of the National Film and Television Institute find employment only in communication industries, a parallel video production has emerged that has no link whatsoever to local talent; basically driven by a search for profit, of mediocre quality because it does not avail itself of the achievements of the preceding generation, its success is today threatened by the invasion of the Nigerian competition. Kwaw Ansah—who had excellent commercial successes with his wonderful *Love Brewed in the African Pot* (1980) and *Heritage Africa* (1987)—told me in Accra in October 2005:

> Hollywood has done so much ill against the black race, and now that we have an opportunity to tell our own stories, we are doing worse than Hollywood! It's really painful. We are few in Ghana but these few are following the Nigerian example.

Much like Bollywood, Nollywood responds to its audiences' demands. The Nigerian films rework anxieties of a society confronted by violence and the growing role of the occult and money, while replaying the ambitions of upward social mobility in tales of romance and jealousy. That is the key to their success. But it would be useful to undertake a critical analysis of their representation of violence (and thus of the model they offer to the young people of their country), their treatment of moral values, and the way they reproduce a consumerist and arriviste model that often involves self-rejection and an acceptance of an external model. The greatest recent Nigerian hits, such as *Dangerous Twins* (Tade Ogidan, 2004) or *Osuofia in London* (Kingsley Ogoro, 2003) that have been sold in hundreds of thousands of copies and have generated sequels that hope to make similar profits, convey a devalorizing comparison between the North and the South. As Martial Nuega and Franck Ndema put it in their critique of *Dangerous Twins* entitled "A Sad Stereotype of Africans" (which can be found on www.africine.org), "this London of liberties and of success acts as a mystifying model of refinement, while Lagos remains in the era of dust, corruption and scams." Their conclusion is "instead of a potential return home this seems to be an appeal to emigration."

the myth of popular cinema

What then is this positiveness we are talking about? The paradox of the demand to keep in mind the so-called "natural" audience is that this entails calling for a popular cinema that eternally reproduces the same old "invention of Africa" along external mercantile models rather than creating characters capable of pooling energies and talents for an autonomous development. Yet that is exactly what the cinema accused of being "made for Westerners" tries to do. Sogo Sanon, the veteran in *Tasuma, le feu* (Daniel Sanou Kollo, Burkina Faso, 2003) is a non-conformist, a pacifist, concerned with preserving people's dignity: he fights for the right of the village women to use a flour mill. Sergeant Vittorio at the center of *Un Héros* (Zézé Gomboa, Angola, 2004), a veteran who has lost a leg to a landmine, has a spirit open enough to find the path of hope in a ravaged country. In *Kabala* (Assane Koyoute, Mali, 2002) Hamalla finds a way to turn around the rejection of his village and gets them to build a durable and solid settlement. In *Madame Brouette* (Moussa Sene Absa, Senegal, 2002) Mati revolts against the men who abuse and rape her. In *Paris selon Moussa* (Cheick Doukouré, Guinea, 2002) Moussa gets involved in the cause of the illegal immigrants whom he discovers in Paris even though he only came to purchase a water pump for his village . . .

Is this simply ethnographic discourse, a trap laid by the West? What contempt for engaged filmmakers who have taken so long to gestate their work evan as the popular films are churned out at top speed and with no other ambition than to please! The sensibility and dignity of these modern heroes (even when they are from the bush, which, for that matter often begins only a stone's throw from the big cities) is every bit as radical as Sembène's lambasting of corrupt elites and obsolete traditions. Yet these costly productions do not draw the same numbers of viewers as the digital productions shot cheaply by the newcomers working on the Nigerian model. In Burkina Faso, the 4,000 euros which Regina Fanta Nacro spent on a tightly organized publicity campaign for Zeka Laplaine's *Le Jardin du papa* drew only 1,500 viewers. But, following in the footsteps of *Sofia* and *Traque à Ouaga* made in 2004 by the journalist Boubacar Diallo, *Ouaga Zoodo* (*Friendship in Ouaga*, produced in the Mòoré language) directed by Boubacar Zida aka Sidnaaba, director of Radio Savane FM, was a box-office hit: 50,000 tickets in a few weeks in August 2005, theatres filled to bursting, viewers asking for reruns. It is not by accident that these budding directors are from the world of media: they know what makes their audience buzz and use the miracle formula. Boubacar Diallo (also the chief editor of the satiric weekly *Le Journal du jeudi*) uses the same tricks as the American or Hindi cinema, but the narrative structure of his films is quite close to the traditional storytelling in Africa. It is always the good and the poor one that wins.

There is not much time to ponder a project: while Diallo has a series of screenplays ready to go and is preparing to shoot *Dossiers brulants*, Sidnaaba has just completed pre-production of his next film *Wiidbo* (*Sacrilege*). The average budget of a feature is 20 million FCFA (30,000 euros) so a film has to have only a two-month run to break even. Sponsors are acknowledged in the films: in *Sofia* the heroine and her sister have an argument in front of a television where an ad for the cell phone company Celtel is running; she also comes out of a building that belongs to the National Social Security Fund, and in Bobo Dioulasso she walks in front of posters for the Burkina national lottery. Some of these films are beginning to be exported to places such as Bamako and Dakar. To say nothing of the hope that Canal France International (CFI) will buy them so that the national African televisions can rebroadcast them. It is finally beginning to be possible to make a living out of cinema in Africa!

This phenomenon is also found in Senegal (Alasanne Ndiagne, Amadou Thior) and in Cameroon (Cyrill Masso, Ako Abunaw . . .), as well as in Madagascar, where video production has garnered some genuine public successes. This is, for instance, the case for Henri Randrianierenana who, after some thirty stage productions and five original plays with the Johary theatre company, turned in 2000 to cinema to make several films each year, from the martial arts film *Ambalamasoandro* (2001) to *Ralaitavin-Dravao* (*The Woman from Ralaitavin,* 2001), in which a woman crosses social barriers in order to pay for her daughter's studies abroad, to a 135-minute long police drama *Raharaha 245* (2001), to the thriller *Soalandy* (2002) in which a maid rises to wealth. Upward mobility plus romantic entanglements: a sure recipe for success. Randrianierenana, a seasoned cinephile, refines his films for stronger impact, but it would be an exaggeration to see in them a genuine aesthetic undertaking.

This is another example of the Nigerian logic, where a director like Lancelot Imasuen, at 31, already has sixty-one features to his credit. But let us not get trapped in a trivial binarism that pits a popular cinema against "cinema of quality": some big popular films are cinematographic treasures. Public success does not devalue a film. But the question is, in what way does it value the film? Popular cinema makes it possible to federate a people around characters that represent its daily ambitions, but in what ways do these ambitions help in facing social change or in buuilding up an imaginary? That requires a questioning of the self, the object of art, which in turn traces the pathways of a collective development, the object of politics. Since when do creators who aim to advance a society's self-reflection crave box-office success? Cooperative programs which contribute to financing the productions of films destined for the local market, such as the Images Afrique fund, administered by the French Ministry of Foreign Affairs (granted to local producers, in particular for TV serials), aim in their selection criteria to promote quality productions in the hope that these will in turn infect others with some increased inventiveness and creativity.

the era of suspicion

Even though this is never admitted, it seems inevitable that subsidy commissions influence the content of films: they judge according to their criteria of eligibility, guided by imaginary representations that have evolved over time. A study, in which I participated as expert and which published its report in 2003,[3] proposed to include as many professionals from the South as possible in these commissions so as to provide a referential counterbalance to the dominant representations of the North. Rather than relying on quotas, or on a devalorizing "affirmative action," the blend in the decision-making bodies should at least limit neocolonial-style abuses.

But the fact that at present these commissions draw on those professionals from the South who are based in Europe reignites the old accusation against Francophone filmmakers that they "only address Europeans": though they are often in perennial transit between their home countries and the countries of their residence, the fact that they live principally in Europe casts a shadow of suspicion on the filmmakers of the "diaspora." Here too contempt is the norm, and the force of accusations proportional to the frustrations felt. They are said to be disconnected from African realities, uninterested in their audiences' expectations, sell-outs to the West. Would such accusations be made against an abstract painter? Is a filmmaker less of an artist?

Yet going away has always been understood to be a saving grace for creative people. It affords critical distance without having to deny awareness of where one is from. Their origin is an inexhaustible raw material that "inhabits" them, as is the case with the Congo for Tchicaya U Tam'si in his French exile—which does not obstruct him being recognized as one of the greatest African poets. For they are structured not simply by referencing their culture, but by their very experience, their way of belonging to the world. They are asked to represent their country but refuse, claiming a right to hybridity or even the split that comes from their contact with an else-where. Their ambitions and their doubts are not necessarily shared by their society of origin: they cannot be its emblems as some would like them to be (or as some reproach them for being when they don't feel represented abroad by the content of their films). "It's tiresome," says the Chadian Mahamat Saleh Haroun. "The problem is how to free oneself from the vision of others, and to affirm oneself as a distinct artist who is not the sum total of those back home."[4]

An individual artist: what if we recognized them as such? This requires starting from the works themselves without trapping them in the globality applied so frequently when it comes to Africa. Not only is it contemptuous to say that they become perverted in contact with the North; it also yet again allows the triumph of a duality that unfortunately characterizes a widespread way of thinking of the world. "There is no center any more, only peripheries: each periphery becomes a center of its own," as Edouard Glissant points out.[5] Today sectarianism entails imposing a filiation: rootedness in origin becomes a *diktat*, yet it is from a network of roots that a new vision of a world can emerge, a vision capable of recognizing the "creolization" within a work. It is in this sense that "a plural identity is not a lack of identity," to quote Glissand again. "It does not boil down to either losing or distorting oneself."

olivier barlet

222

a subversive aesthetic

Such a stance is subversive. It is a form of resistance to unitary thought and to globalization's impoverishment. Right from the first film made by Black Africans, *Afrique sur Seine* (1955), Paulin Soumanou Vieyra and his friends in the Groupe africain du cinema worked to turn around the gaze of the colonizer. But this returned gaze was fundamentally directional: the film was made under the auspices of the Comité du film ethnographique! This led to an appropriation: cinemas in Africa seized on, as Jean-Michel Frodon suggests, "the French idea of cinema" as universalist message.[6] This is where it might be possible to criticize the Francophone filmmakers for making films for Europeans—in the sense of not having invented a language adapted for African audiences. But is this not paradoxical? For this cinematography has not, until recently, developed a truly aesthetic rupture. It has for instance not undertaken a rereading of genre cinema crammed with mise-en-scene innovations of the sort Hong Kong cinema has since the 1970s. Rather, much like African literature, this cinematography has "resorted to the margin," to borrow an expression of Momar Désiré Kane, so as to go beyond the role of mirroring the African cultural space and to "install the reign of ambivalence." "In the wake of the *Négritude* movement which foregrounded the role of the bard, the process of overcoming the duality between Africa and France is organized around the persona of the marginal drop-out, the madman and around the thematic of wandering."[7]

What has changed today is that African cinematography struggles against this marginality, which may have allowed it to envisage the world in its globality but which now traps it by severing it from the wider dialogue of contemporary cultural expressions. To be able to ask about one's place in the world independently of where one comes from demands a new aesthetic, a new language that reflects this. This is why the films of a new generation of filmmakers are experimenting with new forms better suited to the sharp awareness they have of the problems facing Africa and the world at large—and these are necessarily different from the format of popular cinema.

They do so in a variety of ways. On the one hand, by responding to Western audiences' demands for both exoticism and reality through strategies which are not necessarily specific to these filmmakers but are nonetheless frequently shared among them: rendering more complex (*Immatriculation temporaire*, Gahité Fofana, Guinea, 2001); leaving behind autochthonous thinking (*L'Afrance*, Alain Gomis, Senegal, 2001); seizing the present moment ((*Paris:XY*), Zeka Laplaine, Democratic Republic of Congo, 2000), focusing on the intimate to challenge perceptions (*Bye Bye Africa*, Mahamat Saleh Haroun, Chad, 1999); privileging similarity over singularity (*Daressalam*, Issa Serge Coelo, Chad, 2000, *La Vie sur terre*, Abderrahmane Sissako, Mauritania, 1998), working on memory (*Asientos*, François Woukoache, Cameroon, 1995;

Adanggaman, Roger Gnoan Mbala, Ivory Coast, 2000; *Fools*, Ramadan Suleman, South Africa 1997).[8]

On the other hand, by returning to orality. No need to sing one's Africanness—it already is a fact, as Simon Njami notes.[9] But the filmmakers are, for example in *Bye Bye Africa*, developing an "oraliture" akin to that found in the works of authors like Ahmadou Kourouma, a new form of writing characterized by the fact that it no longer is one.[10] *Heremakono—En attendant le bonheur* (Abderrahmane Sissako, 2002) replaces narrative linearity by a form of jazz in that it is the physical sensations induced by acoustic or visual experiences which lead to our understanding of the film characters' position in the world. Like in *Abouna* (Mahamat Saleh Haroun, 2002), it is the way of filming the body in context which suggest a state of suspension, mirroring the situation in which Africans find themselves today, tragically cut off from the possibility of moving outside the continent, as well as from their inscription in the global exchange system, but paradoxically in a peaceful state of waiting, drawn from a kind of serenity in which spirituality too plays a role. Worries and chaos do not obscure a certain glimmer of hope embodied by the young Khatra as he retrieves the light bulb which will allow him to bring his family light. But the doors, the drapes, the unspoken words and the slit windows suggest uncertainty and doubt: this cinema has neither a ready-made solution nor a didactic message, settling instead for an evocation of the complexity of the state of things at hand, sharpening the gaze in order to favor hearing. A new awareness is coming to the foreground, "an awareness accompanied by a system of thought," to quote Haroun, sharpened by a cinema conceived as an artistic expression and which greatly draws on self-reflexive documentary film.[11]

If these films resonate in the manner of blues it is because they are marked by not only the memory of a black people but also its dignity. South Africa's eruption onto the African cinema scene is a reminder of the continuity between slavery, the slave trade and segregation. The highpoint of FESPACO 2005 was Ramdan Suleman's second feature, *Zulu Love Letter*, whose aesthetic innovation matched its theme, the film as a whole helping to clarify that, it is impossible to reach political reconciliation without recognizing the need for mourning in the private sphere.

a new imaginary

Today it is essential that this cinema does not burn itself out because of its invisibility in the South, and its systematic misunderstanding in the North. Invisibility in the South because these cinematic works now have no places of exhibition: the last movie houses are disappearing in African cities,[12] or else turning—much like the video-clubs—into full-time popular movie places. And misunderstanding in the North because the game of fascination/rejection which characterizes the relation to anything African persists,[13] and because contemporary African productions are valorized only if they "enrich Western art deemed to be too cerebral by an infusion of new blood,"[14] or to use Henri Lopès' terms a propos of Francophone literature: "Mme de Sévigné's language with black balls."[15] What the West needs is neither regeneration nor hybridization but rather to make room for African cultural expressions as an autonomous proposal within a new imaginary, capable of channeling the tremor of our world.

notes

1. Manthia Diawara, "L'Autoreprésentation dans le cinéma africain," in *Africa Remix: L'art contemporain d'un continent, catalogue de l'exposition*, ed. Simon Njami (Paris: Editions de Centre Pompidou, 2005), 285–91.
2. Ibid., 290.
3. Ministère des Affaires étrangères, DGCID, *Soutenir le cinéma des pays du Sud— évaluation rétrospective de la coopération française dans la Zone de Solidarité Prioritaire (1991–2001)*. Série évaluations no. 67 (April 2003): 166.
4. "Pour un cinema pensé. Entretien avec Mahamat Saleh Haroun," Olivier Barlet interview. www.africultures.com. www.africultures.com/index.asp? menu=affiche_article&no=3685
5. "Les grands entretiens du Cercle de minuit," Edouard Glissant interviewed by Laure Adler and Thérèse Lombard, program directed by Pierre Desfons, France 2 télévision.
6. Jean-Michel Frodon, *La Projection nationale* (Paris: Odile Jacob, 1998), 187.
7. Momar Désiré Kane, *Marginalité et errance dans la littérature et le cinéma africains francophones: Les carrefours mobiles*. Collection Images plurielles (Paris: L'Harmattan 2004), 9.
8. See Olivier Barlet, "Les nouvelles stratégies des cinéastes africains," in "L'Africanité en questions," special issue, *Africultures*, no. 41, (October 2001): 69–76.
9. Simon Njami, "Chaos et métamorphose," in *Africa Remix*, ed. Njami, 15–25.
10. See Olivier Barlet, "Les nouvelles écritures francophones des cinéastes afro-européens," in "Ecritures dans les cinémas d'Afrique noire," ed. Boulou Ebanda de B'beri, *CiNéMAS* 11, no. 1 (2000).
11. See Olivier Barlet, "Du cinéma métis au cinéma nomade: défense du cinéma," in "Métissages: un alibi culturel?" special issue, *Africultures*, no. 62 (January–March 2005): 94–103.
12. See Olivier Barlet, "Afrique noire: la fin des salles?" *Cahiers du cinéma*, no. 604 (September 2005): 62–63.
13. Olivier Barlet, "Postcolonialisme et cinéma: de la différence à la relation," in "Postcolonialisme: inventaire et débats," special issue, *Africultures*, no. 28 (May 2000): 56–65.
14. Jean-Loup Amselle, *L'Art de la friche: Essai sur l'art africain contemporain* (Paris: Flammarion, 2005), 12.
15. Ibid., 51.

Translated from the French by Nataša Ďurovičová, with Melissa Thackway.

the transnational

other

street kids in

contemporary

brazilian cinema

j o ã o   l u i z   v i e i r a

How does film still reflect, refract, and transform cultural identity while shaping new forms of subjectivity in an increasingly transnational world? Economic transnationality implies a deep interdependence between the developed and the developing world, somehow deconstructing older, simplistic polarizations such as that between North and South, for example. Contingent terms such as First World and Third World might no longer signify the same valence of economic and political power that they did until very recently. Skyrocketing levels of unemployment, drug trafficking, child labor, prostitution, and sexual tourism in the "tropics" are just a few symptoms that, depicted on screen, lend authenticity to the representation of social ills and other forms of violence in contemporary international cinema.

Extending these formulations from the national to the transnational, the global fate of street kids seems to be a continuing topic of inquiry, one that eloquently shows us a present and future dystopia, especially in Brazil, which is plagued by extreme levels of social injustice and one of the worst wealth distribution rates anywhere in the world. The marginalization of children has become a priority on the agendas of public security as well as human rights organizations.[1] From as early as Buñuel's *Los olvidados* (1950), to Babenco's *Pixote* (1980) and Nair's *Salaam Bombay* (1988), to the contemporary scene of Meirelles' *Cidade de Deus* (2003) or Koreeda's *Nobody Knows* (2004), international audiences have become so familiar with their "others's" social contexts that they may discount the situations depicted in these and many other film narratives as "typical Third World scenarios." The socio-economic contexts these films depict have become all too familiar, serving to confirm the trope that "there is a First World in every Third World and vice versa." Their veneer of documentary realism makes it possible for some of the films discussed here to depict Latin American metropolises—be they São Paulo or Rio, Buenos Aires, Bogotá, or Mexico City—as somehow interchangeable and anonymous Third World cities, with their protagonists functioning as generic oppressed subjects, whether they are from Los Angeles, Chicago, Detroit, the outskirts of Paris, London, or Tokyo.

In conceptual terms, I am interested in asking whether it is currently possible to avoid repeating stories of urbanization and modernization in which the city could be anywhere in the late-capitalist world, operating as the arena for corruption, economic underdevelopment, and exploitation. Such a question requires contemporary film and cultural critique to bear in mind a series of issues: analogies between art and politics in the contemporary transnational landscape; the dense web of connections that links communities, societies, and nations in terms of race, gender, sexuality, religion, and other important axes of identity; questions posed by film analysis concerning the film text's ability to narrate more open spaces that differ from the closed familiar household, such as the streets of any urban landscape, in which blurred spatial configurations destabilize the traditionally gendered binary of space, and where boundaries between self/other, inside/outside, interior/exterior, city/countryside, male/female, and child/adult are continuously negotiated.

How then do these films avoid representing their so-called Third World subjects merely as "The Other"? How do these filmic texts succeed in representing the dynamism of a more transnational economic reality and avoid an anachronistic specular regime in which the Third World is constructed for, and subjected to, the gaze of the First World? Ultimately, in light of the renewal of the conventions of Hollywood-centric film language, I wish to investigate how a transnational mode of production/consumption impacts representation.

The relevance of a topic like street kids in Latin American (and Brazilian in particular) cinema for an anthology like this is that it readily qualifies as a true transnational genre, the *street urchin film*, which might include Vittorio De Sica's *Shoeshine* (1946), David Lean's *Oliver Twist* (1948), or Carol Reed's film of the stage musical version, *Oliver!* (1968), as well as its 2005 remake by Roman Polansky, but also, and more to the point of this inquiry, Luis

Buñuel's *Los olvidados*, Mira Nair's *Salaam Bombay*, Victor Gaviria's *Rodrigo D: No Future* (1990) as well as his *La vendedora de rosas* (1998), Peruvian Francisco Lombardi's second episode of *Caídos del cielo* (1990), Fernando Spinoza and Alejandro Legaspi's *Juliana* (1994), John Singleton's *Boyz n the Hood* (1991), Larry Clark's *Kids* (1995), Spike Lee's *Crooklyn* (1994), Argentine Bruno Stagnaro's *Pizza, birra, faso* (1998), Chilean Gonzalo Justiniano's *Caluga o menta* (1990), Ecuadorian Sebastián Cordero's *Ratas, ratones, rateros* (1999), Mexican Gerardo Tort's *De la calle* (*Streeters*, 2001), Rodrigo Plá's *La zona* (2007), or Danny Boyle's *Slumdog Millionaire* (2008) and, of course, a whole series of Brazilian films such as, to name but a few, Hector Babenco's *Pixote* (1981), José Joffily's sequel, *Quem matou Pixote?* (1996), Anselmo Duarte's *Os Trombadinhas* (1978), Sandra Werneck's documentary *A Guerra dos Meninos* (1991), Murilo Salles' *Como Nascem os Anjos* (1996), Sérgio Bianchi's *Chronically Unfeasible* (2000), and his latest *Quanto vale ou é por quilo?* (2005), Fernando Meirelles and Kátia Lund's *City of God* (2003), Rudi Lagemann's *Anjos do Sol* (2006), Paulo Morelli's *City of Men* (2007), and José Padilha's documentary *Bus 174* (2002) as well as his *Elite Squad* (2007).

Limiting ourselves here to the films from Mexico, Brazil, India, and Argentina makes more sense in that they express and reflect the economic, cultural, and psychological conditions of postcolonial nations. For all these films deal with fundamentally similar situations in which youth are undervalued and, as a result, they perceive their daily lives as senseless and often engage in criminal behavior that ultimately leads to a dead-end future.

Babenco's *Pixote* can still be considered a landmark film for contemporary Latin American cinema. Its enduring influence was felt all over the continent, due perhaps to the fact that it shares many of its widely praised qualities with the iconic *Los olvidados*: its topic (delinquent children), its source (sociological documentation), its setting (a Third World metropolis), its style (documentary inflected), its casting strategy (a mix of professionals and nonprofessional performers), its focalization (the children themselves), and even its episodic structure. *Pixote*'s relevance has only increased in tandem with unemployment, illiteracy, and child labor, especially in the drug trade, not to mention the unparalleled explosion of sexual exploitation of teenagers, particularly in Brazil, with its sexual tourism.

Yet already in 1978, some two years before *Pixote* was released, homeless kids in urban centers such as Rio and São Paulo began to attract media attention. Besides the more militant documentary shorts, the subject was also taken up by the well-known director Anselmo Duarte, winner of the prestigious Palme d'Or in Cannes in 1962 with *O Pagador de Promessas*, a film that profited internationally from the impact of Cinema Novo in the early 1960s. His *Os Trombadinhas* (1979) takes its title from an early nickname for homeless children derived from the word, *trombada*, which literally means "collision" or "crash" and was used to describe their method of stealing, a kind of unarmed pickpocketing. Duarte's film rehearses a Manichean world of Dickensian inspiration where, despite some similarities in the use of language and the strategies of a collective organization, good and evil possess clearly defined borders. In this world, children are the objects of adult exploitation of various kinds. Through a Griffithian contrasting parallel montage, spectators were able to draw a moral conclusion favoring sports, alongside music, as perhaps the only venues left for poor, mainly African-Brazilian, boys, especially since the coach in the film is Pelé, the quintessential model hero, who, being himself of African descent like so many other Brazilian soccer heroes, functions as an eloquent emblem of social mobility.

The seminal first feature by Nelson Pereira dos Santos, made around the mid-1950s, the very moment of the inception of a new cinema in Brazil, still resonates today. In order to question the clearly demarcated divisions between rich and poor, tourists and excluded children, *Rio 40 Degrees* (1956) introduced new social actors into the Brazilian cinema, five young black *favela* boys selling peanuts in the streets of Rio de Janeiro on a hot summer day. They serve as nodal points for a narrative that cuts among characters from different social backgrounds. Marginalized by the upper classes, the boys are systematically and physically excluded from participation in society. At a key moment two of the boys, begging for money on the oceanfront Avenida Atlântica in Copacabana, happen to meet two North American women tourists enjoying leisurely drinks on a hotel terrace. The boys ask for money and are refused. As the approach did not work, one of them teaches the other what the proper performance to win the sympathy of other tourists and passers-by might be; his advice is to pretend the money is for a sick mother. These displays of street smarts will be repeated in another key yet almost lost film from the early 1960s, *Fábula, minha vida em Copacabana* by the Swedish documentary filmmaker Arne Sucksdorf, which he shot between 1963 and 1965. In this film, the *malandragem*, as well as the ability to overcome obstacles with wit and speed, elements that characterize street smarts, are always shown in a positive light.[2] Dos Santos' quintet from *Rio 40 Degrees*, along with the children in Marcel Camus' *Black Orpheus* (1958) and Joaquim Pedro de Andrade's short episode *Cat's Skin* (1962), develop the tropes which would soon be rendered more complex in Sucksdorf's docudrama. But since the censorship problems faced by Dos Santos were still on everyone's mind, the production of *Fábula* met with all sorts of self-imposed difficulties, compounded by the rise of the military regime, which was to last for the next twenty years.

Fábula brings to mind other connections with *Black Orpheus*. It opens with shots of the *favela* boys flying their kites around the same spectacular locations used in the French production. The only major difference lies in the use of black and white stock instead of the lush colors used in the Camus film. In contradistinction to *Rio 40 Degrees*, however, it is the first feature film made in Brazil to place street kids at the center of the narrative, giving them voices and points-of-view in order to explicitly expose the constraints of a life lived in the streets. As in practically every Brazilian film shot in the *favelas*, it constantly moves from the hillside slums to the city streets in order to denounce the correctional institutions in which lessons on how to steal more efficiently are learned, and the most common pedagogical technique is a foot in one's face, as one of the young characters proclaims. Hunger and other forms of violence are also part of the routine in these so-called reform schools. This neglected and underrated film attests to the pervasiveness of the drug trade and its wars in the early 1960s, and it retains its relevance for contemporary Brazilians, who are exposed to these maladies on a daily basis, especially in the major cities.

After a rather adventurous morning at the beach, during which the quartet of three boys and a girl tries to survive by stealing and reselling rich kids' kites on the Copacabana beach, the group goes up the hill to where they live among the ruins of a former shack, only to find the place occupied by a group of heavily armed bandits whose sinister silhouettes seem to dominate the landscape from above. Of course, the kids are forced to abandon the place. Today the sequence seems visionary, four decades ahead of such images becoming all too banal in the daily lives of Rio's frightened population. The group then tries to survive by picking through a huge garbage dump on the outskirts of the city, a brief scene which is perhaps the first visit paid by Brazilian cinema to that privileged site of socio-economic contradictions. Failing at that, the brief interlude in the garbage dump leads them back to the streets of Copacabana and once again to the beach. They repeat the begging lessons taught in *Rio 40 Degrees* as one advises another never to smile and to always try to put on a hungry face. One of them attempts working as a shoeshine boy (an explicit reference to De Sica's *Shoeshine*), while the others make their living by picking pockets among other things, always with bad results.[3] In contrast to *Rio 40 Degrees*, where crime still does not exist in the children's daily lives, here it always offers a chance to get out of poverty, though it is an option not considered without some guilt.

Pixote follows some Brazilian slum kids, emblematic of Brazil's 3 million homeless children, from police raids to reform school to life-threatening "freedom" on the streets. Again following *Los olvidados*, there is a factual prologue—initially only included on prints for international distribution and only recently available on the VHS version in Brazil—in which the director himself, Hector Babenco, quotes the alarming figure of 28 million Brazilians under the age of 18 living a life of misery far below the international standards of living set by the United Nations. Babenco argues that this enormous population is easily attracted to crime due to their impoverishment and helplessness. Back in the early 1950s, however, Buñuel's prologue to *Los olvidados* already introduced a transnational scenario. Although the story is set in Mexico, by showing images of New York and Paris, Buñuel suggests that the location is purely a matter of choice, that any other major city could have served just as well. Although it was produced during the years of the *abertura*, the gradual political opening of the military dictatorship in progress since 1974, *Pixote* was the subject of extensive negotiations with the censors due to the explosive nature of its content, a fate shared by other critical films of the period.

Adapted from José Louzeiro's book *A Infância dos Mortos* (*The Childhood of the Dead*), the screenplay was written by Jorge Durán and Babenco, who divided the narrative in two main parts. The first, somber and dark, takes place in São Paulo and depicts the lives of adolescents in a correctional prison and then in the streets, while the second takes place in sunny Rio and narrates the disintegration of the group in that city's underground. The narrative focus concentrates on a few typical figures. One by one the children and teenagers are delineated as the main characters: the ringleader "Queen" Lilica; the pot-loving "Fumaça" (meaning "smoke" in English); the sensitive, searching Dito, Lilica's lover; and Pixote himself, a 10-year-old kid who is the smallest and most vulnerable of the group. Pixote combines pubescent energy with precocious street smarts, and behind his hauntingly feral face one glimpses the perfectly normal child that might have been under less Darwinian circumstances. That both the young actor Fernando Ramos da Silva, who played Pixote, and his brother were themselves killed by the police a few years after the completion of the film, in circumstances still not well understood, attests to the veracity of the film.

Indeed, *Pixote* anticipates the murder of more than a thousand children every year between 1989 and 1991, usually by the police or death squads. One of these tragic events happened in 1994, in Rio, garnering immediate attention from the international press and several NGOs. Seven teenagers were killed in downtown Rio near Candelária church, and one of the survivors of that massacre would later be the kidnapper of *Bus 174*, another tragic episode in the daily chronicle of violence affecting contemporary Rio. At the time of the Candelária killings, elites would ambiguously refer to that group killing as *faxina* instead of *chacina*.[4]

The first half of *Pixote* is set in a microcosmic detention center, a ritualized universe of authoritarian power trips and sordid sexual humiliations. Babenco exposes an array of abuses such as gang rapes by the inmates, exploitation, and even murder by the authorities themselves, which they cover up with glib lies to investigating agencies. The film vividly illustrates the perennial metaphor of prison as a school for crime. Armed with wooden guns, the children play-act bank holdups and rehearse techniques of torture learned from the authorities, who are in some respects presented as the real criminals. Apart from exposing the Dickensian oppression of the reform school, the film uncovers the human suffering masked by bland abstractions like "abandoned minors" and "juvenile delinquency." When Pixote and his friends escape, the film metamorphoses generically from a social pamphlet into a picaresque tale of tragicomic misadventures. Freedom, the boys soon discover, bears an uncanny resemblance to their previous confinement. The escapees form a makeshift family, surviving through petty assaults and drug deals, much in the same way as the older teenagers do in the Argentine film *Pizza, birra, faso.* And, as in *Los olvidados,* we also find a poignant adolescent yearning for the lost mother; in place of Pedro's mother in the Buñuel film we have Sueli in the Babenco film. Thus *Pixote* deepens two interrelated themes: the brutality of the Brazilian prison system and the process by which children and teenagers become criminals. In doing so, it also correlates body and power in a context of repression and social exclusion.

Having little in common beyond their marginalization, the group is perpetually threatened by internal and external pressures. The children forge a precarious solidarity, seizing fleeting moments of tenderness in the face of insurmountable odds. Pixote is finally stripped of his companions, left the last survivor of the tribe. At the same time he undergoes a process of desensitization, showing little emotion not only at the deaths of the despised johns of their "prostitute" Sueli, but even at the accidental slaughter of his friend Dito. That the film renders this melancholy slide into degradation believable is one of its many achievements. Babenco presents his adolescent protagonist without moralizing. Neither monster nor victim, he is an urban survivor denied the luxury of conventional morality.

Pixote, as well as some other examples of this powerful sub-genre, tends to indict specific institutions as ghettoized scenes of local abuse rather than implicate the entire social system that makes such abuses virtually inevitable in the way Sérgio Bianchi does in *Chronically Unfeasible,* as we shall see below. The film's deployment of point-of-view is somewhat problematic; our identification with the children, which is guaranteed through narrative focus, point-of-view shots, and emphatic music, is usually so total that we lose all critical distance. The characters that middle-class spectators would normally identify with, the doctors, teachers, and social workers, are all one-dimensional figures unworthy of sympathy, while the victims of Pixote and his gang are either obnoxious tourists or low-life types equally unworthy of being objects of identification. Thus the film lets middle-class spectators off the hook—exactly those spectators who, in real life, might be either an oppressor or a victim of the Pixotes of this world.

Pixote skirts the question of the spectator's location within the story. We sympathize with the children and are viscerally touched by their story, but we are given little sense of our relation to what we see or what might be done about it. The emotional impact leaves little analytical residue in its wake. It is a conventionally linear, action-packed film, with plenty of narrative, music, fast-paced editing, and expressionistic colors, not to mention occasionally heavy doses of sentimentality. This holds true even when the style approaches that of a quasi-documentary, such as when a zoom-in on Pixote's face poetically reveals the moment when the young boy first learns to write, guided by a teacher. Without a cut, we see this incredible face in the very process of acquiring the ability to write, a shot which creates an unexpected intimacy between the spectator and Pixote and makes for one of very few lyrical moments in this powerful film. Despite its lack of global analysis, the film is startlingly effective in purely aesthetic and cinematic terms, given its hegemonic look. Babenco's funky Third World Expressionism turns the film into a montage of repulsions, a series of horrific images: Pixote forced to drink spittle out of a cup, adolescents witnessing a gang rape, Sueli's aborted fetus speared by a knitting needle and dumped in a bathroom wastebasket, to mention just a few. At the same time, Babenco snatches beauty from squalor. Smoking dope and sniffing glue inspire kaleidoscopic-psychedelic visions of paperweight saints, intimations of an ephemeral transcendence. Babenco is fond of quoting André Breton's aphorism "beauty will be convulsive or it will not be," and *Pixote* does achieve a kind of wrenching beauty which artfully juxtaposes apparent opposites. The sordid milieu becomes a backdrop for epiphanies of tenderness in the form of sexual connections made across lines of age, race, and class. Although lacking in a more profound political analysis, *Pixote* does expose the abuses of governmental correctional institutions and achieves, at its best, a sort of convulsive beauty truly reminiscent of Buñuel.

Comparisons with Larry Clark's *Kids* may be of interest in the context of this essay. Both films give accounts of teenage conditions in two drastically opposed cultures. Points in common, besides the more obvious theme of coming of age, include an approximation of *cinéma-vérité* style, the use of actors and non-actors, the point of departure offered by real-life characters in real locations, the preference for natural light, and the immediacy of the hand-held camera. The kids drink, smoke pot, and take illegal drugs, bringing us to another point in common, the escape from reality through drugs. In both films homosexuality plays a large role. While in *Pixote* gay characters seem to be rather ambiguously accepted at the same time they are put down, in *Kids* they are completely looked down upon by the macho guys; characters in *Kids* refer to two men in a park as faggots. Other common and interesting connections between these two films can be found in the yearning for mother/regression. *Pixote* has a breast-sucking scene, and in *Kids*, when Casper visits Telly's house, he becomes extremely preoccupied and even obsessed with Telly's mother's breastfeeding her younger son, a moment which brings back his yearning for the womb and his very early existence, perhaps the only time he was provided for.

However, one major difference between the films lies in the fact that while *Kids* concentrates more on sexual fulfillment, *Pixote* deals with economic fulfillment. But neither of the films ends with some sort of solution; rather, they leave the possibilities open. Either the children will be saved, probably with the help of outside sources, or the streets will eventually destroy them. Babenco's film links the socio-economic conditions of the youths with the absence of family ties, portraying it as a conditioning factor for their marginal existence. This is made evident in an early scene in the film in which we see a mother looking for her son in a police precinct. The mother signals more than anything else abandonment and the absence of motherly love, a trope the film explicitly touches upon in the breast-sucking shots.

Since the late 1980s, homeless Brazilian street kids have been most visible on the pages of the daily press and on the television news, especially on such sensationalist news programs as *A Cidade na TV* and *TV Alerta*. Filmmaker Sandra Werneck directed a documentary entitled *A Guerra dos Meninos* (*The War of the Boys*, 1991), which, along with its other merits, displayed positively the solidarity of those who try to escape a routine of drug abuse. The filmmaker also brought the actors from her film to screenings at regular movie theaters, a completely new experience for her amateur cast.

The fate of Pixote was also dramatized in the sequel, *Quem Matou Pixote?* (*Who Killed Pixote?*, 1996), directed by José Joffily. Shot in 1995, the project caught immediate attention after the Candelária killings of seven street kids mentioned above. However, *Quem Matou Pixote?* paints a more sentimental portrait of that milieu, chronicling the life of Fernando, the once-famous slum boy turned actor who became rich and famous at the age of 11. Thrown into the limelight thanks to the internationally acclaimed *Pixote*, Fernando almost immediately ceases being Fernando and becomes inextricably intertwined with his character, Pixote. His money soon runs out and he never makes it as an actor; meanwhile one of his many brothers, Cafú, returns to petty thievery, attracting Fernando back to a life of crime. During one of their exploits Fernando is arrested and imprisoned by an officer who promises to pursue him from that day forward. After his release, in search of renewed stardom, he lands a role on a soap opera produced by Rio's TV-Globo. But because he is unable to read properly, he cannot learn his lines, a fact that leaves him deeply embarrassed. Because he was afraid to admit his shortcomings, Fernando is eventually dismissed, returning to his hometown of Diadema on the outskirts of São Paulo. He marries and has a daughter, works as a janitor for a production company, but returns once again to crime and is killed by the police in a hold-up. As Ismail Xavier points out, this film articulates the eclipse of the social bandit in symmetry with the power of authority once attributed to the tri-continental filmmaker.[5] During the 1960s and 1970s Latin American filmmakers used to equate the camera with a gun and associate the aesthetic of violence with wars for national liberation. But since then it has become clear that cinema has become even more problematic, that it is an instrument that may also degrade relations or even kill. *Quem Matou Pixote?* offers a straightforward answer to its title—the police—but not before exposing the complicated relations experienced by the boy in his encounter with cinema, which, despite the intense envy it provokes in others, is not powerful enough to rescue him from his family's poverty, leaving him full of resentment.

In 2006, the fate of Pixote was discussed in another documentary reconstructing the making of the film and opening a space for revisions. In this film Babenco himself reminisces about his methods of directing the young actors and explicitly raises questions about what went wrong—not with his film, of course, which was hugely successful nationally and internationally—but with reality itself.[6]

Psychological and socio-cultural mechanisms similar to those activated by Pixote's fate also reverberate some years later in Murilo Salles's *Como Nascem os Anjos* (*How Angels Are Born*, 1996), a complex story about the kidnapping of an American and his daughter, who become trapped in their own house by two kids and one adult fleeing a chase in the *favela* Dona Marta, where they live. From the opening shots we witness the pervasive power and presence of national and transnational media, especially at the periphery. The young girl Branquinha is interviewed in the *favela* by a German television crew. Social exclusion, sexism, marginal childhood, national and transnational media, and drugs are some of the ingredients that will suffuse the narrative of another seemingly urgent exposé.

The opening scene is a close-up of Branquinha, with the slums as backdrop, framing both the character and her misery. When recording the interview, Branquinha appears against another internationally famous backdrop, the typical Rio skyline, with its hilly landscape, lush vegetation and the iconic Sugarloaf Mountain. Whereas the film-within-the-film beautifies the shot, the film itself more tightly frames the character and dispenses with the contextual landscape, in direct contrast, for example, to the now distant *Black Orpheus*. Branquinha's interview is entirely self-conscious and thanks to the daily repetition of the recent national and international interest in the culture of the margins, she knows very well what she is supposed to represent and what is expected of her. Performing accordingly, she begs for more money—a mere fifty-dollar bill—in exchange for an "explosive" statement. What we see then is the scene of "realism rehearsed"—the all too clean framing of Rio's misery with the postcard image of the Sugar Loaf behind—offering an image of the girl posited as part of a human zoo of sorts, both a survivor of daily violence and a spectacular and exportable tropical product for consumption by an international audience. The introduction of the other kid, Japa, who will be fascinated with the United States throughout the narrative, somehow follows the same pattern; he is shown with the city behind—the quintessential image of a city where *favela* and asphalt are inextricably associated, two worlds in constant conflict and interaction.[7] From the very beginning, the visibility promoted by the mediated power of television becomes a central defining trace of Branquinha's (and later of Japa's) characters and behavior, an example of the televisual media's capacity to weave a new kind of subjectivity.

A reflexive instance cuts across the narrative via different mediated forms. In the course of the siege, the presence of the police and the television equipment construct important analogies related to the apparatus and esthetics of surveillance. Beyond using the same channels and lenses and the same sophisticated hearing and recording devices, such as a Nagra, all this paraphernalia forms part of the repressive arsenal, without which neither the police nor the media people would be able to grasp what is happening inside the house. In this process, identities, behavior, and logic are completely disturbed—determined even—by the narcissistic charge induced by television, which is omnipresent from the beginning to the end of the film. Cameras, telephones, telephoto lenses, front door intercoms, binoculars, and other gadgets of modern communication appear at every turn in the narrative in a true catalogue of contemporary surveillance techniques that appear to render the "real" just like in any other contemporary society.

Sérgio Bianchi's *Cronicamente Inviável* (*Chronically Unfeasible*, 2000), perhaps the most important among the Brazilian street urchin films, caused something of a stir, not only with critics, but also with the public. With very few exceptions, from the *retomada* period (1990–94) to the present almost all Brazilian-made films have had very limited runs.[8] However, despite the fact that it opened only in Rio de Janeiro and São Paulo, in only two theaters in each city, the box-office figures for *Chronically Unfeasible* were an unprecedented success for a film that made no concessions to easily seduce the public. Rather, it forced the audience to confront, via its discursive structure, the unremittingly harsh social conditions for large sectors of the population in contemporary Brazil.

Part of an "intermediate" generation of filmmakers following the *Cinema Novo* movement of the late 1950s to early 1970s, Sérgio Bianchi is one of the few independent filmmakers in Brazil who has succeeded in continually producing feature films amidst the political upheaval and economic crises that have marked the post-dictatorial 1980s. His early ability to balance state co-sponsorship with a range of financing and production strategies has yielded a distinctive authorial style; many of his films test the boundaries between documentary and fictional modes of address while thematically centering on environmental issues and the wide panoply of social distortions that have accompanied the Brazilian "economic miracle" and its tragic aftermath, the "end" of Brazil as a nation outside the neoliberal model, thanks to globalization.

Elaborated along this vein, *Chronically Unfeasible* evokes the sense of anger mixed with disgust that has deeply affected all levels of contemporary life in Brazil—social, political, cultural, intellectual—while defying the conventions of social or magical realism that have customarily been used to represent Latin American social dilemmas for both domestic and foreign consumption.

A number of contemporary events informed the reception of this film. At the beginning of 2000, Brazilians had been exposed to, among all too many disturbing media events, the process of impeachment of São Paulo's mayor, Celso Pitta, charged with corruption; continuing charges against multinational laboratories for producing counterfeit drugs—most of them using only 10 percent of the active ingredient required; the escalating police violence against teachers and public servants alike entering their sixth year without a raise in salary; the news that the Joint Congressional Commission on Provisional Decree voted to roll back forest protection requirements so that mega-landowners, mostly connected with transnational corporations, could legally cut and burn the Amazon forest even more voraciously; the arrest of a man who threw an egg during a *peaceful* demonstration against the Minister of Health under the *Lei de Segurança Nacional* (Law of National Security), a convenient remnant of the arbitrary laws of the military dictatorship still in effect and available according to the repressive needs of the moment. Throughout the whole year, this class-based law had also been enforced against leaders and militants of the *MST—Movimento dos Sem Terra* (Landless People's Movement).[9]

But perhaps, nothing could be compared, in terms of media events, to the remarkably negative reaction to the official celebrations around the "500 years of Brazil," which climaxed in April 2000 with cases of extreme violence and repressive force used against indigenous Brazilians and African-Brazilians. The latter were questioning the meaning of the celebrations, while indigenous Brazilians were demanding, once more, the demarcation of their lands in southern Bahia, near the sites where the Portuguese actually arrived in 1500. The year 2000, then, was a moment more privileged than any other in recent history, where questions of national identity came to the forefront, and Bianchi's film deeply touched upon some endemic problems as well as on more recent national tragedies, among which the fate of street kids was a particularly visible one.

But how does one film, record, or construct "anger," "disgust," and "hate"? *Chronically Unfeasible* is a cry (a "vomit" would be a better word) against a state of general social conformism that seems to be affecting life in Brazil. Through parallel narratives that show excerpts of six characters' life stories, the film integrates violence, social prejudice, corruption, and other themes, laying out the difficulties involved in surviving, both mentally and physically, in an often chaotic Brazilian society. And it does so by assuming or making the case that those problems trouble everyone regardless of their political stance or social position. The events revolve around an upper-middle-class restaurant in São Paulo, owned by Luis, a refined, well-mannered man in his fifties who manages to be simultaneously ironic and poignant. Alfredo is an intellectual, a writer (or perhaps a university professor) engaged in a journey into the country, attempting to understand, from his markedly bitter perspective, the problems of social oppression and domination. Adam has just arrived from the south to find a job in Luis's restaurant as a new waiter. He stands out among the other employees because of his European descent, evident in his physical appearance and level of education, as well as in his rebellious tendencies. Maria Alice comes from Rio's upper-middle class and

237

is always trying to keep a minimum of humanity when dealing with people from the lower classes. She is married to Carlos, a pragmatic man who believes that taking personal advantage of the country's social instability is a rational course of action. Finally, Amanda, the restaurant's manager, is a captivating woman with an obscure past, hidden behind the many tales she tells her friends and customers. Although she is now living in São Paulo and working in a sophisticated restaurant, Bianchi projects a different past onto the character, one in which she might have been like the thousands of children in the country's illegal labor force. Introduced by the voice-over of the intellectual narrator, a flashback shows her very young, working in a charcoal mining camp of the sort linked to the devastation of the Amazon forest.

However, this schematic summary of the film's possible plots is in the end misleading. Through a careful editing style, Bianchi questions the very foundations, the inner workings or logic, the unspoken tenets, and the ideology of nearly all of our recent film production which, by and large, flirts with the audience using seductive strategies of all sorts. The blithe recuperation of our historical subservience by hegemonic models (be they international, i.e. Hollywood, or national, mostly the aesthetic orientation of *TV Globo*) seems to be an endless area of debate in our context; Bianchi has little patience with such light-hearted romanticization in the face of the urgent crises of present-day Brazil. His film contests common-sense "interpretation" with a radical narrative frame that decenters its parallel narratives in order to indicate their historical contingencies. This conflictive interweaving of narratives has the final effect of an overwhelming saturation of meaning in the spectators themselves. By representing Brazil as a singular social and geographic totality, cutting apparently without any motivation from one region to another (from the more developed south to the northern region of Bahia, from São Paulo and Rio to the more remote areas in the country such as the Amazon frontier), Bianchi transposes the mechanics of capitalist social relations in order to reveal the reified social fabric of contemporary Brazil in an eloquent representation of the internal diaspora which promotes waves of migration.

Thus the film *challenges* the concept of "change," presenting it not as a matter of flow and flux, that is to say, of evolution, but rather as the articulation of capitalist social economy, of *inclusion* and *exclusion*, against a cinematic politics of exploitation. Bianchi's camera-gun (or rather, *camera-scalpel*—a metaphor directed at the film's editing process) points to everything and everyone at once: manipulated landless people, indigenous Brazilians, intellectuals, community-based activism, the right and the left, spectators, and the filmmaker.

Echoing Bianchi's short *Mato eles? (Should I Kill Them?*, 1982) *Chronically Unfeasible* constitutes an assault on the assumptions and sensibility of the contemporary moviegoing audiences in Brazil, largely middle class and accustomed to documentaries *à la vérité* that flatter their sense of humanist compassion, be they progressive films or more conventional television docudramas, such as the weekly *Globo Repórter*. At first one is led to identify with the character of the intellectual—a voice-over of progressive consciousness—who, because he seems detached and able to see and analyze everything, implicates the spectator by soliciting complicity. Throughout most of the narrative we have no idea that this strategy is mocking our illusion of omnipotence, our self-aggrandizing fantasy that our heightened consciousness and sensitivity might actually change the situation. By the end we are informed that the traveling intellectual is involved with the illegal traffic of human organs, including those of children, which is hinted at through his connection with Amanda, who, besides working at the restaurant, is also involved with suspicious child adoption enterprises as well as what seems to be a NGO working to integrate indigenous Brazilians into the labor force in São Paulo.[10] No illusion is left standing. The fate of children reappears in Bianchi's latest film, *Quanto vale ou é por quilo?* (2005), which is freely based on a Machado de Assis short story and traces a parallel between life in Brazil during the slavery period and modern Brazil. These two films have been instrumental in critiquing and denouncing official concern for abandoned children in Brazil. This non-existent politics, based on voluntarism and social marketing promoted by some private organizations and represented by dozens of NGOs whose only interest is an assault on public funds, gradually leads to absolving the state of its responsibility regarding children's rights to education, health and welfare—a development that serves only to promote institutionalization of marginality and social exclusion.

It has become a commonplace, especially in the postmodern critical discourse, to acknowledge the fact that "every film is political" in a pluralist sense (so that all cultural phenomena are simply inflected with the "biases" of specific, competing "points-of-view"), but *Chronically Unfeasible*, as with most of Bianchi's films, does not fall into the traditional humanistic trap of "ethics." Instead, he purposefully reveals that not only the characters in the film but also the individual members of the audience have, in effect, lost their sovereign place in society; that is, they are no longer central to any political discourses of social change. *Chronically Unfeasible* replaces, once more, ethics and aesthetics with politics, the struggle for control over the means of production in all social spheres, whether of state power, of material resources, or cultural representation. The film cuts across these instances more than any other film from the most recent Brazilian audiovisual productions. These politics, we are constantly reminded, are none other than those of class struggle, gender, race, and sexual relations, all intertwined as in a single fabric.

It is also important to remember that Bianchi's postmodern aesthetic was preceded by the *aesthetics of garbage*, a trope that goes back to the Brazilian underground cinema, the *udigrudi* (in its parodic Portuguese rendition), the name given to a group of young Brazilian filmmakers in the late 1960s who questioned and offered an alternative to Cinema Novo. For this underground, Cinema Novo had become *embourgeoisé*, respectable and cautious in both its thematic and its cinematic language. As Cinema Novo moved towards relatively high-budget films characterized by technical polish and "production values," the *Novo* Cinema Novo, as it became known, demanded a radicalization of Glauber Rocha's manifesto "The Aesthetic of Hunger." Parallels with the present situation apply; nine out of ten Brazilian films made today follow the recipe for "high quality" films, and they are made with increasingly enormous budgets. The young filmmakers of the underground rejected a well-made cinema in favor of a "dirty screen." A garbage style, they argued, was more appropriate to a postcolonial country picking through the remnants of a world dominated by First World monopoly capitalism.

Besides being "ugly" and "dirty," Bianchi's film abounds with images of garbage, of literal and metaphorical human detritus. As Robert Stam has pointed out, garbage is fundamentally hybrid, the site of the promiscuous mingling of rich and poor, of center and periphery, of the industrial and the handcrafted, the private and the public, the durable and the transient, the organic and the inorganic, the national and the international.[11] The ideal postmodern and postcolonial metaphor, garbage is mixed and syncretic, a radically decentered "social text." It might be productive, once more, to refer back to Fredric Jameson's still-pertinent albeit controversial article "Third World Literature in the Era of Multinational Capitalism," in which he argues that even those texts invested with an apparently private or libidinal dynamic "project a political dimension in the form of a national allegory; the story of the private individual destiny is always an allegory of the embattled situation of the public Third World culture and society."[12]

By avoiding the conventional relations of seduction between text and audience, films such as *Chronically Unfeasible* foreground exploitative social mechanisms in all their complexity, positing a thematic as well as stylistic agenda of resistance to contemporary social relations under global capitalism. Following the paths opened by Nelson Pereira dos Santos' *Rio 40 Degrees*, films such as Bianchi's, along with *How Angels Are Born, City of God, Bus 174*, and *Angels of the Sun*, have been able to garner critical and popular success while exploring new cinematic ways of depicting the harsh realities of contemporary life in Brazil. Back in 1975, Jorge Bodansky and Orlando Senna's allegorical and ecological docudrama *Iracema, uma transa amazônica* employed documentary techniques—hand-held camera, location shooting in the vast Amazon area and a skilful mix of professional and non-professional actors—to denounce the process of modernization known as the "Brazilian Economic Miracle" inflicted by the military regime. In the twenty-first century, environmental devastation and human exploitation continue to thrive at the green frontiers, as can be seen in *Angels of the Sun* (2006), which revisits the Amazon to narrate the road adventure saga of Maria, a 12-year-old girl who, in the summer of 2002, is sold by her family in the hinterland of Brazil to a white slave recruiter. She is bought in an auction and then sent to a brothel located in a mining camp deep in the jungle. After months of being abused, along with other girls, she succeeds in escaping and crosses Brazil by hitchhiking and riding on trucks. Arriving at her new location, the streets of Copacabana in Rio, she returns to prostitution, now part of the fashionable transnational business of sexual tourism. Comparisons with *Iracema* might be of interest here in the sense that both films, though related, display two different stylistic approaches and question the shift from fictional documentary to updated melodrama in contemporary Brazilian cinema, notions of representation, and the articulation of the female body imprinted by history in a landscape of disintegration and, ultimately, destruction.

By turning their lenses on the mix of social misery, extreme poverty, abandoned children, drugs, and other urgent issues emblematic of our times, these filmmakers challenge the grounds for outsiders' interest in the margins of society. Consider the seeming euphoria, for example, with which the inhabitants of the *favela* Dona Marta met the production crew for Spike Lee's video of Michael Jackson's *They Don't Care about Us* (1987), or the *favela*-tours for which foreign tourists pay fifty dollars for a "safari" to the largest *favela* complex in Latin America, the Rocinha, as if it were a kind of postindustrial theme park. In this respect, and within the transnational perspective discussed here, it is worth noting the impact a film like *City of God* has made in other geographical contexts such as the Philippines. The frenetic opening of the Brazilian film, as well as its documentary-like techniques of location shooting in a notoriously violent district of Rio, plus the choice of actors recruited from among the inhabitants of those slum areas, the first person narration from a young boy's point of view, and the careful choice of a "cool" soundtrack all worked together to create unexpected dialogues between Rio and Manila. In a global context of endemic and relentless accumulation of misery, dysfunctional families, drug trafficking, and lack of jobs and other opportunities for young people, this wave of films point to some key issues that draw children into crime and violence worldwide.[13] They also have the power to transform these otherwise often neglected parallel worlds of contemporary global peripheries into the center of a transnational *favela* culture, instantly absorbed by the mainstream industries of fashion and music in a recent phenomenon known as *favela chic*. It is not surprising, though, that the current search for "authenticity" would discover in the *favelados*'s life of poverty, violence, and all sorts of misfortunes, a privileged locus for exoticism, mystery, and danger.[14] Their key innovation lies in focusing on native excluded youth as authentic subjects of, and shareholders in, this transnational rap culture.

The international impact and the 2009 Oscar consecration of Danny Boyle's *Slumdog Millionaire* comes as no surprise then: its authentic *favela* locations, the use of a young and largely inexperienced cast who were asked to improvise dialogues and even actions, a cool soundtrack creating a musical landscape at once local and global, and its frenetic editing style are all part of an aesthetic package ostensibly inspired by *City of God* to ignite an effect of instant reality.

The films I have discussed continuously call attention to matters of vision, spectacle, and meaning, where the pathology of the *favela* has transformed itself into a new form of commodity.

acknowledgments

An early version of this chapter was presented as a public lecture at the European Center/Cinemathèque Municipale during the seminar Latin American Cinemas in a Global Context, organized by Clark University, October 31 to November 2, 2000, under the direction of Professor Marvin d'Lugo. A subsequent redrafted version was presented at the University of Michigan, Atlantic Studies Initiative, March 2002. Parts of it are based on a collective chapter by Robert Stam, João Luiz Vieira, and Ismail Xavier entitled "The Shape of Brazilian Cinema in the Postmodern Age," published in Robert Stam and Randal Johnson, *Brazilian Cinema*, 3d ed. (New York: Columbia University Press, 1995). The extended discussion of *Pixote* is indebted to a review-essay by Robert Stam. See Robert Stam, "*Pixote*," *Cineaste* 12, no. 3 (1983): 44–45.

notes

1. According to UNICEF, Brazil has the second highest level of child mortality in South America, after Bolivia. Data referring to 1999 point to the fact that for every 1,000 births 65.5 die before reaching the age of 5 years, a figure that increases to 76 when considering only African-Brazilians. According to IBGE (Brazilian Institute of Geography and Statistics) data, though the index of absolute misery has decreased since 2002, Brazil still has one of the worst distributions of wealth among 150 countries researched. On the situation of homeless children in Brazil, see Gilberto Dimerstein, *Brésil: La Guerre des Enfants* (Paris: Fayard, 1991).

2. The word *malandragem* refers to the actions of or condition of being a malandro. Usually, being a *malandro* has a negative connotation, and means being a bum who lives on petty actions, such as stealing and cheating. The word can also have positive meanings and refers to a person who is smart and resourceful. In this latter sense, it is a popular term in Rio de Janeiro.

3. When *Pixote* opened in 1981, several Brazilian film critics remarked on the influence of *Shoeshine*. They emphasized the film's first half, where De Sica depicts the disciplinary methods of the reform school, as the center of its narrative. Just as a reminder, some years before De Sica, Jean Vigo had

João luiz vieira

already visited that narrative space in *Zéro de Conduite* (1933), though with comic overtones.

4. In Portuguese a play on words; *chacina* means the simultaneous violent murder of more than one person and *faxina* means cleaning. The message here is that the massacre of street kids (and of homeless poor people in general) is a way of *cleaning* the city of its excluded marginal inhabitants.

5. Ismail Xavier, "O cinema brasileiro dos anos 90," *Praga: estudos marxistas*, no. 9 (2000): 125.

6. See the documentary film by Felipe Briso and Gilberto Topczewski, *Pixote in Memoriam* (2006).

7. In opposition to a more common thought that posits Rio as a *divided, fractured* city, films such as *How Angels Are Born, City of God*, or Beto Brant's *O Invasor* (*The Intruder*, 2002) display a more interconnected, interdependent urban landscape usually linked through drugs and crime.

8. *Retomada* refers to the gradual recovery of the Brazilian film production in the years 1990–94, following President Collor de Melo's March 1990 shutdown the infrastructure created to develop and promote Brazilian films. Among the most destructive of his measures were the closings of EMBRAFILME—the state agency responsible for film development—and CONCINE—the legal agency in charge of protecting Brazilian films through quota laws.

9. That Act represented a total victory for the cattle farmers and the international trade of rare Brazilian wood. The rewritten law entailed a 25 percent increase in Amazon forest destruction, which meant 4,500 square kilometers a year at 1998 rates. As of June 2008, data from the INPE (National Institute of Space Research) proved that out of a total of 4 million square kilometers of the Amazon forest, 700,000 square kilometers have been deforested. Of these, 360,000 square kilometers were destroyed between 1988 and 2008, which means that the equivalent of a soccer field has been destroyed every ten seconds in this twenty-year period alone.

10. For a discussion of the trafficking of human organs in Brazil, see Nancy Scheper-Hughes, *Death without Weeping: The Violence of Everyday Life in Brazil* (Los Angeles, CA: University of California Press, 1993), 216–67.

11. Robert Stam, "Palimpsestic Aesthetics: A Meditation on Hybridity and Garbage," in *Performing Hybridity*, ed. May Joseph and Jennifer Natalya Fink (Minneapolis, MN: University of Minnesota Press, 1999), 59–78.

12. Fredric Jameson, "Third World Literature in the Era of Multinational Capitalism," *Social Text*, no. 15 (Fall 1986): 65–88.

13. Some titles from the vibrant Filipino film scene could be grouped together in a sort of genre of *favela* cinema: *The Blossoming of Maximo Oliveros* (Auraeus Solito, 2005), *The Debt Collector* (Jeffrey Jeturian, 2006), *Sling Shot* (Brillante Mendoza, 2007) and *Tribu* (Jim Libirian, 2007).

14. On the impact of *City of God* on music, see Joey Sweeney, "Favela Chic" (www.citypaper.net/articles/2004-12-09/naked.shtml).

comparative

perspectives

part three

fantasy

in action

twelve

paul willemen

In thought and political analysis we have still not cut off the head
of the king.

Michel Foucault, 1976

The historicity of individual films is readily acknowledged by all. In fact, it was never disputed. The consensus is that a film relates closely to the economic, social, political and cultural circumstances that presided over its making. The same consideration was extended to the reading-viewing of films, provided that we first agreed to reduce ourselves to the status of consumers of discrete objects. Whereas the protocols deployed to perform a reading have been referred to a more or less sophisticated notion of the contemporary context, the historicity of the theoretical discourse that tries to construct the intelligibility systems of those films is rarely taken equally seriously. When such theoretical constructs are discussed at all, it tends to be in a Tom-and-Jerry fashion as academics try to hit each other over the head with one theoretical paradigm or another, each one being presented as bigger and better than the other. In that practice, theories of cinema are, just like the films, treated as discrete objects examined, in this case, exclusively in terms of their internal logic, omitting to consider what problem(s) the theories are supposed to solve for whom. Rarely are these theories examined as historical constructs closely related to the social-historical conditions that presided over their formulation.

Even when such a critique does surface, it tends merely to replicate the usual modus operandi as Western or Asian or African (or feminist, or queer, and so on) frames of understanding are invoked for the same purposes that Jerry calls on Spike the Bulldog. In sum, cultural production is readily understood as historically specific, but the theory of cultural production as the elaboration of how that production actually works and produces meaning, tends to be either exempted from history or to be so thoroughly determined by history that the theory loses any explanatory value what-soever, sinking instead into a morass of relativism that ends up declaring any mode of understanding as equally valid as any other. Modes of under-standing thus become like cans of differently branded beans stacked on an imaginary supermarket shelf of intellectual goods. At that point, all that remains to distinguish one theoretical frame from another is the exercise of raw marketing and (self-)promotional clout, that is to say, the institutionally backed power to impose a mode of consumption on people looking for a mode of understanding.

Is the relation between a film (or a reading of a film) and its contem-porary social-historical context so indisputable and so clearly defined that it deserves to be taken as a baseline? What if aspects of a film did not relate to a contemporary configuration, but to determining dynamics that operate on a much longer time scale, being neither residual nor emergent but simply "still there," like the king's head that has still not been cut off? That possibility would open up the problem of differential temporal rhythms, that is to say, different epochal temporalities being folded over and into each other, generating composite or historically mixed discursive regimes. What we still have to give ourselves is a grid of historical decipherment capable of detecting the bewilderingly complex arrays of enunciating agencies and their associated social positionings and historical temporalities that find their always unstable but never arbitrary orchestration in texts.

Conventionally, the combination of polyphony and polychrony in cinematic texts is reduced to a binary opposition so simple that it is useless: tradition and modernity. The only vestigial use value of that opposition resides in its unspoken and therefore often unactivated dimensions. While it is true that the concept of tradition has been secreted by modernity to designate something that preceded it, this notion of tradition also acknowl-edges that there are things that persist, things that are "still there" and which, by their very persistence, modify the modernity that they inhabit and whence they have been imagined or, to use Hobsbawm's polemical phraseology, invented. While the rituals and cultural forms that are called "traditional" are indeed modern inventions, the hierarchical social relations and the modalities of subjectivity or (non)individuation staged by those invented rituals, are not. Those are still very much alive and active in the contemporary socio-cultural configuration, exemplifying what Ernst Bloch meant by his notion of the synchrony of the asynchronous, or what Marx meant by combined and unequal development. In the study of cultural production, the main role that the modernity/tradition opposition is still capable of playing is to remind us that while we do indeed construe meaning by way of representations, representation is not all that there is. Consequently, by failing to attend to the intricate ways that the representation is animated by what it "presents," our theoretical toolkits have no means of assessing the relations between representations and the historical forces that speak "through" or "in" those representations.

As a result of installing an unbridgeable gap between the representational and the non-representational, or, if you wish, between signification and the real, we are bound to get representation wrong in two crucial ways. First, representation is a concept, and therefore a methodological tool designed to help us, through protocols of differentiation, to understand what is happening "in" the real. Representation does not designate an actually existing category of objects in the real clearly differentiated from what the concept of representation, if it is to be useful, must exclude: the non-representational. Second, by getting the nature of the boundary between representation and its "outside" wrong (a methodological boundary, not a real one), we also get representation itself wrong, in that we fail to see the processes that representation is there to "contain." The fact that we cannot think without concepts does not entitle us to substitute the processes that we try to understand with the thinking tools we require to understand them.

Elsewhere, I have argued that the perspectival regime built into the cinema apparatus by way of its camera lenses is itself a polyphonic and polychromic orchestration instituting a compromise configuration between a still dominant, religiously legitimized status hierarchy and the nascent, secular notion of individuation that had to be accommodated somehow as a result of the contractual requirements of the Genoese and Florentine bankers. In that sense, the perspectival regime of looking presents an amalgam of Renaissance and pre-modern (pre-Renaissance) scopic regimes.[1] Consequently, the regimes of subjectivity that ensue from the way films stitch together the seen/scene and the (implied) viewer, are also composite formations that, in different social-historical configurations, push the discursive regimes that animate a film towards pre-modern or modern forms of subjectivation. A given film's discursive regime, that is to say, the mode of address it deploys in order to manage a viewer's way of attending to the film, tries to secure a viewer's consent to ways of making sense of the social constellation in ways that privilege the modern, the pre-modern or some other structured amalgam of epochally identifiable, socio-economically grounded historical configurations favoring particular types of power relations.[2]

Texts operate indeed as force fields organizing "corridors of voices," in Bakhtin's useful phrase. Perhaps his acoustic-architectural image might be updated by comparing films with fiber optic cables carrying multiple voices in a variety of directions simultaneously. Each of these voices indicates the active presence within the contemporary of social agencies that can be posited as their expressive subjects. The notion of subjectivity required for such a conceptualization of discursive regimes was perhaps best formulated by Arrighi's notion of social agency in the long-term dynamics of capitalism's historical development:

> The recurrent expansions and restructurings of the capitalist world-economy have occurred under the leadership of particular communities and blocs of governmental and business agencies which were uniquely well placed to turn to their advantage the unintended consequences of the actions of other agencies.[3]

Social agencies of that type, though not limited to governmental or business agencies, function as expressive subjects, or rather, as the retroactively construed subject-positions (or, if you will, identities) that underpin any one of the many voices resounding in a "corridor" (or film). A film thus presents an orchestration of voices and, at the same time, a hierarchically organized network or field of power relations between contending social agencies. It also, necessarily and simultaneously, indicates a preferred hierarchical arrangement of the component agency-voices: the preferred way of making sense of the social that is advocated, on the whole, by a given text. However, these agencies, although active within any given contemporaneity, are not necessarily synchronous with it from a historical point of view. For instance, in the United States at the present time pre-modern regimes of belief are deployed and advocated by dominant social-economic agencies (important media agencies, governmental departments, lobby groups, and so on). Some voices resounding in the corridor may seek to advocate a modernizing vector of social development, others may exert archaicizing pressures. In other words, the contemporaneity that is assumed to be the historical reference to which a film or any other cultural production may be referred, is itself an intricate patchwork of interest-positions, that is to say, of enunciative positions often formed in pre-modern or even older socio-cultural constellations. Consequently, the discussion in film studies of some stylistic feature such as, say, the zoom, must be conducted in terms of an awareness of the multidimensionality of historical configurations. Such an analysis cannot be conducted just in terms of the already complex history of technology. It must simultaneously address the emphatic dimension of the performance of an enunciation, a feature characteristic of the kind of auditive cultures that preceded print cultures. In other words, within films, there are still very much at work features, duly transformed or translated, not only of print cultures, but also of pre-print cultures.[4]

Another notable example of the synchrony of the asynchronous was provided by Andreas Huyssen,[5] when he showed not only that cultural theory is out of phase with the history of aesthetic and cultural practices in the arts, but also that the explanatory frameworks, that is to say, the cultural theories synchronically accompanying aesthetic-cultural waves (-isms), may belong to a preceding era. This was the case with modernism, which reformatted cultural theory only some half-century after the industrialization of culture had transformed large sectors of cultural practice. Huyssen noted that although "the various forms of post-structuralism have opened up new problematics in modernism and have re-inscribed modernism into the discourse formations of our own time,"[6] the wave of cultural theory conventionally dated back to the work of Roland Barthes, Jacques Lacan and many other European thinkers signaled the long delayed arrival of modernism on the terrain of cultural philosophy. The effervescence of cultural theory that marked the last three or four decades of the twentieth century thus constitutes the belated arrival of modernism in theory, hiding its backwardness under a futuristic mask soon labeled postmodernism. And, characteristically, modernism arrived in theory just around the time when cultural practices were beginning to move away from the critical challenges to industrialization embodied by modernism, seeking instead to realign themselves with the advertising-oriented and standardizing mainstream of the cultural industries. Hence the ridiculous spectacle from the late 1970s onwards of a modernist theory called postmodernism being used to legitimize and promote the very industrialization of culture criticized by late nineteenth-century modernism.

It is true that the kind of modernism involved did indeed remobilize significant aspects of the cultural formation that had, in Arrighi's words, "been superseded by the preceding regime,"[7] that is to say, by the regime that had recast the medieval European world of fixed status hierarchies into a kind of Romantic individualism, whereby members of high-status groups had been transformed into exemplary individuals. This, no doubt, prompted Umberto Eco to talk of postmodernism as a version of modernism infused with neo-medievalism.

Given that texts, just like social formations themselves, present an orchestration of a wide array of social agencies—interest positions arranged in preferred hierarchical relations of power—it follows that the very same forces that are said to animate and drive history will also constitute the configurative pressures that preside over text-formulations, that is to say, over the formation and shaping of objects such as films. The problem then is to find theoretically adequate toolkits that may enable us to read those structuring pressures "at work," so to speak.

251

There is no need to rehearse all the arguments against the existing theoretical toolkits used to map texts on to social configurations: reflectionism, relativism, constructivism and so on have all been shown to be inadequate to the task, even though some of the tools forged by these cultural philosophies may well turn out to have a use after all. When the issue of the social crops up in film studies, identity categories such as class, gender, ethnicity, and so forth tend to make their appearance, all of them fantasized as homogeneous identities with essential characteristics, like dramatis personae. The use of such thought-categories as they are currently offered in a variety of theoretical toolkits is doubtful, to say the least. For instance, much has been said about the way cinema talks about class. But film theory has been silent on the subject of labor power, even though it is one of the most fundamental concepts in historical or dialectical materialisms without which the notion of class becomes merely a matter of one's wage-packet. Rather than attributing such a surprising omission to a lack of concern or interest, the explanation must be sought in the inadequacies of film theory itself. Let me attempt to reframe the issue by putting the following hypothesis onto the agenda: the historicity of films (and therefore of cinema) can be understood by accounting for the way that labor power is present in the very texture of films. The problem is: what kind of theoretical toolkit does one need to achieve an understanding of its presence in films?

The first item for our toolkit will have to be a concept of historical temporality such as the one advanced by, among many historians, Giovanni Arrighi, when he identified the one-step-forward-two-steps-back movement involved in the major cycles of capitalist development. In order to find an explanatory framework for the dynamics that programmed delays and a-synchronicities, as well as for the wave-motion animating the practice of cultural theory and its isms, one must start from the question of how precisely the forces that shape history also and simultaneously shape ways of knowing, fantasizing, and storytelling, although they do so in different ways and at a different pace, depending on the particular densities of the institutions that regulate critical discourse, as opposed to industrialized cultural practices. In more theoretical terms, this is the question of representation (one thing standing for another) versus presentation (something manifesting itself even if only in a disguised, distorted or translated manner). This question can be formulated in the following terms, adapted from medical parlance: how do the dynamics animating historical change "present" in representations?

In the light of film criticism and journalism's preoccupation with at times grudgingly performed odes to US-led economic policies and the dubious "popular pleasures" they dispense, it has become clear, not surprisingly, that not all that much of the currently available film theory can account for the way non-Western or non-Euro-American films function. This has prompted two equally inadequate responses. One was to identify the lack-of-fit between, say, melodrama in Europe and in the Hindi cinema of the 1950s, and then to locate the alleged specificity of that Hindi cinema precisely in that difference. Such a gesture achieves two results at once: the accuracy and normative status of Western criticism's notions of Euro-American melodrama remain unchallenged while some essentially "other," unspeakably sacred national cultural essence is affirmed.[8] The second response is a more radically nationalist variant of the same strategy: each nation is allocated a unique essence that is deemed to pervade all its cultural productions, enabling the staging of endless Tom-and-Jerry power struggles between national elites who have declared themselves to be the guardians of a given (read: constructed) cultural heritage. The Asian-values ploy merely maps that strategy onto the North-South or, depending on tactical convenience, East-West axis of world maps.

It is undoubtedly true that the existing corpus of film theory, largely because it has not paid much attention to the historical dynamics which have determined and dictated its agenda, is inadequate, and that those inadequacies are directly connected with the way the cultural dynamics operating in regions of Europe and the United States presented themselves in texts, whether these be films, journalistic criticism, or academic publications. Again, this is not a question of whether representations reflect or construct the real. It is a question of how the real, that is to say, history, is present in the very fabric, as well as in the organization, of representations. That is the issue put on the agenda by many critiques and selective appropriations of the still canonical forms of Western film theory. The challenge is not that we must find an alternative modality of film theory. It is much more drastic than that: we must elaborate, quite simply, a *better* theory of cinema as a cultural form.

Needless to say, this challenge will have to be met collaboratively. Given the notion of historical dynamics and constellations sketched out earlier, it is axiomatic that no individual nor any single "national" intelligentsia is in a position to meet that challenge, mainly because one cannot think outside of the box of one's own social-historical conjuncture. It necessarily requires transnational, critical collaboration within the framework of an agreed and shared sense of direction: towards the never-to-be-reached goal of a comprehensive understanding of the way culture (and, therefore, a social formation) works. Understanding can then be generated from the way(s) that different modes of understanding (and different disciplines) rub against each other. Always provided, of course, that there is broad agreement about what it is precisely that one seeks to understand.

I have explored the consequences of such an approach—deploying the notion of social agency to designate subject-positions in history—for the way that, say, a European encounters the films of non-European social formations.[9] In brief, one of the main conclusions of those endeavors was that one must seek to distinguish, within texts, the operations of different

253

temporalities (long, medium, short) associated with specific modalities of social organization. In cinema, which, as a cultural form, is wholly located within the process of industrialization (that is to say, modernization and its concomitant reference points of subjectivation or individuation), the principal though not the only issue to focus upon in this respect is the question of a film's mode of address in all its complexity. A good reason for asserting this is that an adequate analysis of a film's mode of address will have to include due consideration of its figurative dimensions, its mise-en-scene, editing, acting styles, and so forth.[10] One of the things that a mode-of-address analysis will seek to establish can be formulated as an answer to the following question: to the benefit of which social agency does a film seek to construct its preferred regime of social reproduction as it dramatizes a suggested force-field structured around, on the one hand, individuation and group-status identities, and, on the other, individuals and the social-historical context(s) that frame the process of (de)individuation. Point-of-view or free indirect discourse camera positionings and movements are only a small part of the strategies that make up a film's mode of address. And what I said in relation to representation also is true for a film's mode of address: it is not all that there is. But my insistence that we have to reconceptualize the notion of a film's mode of address is a necessary first move, I think, if we do want to give ourselves a toolkit that will enable us to begin reading what Foucault called the "historical contents that have been buried or masked in functional coherences or formal systematizations."[11] And this is the great, as yet still unrivalled strength of cinema, regardless of whether it is vehiculated by celluloid or some other substance: its ability to give us a glimpse of what is involved, of what must be taken into account, if we are to correlate textually activated meanings with an understanding of our own historicity. Cinema has always been capable of questioning the way "formal systematizations" of thought systems work with methodological short cuts, setting up boundaries and inside/outside demarcations—of which the notion of representation is only one—that we need in order to make sense of a world where such demarcations do not actually hold.

Of course, much could be said about the ways in which cinema has been encased by discourses designed to reduce our way of paying attention to textuality and to focus, instead, on the astonished discovery of individuation within thoroughly industrialized products given to us as "culture," although mostly on condition that we do not take it seriously and confine ourselves to wanting "entertainment" instead. The carapace's first of many more layers tells us that in order to be good cultural consumers, we must focalize our attention either on "entertainment" value or, if we insist on being interested in cultural matters, on "characters" and to see every other aspect of cinema as subordinate to, and conditioned by, the nineteenth-century novel's construct of the individuated character. But if we wish to engage with the full range of cinema's complex discursive dynamics, what kind of theoretical toolkit might enable us to begin making sense of what are still called "films" even though they may actually consist of streams of electronic impulses rather than photochemical registrations.

This conceptualization of the ways cultural production has of negotiating the encounter with capitalism, or, in other words, the centuries' long process of modernization, opens the way towards tackling cinematic narration in a comparative framework. The basic question for such a framework would be: how does the encounter with capitalism generate specific cultural forms in particular geographical areas defined by networks of political-economic institutions? That question can be reformulated as: how and by which social sectors are factors operating in a local history formulated to render the specifics of the fabric of social experience in that locality?[12] The answer to that question requires a multilayered analytical investigation animated by two foundational theories: a still to be elaborated theory of semiosis capable of accounting for the connections between history and textuality, and one (or at least one) theory of history as a process (for instance, historical materialism or, for short, Marxism, especially as revised in David Harvey's brilliant book, *The Limits to Capital*, first published in 1982).

peirce and indexicality

When asking the comparative question in relation to cinema, a number of conceptual magnetic fields suggest themselves as areas for research, profiling the gateways to areas of investigation likely to produce an understanding of how and why particular cinematic forms occur at particular times in specified, more or less state-regulated zones of film production. The theoretical intuitions required as starting points for a comparative project are fairly easy to identify. Much of the work has been done already and the main initial work is to elaborate new sets of connections between aspects of familiar theoretical paradigms. For the required theory of history, I have already pointed to the Marx/Harvey nexus as a good starting point, probably to be complemented by the economic histories of Giovanni Arrighi and Robert Brenner as well as that of the proponents of the Regulation School of economic analysis, and by social historians such as Fernand Braudel, D.D. Kosambi, Romila Thapar, and others.

As for the required theory or, more likely, theories of signification, the issue is a little more contentious. There is no need to embark on a critique of reflection theory as the assumed direct mirroring of text and context has already been decisively discredited decades ago by the Russian and Czech formalists. What does need to be addressed is a fairly basic critique of the notion that representation involves a substitutive relationship in which one thing stands for another.[13] A return to aspects of C.S. Peirce's work, first put on the agenda by Peter Wollen in the late 1960s, provides a useful way forward. We have to begin by abandoning the prevailing misreading of Peirce's work which alleges that he identified three different types of sign: the index, the icon, and the symbol. Instead, we have to understand Peirce as talking about the three dimensions present in any given sign (but present in differing hierarchies of prominence). Then the door opens towards a type of textual analysis that can treat signs as partly representational (through their iconic and symbolic dimensions) and partly non-representational (in their indexical dimension). The latter does not involve a substitutive relation, but one of expressive contiguity, profiling an ontological connection between sign and referent. A first theoretical exercise then suggests itself: identify the three dimensions of any given film image by specifying the indexical, iconic, and symbolic relations at work in it.

In digitized imagery, it may well appear as if the indexical dimension has disappeared from the relation between a photograph and what it shows, but it does not thereby disappear from the image-as-object. Verbal language, the archetype of the symbolic sign system, also has iconic dimensions, based on resemblance, and indexical dimensions based on an ontological relation between signifier and physical reality. Julia Kristeva's discussion of the way unconscious psychic drives animate and inhabit sound patterns in the modernist poetry of Mallarmé suggests that there well may be an indexical dimension diffused through verbal language at the phonemic level, linking the physical apparatus of articulation with unconscious drives.[14] Whatever credence one may give to Kristeva's conclusions, her discussion of these sound patterns at least points to the fact that the physical performance of vocalized articulation, even if simulated in acts of unarticulated inner speech or reading, involves iconic and indexical dimensions as bodies, traversed by impulses and desires, negotiate their encounter with the abstract system of differences which is language, a system dominated by the symbolic dimension of signs. Similarly, the indexical dimension of language is active not only at the level of the phonetic articulation of phonemic oppositions, but also in the morphological and semantic registers of language. The very possibility of mapping dialects onto geographical regions, of connecting speech impediments to physiological processes or of diagnosing other socio-culturally or physically "telling" aspects of language point to an indexical dimension of the symbolic language system. One may turn to any sign system whatever and find confirmation of Peirce's insight that the indexical, the symbolic and the iconic coexist in any given sign, but in differently organized mixes.

Equally, it should not come as a surprise that in any given film text, a multiplicity of temporalities are at work. Indeed, different temporalities inhere in the three sign-types themselves, as Roman Jakobson and Krystyna Pomorska point out in their *Dialogues*:

> Peirce's reflections on the three categories of signs and their
> relation to the problem of time are particularly worthy of

note. In his study entitled *My Masterpiece*, he conceives the icon as being the accomplished image of an experience that is already past, while the index is linked to an ongoing experience in the present. The symbol, however, always possesses a general meaning and is based on a general law; everything that is truly general is related to the indefinite future. The past is an accomplished fact, whereas a general law cannot ever be totally accomplished. It is a potentiality whose mode is the *esse in futuro*. The value of a symbol, and a linguistic symbol in particular, lies in the fact that it "gives us the possibility of predicting the future." The word and the future are indissolubly linked—that is one of Peirce's most penetrating theses.[15]

All these temporalities leave traces, all connecting bits of the optical-aural images to various history-streams, no matter how strenuously filmmakers try to organize texts to make us "overlook" those dimensions, and no matter how vociferously marketers, along with assorted reading instructors, try to coerce us into reading only what we are supposed to read in films, subordinating everything to "character" and "plot." The cinema's indexical dimension is a major key for deciphering the way a particular film engages with its contemporaneity. It is at the indexical level that history "presents" in representation.[16] In an interview with Ron Magid, George Lucas commented on his ardent advocacy of the extremely expensive digital imaging and sound facilities at his Skywalker Ranch and his Industrial Light & Magic special effects business. He candidly observed:

> Before, once you photographed something, you were pretty much stuck with it. Now . . . you can have complete control over it just like an artist does, and that to me is the way it should be . . . You can make shots conform to your idea after the fact, rather than trying to conform the world to what your idea is.[17]

Where Lucas betrays his still pre-modern notion of aesthetics and "art" is in his assumption that painting incarnates the norm for notions of the visual arts. The more modern notions of artistic production acknowledge the values of indexicality. That is where not only filmmakers such as Renoir, Rossellini, and Bresson concentrate their energies, but also Hou Hsiao-chen, Tsai Ming-liang, Wong Kar-wai, Edward Yang, Amos Gitai, Elia Suleiman, Bela Tarr, and many others whose work constitutes a wave of insistently indexical cinema from the mid-1970s onwards.

However, it is necessary to guard against the fetishization of indexicality in the process of combating the totalitarian and brutalizing aspects of the turn to the digital. While it is true that both Greenbergian modernism and avant-gardes mobilized and appealed to the indexical dimension of sign-making in the arts, they did not do so for the same reasons. For the avant-gardes, indexical dimensions of signs were mobilized and stressed for their ability to reference the contemporary social-industrial dynamics which were reformatting culture. As such, the avant-gardes were not in search of indexicality as a mark of anti-industrial romantic individualism, but as a way of making history "present" its symptomatic discourses. On the other hand, Greenbergian modernism was committed to the preservation and continuation of some residually aristocratic dimension of aesthetics, erecting as its ideal reference point the romance of purity and individuation articulated in the early part of the nineteenth century, that is to say, in the post-revolutionary bedding down of a new compromise reached by the bourgeoisie and the resurgent absolutist aristocracy which characterized, for instance, the Napoleonic restoration. Echoes of that version of the search for indexicality still remain very much with us today in, for instance, antiquarian valuations of handcrafted objects. But to note and value the indexical dimension of a set of signs does not guarantee any particular kind of aesthetic or political "progressiveness": that must depend on the way and the purposes for which indexicality is mobilized in the overall aesthetic strategy deployed.

Similarly, the stress on the iconic dimension of signs as practiced in primarily digital mimetic media cannot be equated automatically, knee-jerk fashion, with the ruthlessly authoritarian drive to which digitization has been yoked in our cultural formation. Such a stress must also be seen and assessed as part of an overall political-aesthetic strategy seeking to move cultural practices into a particular direction. The indexical dimension of sign-making may have to be stressed in the face of its threatened elimination, not because of its ability to evoke a linkage with nineteenth-century Romanticism (which it also may do), but because of its ability to enable us to detect the traces of contemporary socio-economic dynamics within the very fabric of the "construals" of the world we inhabit. The construal of reality effected by cinema as a primarily indexical discursive form is thus a far more complicated matter than seems to have been acknowledged hitherto. It is not simply a question of noting the indexical connection between a photo-chemically registered image distorted or inflected by technological procedures such as lens technology, framing, the light-sensitivity of the celluloid's chemical coating and so forth.

258

It is far too crude a move to invoke "ideology" as a filtering mechanism interposed between the camera's lens and reality. To invoke ideology as a set of filtering spectacles is unhelpful not least because it misconstrues the one who is allegedly wearing them as a homogeneous entity that is either deluded (with spectacles) or clear-sighted (without them). Construals of reality are never either one or the other. They do not operate with a binary logic. Such construals are themselves configured by the dynamic interactions between the multiple currents and rhythms we condense in the singular term "history," a configuration that moves us all, from which death is the only exit, and within which "emptiness" only marks in any given framework of understanding either the place of the not-yet-understood or that of what must be excluded for the framework to exist at all.

The premature invocation of ideology as a filtering mechanism or as a set of blinkers emphasizes the expressive, symbolic dimension of cinematic discourse at the expense of its indexical and iconic-analogical aspects, thus promoting a simplistic polarization between reality and "constructions" of reality into which much film theory has become bogged down. In that respect, ideologies are correlated with identities: they involve the ascription of a coherent set of beliefs and prejudices to any member of a particular group by virtue of their location in society. Ideology becomes the expression of the "view" from that position, which might approximate the truth if only such positions were not described as a "point" of view allegedly occupied by one-eyed people with monolithic identities. It may be more useful to remember that in geometry, a point is an abstraction, a fiction, something that cannot be "had" or occupied.

Finally, the invocation of ideology as a pair of distorting spectacles, whether worn consciously or unconsciously, abusively homogenizes ideology itself as an allegedly coherent discursive formation actualized by equally homogeneous individuals who are members of, again, homogeneous groups. Instead, like points in geometry, ideologies and the subject positions to which they correspond are abstract, theoretical constructions designed to enable the analysis of the heterogeneous discursive compounds we produce when construing the world we inhabit. An ideology never appears as such in a pure form to our perception. It is a hypothetical fiction, literally: something inaccessible to the naked eye that must underpin social activities such as thinking and speaking if we are to make any sort of sense of the way culture and consciousness work in daily life. The substance, the reality, from which these well-founded hypothetical fictions have been deduced is to be found in the consistent co-variations between, on the one hand, repeated patterns in discursive productions (at whatever level, involving one or all of the indexical, iconic or symbolic dimensions of the signs deployed), and, on the other hand, the objective interests, established through historical-economic analysis, attaching to positions in the relations of production, regardless of the degrees of consciousness or awareness displayed by any given, actually existing person occupying any part of any number of the available positions in the social-historical constellation. This somewhat convoluted sentence is necessitated by the fact that a person may occupy different positions in the constellation at different times and in different situations without this appreciably affecting the dynamics configuring that social-historical constellation itself: history moves at different speeds than the rhythms most pertinent in biographical or psychic temporalities.

The identification of an ideology is thus dependent simultaneously on the way one construes social positioning in the relations of production and the way one construes patterns of repetition in discursive productions. Consequently—and bracketing for the time being problems raised by my reference to modes of production—it becomes crucially important not to misidentify the multidimensional nature of the signs deployed in such discursive activity. To identify a sign as solely indexical, for instance, necessarily results in a highly questionable, at best rough-and-ready, largely intuitive notion of how an ideology might manifest itself in something such as a film. It is, for instance, relatively easy to identify the occurrence of wave-like phenomena in a given cultural formation. Britain and the United States in the 1980s saw a wave of books, conferences, and essays addressing "identity," both national and personal. The after-effects of whatever social-economic forces programmed that wave are felt still today in various Western governments' heinous immigration and asylum policies. Similarly, a wave of somewhat lesser amplitude washed through cultural, gender and film studies from the late 1970s to the early 1990s under the sign of "masculinity," while elsewhere in the constellation (magazine publishing, music videos, television drama) "laddish" behavior was reasserted as an appropriate, even a commendable register in which to conduct social relations. Aggressiveness was celebrated in sports and politics as well as in business and movies. One UK film, Guy Ritchie's *Lock, Stock and Two Smoking Barrels* (1998) even presented torture in a working-class milieu as rollicking good fun.[18] No doubt, the two waves are connected: masculinity was posed (and remains so today) as "an identity." The connections between these two waves point to a concatenation of ideologies concerned with the reformatting of identities, that is to say, with the ascription of appropriate registers of behavior and value-menus to specific categories of people. So much is apparent from the "surface" of media-texts (including the so-called non-fictional or critical media texts produced by academics or journalists). But the forces that program these waves, determining their amplitude, location, and vectorial movement, remain unidentified in the critical literature.

hjelmslev

The second theoretical domain to be mined in the comparative cinema project is Louis Hjelmslev's set of distinctions as reformulated by Christian Metz:[19] the distinctions between matter, substance, and form of both expression and content, constituting six further dimensions.[20] Particularly the distinctions between the substance and the form of expression and of content appear to hold great promise for the comparative project at this stage, especially in the light of Roland Barthes's identification of the cultural codes (substances of content) as one of the five codes structuring narration.[21]

The combination of Peirce and Hjelmslev, spiced up with Barthes, then allows us to explore the iconic, indexical and symbolic dimensions of the substances and forms of expression and content of a given film text. Of course, such a bricolaged combination of elements from different theoretical configurations is open to all manner of objections. For example, to ignore Peirce's notion of the interpretant as a defining element of the sign while retaining his identification of three dimensions of signs may be seen as an unwarranted truncation of Peirce's semiotic theory. However, I see no particular need for fidelity at this stage since my aim is not to argue for a Peircean way into the problems posed by a comparative approach to film studies. I do not need to accommodate Peirce's notion of the interpretant because this would lead me to the verbal, dictionary definitions of semantic units that are a defining aspect of signs. The need to take Peirce's interpretant into account may come back when the question of inner speech is raised as a dimension of signification, that is to say, when the thought processes that accompany the orchestration of discursive functions as described by Jakobson have to be considered in relation to primarily non-verbal signs.[22] The relevance of particular interpretants will then depend on the modulations of the process of address according to the activation of what Jakobson identifies as the metalinguistic function. Peirce's interpretant operates as an element of a (linguistic) code interacting with what Barthes called the cultural codes and which, together, constitute the metalinguistic dimension of a text or a textual fragment (such as a sequence in a film).

There are also other difficulties which need to be addressed in greater detail if the route advocated here is to become more readily practicable. One of the main issues in this respect is the fact that a film's form of expression is itself an exceedingly complex amalgam of different forms: the film's commodity form, which changes, along with a number of its expressive codifications, as, for instance, when a film made in 35mm is circulated on 16mm or on video, altering the musical, spoken and written linguistic forms, the recorded noise patterns, and so forth.

In this context, a rough example illustrating what my proposed bricolage might mean will have to suffice. The *indexical dimension of a cinematic narrative's form of expression* would be determined by the available technology deployed in the making of the film (indexing a particular kind of industrial organization, division of labor and investment flows). In this respect, an identification of the lenses used, the type of camera used, the film stock, lighting equipment, studio facilities, printing techniques, color process, special effects and so on, would all combine to index a particular kind of industrial organization of production in terms of the value tied up in the machinery deployed. The indexical dimension of technologies also points to the need to distinguish between, for instance, the role and possible structuring impact of different kinds of capital: constant (equipment and raw materials) or variable (labor power), circulating (raw materials and labor power) or fixed (plant), not forgetting the importance of fictional capital (land, of course, but also the potential values constituted by dime novels, newspaper items, old novels and plays, songs and so on, which often acquire value only after having been transformed into the raw material of a script or story outline, at which time these items are transformed and fenced into private property domains liable to yield monopoly rents).

On the other hand, the use of sound in Ridley Scott's *Gladiator* (2000) and in numerous other Hollywood productions may, as *the iconic dimension of the form of expression*, alert us to the analogy with the use of music in the retail trade, as in boutiques and fashion shops, whereas the older convention of discreet background music would iconically evoke muzak in elevators and waiting rooms. This iconic dimension of the form of expression could further signal, at *the indexical level of the substance of content*, the industrial psychology work that led to the widespread adoption of such silence-killing devices and to the manipulative public relations ideology underpinning such research. An example, for instance, would be to research the approach to music manifested in the cue-sheets and scores for silent films and to examine whether this changed (as I think it probably did) with the development of industrial psychology and the spread of public relations strategies as manifested in initiatives such as the BBC's *Music While You Work* radio programs in World War II.

The iconic dimension of a film's form of content may alert us to the structural homology between, say, the narrative structure of Robert Altman's *Short Cuts* (1993) and a television program such as *Hill Street Blues* (early 1980s) as well as the design of shopping malls catering for a range of niche audiences or shoppers. In other words, not only do we need to learn to identify the iconic, indexical, and symbolic dimensions of substances and forms of content and expression, but also we need to consider the probable connections between these various dimensions as they interact within the same text.

The combination of Peirce and Hjelmslev thus offers a way of envisaging a film's relation to economic structures, the range and type of technologies available, the circulation of different types of capital involved, the ideological configurations that must be in place for these particular forms and substances to be able to structure the filmic narrative, and so on. In short, different aspects of the text acquire, through their expressive-indexical dimension, value for something that could be called a forensic or an archaeological reading. In addition, such a reading would be able to identify the longer term social dynamics which overdetermine the kinds of shifts and mutations chronicled, for instance, as formal renewals in the writings of Roman Jakobson and Yuri Tynianov on the evolution of literary—or cinematic—styles. In this context, the detailed research conducted by David Bordwell and his colleagues on the so-called classic American cinema also provides useful clues.

jakobson

As intimated earlier, a third theoretical domain to be taken into account is Roman Jakobson's identification of six functions of discourse, especially if enhanced by Emile Benveniste's distinction between *histoire* and discourse. This conjunction offers a most useful way into the analysis of modes of address. Jakobson's work appears to be capable of suggesting how the conjunction between Hjelmslev's and Peirce's dimensions of discourse can be orchestrated into a textual fabric organized around intricate shifts of emphases among six overlapping axes of address. Moreover, the analysis of shifts and reverberations between functions of discourse, Peirce's three and Hjelmslev's six additional dimensions of textuality is likely to yield an insight into the way meanings can migrate from, say, an indexical dimension at the level of the form of expression to an iconic dimension at the level of the substance of content or an iconic dimension at the level of the form of content. In other words, the analysis may begin to show how the representational aspects of a text may be conditioned by their non-representational aspects, and how regimes of address orchestrate (energize and regulate) the dynamics at work in the textual fabric. This is why I would like to suggest that, at this initial stage of the project, the most productive way into the problems of comparative cinema studies is by way of an analysis of a text's mode of address. The subject positions thus identified would then, in the light of a forensic reading, be mapped (analogically, indexically or symbolically) on to the actual social subject positions (interest groups; subject agencies) in contention in the social formation that presided over the formulation of the text in question. Such a procedure would be able to place the text as a "field" dramatizing the tensions between historically attestable positions occupied by different interest groups and to ascertain the vectorial impetus underpinning the text. In other words, such a reading would be capable of identifying from which historical position the text is primarily (never exclusively) enounced and in which direction, towards what kind of society, the text seeks to pull the addressee.

freud and benjamin

This brings me to the fourth theoretical constellation that has to be mapped into the field of comparative film studies: Freud's identification of four processes of distortion in dream work as seen through the prism of Walter Benjamin's notion of fantasy. Noting that Marx had already dismissed the idea that conditions of life were reflected in ideologies, Benjamin wrote in his notes for the unfinished *Arcades Project*:

> The economic conditions under which society exists are expressed in the superstructure—precisely as, with the sleeper, an overfull stomach finds not its reflection but its

expression in the contents of dreams, which, from a causal point of view, it may be said to "condition". The collective, from the first, expresses the conditions of its life. These find their expression in the dream and their interpretation in the awakening.

(K2, 5)[23]

This is also the context within which Benjamin developed his theory of dialectical images:

> It is said that the dialectical method consists in doing justice each time to the concrete historical situation of its object. But that is not enough. For it is just as much a matter of doing justice to the concrete historical situation of the *interest* taken in the object. And *this* situation is always so constituted that the interest is itself performed in that object and, above all, feels this object concretized in itself and upraised from its former being into the higher concretion of now-being (waking being).
>
> (K2, 3)[24]

Shortly afterwards, having thus put into place a critique of the bulk of what now passes for audience studies, Benjamin quotes a passage from Marx about the way individual machines merge in the production process into a collective machine capable of continuous production. Turning to the cinema to exemplify what Marx may have meant, Benjamin wrote:

> Film: unfolding of all the forms of perception, the tempos and rhythms, which lie preformed in today's machines, such that all problems of contemporary art find their definitive formulation only in the context of film.
>
> (K3, 3)[25]

With that remark, Benjamin foreshadowed the development of one of today's more exciting aspects of both media and cultural studies: the type of mediology currently being elaborated by Régis Debray and his colleagues.

multiple fantasy registers

That film texts relate to the historical dynamics which preside over their production primarily by virtue of the indexical aspect of the formation of their substance of expression is a hypothesis worth pursuing, as is the certainty that the translation from the real to the text, whether expressively or representationally, must be subject to the four distortion processes which Freud showed to be responsible for structuring fantasy and dream texts.

One of the consequences of adopting that hypothesis is that it becomes possible to differentiate between, at least, two distinct, though related, levels in texts where fantasy processes are at work. At the level of *the substance of content*, a menu of culturally determined fantasy scenarios—ideological paradigms of a sort—exert pressure on the way networks of ideas are knitted together into secondarily elaborated ideological or philosophical frameworks or semantic fields underpinning the orchestration of a particular "form": the particular version of the fantasy performed by/in the text (such as a particular version of "the Oedipus"—a substance of content—performed in and by a given film). At the level of a text's *substance of expression*, it is the way the physico-sensoral aspects of cinematic signification are transformed into menus of expressive procedures. For instance, the recourse to special effects emphasizing iconicity over indexicality or expanding the range of possible actorial gestuality by means of stunt doubles or suspending actors on wires, using digital editing and amplified soundtracks, and so forth: these constitute a substance of expression that, by virtue of its very selective aspect, vehiculates another kind of fantasy scenario. So, a techno-fetishistic fantasy relating to a desirable corporate-industrial organization of film production may come to "double" the oedipal scenarios at work in the narrative of a film such as the Wachowski brothers' *The Matrix* (1999). Going one step further, it is probable that it is the relation between these two distinct levels of fantasy embedded in, respectively, the substances of expression and content, which accounts for whether a film "clicks" with a contemporary audience or not. On the other hand, historical changes (cultural shifts or changes in personal maturation) might highlight alignments or discrepancies between these two levels which remained unnoticed by contemporary audiences targeted by a film's marketing strategies. In this respect, reviews, if read symptomatically, often contain a kind of *plumpes denken* commentary on whether the two fantasy orchestrations are deemed to be in the proper alignment for a given economically significant consumer group.

Peter Wollen, who was the first to draw film theory's attention to Peirce and Hjelmslev in his pioneering *Signs and Meaning in the Cinema* first published in 1969, identified a telling example of this kind of *plumpes denken*.[26] He noted how studies of film architecture seem to gravitate unreflectively towards the small group of films which feature architecture as "star." Focusing particularly on Dietrich Neumann's book *Film Architecture* (1996), Wollen quizzically comments:

> what comes across from Neumann's selection of great "film architecture" is that it is clustered in the genres of dystopian science fiction, horror and crazy comedy. Architecture as star represents criminal lunacy, pathetic farce or untrammeled despotism. With this in mind, it seems strange that architects themselves should be attracted by this vision of their art, even if it makes them the centre of attention![27]

The apparent contradiction relates to the discrepancies between two layers of fantasy at work in the films concerned. The fantasy generated at the level of the substance of expression stimulates the positive appreciation of the architectural designs; the fantasy underpinning the formatting of the substance of content does indeed suggest criminal lunacy, pathetic farce or untrammeled despotism. The former fantasy layer, because it is anchored in the substance of expression, makes a "positive appreciation" possible through its implication in the economic aspects of film production. The bulk of the films singled out where architecture features as a star (*L'Inhumaine* (1924), *Aelita* (1924), *Metropolis* (1927), *Just Imagine* (1930), *Things To Come* (1936), *Lost Horizon* (1937), *The Fountainhead* (1949), *Blade Runner* (1982), *Batman* (1989), *Dick Tracy* (1990), and so on) are all very expensive productions mobilizing the industry's resources to showcase "what cinema can do" when it embarks on prestige projects designed to make loads of profit (even if this intention is not always realized on the films' release). These films constitute a celebration of the film industry's corporate financial and cultural power, even if, at another level in the text, such power is presented as problematic.

At the level of the substance of expression, it is what might be described as the film industry's own criminal lunacy (its spectacular displays of corporate power deploying massive resources, mostly acquired by fraud, sharp practice and unfettered greed), pathetic farce (evident from just about any account of the production of "big" films) or untrammeled despotism (by factory bosses, financiers, bureaucrats and their representatives on the studio floor and, in aspirational forms, by the way filmmakers address viewers) that is being celebrated by way of the spectacle starring architecture. From the industry's point of view, all these things are positive features of the great achievements of the culture industries and operate to the greater glory of the hegemons controlling the industry's resources. Hence the prominence given to the quantity of resources used in the marketing of such films. Architects such as Neumann simply disregard the substance of content fantasies (which betray a populist ideological strategy) and appreciate, perhaps intuitively, the role allocated to architectural design in the "real" display of corporate power underpinning the populist rhetoric decrying corporate rule. In that respect, Neumann's celebration of films starring architectural design is similar to the corporate support extended to, for instance, Reaganite rhetoric against "big government": Reagan's backers and those hoping to profit from his election realized that the populist rhetoric merely masked a drive to increase corporate power and even bigger government. Similarly, Neumann was right, in a *plumpes denken* kind of way, to intuit that regardless of the populist rhetoric deployed against corporate power by the "star architecture" films, these were, in fact, celebrations of corporate power at the level of the "indexing" and display of the expressive resources so spectacularly on show. In these films, the two levels of fantasy operate simultaneously but are, from one point of view (Wollen's),

266

somewhat out of ideological alignment. However, from another point of view (Neumann's), the fantasies conveyed through the way the industry's self-celebratory image is indexically encrusted into its substance of expression easily outweigh any importance one might attach to the "surface rhetoric" bad-mouthing the totalitarian aspects of the very untrammeled, despotic corporate power shamelessly spectacularized by the industry itself. These films celebrate the power, both cultural and financial, of the industries that produced them, in the same way that Vicente Minnelli's *An American in Paris* (1951) or Cecil B. De Mille's *Cleopatra* (1934) celebrated the resources at Hollywood's disposal, or as Ridley Scott's *Blade Runner* (1982) and Verhoeven's *RoboCop* (1987) celebrate the triumph of corporate America simply by signaling, at the level of the expressive means deployed to make the film, that if you like *that* kind of cinema which so ostentatiously relies on the central control of masses of labor power and gigantic quantities of dead labor, you cannot object to the kind of social relations that must be in place to make it.

Similarly, most disaster movies and post-apocalypse movies celebrate, in the very display of productive resources that constitutes the "spectacle," the kind of organization of social relations that is on course to create the joyous spectacle of global mayhem. "Blockbusters" and the mainstreaming of exploitation cinema as a business strategy (as opposed to the occasional "epic" celebrating the joys of monopoly production) not only signify the rule of finance capital over the film industry, but also demand that we, the viewers, take delight in finance capital's utopias. The films acknowledge that there may be some rotten apples in the barrel of finance capital, but on the whole it is a wonderful and pleasurable thing, naturally and self-evidently normative. The kind of social organization of labor that can bring us Cameron's *Titanic* (1997) or Michael Bay's *Armaggedon* (1998) and even sell us wars, as in Spielberg's *Saving Private Ryan* (1998), may have its flaws, but it must not be challenged as deserving our undivided attention and enjoyment. Films do indeed speak with a forked tongue, and, as Peter Wollen is probably the first to realize—remembering his arguments in appreciation of the formal(ist) qualities of Orson Welles's *Citizen Kane* (1941)—fantasies inscribed at the level of substance and form of expression often speak louder than apparent story-contents, the kind of thing that is given false prominence in plot-synopses and film journalism.

267

the indexical and the iconic: struggle for hegemony

The importance of trying to come to terms with the polarization between iconic and indexical cinemas, and with the factors that determine their vectorial developments is difficult to overestimate. In a remarkable book, Phil Rosen argued that the indexical dimension of cinematic texts bears witness to a "having-been-made" in addition to a "having-been-there."[28] If we look at *that* dimension of films a complex set of issues opens up, bearing on the way socio-political conjunctures imprint themselves in texts, suggesting that it is possible to specify how and where in a text, and at which level of its functioning, the social relations that prevailed at the time of its conception-production have left the marks that then allow us to read them as a kind of allegory. Rosen rightly points out that the "hype" aspect of cinematic strategies is not a new dimension of the current Hollywood productions. It was always there to a greater or lesser extent. The example of the climactic ballet in Minnelli's *An American in Paris* (1951) also functions as a way of showing that art direction, as well as the virtuoso performances of actors, may convey a significant indexical charge as "a document" of Hollywood's capabilities. The display of virtuosity at both actorial and design levels is a rationalization of what Rosen calls "a certain administration of sense governed by narrative emplacement." Calling that "a rationale" is a diplomatic way of saying that at times even a Minnelli film can become merely a secondary elaboration of the self-display of Hollywood's power and wealth.

Similar dimensions of that display-spectacle also crop up in the lavish decors and hordes of extras in Hollywood historicals. In the context of musicals such as *West Side Story* (1961), Robert Wise showed off the competitive advantages that cinema enjoys over the stage: the proscenium-stage effect of the neighborhood-dance sequence where Romeo and Juliet meet for the first time, ends with the song "Maria" as Richard Beymer walks down a corridor, the background of which then changes into a street scene, demonstrating the superiority of cinema in addition to the Broadway-type staging skills. In fact, that entire sequence is riddled with "specifically cinematic" devices as an ode to the cinematic machine's triumph over Broadway. More recently, digital effects are deployed in the very manner that Gordon Jennings, the head of Paramount's special effects department in 1934, candidly described when he admitted that his work consisted of adding sales points to a film, drawing attention to the quality of the special effects which are being sold *as such* (as they had been earlier in relation to Schoedsack and Cooper's *King Kong*, 1933). When the vice-chairman of Universal, Marc Shmuger, was reported talking about the impending release of Ang Lee's *The Hulk* (2003),[29] he echoed Jennings's approach and candor: "The most spectacular effects were back-loaded. We're now getting to where we can show off what we have." However, there is a crucial difference between the two statements. Discussing Jennings's remarks about special effects as a way of showing off Hollywood's production capacities, Rosen cites the issue of Cleopatra's barge in Cecil B. DeMille's *Cleopatra* (1934). In that film, the studio's research department went to inordinate lengths to achieve maximum exactitude in the reconstruction of the barge as a scale model. Rosen then goes on to draw attention to the display of virtuosity such a meticulously reconstructed model represents and he notes that such a display of virtuosity at the level of the profilmic object is one of the attractions of the historical film as such because it plays a kind of hide-and-seek between referentiality with respect to the past and performance for the present, with both predicated on indexicality: *this* is what the barge actually looked like according to the historical sources, and *this* is what we in Hollywood can do today with our fantastic production resources.[30]

This is also true of science fiction cinema and increasingly of action or horror, where special effects designate a technical virtuosity displayed to its own greater glory by the industry. But digitalization causes these effects increasingly to tip over into the demonstration of a special kind of relation to that wealth and power: it is no longer so much the virtuoso skill of the acting body or the resources available to studio departments that are spectacularized, but the magnitude of the financial investment, the scale of the cost of accessing the technology which itself is outside of the producer's direct control. Digital expertise, software expertise, is brought in by the producers rather than "produced" by them. Consequently, the emphasis shifts from stressing the labor and design achievement represented by the industrial phase of Hollywood production to the amount of money spent on subcontracting and buying the effects required, resulting in a celebration of corporate financial power as opposed to a glorification of the studio's own, industrial production plant.

But in addition to narratorial discourses of self-congratulation and corporate power, the signifiers of spectacular digitization also carry a third discursive thread: corporate dreaming. Anticipating a point I will develop below, it is as if the financial powers underpinning those effects are insinuating, through the indexical dimensions encrusted into the very technological resources deployed (and what we know such a deployment must imply), a set of modalities of knowing and experiencing which convey a power-fantasy (as distinct from the display of actual financial clout) that betrays something of the way in which these social-economic sectors would like to arrange and reproduce the organization of society. It is also at this point that the importance of detecting and analyzing the many dimensions of a film's mode of address becomes so crucially important. The fantasies conveyed by way of the workings of a particular industrial machine also address us: we are invited to consent to finding such fantasies spectacularly pleasurable as they suggest that we should be gratified to be regarded as an eminently malleable mass to be transformed according to the requirements of such an industrial and financial organization, at speeds unencumbered by industrial technology, centrally controlled by programmers of electronic flows.[31] Corporate dreams, however, are to be read in a kind of echo chamber constituted by the reverberations between indexical features of the substance and form of expression (the menu of technical resources deployed) and the indexical dimension of the substance and form of content (the selections made from what Barthes called codes of knowledge or cultural codes operating at the level of the substance of content[32]). Rosen writes about such fantasies as a form of forecasting:

> The strategy of the forecast has a crucial function in freeing an account of the digital from having to deal with hybridities as constitutive. It delineates the characteristics of the digital as existing through pure ideals rather than impure actualities, things that will eventually be achieved, rather than an achieved state of things . . . The forecast puts in place a temporal structure that suggests that such accounts are implicated not just in fetishizing digital technology, but in a kind of *historiographic* fetishization. Purely digital practices become something like an inevitability that is nevertheless "not yet". The structure of the forecast constitutes the digital on the basis of a modern form of historical temporality.[33]

The forecasting temporality involved is not that of a weather report, but that of a wish, consciously or unconsciously articulated. It appears that such a temporality, inherent in the shift to the virtual, encourages the reduction of the resistance of "the real" (still operating in chemical indexicality) and releases unconscious drives more readily, giving them more play. By virtue of the binary code and algorhythms which make up digital images, these, although primarily iconic signs, also share to a greater extent than is the case with indexical signs, a future-oriented temporality, as identified by Jakobson and Pomorska.[34] As such, digital imagery can delineate fantasies of a desired or feared future that are less encumbered by the resistance of the real encountered in, for instance, science fiction films made with more mechanical-industrial means at the pro-filmic level. What is at stake, again, is the very *visibility* of the special effects: if they are not seen as such, the fantasy may not be able to take hold. The political implications for the spread of such fantasies on a gigantic scale were noted many decades ago by Adorno when he remarked about utopian fantasies cast in the kind of temporality that Rosen detects in digital effects:

> Whomever the genius to dominate nature has granted the ability to see far into the distance, sees only what he habitually sees, enriched by the illusion of novelty that gives its existence a false and inflated significance. His dream of omnipotence comes true in the form of perfected impotence. To this day utopias come true only so as to extirpate the idea of utopia from human beings altogether and to make them swear allegiance all the more deeply to the established order and its fatefulness.[35]

The main vectorial point for film theory that Rosen's work indicates is that it should now become a major task to unravel exactly how and where in specific texts the "allegorical" dimensions play which connect that text, not only to a specific history of production, but also to different social strata's dreams of what they would like to see happen, their respective social imaginaries, which is not at all the same as their ideologies (although these two discursive registers are connected). By and large, those allegorical connections have been established on the basis of an analogical-mimetic correlation between a social formation and a text's substance of content. The Brazilian literary historian and theorist Roberto Schwarz provided an excellent example of the analogic-mimetic approach when he commented that when an artistic form emerges from the more or less contingent conditions of its production,

> [t]his form retains and reproduces some [such conditions]—
> it would make no sense if it did not—*which then become its*
> *literary effect*, its "reality effect", the world they represent. The
> vital point is this: a part of the original historical conditions
> reappears, as a sociological form, first with its own logic, but
> this time also on the fictional plane and as a literary
> structure. In this sense, forms are the abstract of specific
> social relationships, and that is how . . . the difficult process
> of transformation of social questions into properly literary
> or compositional ones—ones that deal with internal logic
> and not with origins—is realized.[36]

Schwartz's comment pertains to the indexical and the symbolic aspects of a substance of the content, that is to say, to a configured set of ideas (possibly an ideology) from which—or against which—a particular "form" of content is fashioned. Barthes called this combination "an encyclopedia," "an anthology of maxims and proverbs about life, death, suffering, love, women, ages of man, etc. . . . a nauseating mixture of common opinions, a smothering layer of received ideas" that "turns culture into nature" and appears "to establish reality, 'Life'."[37] However, the manifestations of an endoxic field are not the only indicators of substances of content from which narratives fashion their particular forms. Ideological, philosophical, and theoretical paradigms also function as available substances in this respect. As for the iconic dimension of a substance of content, Régis Debray offers an interesting angle when he writes:

> The contents of thought are externalized in the forms
> of organization which make them possible and which
> they themselves make necessary. To conceive of the
> working class as the agent of universal emancipation,
> for example, is to turn a historical model of the factory,

with its centralization, its verticality and its division of labor, into an organizational model for the bearers of that thought.[38]

fantasies of labor power

I would like to suggest some further, rather riskier, propositions by taking the operations of multiple fantasy layers at work in so-called action films—a marketing category, often called a genre in film studies, that emerged in the early 1980s as a result of the emergence of a new retail sector: video rental and sales. My reason for doing so is that I suspect that, hidden beneath this marketing category called action films, there is a kind of cinematic discourse that speaks to us of labor power and, through this conceptualization, of the fundamental dynamics of capitalism in general. Putting it a little more dramatically, the economic histories offered to us by economic historians such as Robert Brenner[39] and Giovanni Arrighi concern themselves analytically and theoretically with the same issues addressed, as fantasies, by action films. Economic historians and action films both address questions of the value of labor power. The economic historians do so analytically, action films do so fantasmatically. Some of these fantasies concern capitalism's attempts to intensify the exploitation of labor power, and thus to devalue it. Other dimensions of those fantasies talk about efforts to extend control over raw materials through cycles of geographical expansion (marketed mainly as war and adventure films). Yet others concentrate on the fact that, in order to accumulate vast amounts of capital, previously "fixed" capital values have to be destroyed on a massive scale. Orgies of capital destruction, especially of fixed capital (as in the built environment or "plant"), characterize the rise to prominence of a new sector of rapacious social agents. The three main strategies of capital to combat the falling rate of profit can thus be seen to structure fantasy pressures in action films: the intensification of the exploitation of labor power, geographical expansion and the destruction of capital values. Anticipating the rest of my argument, I would like to suggest that through the medium of many films currently labeled as "action," finance capital is giving expression to its concerns and aspirations, whereas in films prior to the 1980s, most cinematic fantasies had the workings and requirements of industrial capital as its reference point. American, European and other regional or national cinemas must be seen as presenting particular "states of play" in the tensions between pre-capitalist, industrial, and finance capital forces. The social sectors underpinning those tensions, sometimes ambivalently implicated in all three vectors, delineate the overall narratorial positions or social agencies whose fantasies constitute the films as texts.

My argument is not that all action films are characterized as a genre by a (fantasy) economic discourse centered on the interests of, say, finance capital, or that the difference between, say, the films of George Lucas and those of Ram Gopal Varma equals the difference between US and Indian finance capital's dreams. If the theoretical-analytical framework proposed here has merit, then it must follow that this kind of fantasy dimension— relating to all three main phases of capitalism's development—must be present in all films at some level, however diluted, distorted or otherwise translated. What I do wish to argue is, first, that in the kinds of films currently lumped together under the label "action cinema" one may find more readily a way of reading the operations of the labor theory of value as it works in the shaping of socio-economic fantasies; and second, that the modalities in which labor power is inscribed into the films allow us to conclude that it is finance capital which is the discursive hegemon in Hollywood's cinema since the late 1970s and early 1980s.

This hypothesis is based on recent historiography: the ascendancy of finance capital in Hollywood from the 1970s onwards is demonstrated extensively by David Cook's account of the way the Los Angeles-based sector of the industry was restructured under the control of personnel drawn from the FIRE (finance, insurance and real estate) sector of the US economy.[40] Cook astutely observes that the representatives of finance capital now in charge of Hollywood also brought the stylistic and marketing practices of exploitation cinema into the mainstream. During the neoliberal surge of the 1970s and early 1980s, company managers no longer had to account to their backers on the basis of annual production schedules and profit plans. Now, finance capital put its own henchmen in charge of each individual production decision, resulting in the much-lamented rule of the accountants who restructured the business. From the mid-1970s onwards, the "run-clearance-zone" system of distribution was changed into the simultaneous blanket release of "blockbuster" films enabling a major increase in ticket prices. In 1975, the release of *Jaws* extended the pioneering "blanket-release" efforts made by Tom Laughlin in the late 1960s (*Born Losers*, 1967; *Billy Jack*, 1971) in California to a national exploitation strategy with a saturation release including suburban shopping mall cinemas, preceded by eight months of marketing. This was followed by *The Deep* (Peter Yates, 1977) while, in the same year, *Star Wars* consolidated the "franchise" approach pioneered by the James Bond series in the early 1960s, with sequels and a marketing strategy designed into the very fabrication of the films. As finance capital's gambling syndicates took over the film business, costs exploded (between 1972 and 1979, they increased by 450 percent) which is one important reason why individual films were replaced by "franchises" (such as the *Exorcist* franchise in 1973, followed by the *Star Wars* franchise, the *Rambo* franchise, the *Jurassic Park* franchise and so on), consisting of a series of films acting as the central advertising engine for a wide variety of business ventures. Marketing costs mushroomed: by the late 1990s, the *average* cost of releasing a film in the United States was estimated by the Motion Pictures

Association of America as some $76.8 million. The *average* marketing budget amounted to some $100 million per film.

Cook showed how and why the restructuring of Hollywood under new FIRE management caused a return to the "cinema of attractions" which had dominated the industry prior to the development of cinema as an "integrated narrative," even though elements of the cinema of attractions had remained as components of certain narrative genres, like the musical and the horror film, where direct sensory stimulation (the delivery of spectacle and shock) had become a key element of spectatorial pleasure.[41] The reversal to the cinema of attractions under current finance capital hegemony thus alerts us to the fact that, prior to becoming organized into an industry, cinema was also under the sway of speculative capital.

This dimension of the restructuring of Hollywood in the 1970s had major effects that went beyond the mainstreaming of exploitation cinema.[42] The question arises—and remains open: is the reversal to a cinema relying on the visceral impact of special effects within a narrative frame barely sufficient to string those effects together, due primarily to the fact that, in the 1970s and 1980s, the industry was reverting to an older moment in the industrialization of culture? There is always the very real possibility that a recourse to visceral sensationalism may well be the logical destination of the industrialization of culture itself,[43] or that one consequence of a number of tendencies present in "new technologies" is the leveling down of cultural strata by reducing the value of cultural-intellectual labor. Both these possibilities would bear further examination in the light of Arrighi's description of the way one cycle of capitalist accumulation supersedes another by reviving aspects of the period which preceded the superseded phase, that is to say, the one-step-forward-two-steps-back move which surfaces in the fantasy scenarios accompanying the cinema of attractions.

And this brings me, in conclusion, to the problem that initiated these reflections: the inscription of labor power in films. In order to see how labor power may "present" itself in films, it may be helpful to outline the contours of the problem by aligning three kinds of films in what may seem, at this stage, a fairly arbitrary manner: the Italian peplums of the late 1950s and early 1960s, the James Bond films that started around 1960 and the cyborg films of which *RoboCop* (Paul Verhoeven, 1987) can be taken as a salient example. Again, it is important *not* to see the trajectory from Hercules to James Bond and then to *RoboCop* as a chronological sequence. All three types of figurations were there from the beginning of cinema (and probably also in the two or three decades before cinema, as the late-nineteenth-century preoccupation in Europe with automata and scientific gadgetry would suggest). For my purposes, the three main figurations can be described in terms of three types of bodies. The bodies of Hercules, James Bond and Robocop relate to each other in a way that suggests the elaboration of a fantasy about the value and uses of labor power as the dreams of industrial capital gradually give way to those of finance capital.

hercules

The *Hercules* body emerged most notably with Pietro Francisci's *Le Fatiche di Ercole* (1958), starring Steve Reeves. It is a muscle-bound, bulky and weighty device with a well-defined musculature denoting its energy-producing mechanisms. In that respect, the Hercules-body is a modernized, machinic version of the equally bulky but undefined mass of the pre-modern wrestler or fairground strongman. It is a body that a lot of work has gone into; a body built in gymnasia and displayed for its energy potential. It bespeaks immense amounts of leisure time spent in gyms and is (over)fed on special diets, carefully groomed and oiled to be put on show. It is much too impractical to be a working body. It is a showcase of labor power, duly eroticized. The Italian peplums often filmed the Hercules-body (also called Maciste, Samson, Goliath, Ulysses, and a number of other names) with a static camera showing the muscleman straining while performing an act of strength. The camera tends lovingly to caress the body with slow pans and tilts detailing the sweating torso, arms, biceps, thighs, and so on. The actor, if he moves at all, does so slowly, signifying the expenditure of massive quantities of energy. Incidentally, this slow-down of movement as a way of signaling the expenditure of excess energy was later repeated in the television series *The Six Million Dollar Man* (the pilot film directed by Richard Irving was shown in 1973). In that respect, the Hercules-body does not (yet) speak of efficiency, as does, for instance, Jean-Claude Van Damme's inscription into action stories. For the latter, the productivity of labor power is measured in terms of the efficiency of its deployment: maximum impact-energy applied in short bursts. The distance between Hercules-Steve Reeves and Van Damme is a historical one: while Reeves's body is valued for its labor power potential, Van Damme's relates to a subsequent period of capitalism, when the falling rate of profit and competition from low-wage economies required the available labor power to be exploited with greater efficiency.

Similarly, it is instructive to compare the Hercules-body with its antecedent figurations. These range from turn-of-the-century boxing films (the male equivalent of the many striptease or "dance-of-the-seven-veils" nickleodeon films) to the wave of nationalist Italian films starting with Enrico Guazzoni's *Quo Vadis* (1912), and especially the role of Bartolomeo Pagano as the black slave Maciste in Pastrone's *Cabiria* (1914).[44] The history of the Hercules body in cinema from its transition in *Maciste: Il Terrore dei banditi* (Borgnetto and Pastrone, 1915) onwards, remains to be written. Suffice it to say that it is a fundamentally different body from the athletic Fairbanks-body, suggesting that the Hercules body and the athletic body each crystallized out of different historical pressures, although overlaps and fusions are always possible in specific texts: for instance, in the eulogies of modernity in Italian futurist manifestos written by Marinetti around 1912 and in the *Manifesto Ardito-Futurista* of 1918, where machinic efficiency and athleticism are telescoped together.[45] Another example would be the celebration of circus athleticism after the 1917 revolution in Russia and Meyerhold's advocacy of biomechanics. The athletic body is part of the discourses of expertise, speed and geographical displacement, while the Hercules body is part of a discursive constellation emphasizing the static expenditure and management of labor power. The statically filmed muscle body is a figure in fantasies about primitive accumulation, that is to say, the transformation of agricultural laborers into factory laborers, valued for the quantity of labor power at their (and therefore the factory owner's) disposal. The mobile athletic body is more part of a militarized labor power, available for the territorial expansion of capitalism and, as such, still containing elements associated with imperial-colonial, aristocratic bodies to which skill, rather than great strength, was attributed. This, at least, has been the case in Western countries since the breakdown of the feudal order, which attributed maximum degrees of wealth, wisdom, skill, beauty, and strength to those at the top of the social hierarchy. The labor body is predominantly part of stories marketed as myths and epics; the flexible athlete is more characteristic of stories marketed as "adventure." The labor power body as figured from Bartolomeo Pagano to Steve Reeves is caught in the process of transition from agricultural labor to industrialization, narrated from the industrialized side of the fence. A wrestler body banking on weight and bulk is—which is not the case for all bodies of wrestlers—caught in the same process, but narrated mainly from the pre-modern side of economic organization. Van Damme's body extends that of Reeves, signaling the advent of a further phase of industrial production in which competitiveness is boosted by so-called efficiency gains.

The history of the athletic and of the acrobatic body still remains to be written. Bruce Lee's body deserves a chapter in both histories since it participates in the status-body series as well as in the labor-power body series. Any such history will have to be able to account for the fact that, for instance, in Hong Kong's martial arts and sword-fighting movies, the energy-impact of gestures is displaced onto the soundtrack: it *may* be signified through editing, but it always is on the soundtrack with greatly intensified sound-effects, a feature also present in, for instance, Hindi action films of the 1980s and 1990s. When watching Shaw movies, it is striking how visually fluid movement is constantly accompanied by percussive soundtracks, as if the almost ethereally speedy gestures needed an aural supplement to signify the quantity of expenditure of physical energy. In that respect, Hong Kong's way of inscribing martial arts bodies, at least since the mid-1960s (King Hu's *Come Drink with Me* (1965) is a notable milestone in this history) can be seen as a compromise formation orchestrating the encounter between—and the intermingling of—both archaicizing and modernizing currents within the texture of the films. Ng Ho noted a similar mixture in aspects of Hong Kong's martial arts comedies when he pointed out that the

> protagonist in king-fu comedy is conventionally a bright but hopelessly lazy kid who lacks both the staying power needed for martial arts training and respect for his *sifu* . . . Often, after suffering a defeat, he will muster the perseverance to train in martial arts more seriously, and will eventually reach the point where he surpasses the skills of his *sifu* . . . This emphasis on individual achievement and on outdoing one's own master undoubtedly parallels the ethos of capitalism.[46]

Other aspects of Hong Kong's complex cinematic martial arts genres also need a great deal of further analysis. One potentially fruitful area of research might be to explore how, for instance, notions of tradition come to perform the function which, in James Bond movies, is performed by the addition of gadgetry to bodily productivity. There is a suggestion in the Hong Kong films that the absorption of a historical-cultural tradition forms part and parcel of the acquisition of skills by a body (usually under the guidance of a *sifu* as the marker of social reproduction) constitutes a way of adding accumulated and stored dead labor to the body, in the same way that machinery of various kinds does in Western films. In this respect, a discourse about the way intellectual labor power relates to physical labor power seems to be insinuated into the Hong Kong films. The connection between the two main discursive strands at issue, "tradition" and "dead labor," is worth exploring in the differences between, for instance, Hong Kong's films and those of Taiwan, or between the "wire-work" traditionalism of Hong Kong's cinema in the 1960s, the scratching or imprinting of special effects directly onto the celluloid prior to that time and the increasing digitalization effects in the more contemporary Hong Kong cinema. Furthermore, the pursuit of those connections would also have to draw into the frame a consideration of the links between Japan's and Hong Kong's martial arts films.[47] This, rather than simpler notions of Confucianism, may well be pertinent in the figuration of Hong Kong's acrobatic displays and apprenticeships. Besides, crude aspects of social hierarchy and its reproduction by way of familial-paternal metaphors for the system of governance, do not particularly demarcate Hong Kong's films from much of so-called Western, allegedly modernized representational strategies anyway. One blatant example is the successful US television series *24 Hours* (broadcast in 2002). In one episode, a presidential candidate is given the line that anyone who cannot rule "his" family cannot govern the nation, demonstrating that aspects of Confucianism are also rife in the Washington-Hollywood nexus of American political culture today.

A politically more authoritarian version of the Herculean body was detected by Abé Mark Nornes in Japanese documentary films of the 1930s and 1940s in the form of large groups of "anonymous bodies in synchronized motion":

> The coordinated-exercise scene appears to have been obligatory in Japanese documentaries throughout the 1930s and until the end of the Pacific War; one begins to wait for its appearance when watching these films, and one is rarely let down. Whenever a group assembles, calisthenics are inevitable. They also bring the human closer to the machine. For instance, it is difficult to judge whether the women in *We Are Working So So Hard* [Atsugi Taka and Akimoto Takeshi, *Watashitachi wa konna ni hataraite iru*, 1945] are mastering their sewing machines or vice versa; their dance like movements appear regulated and non-human. *Attack to Sink* [*Gochin*, 1944] concentrates on the relationship of the sailors to their pipes and valves and torpedoes; the scenes developing that relationship rarely show the faces of the men, only their sweating bodies and pumping muscles.[48]

In such scenes, aspects of the labor body, as activated in peplums, combine with elements of the militarized skill-athletic bodies in adventure and war films, outlining a configuration of eroticized but industrially organized labor that also surfaces in the choreography of musicals such as those signed by Busby Berkeley.

bond

The *James Bond* body is a figure where labor power (physical strength) is enhanced by technological gadgetry, that is to say, by quantities of stored dead labor. Only weakly present in *Dr No* (1962)—mostly in the relationship between Bond and his Aston Martin car—the Bond stories came to emphasize this fusion of the body with machinery more and more as the series continued, with a corresponding rise in the cult status of the Q character originally played by Llewellyn. The display of quantities of physical energy, both in the fight scenes and in the proliferation of scenes demonstrating the desirability and sexiness of such a body, no longer suffices in those fantasies of national competition and transnational corporations. At the same time, the Bond-body not only is part of fantasy scenarios dramatizing the globalization of Anglo-American capital represented and policed by its enforcement institutions, but also features increasingly the orgiastic spectacle of the destruction of capital values in the course of international competition. The labor body (the Hercules body) is still part of the figuration, but it has become more sexualized, eroticized: Bond displays his bare torso or other parts of his anatomy, but his main displays of energy consist of his ability to handle machinery. This capacity is then rendered sexy by way of scenes showing a profligate expenditure of sexual energy that women are supposed to find irresistible. His productivity is governed by the combination of physical strength and plant, that is to say, it is enhanced by putting large quantities of dead labor at his disposal, a power-position that is also supposed to enhance his sex appeal. It is this aspect of the Bond-figure that speaks of a different phase in capitalist production. The Bond-body is part of trans-national monopoly capitalism's dream-world, a decidedly post-World War II configuration. In that world, the combination of labor power with corporate technology deployed on an international scale animates fantasies that go beyond the simple accumulation of wealth and power through which national bourgeoisies sought to acquire dominance at the level of the nation-state. Transnational corporate capitalism also requires the destruction of capital values accumulated "elsewhere" in order to clear the ground for new markets. The spectacular explosions and conflagrations that form part of the Bond-fantasy scenarios are barely disguised implementations of world-bank urban renewal and industrial development policies involving large-scale projects simultaneously causing large-scale destruction.

robocop

In Paul Verhoeven's *RoboCop* (1987), the Robo-body offers an electronically redesigned version of labor power, again imbricated in fantasies about the way social relations should be enforced. Here, labor power is not conjoined with the dead labor stored in machines: the machines are fused with the body to form a single unit capable of both massive quantities of labor power and equally massive information processing speeds. Verhoeven's film is quite explicit in this respect: the story is presented as the drama of transition from "old Detroit" (the rustbelt version of industrial capitalism) to a "New Detroit" which is, in fact, Los Angeles merged with Silicon Valley. The film concerns itself with the kind of social authority and organization that would have to accompany the rule of a triumphant transnational corporate capital anxious to control the flows of credit and to ensure the "correct" distribution of surplus capital (financial power). What appears to be at issue in the deployment of Robo-body fantasies is the fact that, once industrial capital has succeeded in imposing its transnational control, another sector of the bourgeoisie appropriates and takes over the management of the resulting flows of super-profits: the financial bourgeoisie becomes dominant—hence the emphasis on the importance of instantaneous omnivorous information processing. The Robo-body characterizes finance capital fantasies and can be said to constitute a figure in the way finance capital addresses industrial capital: in *RoboCop*, finance capital tells industrial capital how it must reformat social relations and systems of governance in order to ensure maximum profit-flows.

The story told by the different modalities of the inscription of physical energy and its relations to gadgetry and, later, to information processing, is a story of the way, in different places and at different times, capital dreams of ways of increasing profitability through the intensification of the exploitation of labor power, and of the social risks attached to such a move. The story can be presented as a chronological sequence, except, of course, that the chronology relates to the (non-linear) development of the relative dominance, at any given time, of a particular sector of the bourgeoisie. First, there are the fantasies of the transformation of premodern, mainly agricultural and artisanal capacities into industrial labor power, signaled by way of fantasies of muscular bodies disposing of enormous quantities of energy. Second, the corporate phase of capital mobilizes large quantities of dead, stored labor to enhance productivity. Third (to date), we get fantasies of re-engineered cyber-bodies capable of serving both as sources of energy and as enforcers of global discipline by virtue of the combination of bodies with gadgetry *and* information processing technology. These latter labor power fantasies need only particular, specialized bits of bodies capable of being combined with the required mechanical and electronic technologies. The much vaunted flexible accumulation system that is supposed to have displaced, at least in capital's heartlands, Fordist production, yields a further variation on the Robo-body: the infinitely adaptable shape-shifter.

Part and parcel of those fantasies of capitalist development is their diagnosis of the impediments obstructing perpetual increases in profit. Robert Brenner has convincingly argued that the postwar, relentlessly deepening crises in capitalism are due primarily to a structural-historical feature of the development of industrial capital.[49] The organization and building of large-scale industrial plants with huge amounts of expensive but not easily adaptable or movable machinery, condemned to remain in fixed locations, becomes a handicap for the older heartlands of capitalism when global markets are integrated into the system. The globalization required by capitalism also results in increased manufacturing competition from low-wage regions. As a consequence, the massive investment represented by large industrial factories or industrial parks in the historically older (advanced, higher wage) capitalist areas turn into expensive, insufficiently mobile millstones around the bourgeoisie's neck. The need to deindustrialize, difficult in practice because of the immense social costs and risks involved, is fantasized in the form of the orgies of capital value destruction in so-called action movies (but also in disaster movies, spy films, war films, post-apocalypse science fiction films and so on). In other words, movies do indeed talk to us of capitalism's fundamental systemic aspects: they do so in the form of fantasies of labor power and stored "value," and these are manifested both by way of the fantasy scenarios represented and by way of the technological means deployed in the making of the films. The place where these fantasy discourses can be heard loudest, since the mid-1980s or so, is in the films marketed under the "action" label.

In order to read the labor power discourse in movies, it is necessary to distinguish the different sets of relations that may be condensed in a number of different signifier-streams. The basic currents concern the paradigm of body-types (bulk or defined musculature), the relations between body-types and technological gadgetry (which itself comes in at least two modalities: mechanical and electronic gadgets), the subordination (or not) of a labor power unit to a social or managerial authority, the relation between (statically expended) energy and acrobatic athleticism, as also between different types of energy-signification such as extended straining or impact efficiency, and between energy expenditure and the destruction of congealed value. The latter comes in a number of different series of significations ranging from real estate to consumer durables depending on whether the fantasies emphasize accumulation-investment or consumption-sales. All these kinds of figurations, dispersed throughout texts—in plots, actors' bodies, set decoration, locations and so forth—constitute discursive currents conveying economic-social fantasies and propositions.

What complicates matters is that, first, not all body-presentations or body-fantasies in movies are directly or primarily to be read in terms of labor power. For instance, longer term mythical or anthropological fantasies, not so directly connected with capitalism, also operate with body metaphors, but they function as figurations of an idea of national-ethnic cohesion. The Japanese films of Miike Takashi come to mind, preoccupied as they are with mapping an emphasis on body-boundaries onto problems of multiethnic immigration into Japan in the 1990s. Miike further extends the body metaphor by doubling his stories, obsessed with body boundaries, with an approach to text construction that fragments "the body of the text" in ostentatious ways.

A second current of body presentations in movies distinct from—but combinable with—labor power fantasies is the eroticization of status bodies, that is to say, the presentation of upper caste or class bodies as more desirable than those of people of lower strata, or the symbolization of moral deficiencies in terms of physical deficiencies. In this respect, body-representations function more as an index of the nature of the compromise reached between, on the one hand, the " 'old' corruption," that is to say, the feudal status hierarchy and its values, and, on the other hand, a modernized, more individuated conception of "social entities."

A third complicating factor is that fantasies of labor power are also carried by the selection of digital-iconic or indexical dimensions of signs in the construction of film texts. This will require us to pay attention to the means of cinematic production in a way that is all too rarely practiced in discussions of film technology and the deployment of special effects. But again, one needs to be careful about modalities of reading in this respect.

There are differences between, say, special effects inscribed directly onto the celluloid through multiple exposures or scratching, and effects achieved by way of stunt men and women, at times assisted by "hidden" devices such as trampolines or wires in order to preserve the apparent integrity of the indexical image guaranteeing "belief," or effects achieved by way of electronic-digital programming. These differences between types of special effects connect not only with questions of labor power. They also carry associated discursive currents conveying meanings about different conceptualizations of the value of mimesis in different forms of social relations. Phases in the social history of mimesis are most commonly discussed in terms of phases in civilizational history, ranging from the reliance on prehistoric or "primitive" forms of mythical or "savage" thinking to different kinds of pre-feudal or non-feudal social formations, to feudal and then capitalist modernization, each shaping different regimes of subjectivity and "looking," as analyzed in Gebauer and Wulf,[50] and Ley.[51]

The reformatting of physical energy into labor power does involve disturbing and rearranging or redefining spaces, but not all violence and destruction in movies has to do with the productive destruction of capital values, that is, with the liquidation of unproductively stored dead labor (obsolete plant and infrastructure). Some "action" is concerned with the redefinition of hierarchical spaces into more secularized, egalitarian, modernized ones. These films are about the democratization and individuation of space, transforming them from hierarchical spaces into modernized places, or from derelict or under-used places into terrain ripe for redevelopment. Many "action" films concern themselves with staging who (or which kind of social system) shall govern the way space is used in streets, town or village squares, saloons, restaurants, agricultural landscapes and so on. Films addressing this kind of spatial reformatting stage the disruption of hierarchical relations (whether state-legitimized or not) in spatial terms, inscribing more egalitarian relations into them. Often, as, for instance, in westerns, this reformatting of space may be narrated in terms of the imposition of some idealized and egalitarian notion of the "rule of law." But perhaps as frequently, when legality refers to a "law" enforced by a status hierarchy, the reformatting of space can be narrated in terms of a resistance to "injustice" or some "refusal to make way" (for instance, by the sheep farmer or "sodbuster" in the face of the cattle baron's territorial rule).

282

If melodrama is to be seen primarily as a struggle over relations of social reproduction (to be governed by status authorities or by individuated patriarchal citizens), "action" must also be seen as a struggle over the democratization of space that allegedly must follow from the reformatting of people into units of labor power. Such is the case when the relation between labor power and the state is at issue. For instance, in the main series of late 1950s and 1960s Mexican masked-wrestler movies featuring Santo (played by the wrestler Huerta), the bulky muscleman—with ill-defined musculature—is activated by governmental agencies who send messages to his lair, which has all the features of a communications laboratory. But his activities never involve much gadgetry. Even firearms are shunned by the masked hulk. In this respect, one can see not only a continuity with but also a significant difference from the comics that inspired Santo's model, the American comic strip hero "The Shadow." In contrast, James Bond is activated bureaucratically in the residually feudal spaces of Whitehall and other UK government offices while the fusion of his body with gadgetry is staged in a separate space dedicated to research and development geared towards increasing productivity. In the Batman films, the relation of power between state and finance capital (including the reactivation of aristocratic status indicators) is illustrated graphically by the wonders of the Batcave as much as by Bruce Wayne's mansion. Superman's connection with newspapers and telephone kiosks talks to us of the early-twentieth-century utopian fantasies accompanying the creation of a nationally integrated market,[52] and dreams of global control to follow.

So, not all elements in action films speak of labor power, and neither is the reference to labor power limited to action films. But paying attention to its figuration in film texts can lead us to become aware of the need for different protocols of reading than the ones currently dominating film studies. It now falls to the new discipline of comparative film studies to begin to explore, more systematically, how social-historical dynamics impact upon and can be read from films. Such a reading has to proceed with forensic care, paying attention to the ways in which, in different geocultural regions, films orchestrate their modes of address, the relations between the indexical, iconic, and symbolic dimensions of substances and forms of content and expression, paying due attention to the co-presence of a dual fantasy structure vehiculated by that network of signifying relations. Such a program, moreover, requires to be carried out collaboratively and trans-nationally if it is to make any significant headway.

notes

1. Paul Willemen, "Regimes of Subjectivity and Looking," *The UTS Review* 1, no. 2 (1995): 101–29.
2. Let us, for the time being, exclude the other pre-capitalist epochal socio-cultural formations that are also still present and active in textual regimes: the classical and the prehistoric, as is evidenced daily in the mobilization of magical thinking (such as astrology) or the equation between truth, beauty and virtue that characterized Europe's classical antiquity.
3. Giovanni Arrighi, *The Long Twentieth Century: Money, Power and the Origins of our Times* (London: Verso, 1994), 9.
4. Paul Willemen, "The Zoom in Popular Culture: A Question of Performance," *New Cinemas: Journal of Contemporary Film* 1, no. 1 (2002); Wlad Godzich, *The Culture of Literacy* (Cambridge, MA: Harvard University Press, 1994), 74–82.

5. Andreas Huyssen, *After the Great Divide: Modernism, Mass Culture, Postmodernism* (Bloomington, IN: Indiana University Press, 1986).

6. Ibid., 38.

7. Arrighi, *The Long Twentieth Century*, 218.

8. For a critical discussion of this strategy, see Valentina Vitali, "Nationalist Hindi Cinema: Questions of Film Analysis and Historiography," *Kinema* 22 (2004): 63–82.

9. Willemen, "The Zoom in Popular Culture"; Paul Willemen, "Inflating the Narrator: Digital Hype and Allegorical Indexicality," *Convergence* 10, no. 3 (2004): 8–28.

10. A good example of the way North American cinema wrote a user's manual into the films it produced, advocating what later came to be described as a character-centered cinema, is provided by Kristin Thompson's analysis of changes in lighting, set design, art direction, editing and acting mainly in the post-World War I period. See Kristin Thompson, *Herr Lubitsch Goes to Hollywood: German and American Film after World War I* (Amsterdam: University of Amsterdam Press, 2005).

11. Michel Foucault, *Society Must Be Defended: Lectures at the Collège de France 1975–6*, trans. David Macey (New York: Picador, 1997), 7.

12. Examples would be the procedures of state formation, the particular ways in which social relations are transformed and the resistances to that transformation, the particular dynamics involved in the shift from pre-modern modes of surplus appropriation to capitalist production, the transformation of people's physical energy into labor power, the competition for power between different fractions of capital and so on.

13. In a challenging essay, written a few years ago, Jane Gaines called for a similar reconsideration. See Jane Gaines, "Machines that Make the Body Do Things," in *More Dirty Looks: Gender, Pornography and Power*, ed. Pamela Church Gibson (London: British Film Institute, 2004).

14. Julia Kristeva, *The Revolution in Poetic Language*, trans. Margaret Waller (New York: Columbia University Press, 1984).

15. Roman Jakobson and Krystyna Pomorska, *Dialogues*, trans. Christian Hubert (Melbourne: Cambridge University Press, 1983), 91–92.

16. See, for instance, the argumentation developed by Mikhail Iampolski in his challenging book *The Memory of Tiresias: Intertextuality and Film* (Berkeley, CA: University of California Press, 1998).

17. Ron Magid, "George Lucas: Past, Present, and Future," *American Cinematographer* 78 (February 1997), 49–52.

18. A more comprehensive account of this nauseating wave is provided in Claire Monk's contribution, "Men in the 90s," to Robert Murphy's *British Cinema in the 90s* (London: British Film Institute, 2000): 156–66.

19. Christian Metz, *Language and Cinema* (The Hague: Mouton, 1974), 208–12.

20. Briefly, and crudely speaking, the content levels divide into semantic matter, ideological or philosophical paradigms (substances) and the actual meaning—frameworks generated by and in the work itself (the manifested forms); the expressive levels divide into techno-physical materials (matter), technological menus available (substances) and the characteristics of actual equipment, techniques, organizational devices and materials used in/for a given film (form). In this context, the matter of content is less relevant because this level is shared by all films everywhere. However, the matter of expression does remain a serious issue in one respect: it relates to the change

from photochemical processes to electronic data-streams as "matters of expression."

21. Roland Barthes, *S/Z*, trans. Richard Miller (London: Jonathan Cape, 1975), 184.

22. Roman Jakobson, "Linguistics and Poetics," in *Modern Criticism and Theory: A Reader*, ed. David Lodge (London: Longman, 1988), 32–57.

23. Walter Benjamin, *The Arcades Project*, trans. Howard Eiland and Kevin McLaughlin (Cambridge, MA: Belknap Press of Harvard University Press, 1999), 392.

24. Ibid., 392.

25. Ibid., 394.

26. Peter Wollen, *Signs and Meanings in the Cinema* (London: British Film Institute, 1998), 83–84.

27. Peter Wollen, *Paris Hollywood: Writings on Film* (London: Verso, 2002), 208–09.

28. Philip Rosen, *Change Mummified: Cinema, Historicity, Theory* (Minneapolis, MN: University of Minnesota Press, 2001).

29. *The Observer*, June 1, 2003, 9.

30. Rosen, *Change Mummified*, 194.

31. This may be connected to the generation of the changeling fantasies which have beset science fiction and action melodramas both in the cinema and on television in the last twenty years or so. Some of the terms in this section have been inspired by Arjun Appadurai's work.

32. Résumés of common knowledge, the cultural codes provide the syllogisms in the narrative ... with their major premise, based always on public opinion ("the probable", as the old logic said), on an endoxal truth, in short, on the discourse of others ... All the cultural codes, taken up from citation to citation, together form an oddly jointed miniature version of encyclopedic knowledge, a farrago: this farrago forms everyday "reality" in relation to which the subject adapts himself, lives. One defect in this encyclopedia, one hole in this cultural fabric, and death can result.

(Barthes, *S/Z*, 184–85)

33. Rosen, *Change Mummified*, 316

34. Jakobson and Pomorska, *Dialogues*.

35. Theodor W. Adorno, *Critical Models: Interventions and Catchwords*, trans. Henry W. Pickford (New York: Columbia University Press, 1998), 57.

36. Roberto Schwarz, *Misplaced Ideas: Essays on Brazilian Culture* (London: Verso, 1992), 53.

37. Barthes, *S/Z*, 206.

38. Régis Debray, *Critique of Political Reason*, trans. David Macey (London: Verso, 1981), 109–10.

39. Robert Brenner, "The Economics of Global Turbulence," *New Left Review* 229 (May–June 1998).

40. David A. Cook, *History of the American Cinema*, Vol. 9, *Lost Illusions: American Cinema in the Shadow of Watergate and Vietnam, 1970–1979* (Berkeley, CA: University of California Press, 2000).

41. Ibid., 43–44.

42. For instance, at the Brighton Conference of FIAF in 1978, assorted academics and cultural institutions dutifully followed suit and turned their attention towards identifying and legitimating the cinema of attractions. Of course, these scholars never imagined that they were simply following in the slipstream of finance capital's reorganization of Hollywood: they thought

they were turning their attention to "early cinema" for curatorial or theoretical purposes, or, as Thomas Elsaesser noted, because of television's increased appetite for archival materials of various kinds—see Elsaesser, *Early Cinema: Space Frame Narrative* (London: British Film Institute, 1990): 1–10. Of course, pointing out that this "turn of attention" was programmed by developments in the dominant industrial sector of cinema does not mean that the work done by scholars in the books and conferences that ensued is to be dismissed. On the contrary, some of this work is essential to an understanding of cinema's narrative regimes. In that respect, the "early cinema" wave has very little in common with the "masculinity" and "action" waves which were far more directly "in tune" with Hollywood's restructuring.

43. See, for instance, Susan Buck-Morss, *Dreamworld and Catastrophe: The Passing of Mass Utopia in the East and West* (Cambridge, MA: MIT Press, 2000).

44. The development of the strongman (ex-dockworker) Pagano from *Maciste: Il Terrore dei banditi* (Borgnetto, 1915) into a detective relying on physical strength to solve problems later found an echo in American detective stories, though in an inverted form: the detective's body no longer beats other bodies into the direction of "truth," private eye Philip Marlowe's body is now beaten into its direction by others.

45. See Monica Dall'Asta, *Un cinéma muscle* (Crisnée, Belgium: Yellow Now, 1992).

46. Ng Ho, "Kung Fu Comedies: Tradition, Structure, Character" in *A Study of the Hong Kong Swordplay Film (1945–1980)*, ed. Lau Shing-hon (Hong Kong: International Film Festival/Urban Council, 1981), 42–46, p. 43.

47. In 1955, Hiroshi Inagaki made the second Miyamoto Musashi film in a trilogy, *Zoky Miyamoto Musashi—Ichijoji no ketto*, which opens with a duel between Miyamoto and a chain-and-sickle wielding weapons master, anticipating the even more exotic gadgetry that was to surface in Hong Kong's films and later in Italian Westerns, all the gadget-weapons connoting different types and phases of industrialization's relation to "tradition."

48. Abé Mark Nornes, *Japanese Documentary Film: The Meiji Era through Hiroshima* (Minneapolis, MN: University of Minnesota Press, 2003), 90–1.

49. Brenner, "The Economics of Global Turbulence," 23–4.

50. Gunter Gebauer and Christoph Wulf, *Mimesis: Culture—Art—Society*, trans. Don Reneau (Berkeley, CA: University of California Press, 1995).

51. Graham Ley, *From Mimesis to Interculturalism: Readings of Theatrical Theory Before and After "Modernism"* (Exeter, UK: University of Exeter Press, 1999).

52. See Richard Ohmann, *Selling Culture: Magazines, Markets and Class at the Turn of the Century* (London: Verso, 1996).

vernacular

modernism

thirteen

tracking cinema

on a global scale

miriam hansen

This chapter suggests ways in which the notion of cinema as vernacular modernism could be useful to the project of writing transnational film history. To begin with, though, I would like to evoke three sets of examples from Japanese and Chinese films of the 1930s. The first revolves around the figure of the prostitute who is also a mother. In Shimizu Hiroshi's sound film *Forget Love for Now* (*Koi mo wasurete*, Shochiku, July 1937), released the same month Japan turned to open warfare against China, a young woman (Kuwano Michiko) works as a taxi dancer in a Yokohama harbor bar to pay for her son's education. The film resolves the contradiction of motherhood and prostitution by sacrificing the son, having him die from pneumonia after fighting a mob of boys over his mother's reputation. A similar configuration of prostitution and motherhood can be found in a silent Shochiku production directed by Naruse Mikio, *Every Night Dreams* (*Yogoto no yume*, 1933). Likewise set in the Yokohama harbor area, this film casts Kurishima Sumiko as a bar hostess struggling to rear her son and not to descend into the lower depths of the sex trade; the son is *almost* killed, in a car accident, but the sacrifice is displaced onto the unemployed husband

(Saito Tatsuo), who drowns himself after a failed attempt at burglary to pay for his son's medical bills.[1]

But *Forget Love for Now* also echoes the famous Chinese silent film, *Shennii: The Goddess* (1934), directed by Wu Yonggang and starring Ruan Ling-yu as a nameless young Shanghai woman who works as a streetwalker to ensure her son a good education. She ends up in jail for killing a brutal mobster, knowing that her son will be adopted by the headmaster who had defended him earlier against the bigotry of other parents and the school board. If the closing shot of *The Goddess* shows Ruan behind bars yet looking to the future, consoled by the vision of her son (in the form of an insert above her to the right), *Forget Love for Now* ends on a relentlessly pessimistic key. Throughout the film, the sex-workers talk about leaving—for Kobe, for Shanghai or Singapore; one of them tries and gets caught and beaten by bodyguards. To be sure, the foreign ports are discussed as highly ambivalent destinations, but that only compounds the overall sense of hopelessness and stagnation.[2] Extending the static mise-en-scene of the deathbed scene to a closing shot of solitary figures in the street and scored with a melancholy strain, the camera descends into the thickening mist.

The configuration of prostitution and motherhood evokes other films of the period—implied in such US films as *Madame X, Applause, Blonde Venus*, and *Stella Dallas*, explicit in Max Ophuls' *Sans lendemain* (1939), and highly popular in Mexican cinema and likely other cinemas that I am not familiar with. We could talk about these films as a variant of the maternal melodrama, inflected by the genre of *Dirnentragödie* or the trope of the prostitute-with-a-heart-of-gold.[3] We could also consider the Chinese and Japanese examples (and related films in both traditions) in light of the respective historical discourses on prostitution, as well as the significance of the child and childhood in parallel and violently antagonistic discourses of the nation.[4] We could think about the figure of the prostitute-mother as a critical allegory that joins the most extreme instance of commodification of the female body and sexuality with the epitome of unalienated, altruistic love— as embodying a key contradiction of capitalist modernity which irrupts, to paraphrase Alexander Kluge, in the sphere of intimacy and the life stories of strong-minded women.[5]

Yet, much as these films can be analyzed in terms of genre conventions, cultural stereotypes, and historico-philosophical allegories, such terms do not fully account for the films' affective-aesthetic appeal, broadly understood—whatever it may be that enables them to move viewers, including film scholars, across geopolitically disparate spaces and histories. In the case of the prostitute-mother figures cited above, the casting of actresses (as opposed to female impersonators), if not stars, heightens the viewing pleasure derived from the dialectical interplay between fictional character and the actress's public persona and artistic agency. Moreover, the films often foreground, in their diegesis, moments of performance and other aspects of mise-en-scene that make for an astonishing degree of fluidity, incongruity, and elusiveness in the construction of the female character. The implications of such moments may become clearer from my second set of examples.

The mother in *Forget Love for Now* may enact the melodramatic tropes of "if only" and "too late" over the body of her dead son, but the ending neither effaces Kuwano's performance of solidarity as she confronts the cut-throat owner/madam over the hostesses' working conditions nor the erotic power of her dancing alone, in a form-fitting Western dress, on the dance floor of the harbor bar.[6] Sun Yu's film *Daybreak* (*Tiangming*, Shanghai 1933), which invokes and revises Von Sternberg's *Dishonored* (1931), engages in a self-conscious floating and scrambling of character identity on a par with yet quite distinct from Dietrich/Sternberg films.[7] The protagonist, played by Li Lili, migrates from a rural area to the city, like millions of Chinese at the time, initially moving along a predictable trajectory from country girl, through factory worker raped by the boss's son, to indentured prostitute. From that moment on, however, her character is defined by dissimulation and masquerade, as we encounter her as a flirtatious, Robin-Hood-style sex-worker sporting the accoutrements of a Modern Girl (beret, flashy jewelry, silk stockings, and makeup), and finally as martyr for the revolutionary cause who for the execution changes back (varying on *Dishonored*) into her old country clothes. Ozu Yasujiro's *Dragnet Girl* (*Hijoson no onna*, 1933), a parodistic homage to the American gangster film (in particular *Scarface*), features a different kind of Modern Girl or *moga* (Tanaka Kinuyo). The character is introduced as a preppie-looking typist in an open-plan office; her other job is that of a gangster moll. She ends up trying to domesticate both the hoodlum and herself, among other things, by making him hold a skein of wool as she winds it into a ball (the motif of knitting being associated earlier in the film with a traditional self-sacrificing woman with whom the hoodlum falls in love). None of the above roles fit the heroine particularly well. While the plot steers her toward traditional Japanese femininity (and, by implication, marriage and motherhood), the comic performance of the steps she takes in that direction suggest less a return to authenticity and tradition than a continuation of the modernist masquerade.

If these films invoke media-circulated stereotypes, in particular the dichotomy of the New Woman or Modern Girl and traditional (Chinese, Japanese) womanhood, they often confound such stereotypes at the levels of plot, performance, costume, and other aspects of mise-en-scene. They self-consciously put into play the contradictions and constructedness of these ascriptions, along with the utopian possibility of breaking with them. And they were doing so for heterogeneous mass audiences emerging in both Shanghai and Tokyo, marked by, among other things, an unprecedented share of female viewers—women who were trying to negotiate the discrepancies between their dreams and lived realities through and against the cataclysms of modernity.[8]

Another example along those lines takes me to a and set of images that signal the concern with everyday modernity through material objects, "things," even trash. Shimizu's *Japanese Girls at the Harbor* (*Minato no nihon musume*, 1933), shot at the same time as *Dragnet Girl* and responding to Ozu's film with another Eurasian fantasy (they were colleagues at Shochiku as well as roommates), shuffles the deck of gender roles even more whimsically. The film tracks the fate of two girlfriends, Sunako (Oikawa Michiko) and Dora (Inoue Yukiko), introduced in sailor-style school uniforms as they watch a departing ocean liner from the Yokohama bluffs; soon after they will compete for the love of Henry (Egawa Ureo), a small-time hood who enters their lives on his motorbike. Henry is reformed by marriage to the virtuous Dora, who as an adult is shown only in rather asexual Western clothes (in the style of New Sobriety); Sunako, having become a bar hostess, now wears traditional geisha garb (if fashionably adorned with a flashy ring). Shimizu cites the heteronormative wool-winding ritual from Ozu's film, but gives it a particular twist. As Sunako pays a visit to the couple's modern home (a caricature of *shoshimin* or petty-bourgeois sensibility and boredom) and we see the three together in the same space for the first time as adults, Dora's gaze swerves from preparing dinner behind a glass partition to the ball of wool that skips around the floor as if it had a life of its own; still from her point of view, a track to the right reveals the source of this uncanny animation—Sunako and Henry dancing together, their legs at once entangled in and unraveling the strings of petty-bourgeois domesticity.

The foregrounding of material objects—through close-ups, camera movement, editing, and mise-en-scene—is part of the vocabulary of inter-national silent film and returns more selectively in a wide variety of sound film practices. Western critics of Japanese film have linked this stylistic gesture, specifically for the later work of Ozu, to traditional Japanese aesthetics (in particular the Heian-era concept of *mono no aware* or "pathos of things") and principles of Zen Buddhism.[9] This tradition may have constituted a significant cultural reference (albeit a refracted, mediated, and perhaps ironic one), but the cinematically intensified presence of the object in Japanese pre-war films seems to have had at least as much to do with modern commodity culture and its social and epistemic conse-quences. As European and Asian writers have noted early on, film's technical ability to animate and foreground inanimate objects enabled it to dramatize the changed and changing economy of things, be it to explore their fetishistic power, to counter the abstraction of commodity capitalism with physiognomic expressiveness, or to enhance their physical opacity and alterity.[10]

The material objects foregrounded in Japanese films of the period—as in Chinese, French, Soviet, and Hollywood examples that come to mind— range from glamorous consumer goods and details of fashion and decor;

through items of everyday use (work, domestic reproduction, leisure, play), industrially manufactured objects and icons of mass consumption; to worn-out, battered, even useless things that have accreted meanings of their own. Ozu's *Dragnet Girl*, for instance, sets up its heterotopic mise-en-scene of urban modernity by tracking along serially arranged identical hats and typewriters (pausing to show one hat fall off the hook for no particular reason); it opens sequences with close-ups of objects (a not uncommon stylistic device), such as a chipped enamel coffee pot that repeatedly ushers us into the couple's shabby apartment, followed by boxing and movie posters on tattered wallpaper; and scenes in a record store involve a running gag of whimsical animation with statuettes of Nipper, the RCA Victor mascot.

Things take on a similarly active, if not activist role in Chinese films of the period, for example in Sun Yu's *Playthings* (*Xiao wanyi*, 1933), which pits handcrafted folk toys against industrially produced toys like military tanks that in turn dissolve into "real" tanks. In a different key, objects acquire agency in the sound film *Crossroads* (*Shizi jietou*, dir. Shen Xilin, 1937), a romantic comedy/tragedy (with queer overtones) about a young man and a young woman falling in love without knowing that they are actually neighbors. They fight each other by throwing objects back and forth across the flimsy tenement wall, such as several framed photographs of university graduates (including one of the male protagonist), taped over with labels reading "Unemployed no. A," "B," etc., or a white shirt (his only) with an ink stain which the female protagonist transfigures into a pig. Traveling shots and close-ups highlight, among a chaotic assembly of things, a figurine of Mickey Mouse, a tea kettle and an ink well, wine bottles, paper scraps being written and drawn on, and a Kewpie doll similar to the one in Pal Fejos' film *Lonesome* (1929), whose plot device *Crossroads* seems to have borrowed.[11]

It goes without saying that such cinematically concretized objects function differently in different films and film traditions, and are bound to have different meanings and affective valences in different contexts of reception. They may vary according to the degree of their narrative motivation and agency; they may serve to characterize individuals or to provide an objective correlative for the harsh and volatile conditions of their existence; or they may draw attention to the mechanisms of circulation by which things acquire and lose value and undergo changes of meaning. What interests me in viewing these films is the extent to which, at the level of filmic representation, they gesture toward a modernist, non-anthropocentric aesthetics of contingency, even as they mobilize material objects to create pathos and critical reflection, in other words, to construct a space and time for spectatorial subjectivity.[12]

The tension at work here seems particularly acute in the representation of objects that push film's aesthetic material toward the "formless"—images of trash, detritus, rubble, waste, literally, the abject.[13] If such images are more programmatic in postwar cinemas (cf. Italian neorealism, German

Trümmerfilme, and revolutionary Chinese films), they also seem to proliferate in Japanese films during the Depression years. They are often placed near the film's end (as in Mizoguchi's *Osaka Elegy* or Ozu's *Woman of Tokyo*), in contrast with Depression-era Hollywood films where they may crop up in the beginning but get cleaned up in the interest of closure (e.g., Mamoulian's *Applause*). In the last sequence of *Japanese Girls at the Harbor*, we see Sunako on board of a departing ocean liner with her down-and-out painter house-husband (Saito Tatsuo), making him toss his awful portraits of her overboard; in the closing shots, which echo the film's opening sequence, the camera lingers endlessly on streamers fluttering in the wind, alternating with shots of her portrait adrift in the water. Such images signal a different register of temporality, a *durée* of the ephemeral, the no longer, if ever, useful. At the same time, inasmuch as they resonate with the narrative's dispatch of the heroine into an unknown yet open-ended future, they also evoke a liberating anonymity.

Images of rubble and detritus in Chinese films of the 1930s tend to be more clearly motivated in narrative terms, whether linked to the 1932 Japanese attacks on Shanghai, as in *Playthings* and *Coming Home* (Zhu Shilin, 1934), or to rural flight and urban immiseration, as in *Fishermen's Song* (Cai Chusheng, 1934) and *Street Angel* (Yuan Muzhi, 1937).[14] Waste becomes thematic in scenes that suggest how to recycle and creatively reuse every scrap, the remains of colonial leisure-class consumption, under conditions of extreme poverty and inequality.[15] One could argue that images of detritus in Japanese films of the period are just as realistically motivated, considering the recent experience of the 1923 Kanto earthquake and the massive urban renewal that followed. Yet, between such immediate sources and an alleged cultural penchant for images of transience, impermanence, or loss, the aesthetic irruption of trash in these films also speaks to a particular experience of capitalist modernity, the moment when mass consumption and urbanization raised the age-old problem of garbage to unprecedented proportions, and when the disposability of things came to be associated with the disposability of human beings.

These sets of examples raise more general questions about how films can be understood as engaging with modernity—more precisely, distinct, highly uneven and unequal formations of modernity—and about how film practices interrelate across the borders of national cinemas and, in this case, across an increasingly violent political divide. I have compiled these examples because of my impression that, with few exceptions, Japanese and Chinese film histories seem to exist in parallel universes, which intersect only problematically during the war and occupation.[16] This is not surprising given the history of aggression and subordination which for the first part of the twentieth century defined relations between, on the one hand, an imperial nation-state whose modernization campaigns competed with and defended against Western capitalist powers and, on the other, a republic weakened by warlordism and civil war, with its film industry concentrated in the semicolonial and multiethnic treaty port of Shanghai. Still, viewing Chinese and Japanese films of the late 1920s to the 1930s side by side, one is struck by their shared concern with modern life and with modernist aesthetics—a strong interest in the everyday, similar thematic issues, stylistic tendencies, and configurations of film culture.[17] These include, broadly speaking, conflicts between traditional gender norms and modern femininity (the precarious status of single working women, arranged marriage versus romantic love, the persistence of feudal mentalities and oppressive family structures), labor conflicts and unemployment, urbanization and immiseration, the city/country dichotomy and discourses of nationality in relation to modernity and the West; stylistic references to a cosmopolitan visual culture of consumption, fashion, and design participating in international Art Deco (Shanghai modern, Taisho/Showa chic); and the significance accorded in both film cultures to actresses, whose public presence "gave human faces to the many social transformations of urban modernity," considering that the convention of female impersonators on stage and screen had only recently begun to be dislodged.[18]

Such points of intersection between Chinese and Japanese cinemas of the period may owe as much to the contemporaneity with Western modernity—and the alternative modernity offered by the Soviet Union and communism—as to the shared, though differently interpreted legacy of Buddhism and Confucianism. They can be explored from various perspectives, though not without awareness of the asymmetries of wealth and power and the racialized hierarchies in the conditions under which films were produced and received.

In addition to a comparative approach that would rethink the grounds, scales, and terms of comparison, transnational relations between the respective film cultures ask to be researched in terms of actual processes of transfer and translation, circulation and reception.[19] Thus, following scholars of literary modernism, film historians have begun to trace cross-filiations between Tokyo's artistic-intellectual (and cinephilic) avant-gardes and Chinese debates on film, such as the adaptation and transformation of the Japanese movement of New Sensationism by Shanghai dandy Liu Na'ou and others, or the significance of the early theorist of film and modernity and (later) famous novelist Tanizaki Jun'ichiro.[20] These cross-filiations, among other things, highlight the significance of the issue of woman's relation to urban modernity for critical debates over left-wing film politics (cf. the "hard" versus "soft" film debate), thus challenging received Chinese film history. The question is whether such an argument merely expands on the long-standing mediation of Chinese modernity and modernism by way of Japan, or whether there were crossings in the other direction as well, direct or indirect, elite or mass-cultural, contemporaneous or temporally displaced—connections that may elude established historiographic narratives.

In this chapter, I want to argue that the thematic, theoretical, and methodological issues raised by my examples can be productively addressed through the notion of cinema as a vernacular form of modernism. This notion contributes a pragmatic lens to the project of transnational film history, by bringing into view junctures between, and heterogeneities within, national film histories, whether virtual or actual, politically blocked or historiographically repressed. I am interested in the heuristic potential of vernacular modernism as a relational framework for mapping film practices—not only vis-à-vis Hollywood (and other foreign cinemas) but also on regional and local scales that complicate nationally defined film cultures. Distinct from, yet imbricated with, questions of *genre*, this framework may help us track the ways in which particular film practices engaged with their respective trajectories of modernity and modernism, whether parallel or intersecting, antagonistic or in conversation with each other.[21] The point is not to come up with a globally valid notion of vernacular modernism but to see it as a more reflexive framework capable of generating new lines of inquiry and revising itself in view of the empirical formations it explores.

Let me briefly back up to what is at stake in the concept of vernacular modernism in the context of recent cinema studies, and for renewed debates on questions of modernism and modernity. First off, I am not talking about the kinds of cinema that are commonly evoked in conjunction with modernism—such as experimental film practices that emerged within or alongside historical avant-garde movements in the other arts, or modernist directions in international auteur and art cinema. Rather, I am concerned with currents of modernist aesthetics *within* the field of commercial, mainstream cinema, at a level of cultural circulation suggested by the term vernacular.

Second, the concept of vernacular modernism was initially aimed against neoformalist accounts of classical Hollywood cinema that tended to reduce that cinema to a stylistic system predicated on neoclassicist norms.[22] In an earlier article entitled "The Mass Production of the Senses," I argued that the worldwide success of Hollywood, much as it relied on aggressive industrial strategies and state intervention, had less to do with the "classical"—timeless, universal—narrative organization of the films than with their ability to provide, to mass audiences both at home and abroad, an at once aesthetic and public horizon for the experience of capitalist-industrial modernity and modernization.[23] This was not an argument about a general and structural, let alone a causal, relationship between cinema and modernity.[24] Rather, the question was, and continues to be, how particular film practices can be productively understood as *responding*—and making sensually graspable our responses—to the set of technological, economic, social, and perceptual transformations associated with the term modernity. In other words, to the extent that film practices acknowledged these transformations, including the cinema's own role in them, and engaged with modernity's contradictory effects, they can be considered a form of modernism, asymmetrically related to modernist practices in the traditional arts. The notion of cinema as vernacular modernism thus entwines concepts of modernity and aesthetic modernism in an institutionally specific mode— as a heterotopic practice that, on a mass basis and in a sensorial-affective form, references and brings into play the impact of capitalist-industrial modernization and other aspects of modernity.

It has become a critical commonplace that one can no more speak of modernism in the singular than assume a singular concept of modernity apart from its entwinement with histories of colonization and globalization.[25] In the spirit of Dipesh Chakrabarty's injunction to "provincialize Europe,"[26] scholars have been exploring different geopolitical constellations and historical trajectories of modernism and modernity in Asia, Latin America, and Africa.[27] I will not go into the problematic of "alternative" and/or "multiple" modernities here, though, notwithstanding Fredric Jameson's dismissal of these efforts as "regressive" (that is, in light of the singular foundation of modernity that is capitalism), I consider that debate by no means closed.[28] The problem is compounded by the need to distinguish between colonial forms of extraction and circulation and twentieth-century industrial formations competing with and overlaying them, specifically the Fordist regime of technological production and consumption (Americanism) including the worldwide circulation of low-cultural, market-based forms such as the cinema.[29]

The question of Hollywood hegemony—at the levels of distribution and exhibition in local and regional markets, and as narrative-stylistic model— poses methodological and theoretical challenges similar to the problematic of alternative and multiple modernities, though it also complicates them. It may well be the case that, as David Bordwell claims, all the world's mass-market cinemas are based on the standard continuity style pioneered by classical Hollywood, as the ground against which the stylistic accomplishments of indigenous filmmakers can be analyzed. But that does not make them simply variants of a dominant style (in the manner, to cite Bordwell's analogy, one would consider Haydn, Mozart, and Beethoven variants of Viennese classicism).[30] If filmmakers in China and Japan confronted Hollywood hegemony in both its enabling and destructive effects, their efforts to forge idioms of their own were crucially inflected by a larger vernacular-modernist culture at once cosmopolitan and local. As Zhang Zhen has shown for the case of Shanghai cinema, this involved a volatile process of negotiation between nativist modernizing projects (such as the May Fourth Vernacular Movement) and international(ist) forms of modernism, elite and popular—between competing models of national culture and creative appropriations of the globalizing vernaculars of Hollywood, European, Soviet, as well as Japanese cinemas.[31]

295

If "The Mass Production of the Senses" sought to make a case for an expanded notion of modernism, this chapter emphasizes the other part of the concept—vernacular. I will revisit some of the term's theoretical implications because I take it to offer, with its historically variable, ambiguous and conflicting connotations, a dynamic model of cultural circulation that can be extended to technologically mediated forms such as the cinema. A familiar narrative associates the term vernacular with linguistic and literary practices—and corresponding intellectual and political movements—that mark a deliberate turn away from, around, and against an official imperial or "high," cosmopolitan language, be it Latin, Persian, Sanskrit, or classical Chinese. Vernacular practices emerged in different parts of the world at different times beginning with the late medieval and early modern periods. In western Europe, the historical trajectory of vernacularization leads through the well-known examples of Dante and Luther, as well as the Romantics' "discovery" or, often, invention of local and folk traditions from the last third of the eighteenth century on. This trajectory is entwined with the cultural-political transformations that produced the nation-state, with its grounding in presumably homogeneous ethnic identities. At the same time, the idea of the vernacular reverberates in twentieth century leftist thought, notably in the work of Bakhtin, as well as later efforts, indebted to Gramsci, to reclaim "the popular" as a socially and politically progressive force as much against "elitist" intellectuals as against capitalist universalization.

The standard etymological account tells us that the term vernacular derives from the Latin word *verna* or second-generation slave born in Republican Rome. The adjective *vernaculus* defines a language used by subaltern subjects to communicate among each other and, in non-official, domestic contexts, with their masters—that is, a language inscribed with enslavement, displacement, and domestication. (It is no coincidence that the Latin word *verna* itself is derived from the Etruscan, a language destroyed with the Roman's vanquishing of the Etruscans and the founding of Rome.) Restricting the term to its etymological roots, however, limits the heuristic and historical range of the concept. As Sheldon Pollock has argued, the term vernacular narrowly understood as referring to a "very particular and unprivileged mode of social identity" is "hobbled by its own particularity," in so far as "there is no reason to believe that every vernacular is the idiom of the humiliated demanding vindication."[32] Rather, as Pollock shows, not only are vernacular forms geopolitically and historically variable, but also they are mutually constitutive with the cosmopolitan forms they oppose. "As the cosmopolitan is constituted through cultural flows from the vernacular, so the vernacular constructs itself by appropriation," often by "unwittingly relocalizing what the cosmopolitan borrowed from it in the first place."[33]

Pollock makes his case through a comparative account of the ways in which two distinct historical cosmopolitanisms, Latin and Sanskrit, gave rise in turn to different types of vernacularism. Leaving aside the question to what extent he may be idealizing Sanskrit as an alternative, non-coercive and pluralistic, form of cosmopolitanism, I consider his argument immensely useful for opening up the concept of the vernacular. In particular, it challenges the fixation of the vernacular on the side of the local—for instance, through ahistorical notions of indigenous identity—and allows us to see vernacular practices as part of the very processes of translocal interactions that produce the local as much as the global. This helps us understand the particular dynamics of vernacular practices as a special "mix," in Pollock's words, which

> consists of a response to a specific history of domination and enforced change, along with a critique of the oppression of tradition itself, tempered with a strategic desire to locate resources for a cosmopolitan future in vernacular ways of being themselves.[34]

Pollock's historicizing and comparative account is framed by the political argument that the vernacular today is threatened by a "new and disquieting cosmopolitanism," "an altogether new universalizing order of culture power (call it globalization, or [neo-]liberalization, or Americanization)." As a result, according to Pollock, we are confronted with a polarization between the "bad options" of,

> on the one hand, a national vernacularity dressed up in the frayed period costume of violent [ethno-chauvinist] revan- chism and bent on preserving difference at all costs and, on the other, a clear-cutting, strip-mining multinational cosmopolitanism that is bent, at all costs, on eliminating it.[35]

We may want to debate this account of contemporary developments. But the bigger problem is that the arc suggested by Pollock eclipses much of the twentieth century, a modernity associated as much with the rise of mass production and mass consumption and a broad-based aspiration to a better world—for women among others—as with catastrophic capitalism, technological warfare, and mass annihilation. This means leaving out the formative stages of technologically mediated, industrially produced mass culture, of new scales and speeds of circulation that not only linked cultural products to the promotion of other, more material goods, but also gave rise to a new type of public sphere turning on the dialectics of acknowledgement and appropriation of social experience.[36] Likewise occluded are the efforts of intellectuals, writers, and artists working in both traditional media and new media such as film, radio, and photography, whether in radical opposition to or on the margins of commercial contexts, to respond to both the devastating and the liberatory effects of modernity and mass-market culture—efforts associated with inter- and transnational movements of

modernism. In other words, Pollock's delineation of the mutual constitution of older cosmopolitan and vernacular forms, to the extent that it is
framed by a monolithic perspective on current globalization, stops short of
recognizing a similarly variable and complex entanglement of vernacular
and cosmopolitan forms in a significant part of the twentieth century. It is in
this heuristic space that I am trying to theorize cinema as a vernacular form
of modernism, hoping in the process to contribute as well to debates on
modern forms of the vernacular.

Before I return to the question of Chinese-Japanese film relations, let
me briefly address the option of grounding a concept of cinema as vernacular practice in the model of architecture (and, by extension, design and
built environment). Dudley Andrew has argued that the term vernacular
is misleading "if we follow its roots and branches toward the history of
languages" because this genealogy, he implies, would resurrect the problematic analogy between cinema and language.[37] Instead, he suggests, we
should work from the connotations of the term vernacular in architecture.
There are a number of good reasons for doing so, not least because of the
affinity between architecture and cinema in the process of creating new
image spaces, in particular (to once more invoke Benjamin) the reconfigura-
tion of "body- and image-space." Work in this direction ranges from
studies of theater architecture and publicity, through cinematic set
design, decor and lighting, to the ways in which films map transformations
of urban space and to architectural conceptions of cinematic space and
narrative.[38]

First off, though, let me point out that drawing on a particular aspect of
a linguistic concept does not mean reviving the analogy between film and
language which, as we know, at the latest since 1960s and 1970s film theory,
can never be more than a complex metaphor. Mobilized in relation to
cinema, the term vernacular too works primarily as a theoretical metaphor,
as it has been doing for architecture and other disciplines and discourses
concerned with modes of cultural circulation beyond the term's linguistic
contexts of origin (even if, as in the case of Shanghai cinema, vernacular
movements of a more literal and literary kind may be part of the mix).

I agree that architecture adds an important dimension to the argument
on vernacular modernism in film, but we should be aware that the
architectural notion of the vernacular is fraught with its own set of
problems. These include, in particular, the unquestioned opposition, in
architectural history and discourse dating back to the turn of the twentieth
century, between the vernacular understood as local ("embracing ethnic,
folk, regionalist, primitive, etc.") and "high-style" or "polite" architecture;
the latter is distinguished by having artistic authors as well as transnational
currency, especially with the rise of the International Style.[39] Accordingly,
vernacular architecture was perceived to be threatened by dilution with the
advent of modernization, in particular the mass fabrication of building

materials and mass circulation of building types through pattern books. Such a narrow understanding of the vernacular in architecture doesn't take into account, for instance, that the term vernacular has been widely used since the late 1960s with reference to Art Deco. A commercial as well as public modernist style, Art Deco spread during the 1920s and 1930s from France through Europe, the United States, Australia, and cosmopolitan centers such as Shanghai, Tokyo, and Bombay and combined with local and regional design and building styles in creative ways. (This narrative of origin is complicated in turn by the fact that French Art Deco drew on, among other things, Japanese art as well as precious wood and other luxurious materials from French colonies in Africa and Asia.)

Increasingly, theorists of design and the built environment have been rejecting the rigid dichotomy of vernacular and high style, along with any attempt to define the vernacular "in itself," emphasizing instead the fluctuating, open-ended, and relational character of vernacular practices in different cultural contexts.[40] In a collection of essays on built environment entitled *Vernacular Modernism*, the editors challenge the conventional polarization of the two terms by "conceiving of the vernacular as a space *within* the modern," and seeking to investigate "the alternative—vernacular—potentialities within modernism itself."[41] However, while they claim that central to their investigation is the "mutual dependence of the vernacular and the global," the enterprise remains amazingly hide-bound, inasmuch as it is based on the assumption that the "vernacular denotes particularism and, by extension, a specific attitude of sensitivity to *place*" (8). The problem is that particularism is tied, not only to the local, but also explicitly to a particular national, if not nationalist and anti-modern, concept of the local—the notoriously untranslatable German word *Heimat* (to be sure, in a theoretically and historically conscious version indebted to the philosophy of Ernst Bloch).[42] This fixation on the local, however mediated it may be through the trajectory of Western modernity (e.g., *Heimat* as an affective and aesthetic response to the universalizing, abstracting, and homogenizing effects of industrialization and urbanization), occludes the *circulatory* dynamics of the vernacular, its portability and interaction with other vernaculars.

Thus deployed, the architectural concept of the vernacular effaces what I consider most relevant to the term—the paradoxical mode in which senses and sensations of the particular, the aesthetic materiality of everyday life, of places, things, and routines, become mobilized, transportable, translatable, and creatively appropriated in and for different contexts of living. Key to this question is a conception of the *everyday* in terms of capitalist modernity—as the "minimal unity," in Harry Harootunian's words, "that has organized the experience of modernity."[43] Substantially different from the "immemorial daily life" lived in the countryside and premodern cities, the modern everyday became the site in which the demands of capitalist production and consumption were set off against, yet made to coexist, "uneasily and unhappily," with received social and cultural forms and relationships. (As the films cited earlier suggest, this coexistence was often articulated as a conflict of irreconcilable forces, especially for women: if capitalist modernity promised liberating possibilities in the face of oppressive traditional gender norms, it also created new forms of bondage, causing new-found subjectivities to get trapped between the rock of societal bigotry and the hard place of sexual commodification.) While both residual cultures of reference and the particular forms that capitalist modernization took were rooted in specific locations, Harootunian argues, the experience of the everyday—and its contemporary theorizations by modernist intellectuals (and, for that matter, vernacular-modernist films)—connected these uneven yet "coeval" modernities across a broader geopolitical context.[44]

We could consider the vernacular, then, more generally as the level of cultural circulation at which these coeval and uneven modernities connect, intersect, and compete, defined by a tension between, on the one hand, connotations of the everyday (the common and ordinary, routines of material production and reproduction) and, on the other, connotations of circulation (commerce, communication, migration, travel). It is this simultaneously particularizing and circulatory dynamics of the concept of the vernacular that makes it useful to continue drawing on the term's rich genealogy in the history of languages and literature, including contemporary usages of the term in fields of socio-linguistics and ethno-linguistics, translation studies, and studies of cultural transfer and regimes of circulation. Thus, while the term vernacular does not have a clear status in contemporary linguistics and may function as a "fuzzy set" in other contexts as well, its usages suggest that it broadly refers to an idiom that operates *below* the level of a dominant standard language (official, national) but *above* that of local dialects, allowing for contact, transfer, and circulation on a larger regional scale. This intermediary status may make it an independent language variety, though an unstable one that draws on local speech and has the potential to develop into a standard language.[45]

It is in that broader sense that I would like to retain the linguistic connotations of the vernacular because it allows us to imagine an *intermediary* level of mass production and mass circulation on which cinema, at the very least during the interwar period, seems to have moved and morphed. Situating cinema at this intermediary level is meant to focus research and analytic attention on the dynamics by which particular film practices engaged both the globalizing and the local vectors in the experience of everyday modernity, and to help us track these dynamics horizontally, within and across geopolitically uneven and unequal formations. In terms of Asian film history, it encourages us to explore transnational relations in the larger region (including Korea, Hong Kong, Taiwan, and India)—despite, though in awareness of, blockages bound up with traumatic histories and perpetuated by nationalist discourses—and thus to complicate binary conceptions of global and local, as of Hollywood hegemony and non-Western national cinemas. This does not mean that Hollywood has not been dominating Asian film markets in specific ways; nor does it mean placing cinema outside a forcefield of asymmetrical power relations and market conditions. But the question is *how* filmmakers have appropriated Hollywood (along with other foreign cinemas as well as their own cultural pasts) in creative, eclectic, and revisionist ways to forge aesthetic idioms, and to respond to social conflicts and political pressures, closer to home. At a minimum, the concept of vernacular modernism provides a comparative lens for tracing related, at once similar and distinct concerns across different film cultures, across uneven and competing yet inevitably entangled modernities.

Finally, if the concept is to have any critical function, that is, as a heuristic and analytic framework for comparing individual films and tracing particular currents in film culture, it is important to insist on the linkage between vernacular and *modernist*. If the vernacular modifies—and expands our understanding of—aesthetic modernism(s), the qualifier modernist also designates and delimits particular directions in the larger field of vernacular practices. It makes no sense to call every film made and commercially circulated during twentieth-century waves of modernization modernist, even in the broadest sense of the term. Nor does every film that references everyday modernity do so in ways that could be productively described as modernist in style and/or stance; on the contrary, there are plenty of films that transmute conflicts and contradictions arising from modernity into conventional narrative and compositional forms. By the same token, we may find a high degree of stylistic experiment in historical period films, as, for instance, in the popular Japanese genre of *chambara* or swordplay films (often combined with a masochistic mise-en-scene of the male warrior body).[46] Moreover, like literature and the arts, cinema too has its share of "antimodern" and "reactionary modernists," to say nothing of the issue of fascist and state-sponsored forms of modernism. And there is the more general question to what extent films from one country may be perceived as modernist in foreign contexts of reception, as were famously certain kinds of Hollywood films by avant-garde intellectuals in France, the Soviet Union, and elsewhere.

Modernist practices within or on the margins of mainstream cinemas may share certain formal-stylistic principles with movements of elite artistic modernism—abstraction, seriality, self-reflexivity, to touch on some critical commonplaces—and did significantly formulate some of their own (montage being just one of them) that in turn inspired the latter.[47] But, as has often been pointed out, modernism does not reduce to a matter of style. A significant impulse in the modernist break with tradition, the quest for the genuinely new and different—in poetry, music, and the visual arts (including experimental film)—has been to oppose, negate, or at the very least

301

undermine, the consumerist logic of capitalist mass-market culture (however dependent upon and complicit with the latter modernist artists may have been in practice). In that sense, for high-modernists from Greenberg and Adorno to Jameson, the notion of vernacular modernism would be substantially a contradiction in terms. For inasmuch as the films in question were produced and circulated commercially, they would inevitably have diverged from the high-modernist agenda in their relationship to the audience. By contrast, I take one of the defining aspects of vernacular modernism to be precisely the way in which these films engaged with the experience and imagination of their audience. By doing so, they implicitly acknowledged, and helped create, a distinct kind of public sphere—constituted through the matrices of capitalist consumption, though not necessarily identical with and uncritical of it. Pragmatically, this orientation entailed working with genre formulas (both local and imported) and popular motifs, if not clichés; but it also meant putting them into play, twisting, denaturalizing, or transforming them, thus making them available for an at once sensorial-affective and reflective mode of reception.

A case in point is the body of films produced at Shochiku's Kamata branch in the late 1920s and 1930s (from which some of my initial examples were drawn), work by directors such as Shimizu, Naruse, Ozu, Shimazu Yasujiro, and Gosho Heinusunke. In the effort to compete with the rival Nikkatsu studio, known for theatrical *shinpa*-style and historical period films, as well as with foreign films, Shochiku developed its niche with a genre of modern film (*gendai-geki*) labeled *shoshimin eiga*—which literally translates as "petty bourgeois film," though more precisely referring to films about the mushrooming class of white-collar workers or salariat.[48] These films brought into view symptomatic sites of everyday modernity—urban streets and department stores, cafés, bars, dance halls, and movie theaters, schools and hospitals, offices and (occasionally) factories, Western-style apartments and traditional Japanese houses and shacks set in the semi-industrial wasteland of suburban Tokyo, or in the more marginal, low-cosmopolitan milieu of Yokahama habor—and used them in ways that led contemporary critics to discern in them "a stunning new realist aesthetic."[49]

Shochiku Kamata films tapped the experience of the white-collar class, including an unprecedented number of working women (typists, salesgirls, café waitresses), as it was dramatized at the time in mass-market fiction and illustrated magazines and theorized by intellectuals (who came to refer to themselves mockingly as members of the *shoshimin* class).[50] Their plots revolved around conflicts and catastrophic accidents related to modernization, expressing the hopes and anxieties of people for whom Meiji-era dreams of upward mobility through education and hard work—and more recent ambitions linked to lifestyle and consumption—had turned, especially with the 1929 crash, into nightmare realities of unemployment and destitution. While the films gave expression to the sense of crisis or, to cite social theorist

miriam hansen

Aono Suekichi, the "panic" of this new class that sought to transcend (working) class, they also registered the blind spots of *shoshimin* mentality with critical irony, combining pathos with a degree of self-awareness we might not find, say, in German films of that period, even prior to 1933.[51]

Whether focusing on "salarymen" and the breakdown of the patriarchal family (cf. Naruse's *Flunky, Work Hard* [1931], Ozu's *Tokyo Chorus* [1931] and his *I Was Born But . . .* [1932]) or on the *moga* image and the contradictions of modern womanhood, Shochiku films, according to studio head Kido Shiro, were supposed to take on these issues in a "lighter" tone than their *shinpa*-influenced competitors or, for that matter, the leftist "tendency films."[52] To whatever degree that policy was actually adhered to and operative in the films, it was a business strategy by which the studio sought to appeal to the growing market of female consumers socializing outside the home, expecting them to bring along not only girlfriends and siblings, but also boyfriends and husbands. In terms of film practice, this entailed a modernization of Japanese cinema in several respects, overlapping in part with the tenets of the "pure film movement": casting actresses instead of *oyama* or female impersonators; using screenplays often based on mass-market fiction addressed to women; and replacing the *benshi*, the silent film narrators, with filmic narration based on forms of continuity editing and other techniques (such as Naruse's expressive track-ins on faces) which not only enhanced the relay of subjectivity between fictional character and viewer but also created "a sense of authenticity drawn from the audience's everyday life."[53]

It would be easy to claim, or dismiss, Shochiku's strategies of constructing and anticipating its audience—by creating a filmic world, or worlds, that partially resembled the one they were trying to inhabit—as yet another lesson from the Hollywood book. But the implications of that lesson are far from clear. For one thing, the Hollywood model was itself a historical formation, developed against the foil of competing models, in particular the model of colonial modernity (the constituting of Western metropolitan audiences by displays of exoticized others) which had been an important factor in French cinema's dominance on the world market up to World War I.[54] For another, to the extent that Shochiku oriented its practices on a liberal market model, this meant something quite different in 1930s Japan, especially as the decade went on, given the escalation of military aggression and territorial expansion vis-à-vis China and the increasing fascization of Japanese society, including anti-leftist arrests and censorship, the 1936 right-wing coup attempt, and full mobilization of imperial-nationalist ideology.

The type of public sphere that crystallized around vernacular-modernist film practices and other matrices of capitalist consumption would have provided a counterpoint to state-controlled national publicity on two counts. First, inasmuch as mainstream commercial films depended on the everyday experience of their constituency, they created a space for spectatorial subjectivity and agency, most strikingly for women. Second, inasmuch as Shochiku directors were inspired by international film culture, they were likely to have an uneasy relationship with an autarchistic nationalism and the ideological imperative of "overcoming modernity."[55]

To be sure, Shochiku responded to increased political repression and censorship by abandoning overtly leftist themes, and dissent migrated into subtle details of mise-en-scene (such as Ozu's placement, in *Dragnet Girl*, of a French poster of the Lewis Milestone adaptation—banned in Japan—of Erich Maria Remarque's German pacifist novel *All Quiet on the Western Front*, actually in the apartment of the film's exemplary traditional Japanese woman).[56] And no doubt there were films whose plots could be said to seek to contain the contradictions of modern womanhood in a manner consistent with, and reinforcing, nationalist discourse—by producing "in their audience a national sentiment toward their own modernity."[57] But to show *moga* figures as failing and, for instance, causing harm to the very people for whose sake they were submitting to alienating and socially proscribed forms of work, does not necessarily mean endorsing a return to traditional or more authentic womanhood. Not only do a great number of Shochiku films focalize narrational subjectivity and affect around the *moga* figure, even if the character is inconsistent and problematic, but also they observe—and quietly expose—the socio-economic conditions and ideological fixations that make the characters fail. By doing so, they still contain the dream of a different life, even if that dream can only be represented as an impossibility. To a remarkable degree (not untypical in Japanese artistic tradition though less so for wartime productions), these films resist closure, even when they end "happily," allowing audiences to recognize in them the contradictions and aporias of their own lives.

I opened this chapter by placing *Forget Love for Now* in a revisionist constellation with *The Goddess*. Shimizu's film was released in July of 1937, when Japan's attacks against China turned to open warfare and when Japanese film workers were encouraged to move to occupied Shanghai and take over the film industry. Whether or not Shimizu had seen *The Goddess*, the defeatist ending of *Forget Love for Now* pays strange homage to the Chinese precursor. At the very least, it seems out of key with the imperialist cause, notwithstanding the film's explicit if ambiguous nods to nationalism.[58] Likewise, self-conscious, ironic, or hyperbolic performances of the *moga* image, as well as aesthetic explorations of the materiality of things and trash, do not necessarily inspire heroic patriotic sentiment. Among other things, my examples can be read to suggest that vernacular-modernist currents in 1930s Japanese cinema were running in directions oblique to dominant imperial-nationalist ideology and its aggressive political and military enforcement. They were neither automatically resistant nor inevitably complicit with that ideology, nor consistent within the oeuvre of individual directors or within one and the same film; and they were obviously not the only type of film made and shown in Japan.[59] Still, in the measure that these films were geared less to National Policy ("kokusaku" films) than to a popular market (albeit one that was changing) and internationalist modernism, they articulated an idiom open to stylistic experiment, narrative ambiguity, parody and irony, and the conflicting potentials of modernity, rather than a unitary national discourse.

Chinese cinema of the period, including the left-wing cinema movement, was no less aware of and dependent on strategies of attracting and constructing an audience, which entailed tapping into the thriving market of urban mass culture and consumption centered in Shanghai. A key term here, related to the Japanese, were the xiao shimin or "petty urbanites": clerks, shopkeepers, employees, a broad social stratum variously referred to as petty bourgeois or new middle class and comprising men and women from diverse social and cultural backgrounds; in other words, a heterosocial urban mass public that had emerged (and met with masculinist-elitist disdain from May-Fourth intellectuals) qua consumers of popular fiction and pictorial journalism, as well as American movies and music.[60] If comparable to similar subject formations in Tokyo (and, for that matter, other metropolitan centers in Asia, Latin America, and Europe), the modern mass public courted and shaped by Shanghai cinema cannot be thought of apart from the violently contested forcefield of Chinese national politics and the conditions of semicolonial modernity. The fact that Japan was part of—and aggressively intervened in—this forcefield further complicates a comparative perspective.

I have tried to show how the concept of vernacular modernism might provide a heuristic framework for tracing transnational relations between and within Japanese and Chinese film practices of the 1930s. This framework could be made productive for cinemas in other parts of the world as well, with different historical trajectories of capitalist modernization, everyday modernity, and aesthetic modernism, including different positions vis-à-vis Hollywood hegemony. In each case, a comparative approach has to be complicated with a theoretically inspired histoire croisée, a history of entanglement that traces actual interconnections, inasmuch as films, filmmakers, and film styles did travel and audiences migrated, along with the virtual ones that were blocked. By tracking the ways in which cinemas in different geopolitical locations and constellations engaged with the contradictory experience of modernity, we may find resonances across violent divisions and asymmetrical conditions of wealth and power. What may surprise us in actually looking at films and exploring particular film cultures is less the fact of the global advance of capitalism than the shared concern, on the part of filmmakers and audiences alike, with modern life and modernist styles, a concern that included, in Harootunian's words, the "as yet unrealized promise of a more humane and just society."[61] This may be one of the reasons why, at a time when that promise has been made to sound like an echo from another era, these films look at once strange, poignant, and timely.

acknowledgments

This chapter is based on a lecture presented at the Centennial Celebration and 2005 Annual Conference of the Asian Cinema Studies Society, "National, Transnational, and International: Chinese Cinema and Asian Cinema in the Context of Globalization," Beijing and Shanghai, June 2005, and was completed in July 2007. For critical readings and suggestions I would like to thank Paula Amad, Weihong Bao, Dipesh Chakrabarty, Nataša Ďurovičová, Norma Field, Michael Geyer, Andreas Huyssen, Andrew Jones, Dan Morgan, Laura Mulvey, Lesley Stern, Julia Adeney Thomas, Po-Chen Tsai, Man-Fung Yip, Judith Zeitlin, and Zhang Zhen. Special thanks to Michael Raine, who has been a challenging and patient interlocutor throughout the various stages of this project.

notes

1. For an illuminating discussion of this film, see Catherine Russell, "Naruse Mikio's Silent Films: Gender and the Discourse of Everyday Life in Interwar Japan," *Camera Obscura* 20, no. 3 (2005): 57–89.
2. As Michael Raine has pointed out to me, the nationalist sentiment mobilized by Kuwano's character in favor of staying, however precarious their existence, is deflated by the subsequent assertion that she would go to Singapore for the sake of her child and would not shed a nostalgic tear when seeing the Japanese flag. Also see Wong Ain-ling, "In the Land of Fallen Souls," in *Shimizu Hiroshi: 101st Anniversary*, ed. Kinnia Yau et al. (Hong Kong: Hong Kong International Film Festival Society, 2004), 19.
3. The discussion of Chinese and Japanese films of the 1920s and 1930s in terms of melodrama is notoriously fraught, whether with unreflected assumptions about the meaning of the term in Euro-American and Hollywood contexts or by its unproblematic transfer to different cultural and film-industrial genealogies and concepts of genre. See Wimal Dissanayake, ed. *Melodrama and Asian Cinema* (Cambridge: Cambridge University Press, 1993); Nick Browne, "Society and Subjectivity: On the Political Economy of Chinese Melodrama," in *New Chinese Cinemas*, ed. N. Browne et al. (Cambridge: Cambridge University Press, 1994). Also see the contributions by Li Cheuk-to, Law Kar, and Law Wai-ming, in *Cantonese Melodrama, 1950–1969: The Tenth Hong Kong International Film Festival*, ed. Li Cheuk-to (Hong Kong: Urban Council of Hong Kong, 1986).
4. See, for instance, Yingjin Zhang, "Prostitution and Urban Imagination: Negotiating the Public and the Private in Chinese Films of the 1930s," in *Cinema and Urban Culture in Shanghai, 1922–1943*, ed. Yingjin Zhang (Stanford: Stanford University Press, 1999), 160–180; Andrew Jones, "The Child as History in Republican China: A Discourse on Development," *Positions* 10, no. 3 (2002): 695–727; Andrew Jones, "*Playthings* of History: The Child as

Commodity in Republican China," lecture presented at the University of Chicago, December 2005.

5. Alexander Kluge, press release for "Kapitalistische Moderne und Intimität: Miriam Hansen über vier Filme, die von selbstbewussten Frauen handeln," *10 vor 11*, broadcast August 22, 2005.

6. According to the program notes for the Hong Kong retrospective, over thirty shots depicting the prostitutes' lives and their efforts to negotiate better conditions were cut by the censor (*Shimizu Hiroshi*, 70). I should add here that, unlike Ruan's Goddess, Kuwano's less saintly mother is granted a romantic attachment toward one of the bodyguards, played by Valentino look-alike Sano Shuji, whose effort to save her, however, is primarily motivated by his fatherly feelings toward the son.

7. I discuss this film in greater detail in Hansen, "Fallen Women, Rising Stars, New Horizons: Shanghai Silent Film as Vernacular Modernism," *Film Quarterly* 54, no. 1, (2000): 10–22.

8. In neither the Japanese nor the Chinese case is there sufficient evidence to suggest that women constituted a majority of the audience (as they did, by the mid- to late 1920s, in Hollywood), or that the studios produced films *primarily addressed* to women (as Hollywood did in the 1940s in response to the collapse of the female market). I therefore hesitate to use the term "woman's film" in this context, as does Mitsuyo Wada-Marciano, "Imaging Modern Girls in the Japanese Woman's Film," *Camera Obscura* 20, no. 3 (2005): 15–56. I take the significance of women's moviegoing in both cinemas to be rather of a differential and qualitative order, inasmuch as it gave women access to a public sphere of theatrical entertainments previously reserved for men and accepting women only in hierarchically regulated and segregated forms.

9. For a critique of such approaches, notably put forth by Paul Schrader and Donald Richie, see David Bordwell's magisterial study *Ozu and the Poetics of Cinema* (Princeton, NJ: Princeton University Press, 1988), 26–29.

10. Film's affinity with the "secret life of things" (Virginia Woolf) is a key topos of film aesthetics in interwar Europe—cf. Béla Balazs, Jean Epstein, Louis Aragon, Germaine Dulac, Siegfried Kracauer, Walter Benjamin—informed in part by a turn to the object in avant-garde movements such as Dada, Surrealism, and Soviet artists such as Boris Arvatov and Alexandr Rodchenko. See Bill Brown, "Thing Theory," in *Things*, ed. Bill Brown (Chicago, IL: University of Chicago Press, 2004), 1–22; Lesley Stern, "Paths that Wind through the Thicket of Things," in ibid., 393–443, and other essays in that collection; also see Bill Brown, "The Secret Life of Things (Virginia Woolf and the Matter of Modernism)," *Modernism/Modernity* 6 (April 1999): 1–28. In the Asian context, an important impulse in this direction can be found in Tanizaki Jun'ichiro's early writings on film and modernity, including screenplays and literary fiction, of which only his essay *In Praise of Shadows* (1933) and his novel *Naomi* (1924–25) are more widely known in English; see Thomas LaMarre, *Shadows on the Screen: Tanizaki Jun'ichiro on Cinema and "Oriental" Aesthetics* (Ann Arbor, MI: Center for Japanese Studies, University of Michigan, 2005). Another important source here is the Japanese school of New Sensationism and its Shanghai counterpart, translated into film aesthetics by Liu Na'ou and others.

11. The film's self-conscious play with the logics of the commodity is epitomized by a scene in which the protagonist's artist friend brings a chicken and two pig's feet to celebrate his birthday, manipulating them like

a puppet and explaining how he paid for them: "This is the summer suit. This is the flannel jacket. This is a pair of white leather pants!"

12. This interest is indebted to Siegfried Kracauer's *Theory of Film* (New York: Oxford University Press, 1960; 1997), a work that tries to negotiate the tension between film's modernist ability to render and preserve the otherness of an historically alienated physis and the inevitable urge to reimbue the world with human feelings and agency. It is understood that the critic's valorization of the former, the tendency to allegorize the significance of the insignificant, ephemeral, and indeterminate, is itself a version of that urge.

13. On the notion of the "formless," taking its cue from Bataille's *l'informe*, see Yve-Alain Bois and Rosalind Krauss, *Formless: A User's Guide* (New York: Zone Books, 1997).

14. In this regard, left-wing Chinese films seem to set themselves off not only against stereotypical images of urban waste attached to the semicolonial port city—graphically displayed in the Soviet documentary film *Shanghai Document* (Yakov Bliokh, 1928)—but also against the racialized aestheticization of refuse and disintegration in the 1929 novel *Shanghai* by Japanese New Sensationist Yokomitsu Riichi, which provides an amazing, and highly ambivalent, intertext for a cinematic aesthetics of things and trash. For a contrasting view of Shanghai though similarly concerned with the materiality of quotidian objects, see essays by Eileen Chang, written during and after the war, *Written on Water*, trans. Andrew Jones, co-ed. Nicole Huang (New York: Columbia University Press, 2005).

15. See Joshua Goldstein, "The Remains of the Everyday: One Hundred Years of Recycling in Beijing," in *Everyday Modernity in China*, ed. J. Goldstein and Madeleine Yue Dong (Seattle, WA: University of Washington, 2006).

16. For efforts (in English-language scholarship) to cross that divide, if mostly at the level of essay collections and journals (such as *Asian Cinema*), see Catherine Russell, ed. *New Women of the Silent Screen: China, Japan, Hollywood, Camera Obscura* 20, no. 3 (2005); also see Dissanayake, ed. *Melodrama and Asian Cinema*; Wimal Dissanayake, ed. *Cinema and Cultural Identity: Reflections on Films from Japan, India, and China* (Lanham, MD: University Press of America, 1988); Linda C. Ehrlich and David Desser, eds. *Cinematic Landscapes: Observations on the Visual Arts and Cinema of China and Japan* (Austin, TX: University of Texas Press, 1994). More research into cross-filiations between Japanese and Chinese cinemas is being done for the post-World War II period, though most accounts tend to focus on Hong Kong and Taiwan. On Japanese-Chinese film politics during the war and occupation, see Peter B. High, *The Imperial Screen: Japanese Film Culture in the Fifteen Years' War, 1931–1945* (Madison, WI: University of Wisconsin Press, 2003), 100–20 (on Kamei Fumio and other Toho military documentaries); Poshek Fu, *Between Shanghai and Hong Kong: The Politics of Chinese Cinemas* (Stanford, CA: Stanford University Press, 2003): Chap. 7; Yingjin Zhang, *Chinese National Cinema* (London: Routledge, 2004): 83–89; Shelley Stephenson, "The Occupied Screen: Star, Fan, and Nation in Shanghai Cinema, 1937–1945," PhD dissertation, University of Chicago, IL, 2000.

17. I had the opportunity to view archival prints from this period in retrospectives of Chinese and Japanese films at the Pordenone silent film festival in, respectively, 1995/1997 and 2001/2005, in addition to retrospectives of the work of Ozu, Shimizu, and Naruse in the United States and Berlin.

18. Russell, "Introduction," *Camera Obscura* 20, no. 3 (2005): 2. Also see Zhang

Zhen, "*An Amorous History of the Silver Screen*: The Actress as Vernacular Embodiment in Early Chinese Film," in *A Feminist Reader in Early Cinema*, ed. Jennifer M. Bean and Diane Negra (Durham, NC: Duke University Press, 2002), 501–529; Weihong Bao, "From Pearl White to White Rose: Tracing the Vernacular Body of *Nüxia* in Chinese Silent Cinema," *Camera Obscura* 20, no. 3 (2005): 193–231; Wada-Marciano, "Imaging Modern Girls," 16, 33ff.

19. For a critique of received comparative approaches in area studies, see Harry Harootunian, "Ghostly Comparisons," *Traces: A Multilingual Series of Cultural Theory and Translation* 3 (2004): 39–52. Also see Michael Werner and Bénédict Zimmermann, "Beyond Comparison: *Histoire Croisée* and the Challenge of Reflexivity," *History and Theory* 45 (February 2006): 30–50, based on the authors' introduction to their edited volume, Werner and Zimmermann, eds. *De la comparaison à l'histoire croisée* (Paris: Seuil, 2004), and Gunilla Budde, Sebastian Conrad and Oliver Janz, eds. *Transnationale Geschichte: Themen, Tendenzen und Theorien* (Göttingen: Vandenhoeck & Ruprecht, 2006) (most contributions in English).

20. See Zhang Zhen, *An Amorous History of the Silver Screen: Shanghai Cinema, 1896–1937* (Chicago, IL: University of Chicago Press, 2005), 82–83 and Chapter 7, esp. 255–64 (on Tian Han's reception and later rejection of Tanizaki), 274–84 (on Liu Na'ou). On the complex relationship of Chinese modernists to their Japanese counterparts, see Shu-Mei Shih, *The Lure of the Modern: Writing Modernism in Semicolonial China, 1917–1937* (Berkeley, CA: University of California Press, 2001), esp. 16–30 and Chapters 9–11. On Tanizaki's "Oriental" film aesthetics, which turned on Chinese written characters (though in a different way than Eisenstein's ideas about ideograms and montage), see LaMarre, *Shadows on the Screen*, 26–33.

21. The question of how vernacular modernism interacts with genre, which involves different mappings—as well as the very concept—of genre that different film cultures developed both in relation to cultural tradition and in response to Hollywood genre films, is the subject of another chapter of this work-in-progress.

22. The foundational text in this regard is David Bordwell, Janet Staiger, and Kristin Thompson, *Classical Hollywood Cinema: Film Style and Mode of Production to 1960* (New York: Columbia University Press, 1985).

23. Hansen, "The Mass Production of the Senses: Classical Cinema as Vernacular Modernism," *Modernism/Modernity* 6, no. 2 (1999): 59–77, reprinted in *Reinventing Film Studies*, ed. Christine Gledhill and Linda Williams (London: Arnold), 332–50.

24. See David Bordwell, *On the History of Film Style* (Cambridge, MA: Harvard University Press, 1997), 141–46; Charlie Keil, " 'To Here from Modernity': Style Historiography, and Transitional Cinema," in *American Cinema's Transitional Era: Audiences, Institutions, Practices*, eds. C. Keil & Shelley Stamp (Berkeley, CA: California University Press, 2004), 51–65. In these somewhat reductive accounts, approaches to early film history informed by theories of modernity are criticized under the label "modernity thesis." For a response to that criticism, see Ben Singer, *Melodrama and Modernity* (New York: Columbia University Press, 2001) 9–10, Chap. 4; Tom Gunning, "Modernity and Cinema: A Culture of Shocks and Flows," in *Cinema and Modernity*, ed. Murray Pomerance (New Brunswick, NJ: Rutgers University Press, 2006), esp. 302–15.

25. On the difficulty of defining the term modernism in any singular way, see Susan Stanford Friedman, "Definitional Excursions: The Meanings of *Modern/Modernity/Modernism*," *Modernism/Modernity* 8, no. 3 (2001): 493–513.

26. Dipesh Chakrabarty, *Provincializing Europe: Postcolonial Thought and Historical Difference* (Princeton, NJ: Princeton University Press, 2000); also see Arjun Appadurai, *Modernity at Large: Cultural Dimensions of Globalization* (Minneapolis, MN: University of Minnesota Press, 1996); Timothy Mitchell, ed. *Questions of Modernity* (Minneapolis, MN: University of Minnesota Press, 2000).

27. On the interrelation of modernism and modernity in an "expanded field," see Andreas Huyssen, "Geographies of Modernism in a Globalizing World," in *Geographies of Modernism: Literatures, Cultures, Spaces*, eds. Peter Brooker and Andrew Thacker (London: Routledge, 2005), 6–18.

28. Fredric Jameson, *A Singular Modernity: Essay on the Ontology of the Present* (London: Verso, 2002), 12–13. While I share Jameson's concern that such approaches may submerge the capitalist foundations of globalization in a happy culturalist pluralism, it seems equally important not to submerge the historically and geopolitically different configurations of both capitalism and modernity under the fixed and timeless category of the capitalist mode of production. The literature on "alternative modernities" is too vast to cite here. For a seminal essay on this concept see Dilip Parameshwar Gaonkar, "On Alternative Modernities," introduction to special issue of *Public Culture* 11, no. 1 (1999): 1–18, esp. 13ff.; also see the special issue on "multiple modernities," *Daedalus* 129, no. 1 (2000); Bruce M. Knauft, ed. *Critically Modern: Alternatives, Alterities, Anthropologies* (Bloomington, IN: Indiana University Press, 2002).

29. On the difference between colonial/metropolitan forms of imperialism and the American model, see Victoria de Grazia, *Irresistible Empire: America's Advance through 20ᵗʰ-Century Europe* (Cambridge, MA: Harvard University Press, 2005); also see de Grazia's earlier essay, "Americanism for Export," *Wedge* 7–8 (Winter–Spring 1985): 74–81.

30. David Bordwell, "Visual Style in Japanese Cinema, 1925–1945," *Film History: An International Journal* 7, no. 1 (1995): 5–31, pp. 23, 7.

31. Zhang, *Amorous History*; also see Laikwan Pang, *Building a New China in Cinema: The Chinese Left-Wing Cinema Movement, 1932–1937* (Lanham, MD: Rowman & Littlefield, 2002). On the dynamics of nativist, cosmopolitan, and hybrid modernisms in Shanghai, see Leo Ou-fan Lee, *Shanghai Modern: The Flowering of a New Urban Culture in China, 1930–1945* (Cambridge, MA: Harvard University Press, 1999); Andrew Jones, *Yellow Music: Media Culture and Colonial Modernity in the Chinese Jazz Age* (Durham, NC: Duke University Press, 2001).

32. Sheldon Pollock, "Cosmopolitan and Vernacular in History," *Public Culture* 12, no. 3 (2000): 591–625, p. 596.

33. Sheldon Pollock, "The Cosmopolitan Vernacular," *Journal of Asian Studies* 57, no. 1 (1998): 6–37, p. 25; Pollock, "Cosmopolitan and Vernacular in History," 616. For a discussion of the relationship of cosmopolitan and vernacular in contemporary globalized settings, see Bruce Robbins, "Actually Existing Cosmopolitanism," in *Cosmopolitics: Thinking and Feeling beyond the Nation*, ed. Pheng Cheah and B. Robbins (Minneapolis, MN: University of Minnesota Press, 1998), 1–19.

34. Pollock, "Cosmopolitan and Vernacular in History," 624.

35. Ibid., 617; also see 592–93.

36. I am using the term public sphere less in the Habermasian sense than that offered by Oskar Negt and Alexander Kluge, *The Public Sphere and Experience*, trans. Peter Labanyi, Jamie Daniel, and Assenka Oksiloff, introd. Miriam Hansen (Minneapolis, MN: University of Minnesota Press, 1993). I have

miriam hansen

310

mobilized this notion of publicness for film history in Hansen, *Babel and Babylon: Spectatorship in American Silent Film* (Cambridge, MA: Harvard University Press, 1991).

37. Dudley Andrew, Position paper, Symposium on "Cinema as Vernacular Modernism," University of Chicago, 2002.

38. See, for instance, Zhang, *Amorous History*, Chapter 4, especially 122–30; Edward Dimendberg, *Film Noir and the Spaces of Modernity* (Cambridge, MA: Harvard University Press, 2004); Mark Lamster, ed. *Architecture and Film* (New York: Princeton Architectural Press, 2000); Gertrud Koch, ed. *Umwidmungen—architektonische und kinematographische Räume* (Berlin: Vorwerk, 2005). Nataša Ďurovičová interpolates the impossible linguistic ambitions and the architectural heteroglossia of cinematic modernity together in her essay "*Los Toquis!* Or, Urban Babel," in *Global Cities: Cinema, Architecture, and Urbanism in a Digital Age*, ed. Linda Krause and Patrice Petro (New Brunswick, NJ: Rutgers University Press, 2003), 71–86.

39. See, for example, John Brinkerhoff Jackson, *Discovering the Vernacular Landscape* (New Haven, CT: Yale University Press, 1975); Bozkurt Güvenç, "Vernacular Architecture as a Paradigm Case," in *Vernacular Architecture*, ed. Mete Turan (Aldershot, UK: Avebury, 1990), esp. 284–88; Francesco Passanti, "The Vernacular, Modernism, and Le Corbusier," *Journal of the Society of Architectural Historians* 56, no. 4 (1997): 438–51, and an updated version of that article in *Vernacular Modernism: Heimat, Globalization and the Built Environment*, ed. Maiken Umbach and Bernd Hüppauf (Stanford, CA: Stanford University Press, 2005), 141–56. Also see "Vernacular Architecture," *Grove Dictionary of Art*, www.groveart.com.

40. Amos Rapoport, "Defining Vernacular Design," in Turan, *Vernacular Architecture*, 78, 95, 98.

41. Umbach and Hüppauf, *Vernacular Modernism* 2 (emphasis added), 9.

42. Umbach and Hüppauf, "Introduction," 9–16. The editors' understanding of *Heimat* is indebted to the utopianist philosophy of Ernst Bloch; see Bernd Hüppauf, "Spaces of the Vernacular: Ernst Bloch's Philosophy of Hope and the German Hometown," in *Vernacular Modernism*, 84–113. This chapter makes no mention of film (or any other technological media), neither of the genre of *Heimatfilm* that transported the parochial antimodernist version of the term well into the Federal Republic, nor of Edgar Reitz's TV miniseries *Heimat* (1984) that gave it international currency.

43. Harry Harootunian, *History's Disquiet: Modernity, Cultural Practices, and the Question of Everyday Life* (New York: Columbia University Press, 2000), 18–19. Historicizing Henri Lefebvre's concept of the everyday Harootunian puts into conversation German writers such as Simmel, Kracauer, Benjamin, Bloch, and Heidegger with contemporary Japanese writers such as Kon Wajiro, Tosaka Jun, Aono Suekichi, and others. Also see Harootunian, *Overcome by Modernity: History, Culture, and Community in Interwar Japan* (Princeton, NJ: Princeton University Press, 2000).

44. Harootunian, *History's Disquiet*, 111–15, 62–64.

45. Examples include transnational language regions as large as Swahili, a multilingual idiom bridging over 130 indigenous African languages; nationally specific idioms such as African American English; and smaller regions like the German Ruhrgebiet and the urban area of Berlin. See Louis-Jean Calvet, "Vernaculaire," in *Sociolinguistique: Concepts de base*, ed. Marie-Louise Moreau (Liège, Belgium: Mardaga, 1997), 291–92; Ronald K.S. Macaulay, "Vernacular," *Concise Encyclopedia of Sociolinguistics*, ed. Rajend

Mesthrie (Amsterdam: Elsevier, 2001), 421; also see Macaulay, "The Rise and Fall of the Vernacular," *On Language: Rhetorica, Phonologica, Syntactica*, ed. Caroline Duncan-Rose and Theo Vennemann (London, New York: Routledge 1988), 107–15. My thanks to Augusto Carli, Salikoko Mufwene, and Susan Gal for alerting me to both the potential and the problematic status of the term in linguistics, in particular sociolinguistics.

46. See Bordwell on the "flamboyant, frantic style" of some of the *chambara* films (*Ozu*, 23). Aimed at urban working-class men, rural audiences, and children, the genre was a matrix for a national discourse on heroic masculinity, including the threat of its failure; significantly, the subgenre of *matatabimono*, wandering yakusa and masterless samurai, was also referred to as "men's weepies." See Isolde Standish, *A New History of Japanese Cinema: A Century of Narrative Film* (London: Continuum, 2005), 33, 43ff., 68.

47. The boundaries between intellectual-elite and vernacular modernisms were more fluid than my schematic paraphrase suggests, considering that numerous modernist artists and writers were fascinated, and themselves experimenting, with the new medium, or were seeking to reach larger audiences in middle-brow print media.

48. The term *shoshimin* was a translation of the French *petit bourgeois* and referred to people who, on the basis of their higher education and less physical types of labor set themselves off from ordinary workers but held no property and worked for low salaries. Whether or not the Japanese-Marxist ascription is adequate to the phenomenon, the English-language rendering of *shoshimin* in American sociological terms (by Wada-Marciano and others) as "new middle class" or "middle class" seems problematic. The historically salient point is that technologically mediated mass culture made visible a new social formation that was defined, to vary on Althusser, as much by their imaginary relation to the capitalist process of production as by their actual economic conditions. On the *shoshimin eiga* and Shochiku, see Sato Tadao, *Nihon eigashi* (1995), 232–33, and Kawamoto Saburo, "Shoshimin eiga no 'atarashii wagaya' " (Shoshimin films and the "new my-home") in *Kindai Nihon Bunkaron*, vol. 7: *Taishu bunka to masu mejia* (*On Modern Japanese Culture*, vol. 7: *Mass Culture and Mass Media*) (1999): 1–17. to Also see, since completion of this essay, Mitsuyo Wada-Marciano, *Nippon Modern: Japanese Cinema of the 1920s and 1930s* (Honolulu: University of Hawai'i Press, 2008).

49. Russell, "Naruse Mikio's Silent Films," 75–76.

50. See Miriam Silverberg, "The Café Waitress Serving Modern Japan," in *Mirror of Modernity: Invented Traditions of Modern Japan*, ed. Stephen Vlastos (Berkeley, CA: University of California Press, 1998), 208–25; Harootunian, *Overcome by Modernity*, Chapter 1; Barbara Sato, "An Alternate Informant: Middle-Class Women and Mass Magazines in 1920s Japan," in *Being Modern in Japan: Culture and Society from the 1910s to the 1930s*, ed. Elise K. Tipton and John Clark (Honolulu, HI: University of Hawaii Press, 2000); also see Barbara Sato, *The New Japanese Woman: Modernity, Media, and Women in Interwar Japan* (Durham, NC: Duke University Press, 2003).

51. Aono Suekichi, *Saraiman kyofu jidai* (*The Salaryman's Panic Time*, Tokyo: Senshinsha, 1930). The German point of comparison is Siegfried Kracauer's study *Die Angestellten* (1929), *The Salaried Masses: Duty and Distraction in Weimar Germany*, trans. Quintin Hoare, introd. Inka Mülder-Bach (London, New York: Verso, 1998). See Harootunian, *History's Disquiet* 91–93, 122–25, 133–40. Kracauer's study, along with numerous reviews and articles on contemporary film and its audiences, early on discerned in the employees' frustrated

bourgeois aspirations and self-delusion a source of their vulnerability to National Socialist propaganda.

52. "Entertainment be bright and healthy, while laughing at society's ironies and contradictions, we can study life." Kido Shiro, *Nihon eigaden: Eiga seisakusha no kiroku (Japanese Cinema Tales: A Record of a Film Producer)* (Tokyo: Bungei Shunjusha, 1956), trans. and quoted in Standish, *A New History of Japanese Cinema*, 32.

53. Mitsuyo Wada-Marciano, "Imaging Modern Girls," 21.

54. I am thinking here, for example, of Pathé travelogues whose appeal more often than not turned on the *contrast* between the world depicted in manifold picturesque views and the world inhabited by the audience (the difference between *le monde* in the geo- and ethnographic sense and *le monde* in the societal sense which is both elided and asserted in the Lumière Brothers' punning slogan, "to bring the world to the world"). This logic of contrast included ethnographic displays of internal others from peripheral and backward regions of Europe and, I would argue, continued in French "realist" peasant dramas of the 1920s, many of whom were based on nineteenth-century literary classics (cf. the series "André Antoine and French Realism," Pordenone silent film festival, 2005). It was to compete with this cinema of colonial modernity on the domestic market, and to transform heterogeneous immigrant audiences into a modern mass audience, that Hollywood developed classical strategies of narration and address (as the new "universal language" understood by viewers from diverse and non-synchronous backgrounds) along with "American subjects"—Westerns, stories and settings of contemporary everyday life. The claim to homology and potential contiguity between the diegetic world and that of the audience ("realism") was never *not* ideological, but the difference between these models matters, in terms of both modernist aesthetics and the quality of cinematic publicness. See Richard Abel, *The Red Rooster Scare: Making Cinema American, 1900–1910* (Berkeley, CA: University of California Press, 1999); also see Hansen, *Babel and Babylon*, Chapters 2 and 3.

55. On the in/famous conference with that title, held in July 1942, see Harootunian, *Overcome by Modernity*, Chapter 2.

56. Wada-Marciano persuasively reads Ozu's extended staging of whispering in his 1933 (silent!) film *Woman of Tokyo*, which ostensibly transmits the rumor of the protagonist's unspeakable night-job as a barmaid, as an implied reference to violent government action against communist intellectuals that had intensified that year—a subversive gag that contemporary audiences would have understood ("Imaging Modern Girls," 31–33). Another example would be Ozu's ironic citation of German cultural emblems, such as a poster of the Bamberger Reiter in the shabby living quarters of the protagonist and an UFA biopic on Franz Schubert, in *The Only Son* (1936).

57. Wada-Marciano, "Imaging Modern Girls," 17. Wada-Marciano challenges Miriam Silverberg's account that there was "a fluidity of identity" (sexual, racial, national) in Japanese interwar modernity that was closed off by the rise of fascist-imperial nationalism; see Miriam Silverberg, "Remembering Pearl Harbor, Forgetting Charlie Chaplin, and the Case of the Disappearing Woman: A Picture Story," in *Formations of Colonial Modernity in East Asia*, ed. Tani E. Barlow (Durham, NC: Duke University Press, 1997), 249–94.

58. Shimizu's dissent most persistently takes the form of sympathetic attention to socially and racially marginalized subjects, such as the group of Chinese

boys whom the ostracized son befriends in *Forget Love for Now*. In *Mr. Thank You* (*Arigato-san*, 1936), a long take of Korean itinerant workers in the landscape turns into a more closely framed friendly exchange between a Korean girl and the eponymic handsome bus driver.

59. See High, *The Imperial Screen*.

60. See Pang, *Building a New China in Cinema*, Chapter 6, esp. 150–54; Zhang, *Amorous History*, 23, 44, 64–65; and Lee, *Shanghai Modern*, Chapters 2, 3, and 8. Lee discusses Eileen Chang as a Shanghai writer who portrayed herself as a petty urbanite writing for petty urbanites whom she characterized this way: "Shanghainese are traditional people tempered by the pressure of modern life. The misshapen products of this fusion may not be entirely healthy, but they do embody a strange and distinctive sort of wisdom" (Chang, *Written on Water*, 54).

61. Harootunian, *History's Disquiet*, 68–69.

globalization and

hybridization

fourteen

f r e d r i c   j a m e s o n

I start from the premise that mapping the totality is still one of the most vital functions and ambitions of art at the present time, as it was under the very different conditions of the modern period. The totality today is surely what we call globalization, and it is therefore the problems involved in the representation of this new and seemingly unimaginable totality which offer the most interesting challenges for the artists and writers of the postmodern, as well as for its literary theorists. But postmodern philosophical positions also warn us to avoid the implication that correct or definitive "representations" of reality are possible or conceivable in the first place: so that what is wanted is an inventory of the dilemmas of representation, of what in the structure of object or subject alike makes representational accuracy or truth an impossible achievement and an ideological ambition or fantasy as well. We map the contours of globalization negatively, by way of a patient exploration of what cannot be perceived and what cannot be narrated.

Still, it would be logical to begin with realistic attempts to convey the dynamics of globalization, in order more surely to isolate those stumbling blocks—the national languages for one thing, the superposition of the media and of image society, for another, the difficulties in representing postmodern power systems for a third—that stand in the way of any convincing artistic realization and seem to render the old ideal of realism (which worked for the old nation-state) as chimeric as the even older epic itself.

But then there is the possibility of what Althusser called a *symptomal* analysis, and it becomes more plausible to expect individual works of a local provenance to betray signs and scars of that larger context they may not even be aware of: unfortunately these signs and scars, these symptoms, will probably turn out as a general rule to be precisely those stumbling blocks on representation already enumerated above for realism. They will simply say over and over again, this is not a complete message, the totality is inaccessible, cannot be represented, the form is impossible and the symptoms are simply symptoms of failure.

I want here briefly to note another possibility, which turns on generic signals. It is a conjecture I will formulate in the language of hybridity, but with some apprehension, for I know that an ideology of the hybrid and the celebration of hybridity as simple mixing has long been a political presence, in particular when dealing with border situations. But I do not have that particular kind of hybridity in mind here, since globalization has to be an affair of difference and identity combined: not merely of new syntheses, but of oppositions preserved in the very condition of that precarious (and maybe even fictive) synthesis.

For hybridity today, in the world of the DNA code and of genetic modification and manipulation, is a very different and often rather somber matter. Indeed, the very idea of hybridity nowadays has become a postmodern concept, with its own history and its kinship relation with all the other forms of postmodern technology such as cybernetic production and information theory.

The point is that this is a new process from anything suspected during the modern period: hybridization is not some synthesis between races or traditions, not some middle or mediatory term in which traits from both sides of the border are selected and combined. Nor is it the situation of multiple personalities or of the polyglot, in which we pass effortlessly from personality A to personality B and back.

In this new postmodern process what happens is evidently that a single characteristic fragment is selected from one gene and inserted into another one—more or less the way a virus is implanted in a cell. This results in a new—dare we call it an artificial?—gene, which is neither the parent cell nor the donor, but which in its realization or embodiment (in the ear of corn, say) is indistinguishable from either of those, and detectable only later on, in its afterlife and its impact on the ecosystem. I will not pursue this analogy any further here, but only signal a few recent films which seem to me to presage this coming logic of the genetic transfer (for which I am, perhaps misleadingly, reserving the term hybridization).

The two filmic texts I have found suggestive are the film *Dust* (2001) by the Macedonian director Milcho Manchevski (whose stunning and critically acclaimed *Before the Rain* appeared in 1994), and Wong Kar-wai's *Happy Together* (1996). In both it is a question of the transfer of a relatively familiar and conventional plot type to an altogether unfamiliar setting. Manchevski's story is one of the fraternal rivalry and vengeance: the older bother, losing the woman he loves to the younger, sets off on a life of exile and forgetfulness during which the younger brother hunts him down and kills him in revenge for his having defiled her in the first place. *Happy Together* tells the tale of the impossibility of the couple, whose miseries have been inventoried from *Adolphe* to *Who's Afraid of Virginia Woolf?* and do not gain any particularly heightened significance from the fact that this particular couple is gay. What does change everything is the unexpected transfer of this situation to Buenos Aires; just as the originality of *Dust* lies in its transfer of a first "western" plot to the east and the Balkans, whose mountaineers begin to look suspiciously like cowboys and whose violence—save for the political content of the struggle between the guerrillas and the Ottoman state—seems to replicate that of the frontier.

Yet I sense a difference, however, between *Dust* and the standard American émigré narratives (from Kazan to Coppola), even though the film begins in New York with the break-in of the apartment of an aged Balkan émigré by a young black man she subsequently adopts (yet another turn of the screw of the conventional multicultural narrative). She, the daughter, tells the story of the distant turn-of-the-century past, in which the wild west still existed, and also the fitful resistance of the Slavic bandits or "social rebels" to their Turkish overlords.

What I want to stress, however, is that *Dust* is predicated on the identity between the two locales, or at least of their uncanny resemblance: they look just like cowboys, comments the boy as he inspects a yellowing photograph. I am not sure whether the film is itself aware of the equally uncanny resemblance of the Western or American version of the vengeance plot to those traditional stories of so-called societies "of honor," which have less often had their equivalent in the permissive Northern European or American protestant areas (even Ford's *The Searchers* has a very different resonance from this).

Yet I want to argue that the American protagonists, the classic western frontier cowboys, are inserted into the cell of the Balkan landscape and society very much in the same way as the newly removed virus is inserted into the host gene. This gives us something rather different from a synthesis of West and East, on the order, say, of Tarantino's *Kill Bill*. To be sure, it seeks to rescue Balkan history (with its legendary violence, etc.) from stereotype, and to project some new ideological vision of history from which American exceptionalism is effaced and turn-of-the-century America becomes very much an old European country. Do the Montenegrin characters then reciprocally become Americans, as in the old Sam Goldwyn joke? I am less certain about that, for it is a question that draws on all the complexities of so-called Balkan identity and the immemorial stereotypes of this unique part of the world (the local spectators would have to have their say on the results). But the film certainly constitutes work on those identities, and a convulsive attempt to undermine national stereotypes in general, ambiguously reinventing them in the process. At any rate, this mixture, which stirs the pot, seems to me sufficiently different from the standard story of immigration and ethnic identity to offer a suggestive object for postmodern meditation and for the theorization of globalized culture.

As for *Happy Together*, it seems to me to operate in exactly the opposite way: the Hong Kong protagonists are abruptly transported to a setting utterly different from that overpopulated rock on which they have lived their previous lives. Indeed, the film opens with the classic shots of the great plains, and the lone car traversing them: wide open spaces which not only contradict our images of Hong Kong itself, but also make us retroactively aware of the claustrophobic and nervous packed images of Christopher Doyle, the cinematographer long associated with Wong Kar-wai, whose jittery frames will shortly replace this first deep breath of the open spaces of the pampas. For the other important point to be made here is that these are very precisely not the open spaces of the American west. (I leave aside the pilgrimage to the world-famous falls at Iguazu which frames this movie and gives it its closure, like a travelogue.) The most important fact of all here is the exclusion of any reference to the United States from a film which is ostensibly, even more than global, globalized and a cultural project of the new global postmodernity. The United States is left out of this, which is between China and Argentina, the Southern Cone and the Pacific Rim; and this is equally suggestive for the spectators, excluded along with their superstate centrality and their new world hegemonic language. This is not for you! This is between us! At best, you will be allowed to overhear, to be the voyeurs of this relationship, which oddly defamiliarizes our mental map of the world today all the while deploying two of its other major languages.

Still, Hong Kong and Cantonese are the virus inserted into this Argentinian cell, whose native characters at best pass on telephone messages and own the businesses in which the travelers work (only the three Chinese characters are listed in the cast): and the inclusion of a Taiwanese actor, with the detour via Taiwan at the end, indeed suggests a different kind of pan-Chinese message within the globalization framework. My point is that this is not a particularly surprising surcharge for a Latin American public, which has many ethnic minorities of its own and could not be imagined to be astonished at the representation of immigrants or guest workers from Asia (for that is what Fai and Po-wing end up being for a time). Nor is the matter of homosexuality really an issue either, despite a long-standing reticence on the part of Chinese writers and filmmakers: Argentina surely has its own gay writers and filmmakers and its own gay subculture. But this last is not represented in Wong Kar-wai's film either, despite the fact that Po-wing clearly begins to frequent it. What emerges here is not some international gay subculture, some gay multiculturalism, but rather the curious persistence of this subcharge of Hong Kong on Buenos Aires in which each retains a strange autonomy.

We must also register an obsessive and claustrophobic use of interior space, which contrasts sharply with the "wide open spaces" of the initial shots as well as with the great open-air market of Taipei or the primordial space of the falls at Iguazu, which virtually inscribe the creation of the world from a churning chaos. Hong Kong itself is absent here, but its own densely populated and serried buildings and dwellings seem to have been transferred and reinvented by these exiles, as though the tiny apartments and nightclubs served as a kind of protective shelter from the open world of Argentina itself all around them.

Stanley Cavell suggests, in *The World Viewed*, that the fascination of film lies in the way the screen shows us the world *without ourselves* and, as it were, without our point of view.[1] This is, for Americans, for the superstate and its world system of globalization and postmodernity, the fascination of *Happy Together*, which shows us a lateral relationship between cultures from which we are absent. On the stereotypical or ideological cognitive mapping of the global system today, everything passes through the United States on its way elsewhere; we necessarily mediate between all the other global cross-relations in the system, like airline flight plans which necessarily stop in Kennedy (New York) or LAX (Los Angeles) on their way somewhere else. *Happy Together* interrupts this stereotype and shows us a mysterious interconnection between cultures which falls outside the conventional scheme and forces us to invent new maps of the current world system. It is thus a far more stimulating representation than one which would simply show us foreigners in the United States or London, or now include Asian and East European actors and characters in the usual international settings and plots. A truly hybrid film like this may be a harbinger of more suggestive representations and mappings to come.

note

1. Stanley Cavell, *The World Viewed: Reflections on the Ontology of Film* (New York: Viking, 1971).

from *playtime*

to *the world*

the expansion and depletion

of space within

global economies

j o n a t h a n   r o s e n b a u m

My subject is the presence or absence of both shared public space and virtual private space in two visionary and globally minded urban epics made about thirty-seven years apart, on opposite sides of the planet—Jacques Tati's *Playtime* (1967) and Jia Zhangke's *The World* (*Shijie*, 2004), coincidentally the fourth feature made by each writer-director. Both films can be described as innovative and very modern attacks on modernity, and both have powerful metaphysical dimensions that limit their scope somewhat as narrative fictions. I should add that they both project powerful yet deceptive visions of internationalism that are predicated both literally and figuratively on *trompe l'oeil*, specifically on tricks with perspective and the uses of miniaturized simulacra. (I am referring here to both emblematic sites, such as the Eiffel Tower in both films, and the scaled-down skyscrapers used in the set built for *Playtime*.) In this sense, among others, both films are social critiques about what it means to impose monumental facades on tourists and workers—visitors and employees—who continue to think small.

One significant difference between the roles played by these films in the respective careers of their makers is that *Playtime*, by far the more utopian and optimistic of the two films, was the first of Tati's features to fail at the box office, and wound up bankrupting him, a disaster that I do not believe he ever fully recovered from. (Furthermore, Tati was pressured to cut the film during its initial Paris run, and although he later said to me and others that he preferred the original and longer version to all the others, this version apparently has not been seen since the 1970s and may no longer exist.[1])

Although it is too early to judge the ultimate effect of *The World* on Jia Zhangke's career, it is worth pointing out that it is the first of his features to get official sanction from the Chinese government and the only one to date to show commercially in theaters (all the others have circulated illegally in pirated versions on video), despite the fact that it is probably more critical of contemporary life and conditions in mainland China than any of his previous features. Another paradox: the film has been shown in China only or at least mainly in a shortened version, although I have been told that the cuts have not constituted any sort of political censorship and have been made only in order to show the film more times per day during its commercial playdates. So, ironically, the full 139-minute version can be seen in most countries where the film is being shown, but not in China.

I should add that in some ways I am more interested in the differences between these two very great films than in their similarities. Quite apart from the fact that *Playtime*, set in Paris, was mainly shot on a massive set outside that city, built expressly for the film, and that *The World* was mainly shot in an already existing theme park in the vicinity of Beijing, the former film depends on a vision of public life that eliminates any sense of private space or private behavior, while the latter—which is often concerned with the vast discrepancies between, first, decrepit, claustrophobic private spaces and alienated private behavior, and second, the enormous and utopian public spaces in a theme park, specifically as seen from the vantage point of the workers in that theme park—never strays very far from that specialized turf. Both films might therefore be regarded as metaphorical as well as metaphysical statements about the modern world that employ public spaces in order to say something about it.

Another key difference between these films and their respective worlds and eras is the presence and uses in *The World* of mobile phones and text messaging. This seems especially relevant because the utopian vision of shared public space that informs the latter scenes in *Playtime*—beginning at night in a new restaurant called the Royal Garden, and continuing the next morning in a drugstore and on the streets of Paris—is made unthinkable by mobile phones, whose use can be said to constitute both a depletion and a form of denial of public space, especially because the people using them tend to ignore the other people in immediate physical proximity to them.

Moreover, the dystopian vision of alienated and alienating public space in *The World* also posits a single, utopian form of escape that is tied to these phones and expressed by the film's abrupt shifts into animation. One might say, however, that the same mobile phones providing a mental escape from the public spaces of *The World* have also obliterated the sense of shared public space that made Tati's vision of utopia possible. On the other hand, they also express and seemingly establish, if only temporarily, a kind of shared private space that otherwise seems very difficult for the characters in *The World* to achieve in other circumstances. Indeed, just about the only sustained intimacy that we find in the film, apart from the kind established through text messaging, is the friendship between Tao (Zhao Tao), the heroine, a professional dancer at the park, and an exploited fellow dancer from Russia named Anna (Alla Chtcherbakova). And significantly, these characters do not speak a word of one another's language.

I have little doubt that Tati, if he were alive today, could and probably would construct wonderful gags involving the uses of mobile phones. But I do not think he would be able to envision the public reclaiming community space in a modern city in quite the same way that he imagined this in the 1960s. More specifically, if he were making *Playtime* today, I suspect he would most likely be inventing gags that involve mobile phones in the first part, and then would have to find a way of destroying or at least disempowering those phones in order to make way for the utopian creation of a community with a shared communal space in his second part.

Playtime, shot in 70mm, often makes use of multiple and sometimes even conflicting focal points in order to grant the viewer an unusual amount of freedom and creative participation in scanning the screen for narrative details. Virtually the entire film is set over a 24-hour period, following a group of American tourists in Paris from the time they arrive inside Orly airport at the beginning until the time they leave for the airport the next morning. And the overall visual structure, as was described by Tati himself, develops from an urban landscape of straight lines and right angles that gradually becomes curved and then round as the regimentation of both the architecture and various daytime rituals give way to a more relaxed, spontaneous, and festive atmosphere.

Within this world, there is no real hero or central character. Tati's Monsieur Hulot, who is just one figure in the crowd, appears at an office building early in the film in order to meet an executive for some unstated reason. They quickly lose sight of one another, and their day becomes a painful series of missed connections, where the architecture itself—in particular the spatial confusions created by reflections in glass panes—seems to conspire in their mutual disorientation. There are also many other male characters who resemble Hulot in terms of their height, weight, and dress, especially from a distance, adding to the executive's disorientation as well as our own, and thereby illustrating Tati's own democratic and non-hierarchical theory of comedy in which, as he put it, "the comic effect belongs to everyone." Most of the film's second half is set at a brand-new restaurant on its opening night, the aforementioned Royal Garden, where connections between people rather than disconnections predominate. Hulot, who finally runs into the executive on the street at night, purely by chance, also re-encounters an old army buddy now working at the restaurant, who brings him along; the restaurant's decor gradually comes loose and falls apart, and the people there, including the employees as well as the clientele, take over the place, so that a kind of anarchistic and carnivalesque atmosphere prevails where public space essentially becomes reclaimed and reinvented.

All the main characters in *The World* are employees working at a theme park that features simulacra of famous sights around the world such as the Taj Mahal, the Leaning Tower of Pisa, the Parthenon, and even Lower Manhattan with the World Trade Center towers still intact. The two main characters are a couple, the aforementioned Tao and Taisheng (Chen Taisheng), a security guard. Both of them, like Jia himself, come from Fenyang, a small rural town in northern China's Shanxi province where they were already a couple (and where Jia's three previous features were shot). Tao came to Beijing first, eventually followed by Taisheng, and their relationship now is much more tenuous than it was in Fenyang. Taisheng eventually betrays her with an older woman named Qun (Yi-qun Wang) who works outside the theme park in a sweatshop, making clothes that are precise imitations of brand-name items found in a fashion catalog. She works, in other words, in a business that is equally involved with simulacra.

Given all the grandiose dance numbers and other kinds of performances that we see at the theme park, all of which are based on representing ersatz versions of various foreign nationalities, *The World* can be regarded in some ways as a backstage musical. It is also a failed love story in which it is suggested that the synthetic environment where these characters work plays a role in making serious relationships difficult. Significantly, in *Playtime*, dance is seen playing a substantial role in bringing people together at the Royal Garden, and while nothing that qualifies as a love story develops, one nevertheless finds a kind of chaste romantic flirtation between a young woman named Barbara (Barbara Denneke) and Hulot—one that is partially thwarted when the mazelike obstructions in a shop prevent Hulot from delivering a going-away present to her before she departs on her bus. Hulot, however, succeeds in getting one of the "false Hulots", a younger version of himself, to deliver it to her just in time—a very touching illustration of the generosity of Tati's democratic vision whereby one Hulot can readily be replaced or supplanted by another.[2]

It is possible that the utopian vision expressed by Tati of a universal urban experience that can be transcended by an international community is no longer plausible in the same fashion—because even if the same technology is shared around the world, the social meaning of that technology can differ enormously from one culture to the next. There are times when I think that people around the globe have more in common today than they have ever had before at any other time in history—if only because the globe is being run by the same people and corporations who are doing the same things everywhere. This idea is in fact already anticipated and satirized in *Playtime* by the posters we see in a travel agency extolling the virtues of various countries around the world. Each of these posters features an identical anonymous skyscraper resembling all of those that we see in *Playtime*'s version of Paris, where the more celebrated emblems of the past—the Eiffel Tower, Concorde, Sacre Coeur—seem to survive only as reflections on glass panes.

But there are other times when I think more pessimistically that we are kept further apart than we ever were before—subdivided into separate target audiences, markets, and DVD zones, territorialized into separate classes and cultures—in spite of our common experiences. This suggests that the technology that supposedly links us all together via phones and computers is actually keeping us all further apart, and not only from each other but also, in a sense, from ourselves. In other words, our sense of our own identities, including especially our social identities, becomes fragmented and compartmentalized, with the operations of Internet chat groups providing a major illustration of this trend.

Perhaps this paradox about so-called "communications" impeding communication has always been the case. But I think the example of mobile phones illustrates such a cultural difference more vividly than any of Tati's examples, which are mainly related to architecture. Personally, I despise mobile phones when I encounter other people using them on the buses and streets of Chicago, because I experience them as a rejection of myself as a fellow passenger or pedestrian. One used to assume, whenever one saw a person walking down the street speaking loudly to no one in particular, that this person was insane. Nowadays one commonly assumes that this same person is a sane individual speaking to someone else on a phone, but it might also be possible to assume that the implied rejection of one's immediate surroundings suggests another kind of insanity, based no less on an antisocial form of behavior.

Yet I have to acknowledge that for a young person who lives with her or his family and feels in desperate need of some kind of privacy, a mobile phone may also represent a kind of liberation. And for the characters we encounter in *The World* whose private spaces are invariably drab and unattractive, even if they spend most of their waking hours in the utopian spaces of a theme park, it seems that the only dreams that can truly belong to them as individuals are the ones that they can transmit on mobile phones to one another via instant messaging. Indeed, according to a front-page story in the *New York Times* by Jim Yardley (April 25, 2005),

> About 27 percent of China's 1.3 billion people own a cell
> phone, a rate that is far higher in big cities, particularly

among the young. Indeed, for upwardly mobile young urbanites, cell phones and the Internet are the primary means of communication.

I guess I am a universalist in Tati's sense in so far as I can view a film such as *The World* as being about what is happening in the world right now and not simply about what is happening in China—just as I can view *Playtime* as a film about the world in 1967 and not simply about France. In fact, I regard both films as being in advance of their own times, even literally so. *Playtime* was shot before France had parking meters, but Tati knew they were coming so he included them in his giant set. I do not know exactly what Jia is predicting about the future of either China or the world, but I think he feels the shock of capitalism more keenly in some ways than many of us currently do in the West, and out of that shock grows a need for a different kind of fantasy. His view is certainly much bleaker, because whereas for Tati utopia was a reinvention of what we already have, Jia sees it, in the shape of a theme park, as an emblem of something we have already lost.[3]

notes

1. I was privileged to work for Tati in Paris as a "script consultant" for a little over a week in early 1973. For more details, as well as some extended material about *Playtime*, see Jonathan Rosenbaum, "Tati's Democracy," *Film Comment* (May–June 1973): 36–41; Rosenbaum, "The Death of Hulot," *Sight and Sound* (Spring 1983): 94–97. An excerpt from the former, introducing an interview with Tati, is reprinted in revised form in my collection *Movies as Politics* (Berkeley, CA: University of California Press, 1997); the latter is reprinted in my collection *Placing Movies: The Practice of Film Criticism* (Berkeley, CA: University of California Press, 1995).
2. In his biography of Tati, David Bellos reveals that Tati was in fact romantically involved with Denneke—a German au pair who had worked for neighbors of his—during part of the shooting of *Playtime*. See David Bellos, *Jacques Tati* (London: Harvill Press, 1999), 265.
3. This essay is derived from a lecture given on the final day of "Urban Trauma and the Metropolitan Imagination," a conference organized by Scott Bukatman and Pavle Levi and held at Stanford University on May 5–7, 2005.

selected bibliography

Abel, Richard. *The Red Rooster Scare: Making Cinema American 1900–1910.* Berkeley, CA: University of California Press, 1999.

Abu-Lughod, Janet. *Before European Hegemony: The World System A.D. 1250–1350.* New York: Oxford University Press, 1989.

Acland, Charles. *Screen Traffic: Movies, Multiplexes, and Global Culture.* Durham, NC: Duke University Press, 2003.

Adorno, Theodor W. *Critical Models: Interventions and Catchwords,* trans. Henry W. Pickford. New York: Columbia University Press, 1998.

Agrasánchez Film Archives. "History of the Archives," 2002. www.agrasfilms. com/nav4/archives.htm.

Ain-ling, Wong. "In the Land of Fallen Souls," in *Shimizu Hiroshi: 101st Anniversary,* ed. Kinnia Yau, Li Cheuk-to et al. Hong Kong: Hong Kong International Film Festival Society, 2004.

Alexander, Jocelyn, JoAnn McGregor, and Terence Ranger. *Violence and Memory: One Hundred Years in the "Dark Forests" of Matabeleland, Zimbabwe.* Oxford: James Curry, 2000.

Altman, Rick, ed. *Sound Theory/Sound Practice.* New York: Routledge, 1992.

——— . *Silent Film Sound.* New York: Columbia University Press, 2004.

The American Film Institute Catalog of Motion Pictures Produced in the United States Feature Films, 1961–1970. Berkeley, CA: University of California Press, 1997.

Amselle, Jean-Loup. *L'Art de la friche: Essai sur l'art africain contemporain*. Paris: Flammarion, 2005.

An, Jinsoo. *"The Killer*: Cult Film and Transcultural (Mis)Reading," in *At Full Speed: Hong Kong Cinema in a Borderless World*, ed. Esther C.M. Yau. Minneapolis, MN: University of Minnesota Press, 2001, 95–113.

Anderson, Benedict. *The Spectre of Comparison: Nationalism, Southeast Asia and the World*. London: Verso, 1998.

Andrew, Dudley, and Steven Ungar. "*Esprit* in the Arena of Extremist Politics" and "Conclusion as Forecast," in *Popular Front Paris and the Poetics of Culture*. Cambridge, MA: Harvard University Press, 2005.

Appadurai, Arjun. *Modernity at Large: Cultural Dimensions of Globalization*. Minneapolis, MN: University of Minnesota Press, 1996.

———. ed. *Globalization*. Durham, NC: Duke University Press, 2001.

Appiah, Kwame Anthony. *Cosmopolitanism: Ethics in a World of Strangers*. New York: W.W. Norton, 2006.

Applebaum, Richard, and William Robinson, eds. *Critical Globalization Studies*. New York: Routledge, 2005.

Apter, Emily. "Global *Translatio*: The 'Invention' of Comparative Literature, Istanbul 1933," in *Debating World Literature*, ed. Christopher Prendergast. New York: Verso, 2004, 76–109.

Archer, Gleason L. *History of Radio to 1926*. New York: Arno Press and New York Times, 1971.

Armero, Álvaro. *Una aventura Americana: españoles en Hollywood*. Madrid: Compañía Literaria, 1995.

Arnove, Robert Frederick and Harvey Graff, eds. *National Literacy Campaigns: Historical and Comparative Perspectives*. New York: Plenum Press, 1987.

Arrighi, Giovanni. *The Long Twentieth Century: Money, Power, and the Origins of our Times*. London: Verso, 1994.

Attali, Jacques. *Noise: The Political Economy of Music*. Minneapolis, MN: University of Minnesota Press, 1984.

Augé, Marc. *Non-Places: Introduction to an Anthropology of Supermodernity*. London: Verso, 1995.

Balio, Tino. " 'A Major Presence in All of the World's Important Markets': The Globalization of Hollywood in the 1990s," in *Contemporary Hollywood Cinema*, ed. Steve Neale and Murray Smith. London: Routledge, 1998, 58–73.

Balsebre, Armand. *Historia de la radio en España. I, II*. Madrid: Cátedra, 2001.

Bao, Weihong. "From Pearl White to White Rose Woo: Tracing the Vernacular Body of 'nüxia' in Chinese Silent Cinema, 1927–1931," *Camera Obscura* 20, no. 3 (2005): 193–231.

Barber, Karin. "Popular Arts in Africa." *African Studies Review* 30, no. 3 (1987): 1–78.

———. ed. *Readings in African Popular Culture*. Bloomington, IN: Indiana University Press, 1997.

Bardèche, Maurice, and Robert Brasillach. *Histoire du cinéma*. Paris: Denoël & Steele, 1935.

Barlet, Olivier. "Postcolonialisme et cinéma: de la différence à la relation," in "Postcolonialisme: inventaire et débats," special issue, *Africultures*, no. 28 (May 2000): 56–65.

———. "Les nouvelles écritures francophones des cinéastes afro-européens," in "Ecritures dans les cinémas d'Afrique noire," ed. Boulou Ebanda de B'béri, *CiNéMAS* 11, no. 1 (2000).

——. "Les nouvelles stratégies des cinéastes africains," in "L'Africanité en questions," special issue, *Africultures*, no. 41 (October 2001): 69–76.

——. "Du cinéma métis au cinéma nomade: défense du cinéma," in "Métissages: un alibi culturel?" special issue, *Africultures*, no. 62 (January–March 2005): 94–103.

——. "Afrique noire: la fin des salles?" *Cahiers du cinéma*, no. 604 (September 2005): 62–63.

Barnier, Martin. *Des films français made in Hollywood: Les versions multiples 1929–1935.* Paris: L'Harmattan, 2004.

Barthes, Roland. *S/Z*, trans. Richard Miller. London: Jonathan Cape, 1975.

Basel Action Network. *The Digital Dump: Exporting Re-use and Abuse to Africa.* Seattle, WA: Basel Action Network, 2005.

Basel Action Network and Silicon Valley Toxics Coalition. *Exporting Harm: The High-Tech Trashing of Asia.* Seattle, WA: Basel Action Network, 2002.

Bayma, Todd. "Art World Culture and Institutional Choices: The Case of Experimental Film," *Sociological Quarterly* 36, no. 1 (1995): 79–95.

Bazin, André. *Cinéma 53 à travers le monde.* Paris: Cerf, 1954.

——. "Le Festival de Cannes 1946," in *Le Cinéma de l'occupation et de la résistance.* Paris: 10/18, 1975, 166–72.

Becker, Wolfgang. *Film und Herrschaft: Organisationsprinzipen und Organisationsstrukturen der nationalsozialistischen Filmpropaganda.* Berlin: Volker Spiess, 1973.

Bello, Walden. *Deglobalization: Ideas for a New Economy.* London: Zed, 2002.

Bellos, David. *Jacques Tati.* London: Harvill Press, 1999.

Benjamin, Walter. *Illuminations: Essays and Reflections*, ed. and introd. Hannah Arendt, trans. Harry Zohn. New York: Schocken, 1969.

——. *The Arcades Project*, trans. Howard Eiland and Kevin McLaughlin. Cambridge, MA: Belknap Press of Harvard University Press, 1999.

Bernardi, JoAnn. *Writing in Light: The Silent Scenario and the Japanese Pure Film Movement.* Detroit, MI: Wayne State University Press, 2001.

Berry, Chris. "If China Can Say No, Can China Make Movies? Or, Do Movies Make China? Rethinking National Cinema and National Agency," *Boundary 2* 25, no. 3 (1998): 129–50.

Berry, Chris, and Mary Farquhar. *China on Screen: Cinema and Nation.* New York: Columbia University Press, 2005.

Bessière, Irène and Roger Odin, eds., *Les Européens dans le cinéma américain: Émigration et exil.* Paris: Presses Sorbonne Nouvelle, 2004.

Betz, Mark. "The Name above the (Sub)Title: Internationalism, Coproduction, and Polyglot European Art Cinema," *Camera Obscura* 46, no. 16.1 (2001): 1–44.

Blinn, Miika. "The Dubbing Standard: Its History and Efficiency Implications for Film Distributors in the German Film Market," IME Working Papers on Intellectual, no. 57, Dynamics of Institutions and Markets in Europe, www.dime-eu.org/files/active/0/WP57-IPR.pdf.

Bois, Yve-Alain and Krauss, Rosalind. *Formless: A User's Guide.* New York: Zone Books, 1997.

Bolter, Jay David. "Remediation and the Language of New Media," *Northern Lights* 5, no. 1 (2008): 25–37, www.intellectbooks.co.uk/journalarticles.php?issn=1601829X&v=5&i=1&d=10.1386/nl.5.1.25_1.

Bonet, Lluís, and Albert de Gregorio. "La industria cultural española en América Latina," in *Las industrias culturales en la integración latinoamericana*, ed. Néstor García Canclini and Carlos Moncloa. Mexico: Grijalbo, 1999, 87–128.

Bordwell, David. *Ozu and the Poetics of Cinema.* Princeton, NJ: Princeton University Press, 1988.

———. "Visual Style in Japanese Cinema, 1925–1945," *Film History: An International Journal* 7, no. 1 (1995): 5–31.

———. *On the History of Film Style.* Cambridge, MA: Harvard University Press, 1997.

———. *Planet Hong Kong: Popular Cinema and the Art of Entertainment.* Cambridge, MA: Harvard University Press, 2000.

———. "Aesthetics in Action: *Kungfu,* Gunplay, and Cinematic Expressivity," in Yau, *At Full Speed,* 2001, 73–93.

Bordwell, David, Janet Staiger, and Kristin Thompson. *Classical Hollywood Cinema: Film Style and Mode of Production to 1960.* New York: Columbia University Press, 1985.

Breckenridge, Carol A., Sheldon Pollock, Homi K. Bhabha, and Dipesh Chakrabarty, eds. *Cosmopolitanism.* Durham, NC: Duke University Press, 2002.

Brenez, Nicole. "The Secrets of Movement: The Influence of Hong Kong Action Cinema upon the Contemporary French Avant-Garde." In Morris, Li, and Ching-kiu, *Hong Kong Connections,* 2005, 163–73, 310–11.

Brennan, Juan Antonio. "La música cinematográfica." *Cinémas Amérique Latine* 8 (2000): 20–26.

Brennan, Timothy. *At Home in the World: Cosmopolitanism Now.* Cambridge, MA: Harvard University Press, 1997.

Brenner, Robert. "The Economics of Global Turbulence." *New Left Review* 229 (May–June 1998).

Brown, Bill. "Global Bodies/Postnationalities: Charles Johnson's Consumer Culture," *Representations* 58 (Spring 1997): 24–48.

———. "The Secret Life of Things (Virginia Woolf and the Matter of Modernism)," *Modernism/Modernity* 6 (April 1999): 1–28.

———. "Thing Theory," in *Things,* ed. Bill Brown. Chicago, IL: University of Chicago Press, 2004.

Browne, Nick. "Society and Subjectivity: On the Political Economy of Chinese Melodrama," in *New Chinese Cinemas,* ed. Nick Browne et al. Cambridge: Cambridge University Press, 1994.

Brunella, Elisabetta. "Old-World Moviegoing: Theatrical Distribution of European Films in the United States," *Film Journal International* (March 2001): 28–32.

Brunetta, Gian Piero, ed. *Storia del cinema mondiale,* vols. I–IV. Torino, Italy: Einaudi, 1999–2001.

Buck-Morss, Susan. *Dreamworld and Catastrophe: The Passing of Mass Utopia in the East and West.* Cambridge, MA: MIT Press, 2000.

Budde, Gunilla, Sebastian Conrad, and Oliver Janz, eds. *Transnationale Geschichte: Themen, Tendenzen und Theorien.* Göttingen, Germany: Vandenhoeck & Ruprecht, 2006.

Burdeau, Emmanuel. "Une lecture de Quentin Tarantino," *Cahiers du Cinéma,* no. 591 (June 2004).

Burton-Carvajal, Julianne. "Mexican Melodramas of Patriarchy: Specificity of a Transcultural Form," in *Framing Latin American Cinema: Contemporary Critical Perspectives,* ed. Ann Marie Stock, trans. Ambrosio Fornet. Minneapolis, MN: University of Minnesota Press, 1997, 186–234.

Butler, Judith. *Excitable Speech: A Politics of the Performative.* London: Routledge, 1997.

Calvet, Louis-Jean. "Vernaculaire," in *Sociolinguistique: Concepts de base,* ed. Marie-Louise Moreau. Liège, Belgium: Mardaga, 1997, 291–92.

Castro, Donald S. "Popular Culture as a Source for the Historian: Why Carlos Gardel?" *Studies in Latin American Popular Culture* 5 (1986): 144–62.

Catholic Commission for Justice and Peace/Legal Resources Foundation. *Breaking the Silence, Building True Peace: A Report on the Disturbances in Matabeleland and the Midlands, 1980–1988.* Harare: Catholic Commission for Justice and Peace/Legal Resources Foundation, 1997.

Cavell, Stanley. *The World Viewed: Reflections on the Ontology of Film.* New York: Viking, 1971.

Cazdyn, Eric. "A New Line of Geometry," in *Subtitles: On the Foreignness of Film,* ed. Egoyan and Balfour, 2005, 403–19.

Chakrabarty, Dipesh. *Provincializing Europe: Postcolonial Thought and Historical Difference.* Princeton, NJ: Princeton University Press, 2000.

Chanan, Michael. *The Cuban Image.* London: British Film Institute, 1985.

Chang, Eileen. *Written on Water,* trans. Andrew Jones, coed. Nicole Huang. New York: Columbia University Press, 2005.

Charensol, Georges. "Cinéma américain, cinéma européen." *Formes et Couleurs,* no. 6 (1946).

Chartier, Roger. "Texts, Printings, Readings," in *The New Cultural History,* ed. Lynn Hunt. Berkeley, CA: University of California Press, 1989, 154–75.

Chase-Dunn, Christopher. *Global Formation: Structures of the World-Economy.* Oxford: Basil Blackwell, 1989.

Chatterjee, Gayatri. *Awara.* New Delhi: Penguin, 2003.

Chatterjee, Partha. "Beyond the Nation? Or Within?" *Social Text* 16, no. 56 (1998): 57–69.

Chaudhuri, K.N. *Asia Before Europe: Economy and Civilization of the Indian Ocean from the Rise of Islam to 1750.* Cambridge: Cambridge University Press, 1991.

Chen, Kuan-Hsing. "Introduction: The Decolonization Question," in *Trajectories: Inter-Asia Cultural Studies,* ed. Chen et al. New York: Routledge, 1998, 1–53.

Cheuk-to, Li, ed. *Cantonese Melodrama, 1950–1969: The Tenth Hong Kong International Film Festival.* Hong Kong: Urban Council of Hong Kong, 1986.

Chifunyise, Stephen. "Trends in Zimbabwean Theatre Since 1980," in Gunner, *Politics and Performance,* 55–73.

Chitauro, Moreblessings, Caleb Dube, and Liz Gunner. "Song, Story and Nation: Women as Singers and Actresses in Zimbabwe," in Gunner, *Politics and Performance,* 1995, 111–38.

Chow, Rey. *Primitive Passions: Visuality, Sexuality, Ethnography, and Contemporary Chinese Cinema.* New York: Columbia University Press, 1995.

————. *The Age of the World Target: Self-Referentiality in War, Theory, and Comparative Work.* Durham, NC: Duke University Press, 2005.

Cinema & Cie, devoted to multiple and multilingual versions: no. 4 (Spring 2004), no. 6 (Spring 2005), no. 7 (Fall 2005).

Cobbing, Julian. "The Ndebele under the Khumalos, 1820–96." PhD dissertation, University of Lancaster, 1976.

Collier, Simon. "Carlos Gardel and the Cinema," in *The Garden of Forking Paths: Argentine Cinema,* ed. John King and Nissa Torrents. London: British Film Institute, 1988, 15–22.

Comaroff, Jean, and John Comaroff. "Ethnography on an Awkward Scale: Postcolonial Anthropology and the Violence of Abstraction," *Ethnography* 4, no. 2 (2003): 147–79.

Cook, David A. *History of the American Cinema,* Vol. 9, *Lost Illusions: American Cinema in the Shadow of Watergate and Vietnam, 1970–1979.* Berkeley, CA: University of California Press, 2000.

Corrigan, Tim, and Patricia White. *The Film Experience: An Introduction*. New York: Bedford/St. Martin's, 2004.

Cosandey, Roland and François Albera, eds. *Cinéma sans frontières 1896–1918 / Images across Borders*. Lausanne: Payot, 1995.

Coward, Rosalind, and John Ellis. *Language and Materialism: Developments in the Semiology and Theory of the Subject*. London: Routledge & Kegan Paul, 1977.

Creekmur, Corey. "Picturizing American Cinema: Hindi Film Songs and the Last Days of Genre," in *Soundtrack Available: Essays on Film and Popular Culture*, ed. Pamela Robertson Wojcik and Arthur Knight. Durham, NC: Duke University Press, 2001, 375–406.

Crofts, Stephen. "Reconceptualizing National Cinema/s," *Quarterly Review of Film and Video* 14, no. 3 (1993): 49–67.

———. "Concepts of National Cinema," in *The Oxford Guide to Film Studies*, ed. John Hill and Pamela Church Gibson. Oxford: Oxford University Press, 1998, 385–94.

Cronin, Michael. *Translation and Globalization*. New York: Routledge, 2004.

Curtius, Ernst Robert. *European Literature and the Latin Middle Ages*, 1953. Princeton, NJ: Princeton University Press, 1990.

Dall'Asta, Monica. *Un cinéma muscle*. Crisnée, Belgium: Yellow Now, 1992.

Danan, Martine. "From Nationalism to Globalization: France's Challenge to Hollywood's Hegemony." PhD dissertation, Michigan Technological University, 1994.

———. "From a 'Prenational' to a 'Postnational' French Cinema," *Film History* 8, no. 1 (1996): 72–84.

———. "National and Post-National French Cinema," in *Theorising National Cinema*, ed. Paul Willemen and Valentina Vitali. London: British Film Institute, 2006, 172–85.

Daney, Serge. *La Rampe: Cahiers critique 1970–1982*. Paris: Cahiers du Cinéma, 1983.

———. *L'Exercise, a été profitable, monsieur*. Paris: POL, 1993.

———. "Cinéphile en voyage," in *Persévérance*. Paris: POL, 1994.

———. "From Movies to Moving," *Documenta Documents*, no. 2 (1996): 76–79.

Daniels, Bill, David Leedy, and Steven D. Sills. *Movie Money: Understanding Hollywood's (Creative) Accounting Practices*. Los Angeles, CA: Silman-James Press, 1998.

Dávila, Arlene. *Latinos Inc.: The Marketing and Making of a People*. Berkeley, CA: University of California Press, 2001.

Davis, Natalie. *The Gift in Sixteenth-Century France*. Madison, WI: University of Wisconsin Press, 2000.

Debray, Régis. *Critique of Political Reason*, trans. David Macey. London: Verso, 1981.

de Grazia, Victoria. "Americanism for Export," *Wedge* 7–8 (Winter–Spring 1985): 74–81.

———. "Mass Culture and Sovereignty: The American Challenge to European Cinemas," *Journal of Modern History* 61, no. 1 (1989): 53–87.

———. *Irresistible Empire: America's Advance through 20th-Century Europe*. Cambridge, MA: Harvard University Press, 2005.

de la Calle, Luis. "Innovación y creatividad de película para el desarrollo," *El Semanario*, December 4, 2007.

de la Vega Alvaro, Eduardo. "Aventurera," in *Tierra en trance: el cine latinoamericano en 100 películas*, ed. Alberto Elena and Marina Díaz López. Madrid: Alianza, 1999, 99–103.

———. "Allá en el Rancho Grande, Over There on the Big Ranch," in *The Cinema of Latin America*, ed. Alberto Elena and Marina Díaz López. London: Wallflower Press, 2002, 25–33.

Deleuze, Gilles. *L'Image-Mouvement*. Paris: Minuit, 1983.

de Valck, Marijke. "Film Festivals: History and Theory of a European Phenomenon that Became a Global Network." PhD dissertation, University of Amsterdam, 2006.

Derrida, Jacques. *Given Time*, trans. Peggy Kamuf. Chicago, IL: University of Chicago Press, 1992.

Diawara, Manthia. "The Present Situation of the Film Industry in Anglophone Africa." Reprinted from "African Cinema: Politics and Culture," in *African Experiences of Cinema*, ed. Imruh Bakari and Mbye Cham. London: British Film Institute, 1996, 102–11.

——. "L'Autoreprésentation dans le cinéma africain," in *Africa Remix: L'art contemporain d'un continent, catalogue de l'exposition*, ed. Simon Njami. Paris: Editions de Centre Pompidou, 2005, 285–91.

Díaz López, Marina. "La comedia ranchera como género musical," *Cinémas Amérique Latine* 8 (2000): 27–40.

Dimendberg, Edward. *Film Noir and the Spaces of Modernity*. Cambridge, MA: Harvard University Press, 2004.

Dimerstein, Gilberto. *Brésil: La Guerre des Enfants*. Paris: Fayard, 1991.

Dissanayake, Wimal, ed. *Cinema and Cultural Identity: Reflections on Films from Japan, India, and China*. Lanham, MD: University Press of America, 1988.

——, ed. *Melodrama and Asian Cinema*. Cambridge: Cambridge University Press, 1993.

Distelmeyer, Jan, ed. *Babylon in FilmEuropa: Mehrsprachen-Versionen der 1930er Jahre*. Munich: edition text + kritik, 2006.

Dodd, Carley H. *Dynamics of Intercultural Communication*. Boston, MA: McGraw-Hill, 1998.

Domenig, Roland. "Anticipation of Freedom: The ATG and Japanese Independent Cinema," *Midnight Eye*, June 26, 2004, www.midnighteye.com/features/art-theatre-guild.shtml.

Driscoll, Mark. "Reverse Postcoloniality," *Social Text* 22, no. 78 (2004): 59–84.

Ďurovičová, Nataša. "Local Ghosts: Dubbing Bodies in Early Sound Cinema," in *Il film e I suoi multipli / Film and its Multiples*, ed. Anna Antonini. IX Convegno Internazionale di Studi sul Cinema. Forum: Udine, 2003, 83–98.

——. "*Los Toquis!* Or, Urban Babel," in *Global Cities: Cinema, Architecture, and Urbanism in a Digital Age*, ed. Linda Krause and Patrice Petro. New Brunswick, NJ: Rutgers University Press, 2003, 71–86.

——. "Paramount und das homöostatische Moment: MLV-Produktion in Joinville," in *Babylon in Europa: Mehrsprachen-Versionen der 1930en Jahre*, ed. Jan Distelmeyer. Munich: text+kritik, 2006, 65–78.

Egoyan, Atom and Ian Balfour, eds. *Subtitles: On the Foreignness of Film*. Cambridge, MA: MIT Press, 2005.

Ehrlich, Linda C., and David Desser, eds. *Cinematic Landscapes: Observations on the Visual Arts and Cinema of China and Japan*. Austin, TX: University of Texas Press, 1994.

Eley, Geoff, and Ronald Grigor Suny, eds. *Becoming National*. Oxford: Oxford University Press, 1996.

Elsaesser, Thomas. *Early Cinema: Space Frame Narrative*. London: British Film Institute, 1990.

——. "Going Live Body and Voice in Early Sound Cinema." In *Le Son en perspective / New Perspectives in Sound Studies*, ed. Dominique Nasta and Didier Huvelle. Berlin: Peter Lang, 2004, 155–68.

————. *European Cinema: Face to Face with Hollywood*. Amsterdam: Amsterdam University Press, 2005.

Espiritu, Talitha. "Multiculturalism, Dictatorship and Cinema Vanguards: Philippine and Brazilian Analogies," in Shohat and Stam, *Multiculturalism, Postcoloniality and Transnational Media*, 2003, 279–98.

Faber, Ronald J., Thomas C. O'Guinn, and Andrew P. Hardy. "Art Films in the Suburbs: A Comparison of Popular and Art Film Audiences," in *Current Research in Film: Audiences, Economics, and Law*, Vol. 4, ed. Bruce A. Austin. Norwood, NJ: Ablex, 1988, 45–53.

Fawaz, Leila, C.A. Bayly and Robert Ilbert, eds. *Modernity and Culture from the Mediterranean to the Indian Ocean, 1890–1920*. New York: Columbia University Press, 2001.

Finkielman, Jorge. *The Film Industry in Argentina*. Jefferson, NC: McFarland Press, 2004.

Flores, Juan. *From Bomba to Hip-Hop: Puerto Rican Culture and Latino Identity*. New York: Columbia University Press, 2000.

Fore, Steve. "Golden Harvest Films and the Hong Kong Movie Industry in the Realm of Globalization," *Velvet Light Trap* (Fall 1994): 40–59.

Foucault, Michel. *Society Must Be Defended: Lectures at the Collège de France 1975–6*, trans. David Macey. New York: Picador, 1997.

Frank, André Gunder. *ReOrient: Global Economy in the Asian Age*. Berkeley, CA: University of California Press, 1998.

Frank, Robert H., and Philip J. Cook. *The Winner-Take-All Society: How More and More Americans Compete for Ever Fewer and Bigger Prizes, Encouraging Economic Waste, Income Inequality, and an Impoverished Cultural Life*. New York: Free Press, 1995.

Friedman, Susan Stanford. "Definitional Excursions: The Meanings of *Modern/Modernity/Modernism*," *Modernism/Modernity* 8, no. 3 (2001): 493–513.

Frodon, Jean-Michel. *La Projection nationale: Cinéma et nation*. Paris: Odile Jacob, 1998.

Fu, Poshek. "Going Global: A Cultural History of the Shaw Brothers Studio, 1960–1970," in *Hong Kong Cinema Retrospective: Border Crossings in Hong Kong Cinema*, ed. Law Kar. Hong Kong: The 24th Hong Kong International Film Festival, 2000, 43–51.

————. *Between Shanghai and Hong Kong: The Politics of Chinese Cinemas*. Stanford, CA: Stanford University Press, 2003.

Fuguet, Alberto. "Magical Neoliberalism." *Foreign Policy*, no. 125 (2001): 66–73.

Furhammar, Leif. *Från skapelsen till Edvard Persson*. Mt Pleasant, SC: Wiksell & Wiksell, 1970.

Gaines, Jane. "Machines that Make the Body Do Things," in *More Dirty Looks: Gender, Pornography and Power*, ed. Pamela Church Gibson. London: British Film Institute, 2004.

Galán, Diego. "El doblaje obligatorio", http://cvc.cervantes.es/obref/ anuario/ anuario_03/galan/p04.htm

Gamal, Mohammad Y. "Egypt's Audiovisual Translation Scene," *Arab Media and Society* (May 2008), www.arabmediasociety.com/?article=675.

Gambier, Yves and Henrik Gottlieb, eds. *(Multi)Media Translations: Concepts, Practices, and Research*. Amsterdam: Benjamins, 2001.

Gaonkar, Dilip Parameshwar. "On Alternative Modernities," introduction to special issue, *Public Culture* 11, no. 1 (1999): 1–18.

García Canclini, Néstor. *La globalización imaginada*. Mexico: Paidós Mexicana, 1999.

—————. *Consumers and Citizens: Globalization and Multicultural Conflicts.* Minneapolis, MN: University of Minnesota Press, 2001.

—————. *Diferentes, Desiguales y Desconectados: Mapas de la interculturalidad.* Barcelona: Gedisa, 2004.

García Riera, Emilio. *Historia documental del cine mexicano,* Vol. I: 1929–37. Guadalajara, Mexico: Universidad de Guadalajara, 1992.

Gebauer, Gunter, and Christoph Wulf. *Mimesis: Culture—Art—Society,* trans. Don Reneau. Berkeley, CA: University of California Press, 1995.

Gerow, Aaron. *Modeling Spectators: Cinema, Japan, Modernity 1895–1925.* Berkeley, CA: University of California Press, forthcoming.

Getino, Octavio. *La tercera mirada: Panorama del audiovisual latinoamericano.* Buenos Aires: Paidós, 1996.

Ghosh, Amitva. *In an Antique Land: History in the Guise of a Traveler's Tale.* New York: Random House, 1992; New York: Vintage, 1994.

Giddens, Anthony. *The Constitution of Society: Outline of the Theory of Structuration.* Berkeley, CA: University of California Press, 1984.

Glissant, Edouard. *Les Grands entretiens du Cercle de Minuit.* Interviewed by Laure Adler and Thérèse Lombard, program directed by Pierre Desfons, France 2 télévision.

Godzich, Wlad. *The Culture of Literacy.* Cambridge, MA: Harvard University Press, 1994.

Goldberg, Fred. *Motion Picture Marketing and Distribution: Getting Movies to a Theatre Near You.* Boston, MA: Focal Press, 1991.

Goldstein, Joshua. "The Remains of the Everyday: One Hundred Years of Recycling in Beijing," in *Everyday Modernity in China,* ed. J. Goldstein and Madeleine Yue Dong. Seattle, WA: University of Washington, 2006.

Gomery, Douglas. *Shared Pleasures: A History of Movie Presentation in the United States.* Madison, WI: University of Wisconsin Press, 1992.

Guha, Ramachandra. *Environmentalism: A Global History.* New York: Longman, 1999.

Guneratne, Anthony R. and Wimal Dissayanake, eds. *Rethinking Third Cinema.* New York: Routledge, 2003.

Gunner, Liz, ed. *Politics and Performance: Theatre, Poetry and Song in Southern Africa.* Johannesburg: Witwatersrand University Press, 1995.

Gunning, Tom. "Modernity and Cinema: A Culture of Shocks and Flows," in *Cinema and Modernity,* ed. Murray Pomerance. New Brunswick, NJ: Rutgers University Press, 2006.

Güvenç, Bozkurt. "Vernacular Architecture as a Paradigm Case," in *Vernacular Architecture,* ed. Mete Turan. Aldershot, UK: Avebury, 1990.

Guzman, Anthony. "The Exhibition and Reception of European Films in the United States during the 1920s." PhD dissertation, University of California at Los Angeles, 1993.

Hage, Ghassan. *White Nation: Fantasies of White Supremacy in a Multicultural Society.* London: Routledge, 2000.

Hannerz, Ulf. *Cultural Complexity: Studies in the Social Organization of Meaning.* New York: Columbia University Press, 1992.

Hansen, Janine. "The New Earth, a German-Japanese Misalliance in Film," in *In Praise of Film Studies,* ed. M. Makino, A. Gerow, and M. Nornes. Vancouver: Trafford, 2001.

Hansen, Miriam. *Babel and Babylon: Spectatorship in American Silent Film.* Cambridge, MA: Harvard University Press, 1991.

—————. "The Mass Production of the Senses: Classical Cinema as Vernacular

Modernism," in *Reinventing Film Studies*, ed. Christine Gledhill and Linda Williams. London: Arnold, 2000, 332–50.

———. "Fallen Women, Rising Stars, New Horizons: Shanghai Silent Film as Vernacular Modernism," *Film Quarterly* 54, no. 1 (2000): 10–22.

Hardt, Michael, and Antonio Negri. *Multitude: War and Democracy in the Age of Empire*. London: Penguin, 2004.

Harootunian, Harry. *History's Disquiet: Modernity, Cultural Practices, and the Question of Everyday Life*. New York: Columbia University Press, 2000.

———. *Overcome by Modernity: History, Culture, and Community in Interwar Japan*. Princeton, NJ: Princeton University Press, 2000.

———. "Ghostly Comparisons," *Traces: A Multilingual Series of Cultural Theory and Translation* 3 (2004): 39–52.

Harvey, David. *The Limits to Capital*. London: Verso, 1999.

———. "Cartographic Identities: Geographical Knowledges under Globalization," in *Spaces of Capital: Towards a Critical Cultural Geography*. New York: Routledge, 2001, 208–33.

———. *Spaces of Global Capitalism: Towards a Theory of Uneven Geographical Development*. London: Verso, 2006.

Hay, James. "Piecing Together What Remains of the Cinematic City," in *The Cinematic City*, ed. Dave Clarke. London: Routledge, 1997, 209–29.

Haynes, Jonathan, ed. *Nigerian Video Film*. Athens, OH: Ohio University Press, 2000.

Hayward, Susan. *French National Cinema*. London: Routledge, 1993.

———. "Framing National Cinema," in Hjort and MacKenzie, *Cinema and Nation*, 2000, 81–94.

Heinink, Juan B. and Robert G. Dickson. *Cita en Hollywood: antología de las películas norteamericanas habladas en castellano*. Bilbao: Mensajero, 1990.

Hershfield, Joanne. *Mexican Cinema/Mexican Women 1940–1950*. Tucson, AZ: University of Arizona Press, 1996.

Hess, John, and Patricia R. Zimmerman. "Transnational Documentaries: A Manifesto," in *Transnational Cinema: The Film Reader*, ed. Elizabeth Ezra and Terry Rowden. London: Routledge, 2006, 97–108.

High, Peter B. *The Imperial Screen: Japanese Film Culture in the Fifteen Years' War, 1931–1945*. Madison, WI: University of Wisconsin Press, 2003.

Higson, Andrew. "The Concept of National Cinema," *Screen* 30, no. 1 (1989). 36–46.

———. *Waving the Flag: Constructing a National Cinema in Britain*. Oxford: Oxford University Press, 1995.

———. "The Limiting Imagination of National Cinema," in Hjort and MacKenzie, *Cinema and Nation*, 2000, 63–74.

Hill, John. "The Issue of National Cinema and British Film Production," in *New Questions of British Cinema*, ed. Duncan Petrie. London: British Film Institute, 1992, 10–21.

Himpele, Jeff. "Film Distribution as Media: Mapping Difference in the Bolivian Cinemascape," *Visual Anthropology Review* 12, no. 1 (1996): 47–66.

Hirshman, Albert. *Exit, Voice, and Loyalty*. Cambridge, MA: Harvard University Press, 1970.

Hjort, Mette. "The Globalisation of Dogma: The Dynamics of Metaculture and Counter-Publicity," in *Purity and Provocation*, ed. Mette Hjort and Scott MacKenzie. London: British Film Institute, 2003, 133–57.

———. *Small Nation, Global Cinema: The New Danish Cinema*. Minneapolis, MN: University of Minnesota Press, 2005.

———. "Gifts, Games, and Cheek: Counter-Globalization in a Small-Nation Context," in *Northern Constellations: New Readings in Nordic Cinema*, ed. Claire Thomson. Norwich, UK: Norvik Press, 2006, 111–29.

———. "Denmark," in *The Cinema of Small Nations*, ed. Mette Hjort and Duncan Petrie. Edinburgh: University of Edinburgh Press, 2007, 23–42.

———. ed. *Dekalog: The Five Obstructions*. London: Wallflower Press, 2008.

———. "Affinitive and Milieu-Building Transnationalism: The Advance Party Initiative," in *Cinema at the Periphery: Industries, Narratives, Iconographies*, ed. Dina Iordanova, David Martin-Jones, and Belén Vidal. Detroit, MI: Wayne State University Press, forthcoming.

Hjort, Mette and Scott Mackenzie, eds. *Cinema and Nation*. London: Routledge, 2000.

Hjort, Mette and Duncan Petrie, eds. *The Cinema of Small Nations*. Edinburgh: University of Edinburgh Press, 2007.

Ho, Ng. "Kung Fu Comedies: Tradition, Structure, Character," in *A Study of the Hong Kong Swordplay Film (1945–1980)*, ed. Lau Shing-hon. Hong Kong: International Film Festival/Urban Council, 1981, 42–46.

Hobson, John M. *The Eastern Origins of Western Civilization*. Cambridge: Cambridge University Press, 2004.

"Hong Kong Action Film at the Frontiers of Cinema," http://apache.cscsarchive.org/Hongkong_Action/index.htm.

Hoskins, Colin, Stuart McFadyen, and Adam Finn. *Global Television and Film: An Introduction to the Economics of the Business*. Oxford: Clarendon Press, 1997.

Hu, Brian. "Closed Borders and Open Secrets: Regional Lockout, the Film Industry, and Code-Free DVD Players: A Review of Multi-Region Accessibility on the Philips 642 DVD player," *Mediascapes* (Spring 2006), www.tft.ucla.edu/mediascape/Spring06_ClosedBordersAndOpenSecrets.html.

Hu, Jubin. *Projecting a Nation: Chinese National Cinema before 1949*. Hong Kong: Hong Kong University Press, 2003.

Hüppauf, Bernd. "Spaces of the Vernacular: Ernst Bloch's Philosophy of Hope and the German Hometown," in *Vernacular Modernism: Heimat, Globalization and the Built Environment*, ed. Maiken Umbach and Bernd Hüppauf. Stanford, CA: Stanford University Press, 2005, 84–113.

Hůrka, Miroslav. *Když se řekne zvukový film . . .* Prague: Český Filmový Ústav, 1991.

Huyssen, Andreas. *After the Great Divide: Modernism, Mass Culture, Postmodernism*. Bloomington, IN: Indiana University Press, 1986.

———. "Geographies of Modernism in a Globalizing World," in *Geographies of Modernism: Literatures, Cultures, Spaces*, ed. Peter Brooker and Andrew Thacker. London: Routledge, 2005.

Iampolski, Mikhail. *The Memory of Tiresias: Intertextuality and Film*. Berkeley, CA: University of California Press, 1998.

Iizima, Tadasi, et al. *The Cinema Yearbook of Japan 1936–37*. Tokyo: Sanseido, 1938.

Ivarsson, Jan. *Bibliography of Subtitling and Related Subjects*, www.transedit.se

Jackson, John Brinkerhoff. *Discovering the Vernacular Landscape*. New Haven, CT: Yale University Press, 1975.

Jakobson, Roman. "Linguistics and Poetics," in *Modern Criticism and Theory: A Reader*, ed. David Lodge. London: Longman, 1988, 32–56.

Jakobson, Roman, and Krystyna Pomorska. *Dialogues*, trans. Christian Hubert. Melbourne: Cambridge University Press, 1983.

Jameson, Fredric. "Third World Literature in the Era of Multinational Capitalism," *Social Text*, no. 15 (Fall 1986): 65–88.

———. Keynote lecture at the conference, Cinema and Nation, Dublin, November 1996.

———. *A Singular Modernity: Essay on the Ontology of the Present.* London: Verso, 2002.

Jarvie, Ian. "National Cinema: A Theoretical Assessment," in Hjort and MacKenzie, *Cinema and Nation*, 2000, 69–80.

Jöckel, Sven. *Der Herr der Ringe im Film: Event Movie, postmoderne Ästhetik, aktive Rezeption.* Munich: Reinhard-Fischer, 2005.

Johnson, Randal and Robert Stam. *Brazilian Cinema*, 3d ed. New York: Columbia University Press, 1995.

Jones, Andrew. *Yellow Music: Media Culture and Colonial Modernity in the Chinese Jazz Age.* Durham, NC: Duke University Press, 2001.

———. "The Child as History in Republican China: A Discourse on Development," *Positions* 10, no. 3 (2002): 695–727.

———. "*Playthings* of History: The Child as Commodity in Republican China," lecture presented at the University of Chicago, December 2005.

Joseph, May. *Nomadic Identities: The Performance of Citizenship.* Minneapolis, MN: University of Minnesota Press, 1999.

Kaarsholm, Preben. "Mental Colonisation or Catharsis? Theatre, Democracy and Cultural Struggle from Rhodesia to Zimbabwe," in Gunner, *Politics and Performance*, 1995, 224–51.

———. "*Si Ye Pambile*—Which Way Forward? Urban Development, Culture and Politics in Bulawayo," in *Sites of Struggle: Essays in Zimbabwe's Urban History*, ed. Brian Raftopoulos and Yoshikuni Tsuneo. Harare: Weaver Press, 1999, 227–56.

Kaminsky, Stuart M. "Kung Fu Film as Ghetto Myth," in *Movies as Artifacts*, ed. Michael T. Marsden, John G. Nachbar, and Sam L. Grogg Jr. Chicago, IL: Nelson-Hall, 1982, 137–45.

Kane, Momar Désiré. *Marginalité et errance dans la littérature et le cinéma africains francophones: Les carrefours mobiles.* Collection Images plurielles. Paris: L'Harmattan, 2004.

Kaviraj, Sudipta. "Modernity and Politics in India," *Daedalus* 129, no. 1 (2000): 137–62.

Kayahara, Matthew. "The Digital Revolution: DVD Technology and the Possibilities for Audio-Visual Translation," *Journal of Specialized Translation* 3 (2005), www.jostrans.org/issue03/issue03_toc.php

Keil, Charlie. " 'To Here from Modernity': Style Historiography, and Transitional Cinema," in *American Cinema's Transitional Era: Audiences, Institutions, Practices*, ed. Charlie Keil and Shelley Stamp. Berkeley, CA: California University Press, 2004.

Kerr, David, with Stephen Chifunyise. "Southern Africa," in *A History of Theatre in Africa*, ed. Martin Banham. Cambridge: Cambridge University Press, 2004, 265–311.

Khor, Denise. "The Geographies of Film Spectatorship: Bruce Lee in Transnational and Ethnic Studies Perspective." Master's thesis, University of California at San Diego, 2003.

King, John. *Magical Reels: A History of Cinema in Latin America.* London: Verso, 1990.

Knauft, Bruce M., ed. *Critically Modern: Alternatives, Alterities, Anthropologies.* Bloomington, IN: Indiana University Press, 2002.

Knights, Vanessa. "Modernity, Modernization and Melodrama: The Bolero in Mexico in the 1930s and 1940s," in *Contemporary Latin American Cultural Studies*, ed. Stephen Hart and Richard Young. London: Arnold, 2003, 127–39.

Koch, Gertrud. *Umwidmungen—architektonische und kinematographische Räume.* Berlin: Vorwerk, 2005.

Koshy, Susan. "The Postmodern Subaltern: Globalization Theory and the Subject of Ethnic, Area, and Postcolonial Studies," in *Minor Transnationalism,* ed. Françoise Lionnet and Shu-mei Shih. Durham, NC: Duke University Press, 2005, 109–31.

Kracauer, Siegfried. *Theory of Film.* New York: Oxford University Press, 1960.

——. *Die Angestellten* (1929), *The Salaried Masses: Duty and Distraction in Weimar Germany,* trans. Quintin Hoare, introd. Inka Mülder-Bach. London: Verso, 1998.

Krauze, Enrique. *Mexico: Biography of Power,* trans. Hank Heifitz. New York: Harper Perennial, 1997.

Kreimeier, Klaus. *Die UFA Story: Geschichte eines Filmkonzerns.* Munich: Hanser, 1992.

Kristeva, Julia. *The Revolution in Poetic Language,* trans. Margaret Waller. New York: Columbia University Press, 1984.

Kuersten, Erich. "*Shaolin Soccer,* Miramax and the Question of Subtitles," *Pop Matters,* May 23, 2003, www.popmatters.com/film/features/030522-shaolin-soccer.shtml

Kwai-cheung, Lo. "Double Negations: Hong Kong Cultural Identity in Hollywood's Transnational Representations," in *Between Home and World: A Reader in Hong Kong Cinema,* ed. Esther M.K. Cheung and Chu Yiu-wai. Hong Kong: Oxford University Press, 2004, 59–84.

Laclau, Ernesto, and Chantal Mouffe. *Hegemony and Socialist Strategy: Towards a Radical Democratic Politics,* trans. Winston Moore and Paul Cammack. London: Verso, 1985.

LaMarre, Thomas. *Shadows on the Screen: Tanizaki Jun'ichiro on Cinema and "Oriental" Aesthetics.* Ann Arbor, MI: Center for Japanese Studies, University of Michigan, 2005.

Lamster, Mark. *Architecture and Film.* New York: Princeton Architectural Press, 2000.

Larkin, Brian. "Indian Films and Nigerian Lovers: Media and the Creation of Parallel Modernities," in *The Anthropology of Globalization: A Reader,* ed. Jonathan Xavier Inda and Renato Rosaldo. Malden, MA: Blackwell, 2001, 350–78.

——. "Itineraries of Indian Cinema: African Videos, Bollywood and Global Media," in Shohat and Stam, *Multiculturalism, Postcoloniality and Transnational Media,* 2003, 170–92.

——. "Report on Nollywood Rising Conference." Unpublished paper, 2005.

Latin American Video Archives, 2002, www.lavavideo.org.

Latour, Bruno. *We Have Never Been Modern,* trans. Catherine Porter. Cambridge, MA: Harvard University Press, 1993.

Lee, Leo Ou-fan. *Shanghai Modern: The Flowering of a New Urban Culture in China, 1930–1945.* Cambridge, MA: Harvard University Press, 1999.

Leenhardt, Roger. "Le Cinéma, art national," *Esprit* 65 (February 1938), reprinted in *Chroniques de cinéma.* Paris: L'Etoile, 1986, 57–60.

Léglise, Paul. *Histoire de la politique du cinéma français: Le cinéma et la IIIeme république.* Paris: Pierre Lherminier, 1977.

Lent, John. "Foreword," in *City on Fire: Hong Kong Cinema,* ed. Lisa Odham Stokes and Michael Hoover. London: Verso, 1999.

Leth, Jørgen. *Det uperfekte menneske: Scener fra mit liv.* Copenhagen: Gyldendal, 2005.

Leung, Grace L.K., and Joseph M. Chan. "The Hong Kong Cinema and its Overseas Market: A Historical Review, 1950–1995," in *Hong Kong Cinema*

Retrospective: Fifty Years of Electric Shadows. Hong Kong: The 21st Hong Kong International Film Festival, 1997, 143–49.

Lewis, Howard T. *The Motion Picture Industry*. New York: Van Nostrand, 1933.

Lewis, Justin, and Toby Miller, eds. *Critical Cultural Policy Studies: A Reader*. Malden, MA: Blackwell, 2003.

Ley, Graham. *From Mimesis to Interculturalism: Readings of Theatrical Theory Before and After "Modernism."* Exeter, UK: University of Exeter Press, 1999.

Li, Siu Leung. "The Myth Continues: Cinematic Kung Fu in Modernity," in Morris, Li, and Ching-kiu, *Hong Kong Connections*, 2005, 49–61, 295–96.

Lionnet, Françoise, and Shu-mei Shih. "Introduction: Thinking through the Minor, Transnationally," in *Minor Transnationalism*, ed. Lionnet and Shih. Durham, NC: Duke University Press, 2005, 1–26.

López, Ana M. "A Cinema for the Continent," in Noriega and Ricci, *The Mexican Cinema Project*, 1994, 7–12.

———. "Of Rhythms and Borders," in *Everynight Life: Culture and Dance in Latin/o America*, ed. Celeste Fraser Delgado and José Esteban Muñoz. Durham, NC: Duke University Press, 1997, 31–44.

———. "*Train of Shadows*: Early Cinema and Modernity in Latin America," in Shohat and Stam, *Multiculturalism, Postcoloniality and Transnational Media*, 2003, 99–128.

Lu, Sheldon Hsiao-peng, ed. *Transnational Chinese Cinemas: Identity, Nationhood, Gender*. Honolulu, HI: University of Hawaii Press, 1997.

———. "Crouching Tiger, Hidden Dragon, Bouncing Angels: Hollywood, Taiwan, Hong Kong, and Transnational Cinema," in Lu and Yeh, *Chinese-Language Film*, 2005, 220–36.

———. "Dialect and Modernity in 21st Century Sinophone Cinema," *Jump Cut*, no. 49 (Spring 2007), http://ejumpcut.org/archive/jc49.2007/Lu/text.html

Lu, Sheldon Hsiao-peng, and Emilie Yueh-yu Yeh, eds. *Chinese-Language Film: Historiography, Poetics, Politics*. Honolulu, HI: University of Hawaii Press, 2005.

Lu, Tonglin. *Confronting Modernity in the Cinemas of Taiwan and Mainland China*. New York: Cambridge University Press, 2002.

Lukk, Tiiu. *Movie Marketing: Opening the Picture and Giving it Legs*. Los Angeles, CA: Silman-James Press, 1997.

Macaulay, Ronald K.S. "The Rise and Fall of the Vernacular," in *On Language: Rhetorica, Phonologica, Syntactica*, ed. Caroline Duncan-Rose and Theo Vennemann. London: Routledge, 1988, 107–15.

———. "Vernacular," in *Concise Encyclopedia of Sociolinguistics*, ed. Rajend Mesthrie. Amsterdam: Elsevier, 2001.

MacGregor, Hilary E. "Latino Movie Theater Chain Promised," *Los Angeles Times*, September 1, 1999.

Maciel, David. "Los desarraigados: Los chicanos vistos por el cine Mexican," in *México Estados Unidos: Encuentros y desencuentros en el cine*, ed. Ignacio Durán, Iván Trujillo, and Mónica Verea. Mexico: Universidad Nacional Autónoma de México/Consejo Nacional para la Cultura y las Artes/Instituto Mexicano de Cinematografía, 1996, 166–67.

McIntyre, Steve. "National Film Cultures: Politics and Peripheries," *Screen* 26, no. 1 (1985): 66–76.

Maldonado-Torres, Nelson. "The Topology of Being and the Geopolitics of Knowledge: Modernity, Empire, Coloniality," *CITY* 8, no. 1 (2004): 29–56.

Maluf, Ramez. "A Potential Untapped? Why Dubbing Has Not Caught on in the Arab World," *Transnational Broadcasting Studies* 15 (Fall 2005), www. tbsjournal.com/Archives/Fall05/Maluf.html

Manovich, Lev. "Understanding Meta-Media," *CTheoryNet*, www.ctheory.net/ articles.aspx?id=493#_edn1#_edn1.

Marchetti, Gina. "Thinking Beyond Culture," Part 2 of "Transnational Cinema, Hybrid Identities and the Films of Evans Chan," http:// members.tripod.com/~ginacao/

Martin, Adrian. "At the Edge of the Cut: An Encounter with the Hong Kong Style in Contemporary Action Cinema," in Morris, Li, and Ching-kiu, *Hong Kong Connections*, 2005, 175–88, 311–12.

Martín-Barbero, Jesús. *De los medios a las mediaciones: comunicación, cultura y hegemonía.* Mexico: G. Gili, 1987.

Martín-Barbero, Jesús, and Hermann Herlinghaus. *Contemporaneidad latinoamericana y análisis cultural: Conversaciones al encuentro de Walter Benjamin.* Berlin: Iberoamericana, 2000.

Mauss, Marcel. *The Gift: Forms and Functions of Exchange in Archaic Societies,* trans. Ian Cunnison, intro. E.E. Evans-Pritchard. London: Cohen & West, 1970.

Maxwell, Richard, and Toby Miller, eds. "Cultural Labor," special issue, *Social Semiotics* 15, no. 3 (2005).

Meng Jian, Li Yizhong, and Stefan Friedrich, eds. *Chongtu, hexie: quanqiuhua yu Yazhou yingshi* (Conflict vs harmony: globalization and Asian film and television). Shanghai: Fudan daxue chubanshe, 2003.

Metz, Christian. *Language and Cinema.* The Hague: Mouton, 1974.

Mignolo, Walter. *Local Histories/Global Designs: Coloniality, Subaltern Knowledges, and Border Thinking.* Princeton, NJ: Princeton University Press, 2000.

——. "Coloniality of Power and De-Colonial Thinking," introduction to "Globalization and the De-colonial Option," special issue, *Cultural Studies* 21, nos. 2–3 (2007): 155–67.

Miller, Toby. *The Avengers.* London: British Film Institute, 1997.

Miller, Toby, and George Yúdice. *Cultural Policy.* London: Sage, 2002.

Miller, Toby, et al. *Global Hollywood.* London: British Film Institute, 2001.

——. *Globalisation and Sport: Playing the World.* London: Sage, 2001.

——. *Global Hollywood 2.* London: British Film Institute, 2005.

——. *Global Hollywood 2,* 2d ed. London: British Film Institute, 2008.

Mintz, Marilyn. *The Martial Arts Films.* North Clarendon, VT: Charles E. Tuttle, 1983.

Mitchell, Timothy, ed. *Questions of Modernity.* Minneapolis, MN: University of Minnesota Press, 2000.

——. *Rule of Experts: Egypt, Techno-Politics, Modernity.* Berkeley, CA: University of California Press, 2002.

Monk, Claire. "Men in the 90s," in *British Cinema in the 90s,* ed. Robert Murphy. London: British Film Institute, 2000, 156–66.

Monsiváis, Carlos. *Mexican Postcard.* London: Verso, 1997.

——. *Aires de familia.* Barcelona: Anagrama, 2000.

Monteagudo, Luciano and Verónica Bucich. *Carlos Gardel y el primer cine sonoro argentino.* Huesca, Spain: Filmoteca de Andalucía, Chicago Latino Film Festival y Festival de Cine de Huesca, 2001.

Mora, Carl J. *Mexican Cinema: Reflections of a Society 1896–1980.* Berkeley, CA: University of California Press, 1982.

Moretti, Franco. *Atlas of the European Novel 1800–1900.* New York: Verso, 1998.

Morris, Meaghan. "Learning from Bruce Lee: Pedagogy and Political Correctness in Martial Arts Cinema," in *Keyframes: Popular Cinema and Cultural Studies*, ed. Matthew Tinkcom and Amy Villarejo. London: Routledge, 2001, 171–86.

———. "Introduction: Hong Kong Connections," in Morris, Li, and Ching-kiu, *Hong Kong Connections*, 2005, 1–18.

Morris, Meaghan, Siu Leung Li, and Stephen Chan Ching-kiu, eds. *Hong Kong Connections: Transnational Imagination in Action Cinema*. Hong Kong: University of Hong Kong Press, and Durham, NC: Duke University Press, 2005.

Mowitt, John. "The Sound of Music in the Era of its Electronic Reproducibility," in *Music and Society: The Politics of Composition, Performance and Reception*, ed. Richard Leppert and Susan McClary. Cambridge: Cambridge University Press, 1987, 173–97.

———. "The Hollywood Sound Tract," in Egoyan and Balfour, *Subtitles*, 2005, 381–400.

Mühl-Benninghaus, Wolfgang. *Das Ringen um den Tonfilm*. Düsseldorf: Droste, 1999.

Naficy, Hamid. *The Making of Exile Cultures: Iranian Television in Los Angeles*. Minneapolis, MN: University of Minnesota Press, 1993.

———. *An Accented Cinema: Exilic and Diasporic Filmmaking*. Princeton, NJ: Princeton University Press, 2001.

———. "Dubbing, Doubling and Duplicity." *Pages*, no. 4 (July 2005): 113–17. www.pagesmagazine.net/2006/article.php?ma_id=7830018.

———. "Interstitial/Transnational Mode of Production and National Cinemas." Paper to the Society for Cinema and Media Studies conference, London, March 31 to April 3, 2005.

Neale, Steve. "Art Cinema as Institution," *Screen* 22, no. 1 (1981): 11–40.

Negt, Oskar and Alexander Kluge, *The Public Sphere and Experience*, trans. Peter Labanyi, Jamie Daniel, and Assenka Oksiloff, introd. Miriam Hansen. Minneapolis, MN: University of Minnesota Press, 1993.

Neumann, Dietrich. *Film Architecture: Set Design from Metropolis to Blade Runner*. Munich: Prestel, 1996.

Njami, Simon. "Chaos et métamorphose." Exhibition catalogue, *Africa Remix*: 15–25.

Noriega, Chon A. "Mexican Cinema in the United States: Introduction to the Essays," in *The Mexican Cinema Project*, ed. Chon Noriega and Steven Ricci. Los Angeles, CA: UCLA Film and Television Archive: Research and Study Center, 1994, 1–6.

———. *Shot in America: Television, the State, and the Rise of Chicano Cinema*. Minneapolis, MN: University of Minnesota Press, 2000.

———. "Making a Difference," *Politics and Culture* 2, no. 1 (2002), http://laurel.conncoll.edu/politicsandculture.

Noriega, Chon A., and Steven Ricci, eds. *The Mexican Cinema Project*. Los Angeles, CA: University of California, Los Angeles Film and Television Archive, 1994.

Nornes, Abé Mark. *Japanese Documentary Film: The Meiji Era through Hiroshima*. Minneapolis, MN: University of Minnesota Press, 2003.

———. "For an Abusive Subtitling," in *The Translation Studies Reader*, 2d ed, ed. Lawrence Venuti. New York: Routledge, 2004, 447–69.

———. *Cinema Babel: Translating Global Cinema*. Minneapolis, MN: University of Minnesota Press, 2007.

O'Brien, Charles. *Cinema's Conversion to Sound: Technology and Film Style in France and the US*. Bloomington, IN: Indiana University Press, 2005.

Ohmann, Richard. *Selling Culture: Magazines, Markets and Class at the Turn of the Century*. London: Verso, 1996.

Ong, Aihwa. *Flexible Citizenship: The Cultural Logics of Transnationality*. Durham, NC: Duke University Press, 1999.

O'Regan, Tom. *Australian National Cinema*. London: Routledge, 1996.

Pang, Laikwan. *Building a New China in Cinema: The Chinese Left-Wing Cinema Movement, 1932–1937*. Lanham, MD: Rowman & Littlefield, 2002.

Paranaguá, Paulo Antonio. "The Sound Era in Latin America," in *Latin American Visions: Catalogue*. Philadelphia, PA: The Neighborhood Film/Video Project of International House, 1989, 13–19.

———. "América Latina busca su imagen," *Historia general del cine*, Vol. 10. Coordinado por Carlos Feredero y Casimiro Torreiro. Madrid: Cátedra, Signoe imagen, 1996, 205–393.

———. *Tradición y modernidad en el cine de América latina*. Madrid: Fondo de cultura económica, 2003.

Paredes, Mari Castañeda. "The Reorganization of Spanish-Language Media Marketing," in *Continental Order? Integrating North America for Cybercapitalism*, ed. Vincent Mosco and Dan Schiller. Lanham, MD: Rowman & Littlefield, 2001, 120–35.

Passanti, Francesco. "The Vernacular, Modernism, and Le Corbusier," *Journal of the Society of Architectural Historians* 56, no. 4 (1997): 438–51.

———. "The Vernacular, Modernism, and Le Corbusier," in *Vernacular Modernism: Heimat, Globalization and the Built Environment*, ed. Maiken Umbach and Bernd Hüppauf. Stanford, CA: Stanford University Press, 2005.

Passek, Jean-Loup. "Yugoslavian cinema." Catalog of the Centre Pompidou, Paris (April–July, 1986).

Pew Internet & American Life Project. *Hispanics and the Internet*. Washington, DC: Pew Internet & American Life Project, 2001.

———. 2006, www.pewinternet.org/trends.asp#demographics

Pieterse, Jan Nederveen. "Oriental Globalization," *Theory, Culture and Society* 23, nos. 2–3 (2006): 412.

Pine, Jim and Paul Willemen, eds. *Questions of Third Cinema*. London: British Film Institute, 1989.

Pineda Castro, Adela. "The Cuban *Bolero* and its Transculturation to Mexico: The Case of Agustín Lara," *Studies in Latin American Popular Culture* 12 (1993):119–29.

Pollock, Sheldon. "The Cosmopolitan Vernacular," *Journal of Asian Studies* 57, no. 1 (1998): 6–37.

———. "Cosmopolitan and Vernacular in History," *Public Culture* 12, no. 3 (2000): 591–625.

Poses, Johanna. "Your Own Personal Jesus? Translation Strategies in the Jesus Biopic." MA thesis, University of Amsterdam, 2005.

Poulantzas, Nicos. *State, Power, Socialism*, trans. Patrick Cammiler. London: Verso, 1980.

Powdermaker, Hortense. *Stranger and Friend: The Way of an Anthropologist*. London: Secker & Warburg, 1967.

Prashad, Vijay. *Everybody Was Kung Fu Fighting: Afro-Asian Connections and the Myth of Cultural Purity*. Boston, MA: Beacon Press, 2001.

Pratt, Mary Louise. "Linguistic Utopias," in *The Linguistics of Writing: Arguments Between Language and Literature*, ed. Nigel Fabb et al. New York: Methuen, 1987, 48–66.

Puente, Enrique. "Latin Universe." Paper for Fifth Congress of the Americas, Puebla, Mexico, 2001.

Quargnolo, Mario. *La parola ripudiata: L'incredibile storia dei film stranieri in Italia nei primi anni del sonoro*. Gemona, Italy: La cineteca del Friuli, 1986.

Raffaelli, Sergio. *La lingua filmata: didascalie e dialoghi nel cinema*. Florence, Italy: Le lettere, 1992.

Raine, Michael. "Youth, Body, and Subjectivity in the Japanese Cinema, 1955–60." PhD dissertation, University of Iowa, 2002.

———. "Masumura Yasuzo's *Giants and Toys*," in *Japanese Cinema: Texts and Contexts*, ed. Alistair Phillips and Julian Stringer. New York: Routledge and American Film Institute, 2007.

Rajadhyaksha, Ashish and Paul Willemen, eds., *Encyclopaedia of Indian Cinema*. London: British Film Institute and Oxford University Press, 1999.

Rajagopalan, Sudha. "Emblematic of the Thaw: Early Indian Films in Soviet Cinemas," *South Asian Popular Culture* 4, no. 2 (2006): 83–100.

Rama, Ángel. *The Lettered City*, ed. and trans. John Charles Chasteen. Durham, NC: Duke University Press, 1996.

Rancière, Jacques. "From One Image to Another? Deleuze and The Ages of Cinema," in *Film Fables*, trans. Emiliano Battista. Oxford: Berg, 2006, 107–24.

Ranger, Terence. "Pugilism and Pathology: African Boxing and the Black Urban Experience in Southern Rhodesia," in *Sport in Africa: Essays in Social History*, ed. William J. Baker and James Mangan. New York: Africana Publishing, 1987, 196–213.

Rapoport, Amos. "Defining Vernacular Design," in *Vernacular Architecture*, ed. Mete Turan. Aldershot, UK: Avebury, 1990.

Reinholds, Jan. *Filmindustri 1900–1975*. Lerum, Sweden: Reinholds Text & Förlag, no date.

Rentschler, Eric. "From New German Cinema to the Post-Wall Cinema of Consensus," in Hjort and MacKenzie, *Cinema and Nation*, 2000, 260–77.

Restivo, Angelo. *The Cinema of Economic Miracles: Visuality and Modernization in the Italian Art Film*. Durham, NC: Duke University Press, 2002.

Reyes, Luis, and Peter Rubie. *Hispanics in Hollywood: A Celebration of 100 Years in Film and Television*. Los Angeles, CA: Lone Eagle, 2000.

Reynaud, Bérénice. "Cutting Edge and Missed Encounters: Digital Short Films by Three Filmmakers," *Senses of Cinema* (May 2002).

Rich, B. Ruby. "Mexico at the Multiplex," *The Nation*, May 14, 2001, 34–36.

Rivette, Jacques. "Mizoguchi viewed from here," *Cahiers du Cinéma*, no. 81 (March 1958), reprinted in Jim Hillier, *Cahiers du Cinéma: The 1950s*. Cambridge, MA: Harvard University Press, 1985, 264.

Robbins, Bruce. "Actually Existing Cosmopolitanism," in *Cosmopolitics: Thinking and Feeling Beyond the Nation*, ed. Pheng Cheah and Bruce Robbins. Minneapolis, MN: University of Minnesota Press, 1998, 1–19.

Rohdie, Sam. *Promised Lands: Cinema, Geography, Modernism*. London: British Film Institute, 2001.

Romney, Jonathan. "Lars von Trier, Nil, Jørgen Leth, Five." *The Independent*, November 9, 2003.

Rosen, Philip. *Change Mummified: Cinema, Historicity, Theory*. Minneapolis, MN: University of Minnesota Press, 2001.

Rosen, Stanley. "The Wolf at the Door: Hollywood and the Film Market in China, 1994–2000," in *Southern California in the World and the World in Southern California*, ed. Eric J. Heikkila and Rafael Pizarro. Westport, CT: Praeger, 2002.

Rosenbaum, Jonathan. "Tati's Democracy," *Film Comment* (May–June 1973): 36–41.

———. "The Death of Hulot," *Sight and Sound* (Spring 1983): 94–97.

———. *Placing Movies: The Practice of Film Criticism* Berkeley, CA: University of California Press, 1995.

———. *Movies as Politics*. Berkeley, CA: University of California Press, 1997.

Rossholm, Anna Sofia. *Reproducing Languages, Translating Bodies: Approaches to Speech, Translation and Cultural Identity in Early European Sound Film*. Stockholm: Almkvist & Wiksell, 2006.

Rubenstein, Anne. "Mass Media and Popular Culture in the Postrevolutionary Era," in *The Oxford History of Mexico*, ed. Michael C. Meyer and William H. Beezley. Oxford: Oxford University Press, 2000, 637–70.

———. "Bodies, Cities, Cinema: Pedro Infantes' Death as Political Spectacle," in *Fragments of a Golden Age: The Politics of Culture in Mexico Since 1940*, ed. Gilbert Joseph, Anne Rubenstein, and Eric Zolov. Durham, NC: Duke University Press, 2001, 199–233.

Russell, Catherine. "Naruse Mikio's Silent Films: Gender and the Discourse of Everyday Life in Interwar Japan," *Camera Obscura* 20, no. 3 (2005): 57–89.

———, ed. *New Women of the Silent Screen: China, Japan, Hollywood. Camera Obscura* 20, no. 3 (2005).

Sachsenmaier, Dominic, Jens Riedel, and S.N. Eisenstadt, eds. *Reflections on Multiple Modernities*. Leiden: Brill Academic, 2002.

Sanaker, John Kristian. "Les Indoublables: Pour une ethique de la representation langagiére au cinéma," *Glottopol* 12 (May 2008): 147–60, www.univ-rouen.fr/ dyalang/glottopol.

Sánchez Vidal, Agustín. *El cine de Florián Rey*. Zaragoza, Spain: Caja de Ahorros La Inmaculada, 1991.

Sánchez-Ruiz, Enrique. "Globalization, Cultural Industries, and Free Trade: The Mexican Audiovisual Sector in the NAFTA Age," in *Continental Order? Integrating North America for Cybercapitalism*, ed. Vincent Mosco and Dan Schiller. Lanham, MD: Rowman & Littlefield, 2001, 86–119.

Santos, Boaventura de Sousa. "Globalizations," *Theory, Culture and Society* 26, nos. 2–3 (2006): 393–99.

Sarkar, Bhaskar. "Hong Kong Hysteria: Martial Arts Tales from a Mutating World," In Yau, *At Full Speed*, 2001, 159–76.

———. *Mourning the Nation: Indian Cinema in the Wake of Partition*. Durham, NC: Duke University Press, 2009.

Sarlo, Beatriz. *Una modernidad periférica: Buenos Aires 1920 y 1930*. Buenos Aires: Nuevas Visión, 1988.

Sartre, Jean-Paul. "Orphée noir," in *Anthologie de la nouvelle poésie nègre et malgache*, ed. L. Senghor. Paris: Presses Universitaires de France, 1948. Translated into English by S.W. Allen as *Black Orpheus*. Paris: Présence Africaine, 1976.

Sassen, Saskia. "Spatialities and Temporalities of the Global," in *Globalization*, ed. Arjun Appadurai. Durham, NC: Duke University Press, 2001, 260–78.

———. "Free speech in the frontier-zone," *Open Democracy*, February 20, 2006. www.opendemocracy.net/faith-europe_islam/freespeech_3282.jsp.

Sato, Barbara. "An Alternate Informant: Middle-Class Women and Mass Magazines in 1920s Japan," in *Being Modern in Japan: Culture and Society from the 1910s to the 1930s*, ed. Elise K. Tipton and John Clark. Honolulu, HI: University of Hawaii Press, 2000.

———. *The New Japanese Woman: Modernity, Media, and Women in Interwar Japan*. Durham, NC: Duke University Press, 2003.

Scheper-Hughes, Nancy. *Death without Weeping: The Violence of Everyday Life in Brazil*. Los Angeles, CA: University of California Press, 1993.

"Schnittberichte.com," http://de.wikipedia.org/wiki/Schnittberichte.com.

Schwarz, Roberto. *Misplaced Ideas: Essays on Brazilian Culture.* London: Verso, 1992.

Seth, Vikram. *From Heaven Lake: Travels through Sinkiang and Tibet.* London: Chatto & Windus, 1983.

Shen, Vivian. *The Origins of Left-wing Cinema in China, 1932–37.* New York: Routledge, 2005.

Shih, Shu-Mei. *The Lure of the Modern: Writing Modernism in Semicolonial China, 1917–1937.* Berkeley, CA: University of California Press, 2001.

Shiro, Kido. *Nihon eigaden: Eiga seisakusha no kiroku (Japanese Cinema Tales: A Record of a Film Producer).* Tokyo: Bungei Shunjusha, 1956.

Shiva, Vandana. *Biopiracy: The Plunder of Nature and Knowledge.* London: South End Press, 1997.

Shohat, Ella and Robert Stam. "The Cinema after Babel: Language, Difference, Power," *Screen* 26, nos. 3–4 (1985): 35–58.

——— . "Film Theory and Spectatorship in the Age of the 'Posts'," in *Reinventing Film Studies,* ed. Christine Gledhill and Linda Williams. New York: Hodder Arnold, 2000, 381–401.

——— . eds. *Multiculturalism, Postcoloniality and Transnational Media.* New Brunswick, NJ: Rutgers University Press, 2003.

——— . "Traveling Multiculturalism: A Trinational Debate in Translation," in *Postcolonial Studies and Beyond,* ed. Ania Loomba et al. Durham, NC: Duke University Press, 2005, 293–316.

Shuk-ting, Kinnia Yau. "Shaws' Japanese Collaboration and Competition as Seen through the Asian Film Festival Evolution," in *The Shaw Screen: A Preliminary Study.* Hong Kong Film Archive, 2003, 279–91.

Silverberg, Miriam. "Remembering Pearl Harbor, Forgetting Charlie Chaplin, and the Case of the Disappearing Woman: A Picture Story," in *Formations of Colonial Modernity in East Asia,* ed. Tani E. Barlow. Durham, NC: Duke University Press, 1997, 249–94.

——— . "The Café Waitress Serving Modern Japan," in *Mirror of Modernity: Invented Traditions of Modern Japan,* ed. Stephen Vlastos. Berkeley, CA: University of California Press, 1998, 208–25.

Sinclair, John. *Latin American Television: A Global View.* Oxford: Oxford University Press, 1999.

Singer, Ben. *Melodrama and Modernity.* New York: Columbia University Press, 2001.

Singer, Peter. *One World: The Ethics of Globalization.* New Haven, CT: Yale University Press, 2004.

Skaff, Sheila. "Intertitles and Language Conflict in Bydgoszcz, El Paso and Juarez, 1908–1920." Paper presented at the meeting of the Society for Cinema and Media Studies, Chicago, IL, March 2007.

——— . *Through the Looking Glass: Cinema in Poland, 1896–1939.* Athens, OH: Ohio University Press, forthcoming.

Skopal, Pavel. "Kolem sveta v 32 jazycich. *Lví král* a strategie lokální globalizace," *Iluminace,* no.2 (2005): 31–49.

Smith, Neil. "Homeless/Global: Scaling Places," in *Mapping the Futures: Local Cultures, Global Change,* ed. Jon Bird et al., London: Routledge, 1993, 87–119.

Sorlin, Pierre. *Italian National Cinema 1896–1996.* London: Routledge, 1996.

Soysal, Yasemin Nuhoglu. "Citizenship and Identity: Living in Diasporas in Postwar Europe?" in *The Postnational Self: Belonging and Identity,* ed. Ulf Hedetoft and Mette Hjort. Minneapolis, MN: University of Minnesota Press, 2002, 137–51.

Sparke, Matthew. *In the Space of Theory: Postfoundational Geographies of the Nation-State.* Minneapolis, MN: University of Minnesota Press, 2005.

Srinivas, S.V. "Devotion and Defiance in Fan Activity," in *Making Meaning in Indian Cinema*, ed. Ravi Vasudevan. New Delhi: Oxford University Press, 1999, 297–317.

———. "Hong Kong Action Film in the Indian B Circuit," *Inter-Asia Cultural Studies* 4, no. 1 (2003): 40–62.

———. "Film Culture, Politics and Industry," *Seminar*, no. 525 (May 2003): 47–51, www.india-seminar.com/2003/525.htm

———. "Hong Kong Action Film and the Career of the Telegu Mass Hero," in Morris, Li, and Ching-kiu, *Hong Kong Connections*, 2005, 111–23, 302–05.

Stahuljak, Zrinka. "An Epistemology of Tension Translation and Multiculturalism," *The Translator* 10, no. 1 (2004): 33–59.

Stam, Robert. "*Pixote*," *Cineaste* 12, no. 3 (1983): 44–45.

———. "Palimpsestic Aesthetics: A Meditation on Hybridity and Garbage," in *Performing Hybridity*, ed. May Joseph and Jennifer Natalya Fink. Minneapolis, MN: University of Minnesota Press, 1999, 59–78.

Standish, Isolde. *A New History of Japanese Cinema: A Century of Narrative Film*. London: Continuum, 2005.

Stephenson, Shelley. "The Occupied Screen: Star, Fan, and Nation in Shanghai Cinema, 1937–1945." PhD dissertation, University of Chicago, IL, 2000.

Stern, Lesley. "Paths that Wind through the Thicket of Things," in *Things*, ed. Bill Brown. Chicago, IL: University of Chicago Press, 2004.

Stewart, Garrett. *Framed Time: Toward a Postfilmic Cinema*. Chicago, IL: University of Chicago Press, 2007.

Stiegler, Bernard. "Our Ailing Educational Institutions: The Global Mnemotechnical System," *Culture Machine* 5 (2003), http:// culturemachine. tees.ac.uk/Cmach/Backissues/j005/Articles/Stiegler.htm (a translation, by Stefan Herbrechter, of Chapter 4 in Bernard Stiegler's *La Technique et le temps*, vol. 3, *Le Temps du cinema*. Paris: Galilee, 2001).

Suekichi, Aono. *Saraiman kyofu jidai* (*The Salaryman's Panic Time*). Tokyo: Senshinsha, 1930.

Sukvong, Dome. "A oriente del sole, a occidente della luna: il cinema muto in Tailandia / East of the Sun, West of the Moon: A Region in Memory," www.cinetecadelfriuli.org/gcm/previous_editions/edizione2003/Thai.html.

Tam, Kwok-kan, and Wimal Dissanayake. *New Chinese Cinema*. Hong Kong: Oxford University Press, 1998.

Tanizaki, Junichiro. "Jinmenso," trans. Thomas LaMarre in his *Shadows on the Silver Screen: Junichiro Tanizaki and Silent Film Aesthetics*. Ann Arbor, MI: University of Michigan Press, 2005.

Tasker, Yvonne. *Spectacular Bodies: Gender, Genre and the Action Cinema*. London: Routledge, 1993.

Taylor, Charles. *Modern Social Imaginaries*. Durham, NC: Duke University Press, 2004.

Teo, Stephen. "The True Way of the Dragon: The Films of Bruce Lee," in *Overseas Chinese Figures in Cinema*. Hong Kong: Urban Council, 1992.

———. *Hong Kong Cinema: The Extra Dimension*. London: British Film Institute, 1997.

———. "The 1970s: Movement and Transition," in *The Cinema of Hong Kong: History, Arts, Identity*, ed. Poshek Fu and David Desser. New York: Cambridge University Press, 2000, 90–110.

———. " 'We Kicked Jackie Chan's Ass': An Interview with James Schamus," *Senses of Cinema* (March–April 2001), www.sensesofcinema.com/contents/01/13/schamus.html.

———. "*Wuxia* Redux: *Crouching Tiger, Hidden Dragon* as a Model of Late Transnational Production," in Morris, Li, and Ching-kiu, *Hong Kong Connections*, 2005, 191–204, 312–14.

Thompson, Kristin. *Exporting Entertainment America in the World Film Market 1907–1934.* London: British Film Institute, 1985.

———. *Herr Lubitsch Goes to Hollywood: German and American Film after World War I.* Amsterdam: University of Amsterdam Press, 2005.

Torrents, Nissa. "Mexican Cinema Comes Alive," in *Mediating Two Worlds: Cinematic Encounters in the Americas*, ed. John King, Ana M. López, and Manuel Alvarado. London: British Film Institute, 1993, 222–29.

Touraine, Alain. "The Idea of Revolution," in *Global Culture: Nationalism, Globalization and Modernity*, ed. Mike Featherstone. London: Sage, 1990, 121–41.

Urry, John. *Sociology Beyond Societies: Mobilities for the Twenty-First Century.* London: Routledge, 2000.

Valis, Noël. *The Culture of Cursilería: Bad Taste, Kitsch and Class in Modern Spain.* Durham, NC: Duke University Press, 2002.

Vasudevan, Ravi. "The Politics of Cultural Address in a Transitional Cinema: A Case Study of Indian Popular Cinema," in *Reinventing Film Studies*, ed. Christine Gledhill and Linda Williams. London: Hodder Arnold, 2000, 130–64.

Venuti, Lawrence, ed. *The Translation Studies Reader*, 2d ed. New York: Routledge, 2004.

"Vernacular Architecture," in *Grove Dictionary of Art*, www.groveart.com

Vincendeau, Ginette. "Hollywood Babel: The Coming of Sound and the Multiple-Language Version," in *"Film Europe" and "Film America": Cinema, Commerce and Cultural Exchange 1920–1939*, ed. Andrew Higson and Richard Maltby. Exeter, UK: University of Exeter Press, 1999, 207–24.

Vitali, Valentina. "Nationalist Hindi Cinema: Questions of Film Analysis and Historiography." *Kinema* 22 (2004): 63–82.

———. "Hong Kong-Hollywood-Bombay: On the Function of 'Martial Art' in the Hindi Action Cinema," in Morris, Li, and Ching-kiu, *Hong Kong Connections*, 2005, 125–50.

Vitali, Valentina, and Paul Willemen, eds. *Theorising National Cinemas.* London: British Film Institute, 2006.

Wada-Marciano, Mitsuyo. "The Production of Modernity in Japanese National Cinema: Shochiku Kamata Style in the 1920s and 1930s," *Asian Cinema* 9, no. 2 (1998): 69–93.

———. "Imaging Modern Girls in the Japanese Woman's Film," *Camera Obscura* 20, no. 3 (2005): 15–56.

Wahl, Christoph. "Discovering a Genre: The Polyglot Film," *CinemaScope* 1 (2005), www.madadayo.it/Cinemascope_archive/cinema-scope.net/index_n1.html.

———. *Das Sprechen des Spielfilms.* Trier, Germany: Wissenschaftlicher, 2005.

Waldman, Harry. *Paramount in Paris: 300 Films Produced at the Joinville Studios, 1930–33, with Credits and Biographies.* Metuchen, NJ: Scarecrow, 1998.

Wallerstein, Immanuel. *The Modern World-System: Capitalist Agriculture and the Origins of the European World-Economy in the Sixteenth Century.* New York: Academic Press, 1974.

———. *The End of the World as We Know It: Social Science for the Twenty-First Century.* Minneapolis, MN: University of Minnesota Press, 1999.

———. *World-Systems Analysis: An Introduction*. Durham, NC: Duke University Press, 2004.

Wang, Shujen. *Framing Piracy: Globalization and Film Distribution in Greater China*. Lanham, MD: Rowman & Littlefield, 2003.

Werner, Michael and Bénédict Zimmermann, eds. *De la comparaison à l'histoire croisée*. Paris: Seuil, 2004.

———. "Beyond Comparison: *Histoire Croisée* and the Challenge of Reflexivity," *History and Theory* 45 (February 2006): 30–50.

Willemen, Paul. *Looks and Frictions: Essays in Cultural Studies and Film Theory*. London: British Film Institute, 1994.

———. "Regimes of Subjectivity and Looking," *The UTS Review* 1, no. 2 (1995): 101–29.

———. "The Zoom in Popular Culture: A Question of Performance," *New Cinemas: Journal of Contemporary Film* 1, no. 1 (2002): 6–13.

———. "Inflating the Narrator: Digital Hype and Allegorical Indexicality." *Convergence* 10, no. 3 (2004): 8–28.

———. "Action Cinema, Labour Power and the Video Market," in Morris, Li, and Ching-kiu, *Hong Kong Connections*, 2005, 223–47, 315–17.

———. "For a Comparative Film Studies," *Inter-Asia Cultural Studies* 6, no. 1 (2005): 103.

Williams, Alan. "Historical and Theoretical Issues Related to the Coming of Recorded Sound to the Cinema," in *Sound Theory Sound Practice*, ed. Rick Altman. New York: Routledge, 1992, 126–37.

———. ed. *Film and Nationalism*. Brunswick, NJ: Rutgers University Press, 2002.

Wolfe, Ernie, ed. *Extreme Canvas: Hand Painted Movie Posters from Ghana*. New York: Dilettante Press and Kesho Press, 2000.

Wollen, Peter. *Signs and Meanings in the Cinema*. London: British Film Institute, 1998.

———. *Paris Hollywood: Writings on Film*. London: Verso, 2002.

Wood, Frances. *The Silk Road: Two Thousand Years in the Heart of Asia*. Berkeley, CA: University of California, 2002.

Xavier, Ismail. *Allegories of Underdevelopment: Aesthetics and Politics in Modern Brazilian Cinema*. Minneapolis, MN: University of Minnesota Press, 1997.

———. "O cinema brasileiro dos anos 90," *Praga: estudos marxistas*, no. 9 (2000).

Yau, Esther C.M., ed. *At Full Speed: Hong Kong Cinema in a Borderless World*. Minneapolis, MN: University of Minnesota Press, 2001.

Yeh, Emilie Yueh-yu, and Darrell W. Davis. *Taiwan Film Directors: A Treasure Island*. New York: Columbia University Press, 2004.

Young, Robert. Introduction, in *White Mythologies: Writing History and the West*. London: Routledge, 1990.

Yúdice, George. *The Expediency of Culture: Uses of Culture in the Global Era*. Durham, NC: Duke University Press, 2003.

Žáček, Ivan. "Český film—chorobopis," *Iluminace*, no. 2 (2005): 51–80.

Zakaria, Fareed. *The Post-American World*. New York: W.W. Norton, 2008.

Zhang, Fengzhu, Huang Shixian, and Hu Zhifeng, eds. *Quanqiuhua yu Zhongguo yingshi de mingyun* (Globalization and the Destiny of Chinese Film and Television). Beijing: Beijing guangbo xueyuan chubanshe, 2003.

Zhang, Yingjin. "Prostitution and Urban Imagination: Negotiating the Public and the Private in Chinese Films of the 1930s," in *Cinema and Urban Culture in Shanghai, 1922–1943*, ed. Yingjin Zhang. Stanford, CA: Stanford University Press, 1999, 160–80.

———. *Screening China: Critical Interventions, Cinematic Reconfigurations, and the Transnational*

348

Imaginary in Contemporary Chinese Cinema. Ann Arbor, MI: Center for Chinese Studies, University of Michigan, 2002.

———. *Chinese National Cinema*. London: Routledge, 2004.

Zhen, Zhang. *An Amorous History of the Silver Screen: Shanghai Cinema, 1896–1937*. Chicago, IL: University of Chicago Press, 2005.

Zhen, Ni. *Memoirs from the Beijing Film Academy: The Genesis of China's Fifth Generation*, trans. Chris Berry. Durham, NC: Duke University Press, 2002.

Zhu, Ying. *Chinese Cinema During the Era of Reform: The Ingenuity of the System*. Westport, CT: Praeger, 2003.

contributors

Dudley Andrew, the R. Selden Rose Professor of Film and Comparative Literature at Yale University, has written *The Major Film Theories*, *Concepts of Film Theory*, *André Bazin*, *Mists of Regret: Culture and Sensibility in Classic French Film*, and, with Steven Ungar, *Popular Front Paris and the Poetics of Culture*. He is currently preparing *Cinema in the World*.

Olivier Barlet, a film critic and translator, is the author of *African Cinemas: Decolonizing the Gaze*, the website editor for www.africultures.com, an African cultural journal, and a film correspondent for *Continental*. He directs the "Images plurielles" series on cinema for L'Harmattan, and is a member of the Syndicat français de la critique de cinéma and of the African Federation of Film Critics through the French Afrimages association.

Marvin D'Lugo, Professor of Spanish and Adjunct Professor of Screen Studies at Clark University, is the author of *The Films of Carlos Saura: The Practice of Seeing*, *Guide to the Cinema of Spain*, *Pedro Almodóvar*, and numerous articles on Spanish, Cuban and Argentine cinemas. He is currently working on a book tentatively titled *The Hispanic Transnation on Screen*, dealing with the historical construction of the transnational audience of Spanish-language cinemas in Spain, Latin America and the United States.

Nataša Ďurovičová is the editor of www.91st-meridian.org, the journal of the International Writing Program, and affiliate faculty in the Department of Cinema and Comparative Literature, both at the University of Iowa. Her film scholarship has dealt with national and trans-atlantic cinemas as historiographic categories, and with the politics and aesthetics of film translation.

Miriam Hansen is the Ferdinand Schevill Distinguished Service Professor in the Humanities at the University of Chicago. Her publications include *Babel and Babylon: Spectatorship in American Silent Film* as well as a forthcoming book on the Frankfurt School, cinema, and modernity.

Mette Hjort is Professor and Program Director of Visual Studies at Lingnan University in Hong Kong. She is the author of *Stanley Kwan's Center Stage, Small Nation, Global Cinema*, and *The Strategy of Letters*. She has also edited and co-edited a number of books, including *Dekalog 01: The Five Obstructions, The Cinema of Small Nations, Cinema and Nation*, and *Purity and Provocation*. Mette Hjort has been a Leverhulme Visiting Professor of Film Studies at St Andrews in Scotland and a Visiting Professor of Scandinavian Studies at University College London. Her current projects focus on film and risk.

Fredric Jameson is the William A. Lane, Jr. Professor of Comparative Literature and Romance Studies at Duke University, where he directs the Institute for Critical Theory. Author of *Postmodernism, or, The Cultural Logic of Late Capitalism* and numerous other books, his most recent works include *Archaeologies of the Future* and *The Modernist Papers*.

Toby Miller is Professor of Media and Cultural Studies at the University of California, Riverside. He is the author and editor of more than thirty books, among them *A Companion to Film Theory* (with Robert Stam); *Global Hollywood 2* (with Nitin Govil, John McMurria, Richard Maxwell, and Ting Wang); *Critical Cultural Policy Studies: A Reader* (with Justin Lewis); *Television Studies: Critical Concepts in Media and Cultural Studies* (five volumes), and *Spyscreen: Espionage on Film and TV from the 1930s to the 1960s*

Kathleen Newman is an Associate Professor of Cinema and Spanish at the University of Iowa. Her research and teaching focuses on Latin American, Chicano, and Spanish cinemas as well as on theoretical questions regarding the relation between cinema and globalization. She is the author of *La violencia del discurso: el estado autoritario y la novela política argentina*.

Jonathan Rosenbaum was until early 2008 film critic at the *Chicago Reader*. His publications include *Discovering Orson Welles, Essential Cinema, Movie Wars, Dead Man, Movies as Politics, Moving Places* and *Placing Movies*. He co-edited, with Adrian Martin, *Movie Mutations*, and co-wrote, with J. Hoberman,

Midnight Movies, and with Mehrnaz Saeed-Vafa, *Abbas Kiarostami*. His website is www.jonathanrosenbaum.com.

Bhaskar Sarkar, Associate Professor of Film and Media Studies at the University of California at Santa Barbara, is the author of *Mourning the Nation: Indian Cinema in the Wake of Partition*. He is the co-editor of two forthcoming volumes: *The Subaltern and the Popular* and *Documentary Testimonies: Global Archives of Suffering*. At present, he is working on a monograph about the plasticity of Indian cultural nationalism in the era of globalization.

Lesley Stern is Professor in the Visual Arts Department at the University of California at San Diego. She is the author of *The Scorsese Connection* and *The Smoking Book*, and co-editor of *Falling For You: Essays on Cinema and Performance*. She has published extensively in the areas of film, performance, photography, cultural history and feminism, gardening and politics, and her essays have appeared in journals such as *Screen*, *M/F*, *Camera Obscura*, *Film Reader*, *Image Forum* (in Japanese), *Trafic* (in French), *Emergences*, and *Critical Inquiry*.

João Luiz Vieira is an Associate Professor in the Departamento de Cinema e Vídeo of the Instituto de Arte e Comunicação Social at the Universidade Federal Fluminense in Rio de Janeiro, Brazil. He is the co-author, with Robert Stam and Ismail Xavier, of *Brazilian Cinema*, and the editor of *Cinema Novo and Beyond*, published by the Museum of Modern Art, New York. His latest book is *Câmera-faca: o cinema de Sérgio Bianchi*.

Paul Willemen, is the author of *Looks and Frictions: Essays in Cultural Studies and Film Theory*, as well as co-editor of *Questions of Third Cinema* with Jim Pines, *The Encyclopaedia of Indian Cinema* with Ashish Rajadhyaksha, and *Theorising National Cinema* with Valentina Vitali. His editorial work includes *Screen* in the 1970s and *Framework* in the 1980s.

Yingjin Zhang, Director of the Chinese Studies Program and Professor of Comparative Literature, Cultural Studies, and Film Studies at University of California at San Diego, is the author of *The City in Modern Chinese Literature and Film*, *Screening China*, *Chinese National Cinema*, and *Cinema, Space, and Polylocality in a Globalizing China* (forthcoming); co-author of *Encyclopedia of Chinese Film*; editor of *China in a Polycentric World* and *Cinema and Urban Culture in Shanghai, 1922–1943*; and co-editor of *From Underground to Independent*.

index of film and

television titles

general index

general index